Dejah Thoris™

SOLDIER of MEMORY

SOLDIER OF MEMORY

written by
FRANK J. BARBIERE

illustrated by
FRANCESCO MANNA

colored by
MORGAN HICKMAN
and VALENTINA PINTO

lettered by
ERICA SCHULTZ

collection cover by
NEN CHANG

collection design by
GEOFF HARKINS

based on the stories and characters by
EDGAR RICE BURROUGHS

senior editor
JOSEPH RYBANDT

associate editor
RACHEL PINNELAS

Online at www.DYNAMITE.com
On Facebook /Dynamitecomics
Instagram /Dynamitecomics
On Tumblr dynamitecomics.tumblr.com
On Twitter @dynamitecomics
On YouTube /Dynamitecomics

First Printing ISBN-13: 978-1-5241-0135-0
10 9 8 7 6 5 4 3 2 1

DYNAMITE

Nick Barrucci, CEO / Publisher
Juan Collado, President / COO

Joe Rybandt, Executive Editor
Matt Idelson, Senior Editor
Rachel Pinnelas, Associate Editor
Anthony Marques, Assistant Editor
Kevin Ketner, Editorial Assistant

Jason Ullmeyer, Art Director
Geoff Harkins, Senior Graphic Designer
Cathleen Heard, Graphic Designer
Alexis Persson, Production Artist

Chris Caniano, Digital Associate
Rachel Kilbury, Digital Assistant

Brandon Dante Primavera, V.P. of IT and Operations
Rich Young, Director of Business Development

Alan Payne, V.P. of Sales and Marketing
Keith Davidsen, Marketing Director
Pat O'Connell, Sales Manager

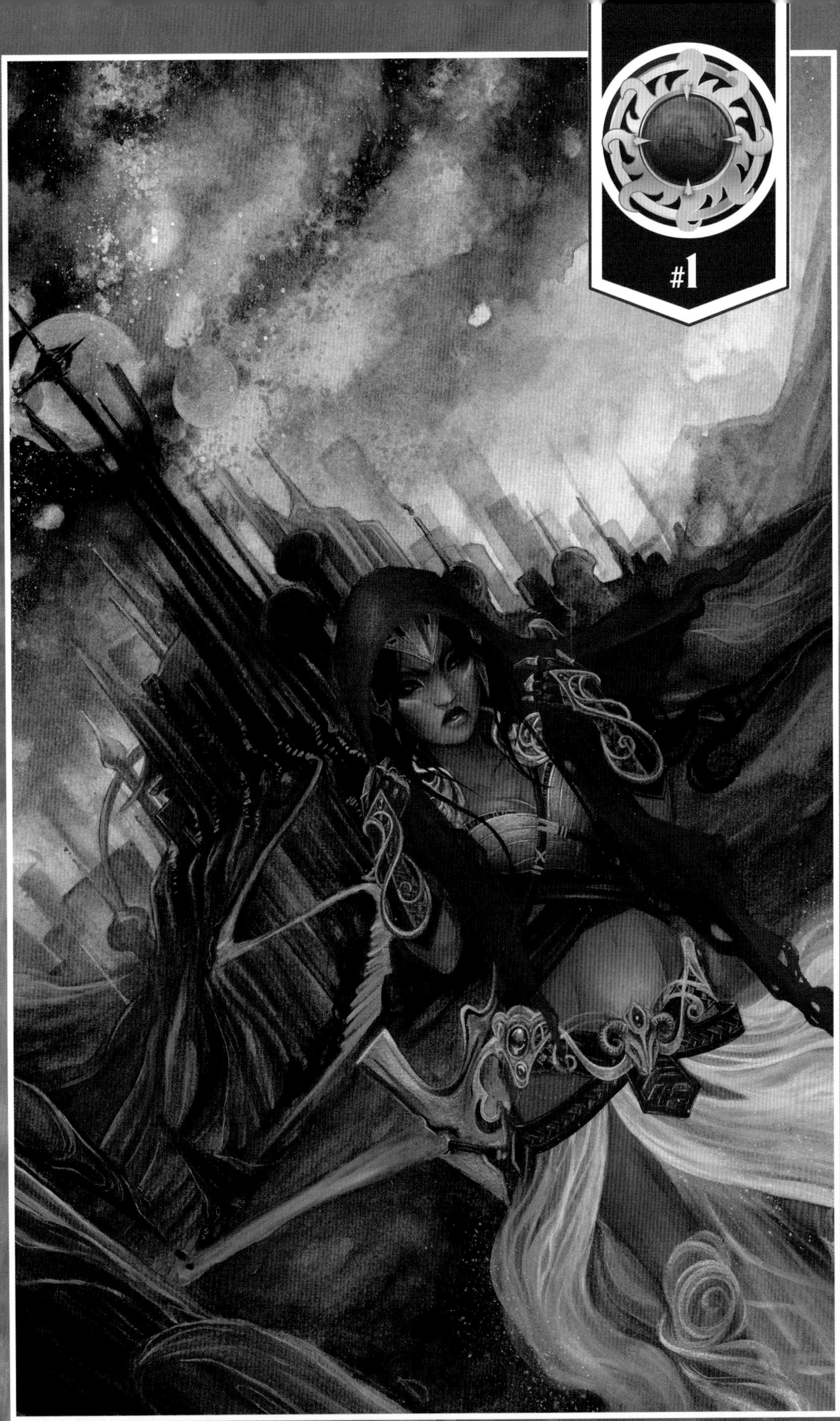
#1

cover by **NEN CHANG**

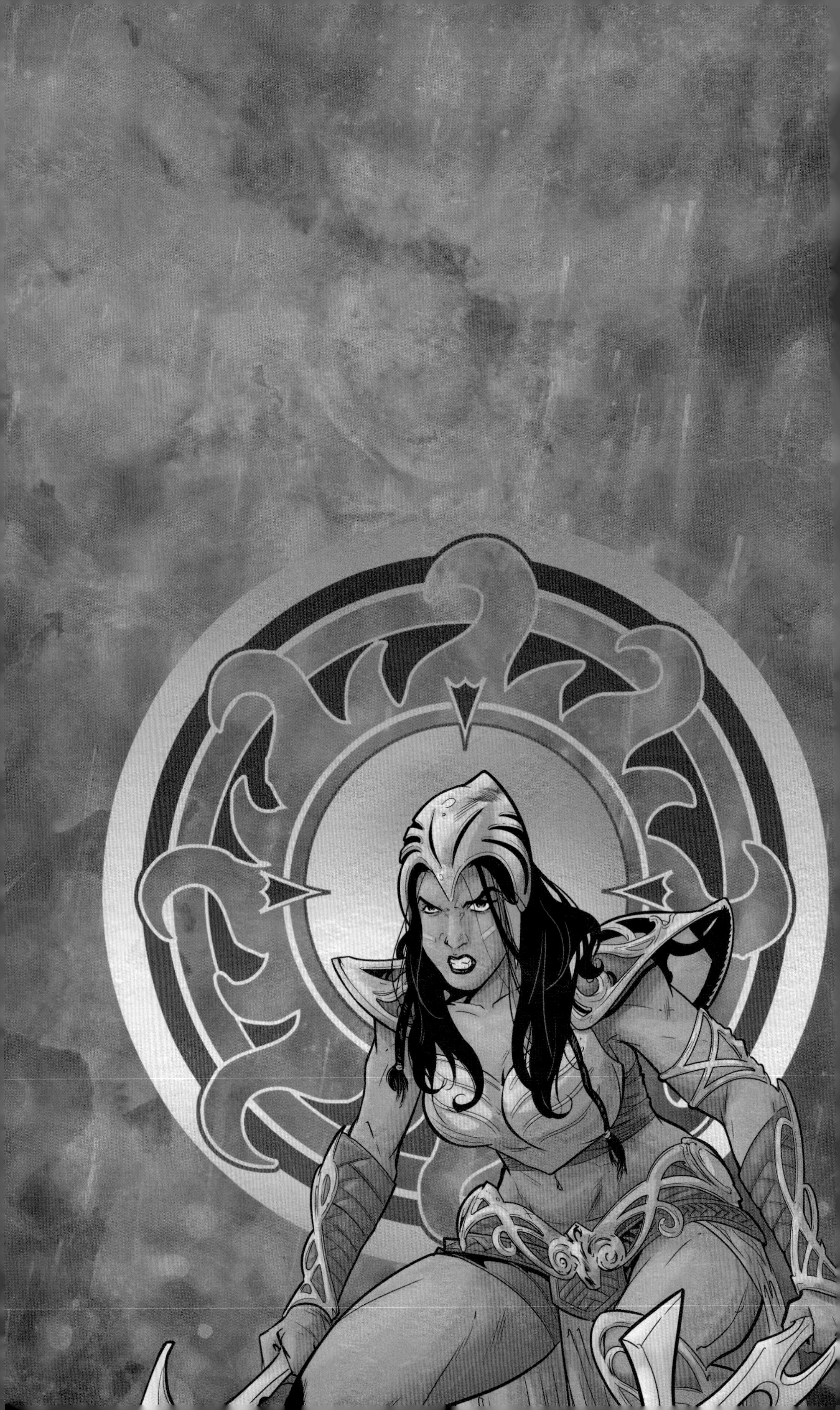

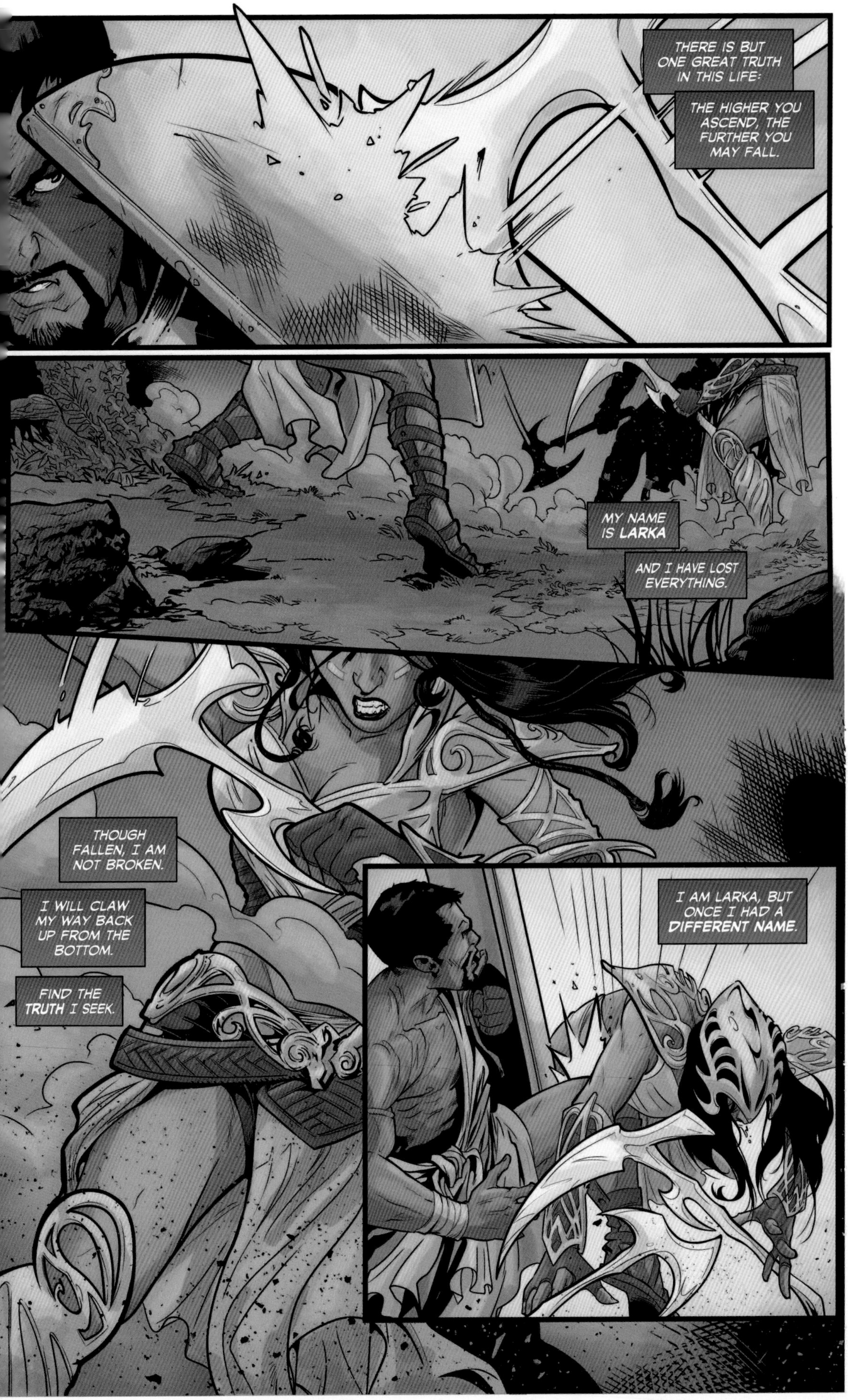
THERE IS BUT ONE GREAT TRUTH IN THIS LIFE:
THE HIGHER YOU ASCEND, THE FURTHER YOU MAY FALL.
MY NAME IS **LARKA**
AND I HAVE LOST EVERYTHING.
THOUGH FALLEN, I AM NOT BROKEN.
I WILL CLAW MY WAY BACK UP FROM THE BOTTOM.
FIND THE **TRUTH** I SEEK.
I AM LARKA, BUT ONCE I HAD A **DIFFERENT NAME**.

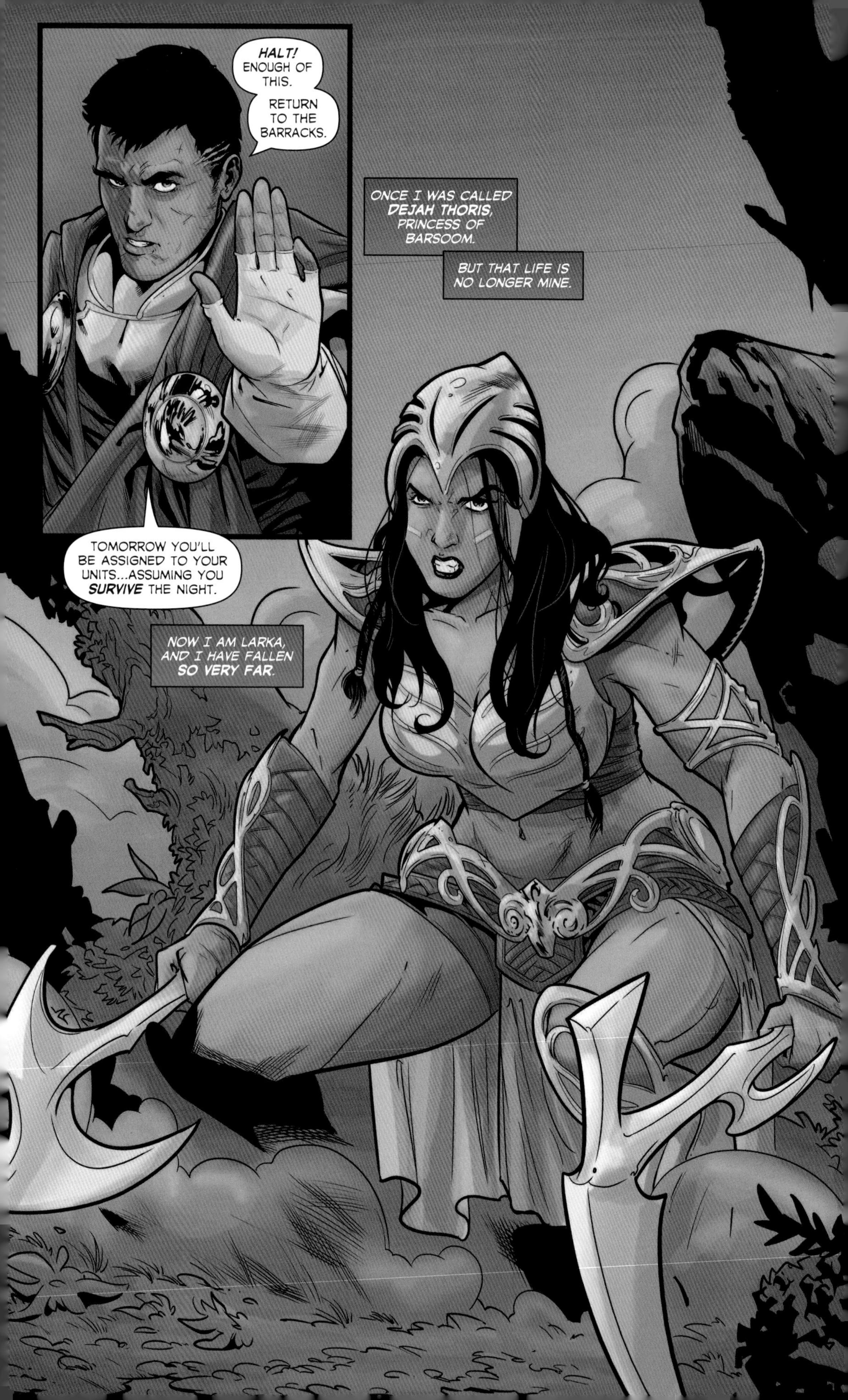
HALT! ENOUGH OF THIS.
RETURN TO THE BARRACKS.
ONCE I WAS CALLED DEJAH THORIS, PRINCESS OF BARSOOM.
BUT THAT LIFE IS NO LONGER MINE.
TOMORROW YOU'LL BE ASSIGNED TO YOUR UNITS...ASSUMING YOU SURVIVE THE NIGHT.
NOW I AM LARKA, AND I HAVE FALLEN SO VERY FAR.

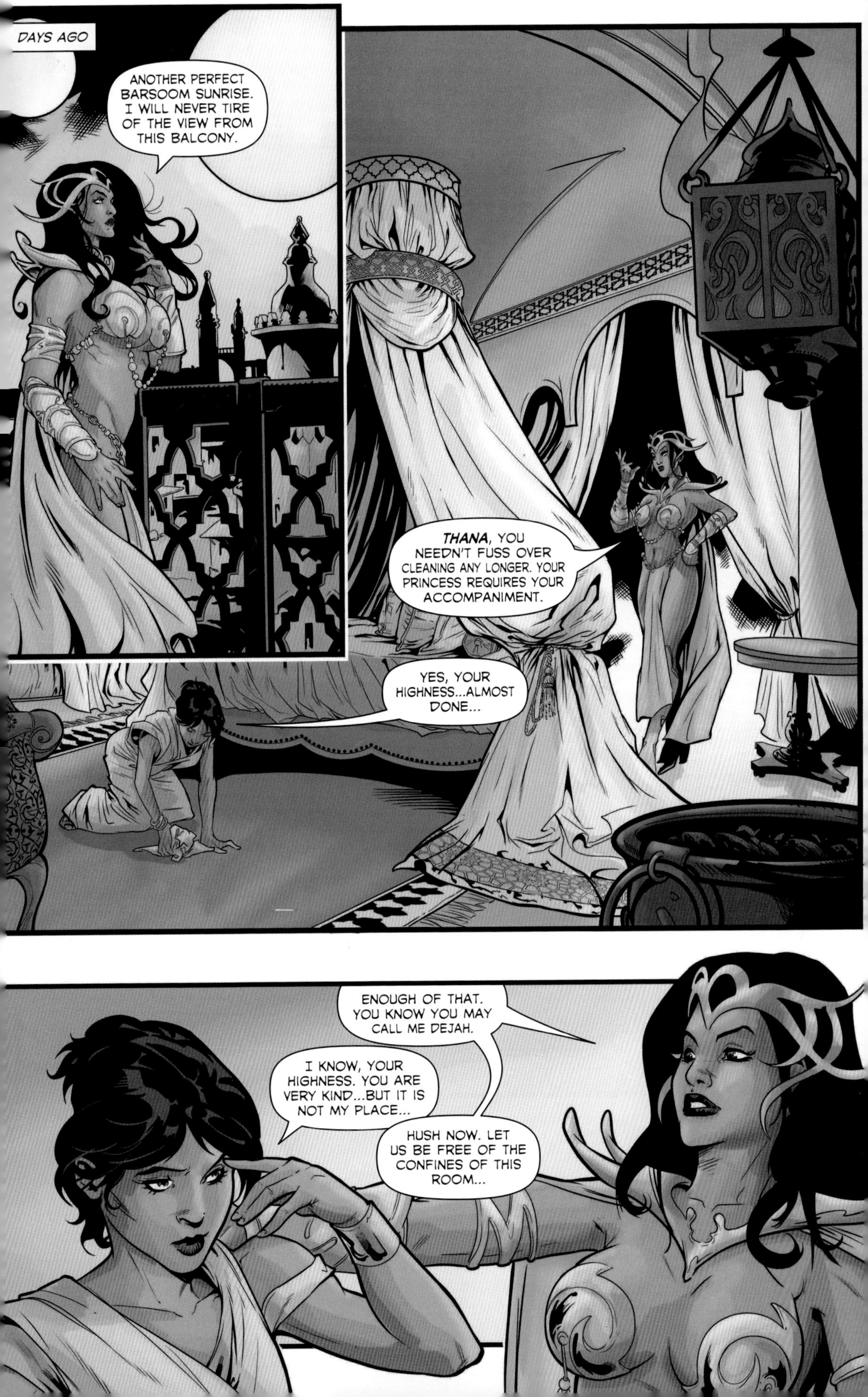

DAYS AGO
ANOTHER PERFECT BARSOOM SUNRISE. I WILL NEVER TIRE OF THE VIEW FROM THIS BALCONY.
THANA, YOU NEEDN'T FUSS OVER CLEANING ANY LONGER. YOUR PRINCESS REQUIRES YOUR ACCOMPANIMENT.
YES, YOUR HIGHNESS...ALMOST DONE...
ENOUGH OF THAT. YOU KNOW YOU MAY CALL ME DEJAH.
I KNOW, YOUR HIGHNESS. YOU ARE VERY KIND...BUT IT IS NOT MY PLACE...
HUSH NOW. LET US BE FREE OF THE CONFINES OF THIS ROOM...

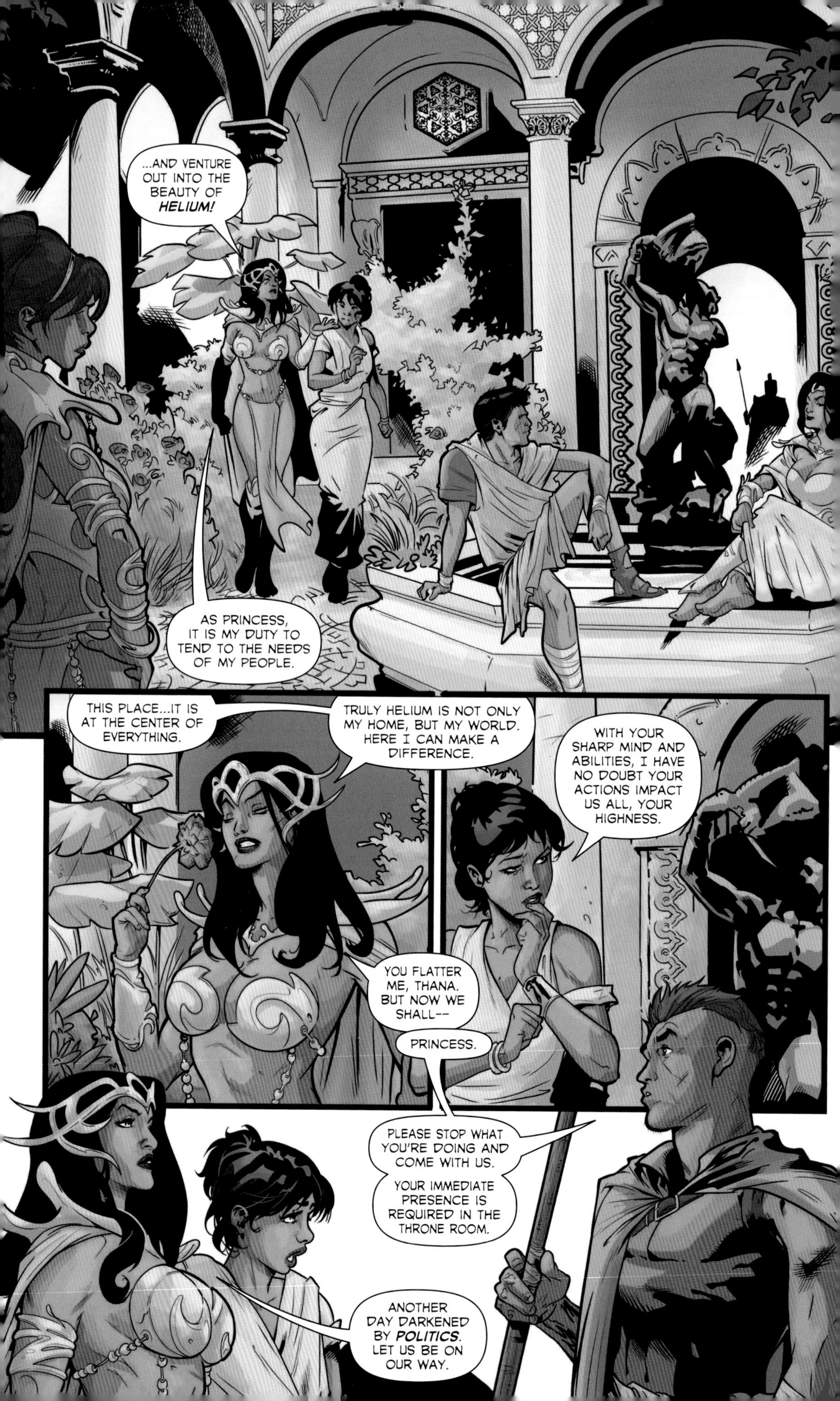

...AND VENTURE OUT INTO THE BEAUTY OF HELIUM!
AS PRINCESS, IT IS MY DUTY TO TEND TO THE NEEDS OF MY PEOPLE.
THIS PLACE...IT IS AT THE CENTER OF EVERYTHING.
TRULY HELIUM IS NOT ONLY MY HOME, BUT MY WORLD. HERE I CAN MAKE A DIFFERENCE.
WITH YOUR SHARP MIND AND ABILITIES, I HAVE NO DOUBT YOUR ACTIONS IMPACT US ALL, YOUR HIGHNESS.
YOU FLATTER ME, THANA. BUT NOW WE SHALL--
PRINCESS.
PLEASE STOP WHAT YOU'RE DOING AND COME WITH US.
YOUR IMMEDIATE PRESENCE IS REQUIRED IN THE THRONE ROOM.
ANOTHER DAY DARKENED BY POLITICS. LET US BE ON OUR WAY.

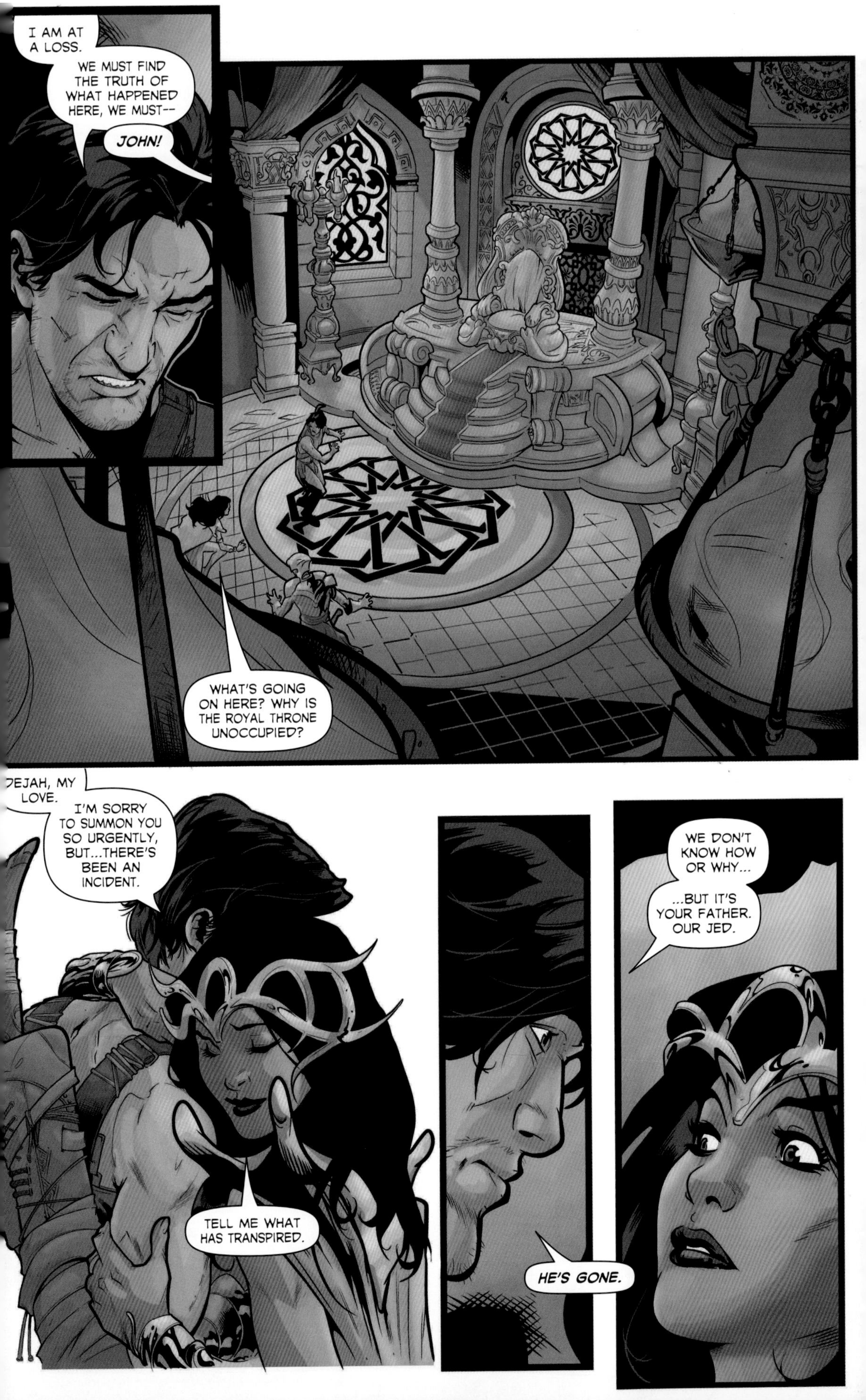
I AM AT A LOSS.
WE MUST FIND THE TRUTH OF WHAT HAPPENED HERE, WE MUST--
JOHN!
WHAT'S GOING ON HERE? WHY IS THE ROYAL THRONE UNOCCUPIED?
DEJAH, MY LOVE.
I'M SORRY TO SUMMON YOU SO URGENTLY, BUT...THERE'S BEEN AN INCIDENT.
TELL ME WHAT HAS TRANSPIRED.
WE DON'T KNOW HOW OR WHY...
...BUT IT'S YOUR FATHER. OUR JED.
HE'S GONE.

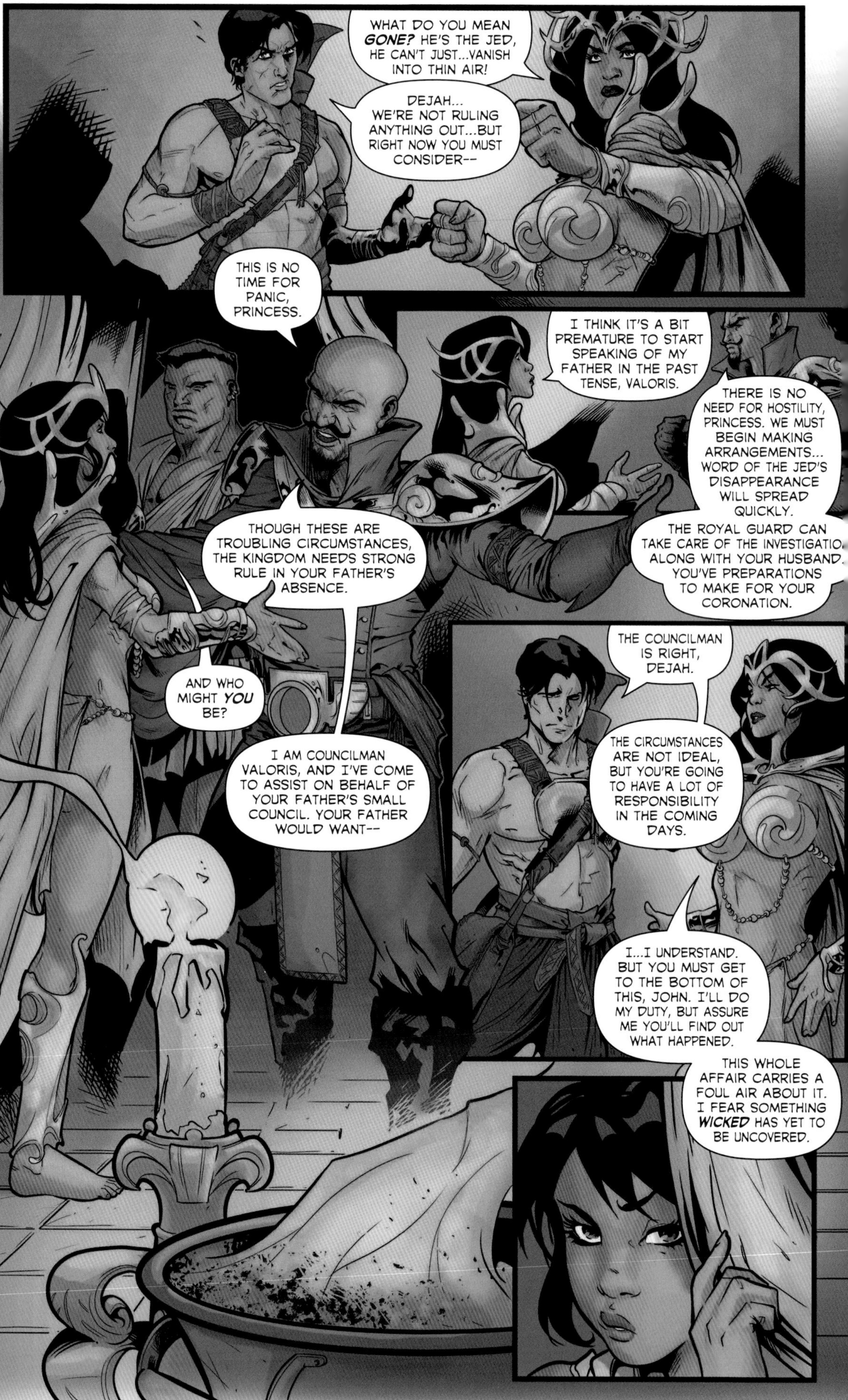
WHAT DO YOU MEAN *GONE?* HE'S THE JED, HE CAN'T JUST...VANISH INTO THIN AIR!
DEJAH... WE'RE NOT RULING ANYTHING OUT...BUT RIGHT NOW YOU MUST CONSIDER--
THIS IS NO TIME FOR PANIC, PRINCESS.
I THINK IT'S A BIT PREMATURE TO START SPEAKING OF MY FATHER IN THE PAST TENSE, VALORIS.
THERE IS NO NEED FOR HOSTILITY, PRINCESS. WE MUST BEGIN MAKING ARRANGEMENTS... WORD OF THE JED'S DISAPPEARANCE WILL SPREAD QUICKLY.
THE ROYAL GUARD CAN TAKE CARE OF THE INVESTIGATIO ALONG WITH YOUR HUSBAND. YOU'VE PREPARATIONS TO MAKE FOR YOUR CORONATION.
THOUGH THESE ARE TROUBLING CIRCUMSTANCES, THE KINGDOM NEEDS STRONG RULE IN YOUR FATHER'S ABSENCE.
AND WHO MIGHT *YOU* BE?
I AM COUNCILMAN VALORIS, AND I'VE COME TO ASSIST ON BEHALF OF YOUR FATHER'S SMALL COUNCIL. YOUR FATHER WOULD WANT--
THE COUNCILMAN IS RIGHT, DEJAH.
THE CIRCUMSTANCES ARE NOT IDEAL, BUT YOU'RE GOING TO HAVE A LOT OF RESPONSIBILITY IN THE COMING DAYS.
I...I UNDERSTAND. BUT YOU MUST GET TO THE BOTTOM OF THIS, JOHN. I'LL DO MY DUTY, BUT ASSURE ME YOU'LL FIND OUT WHAT HAPPENED.
THIS WHOLE AFFAIR CARRIES A FOUL AIR ABOUT IT. I FEAR SOMETHING *WICKED* HAS YET TO BE UNCOVERED.

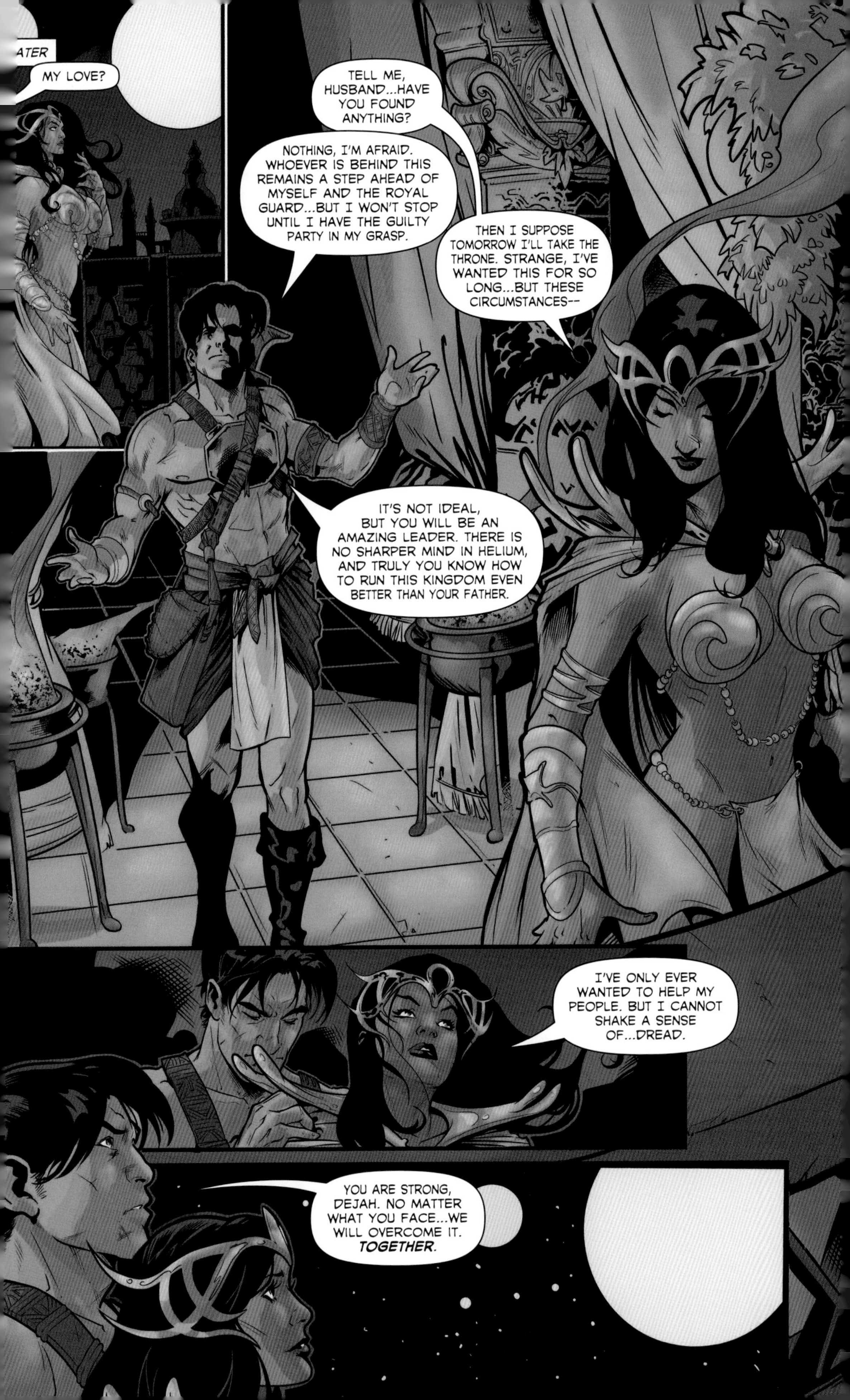
ATER
MY LOVE?
TELL ME, HUSBAND...HAVE YOU FOUND ANYTHING?
NOTHING, I'M AFRAID. WHOEVER IS BEHIND THIS REMAINS A STEP AHEAD OF MYSELF AND THE ROYAL GUARD...BUT I WON'T STOP UNTIL I HAVE THE GUILTY PARTY IN MY GRASP.
THEN I SUPPOSE TOMORROW I'LL TAKE THE THRONE. STRANGE, I'VE WANTED THIS FOR SO LONG...BUT THESE CIRCUMSTANCES--
IT'S NOT IDEAL, BUT YOU WILL BE AN AMAZING LEADER. THERE IS NO SHARPER MIND IN HELIUM, AND TRULY YOU KNOW HOW TO RUN THIS KINGDOM EVEN BETTER THAN YOUR FATHER.
I'VE ONLY EVER WANTED TO HELP MY PEOPLE. BUT I CANNOT SHAKE A SENSE OF...DREAD.
YOU ARE STRONG, DEJAH. NO MATTER WHAT YOU FACE...WE WILL OVERCOME IT. *TOGETHER*.

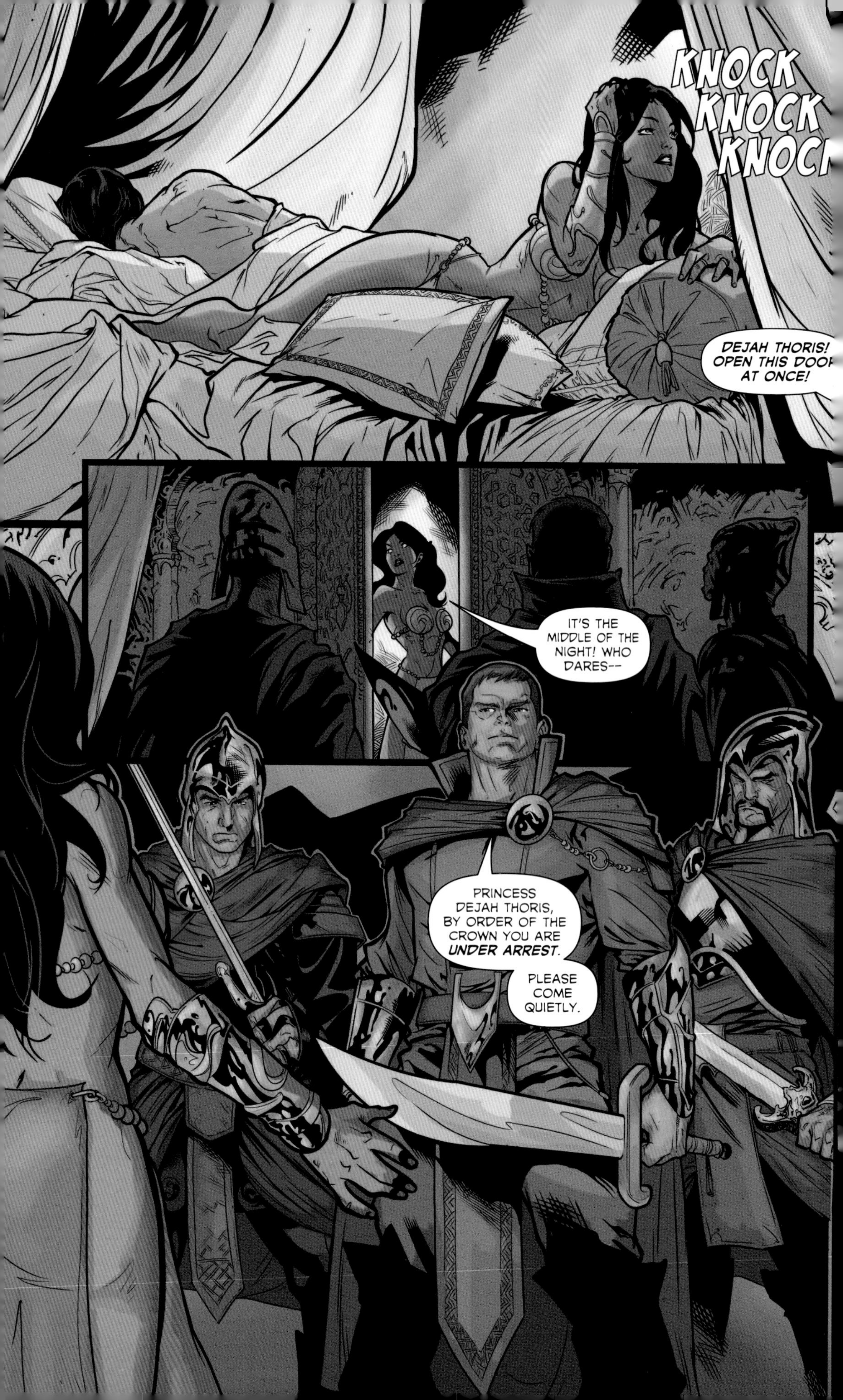
KNOCK KNOCK KNOC
DEJAH THORIS! OPEN THIS DOO AT ONCE!
IT'S THE MIDDLE OF THE NIGHT! WHO DARES--
PRINCESS DEJAH THORIS, BY ORDER OF THE CROWN YOU ARE UNDER ARREST.
PLEASE COME QUIETLY.

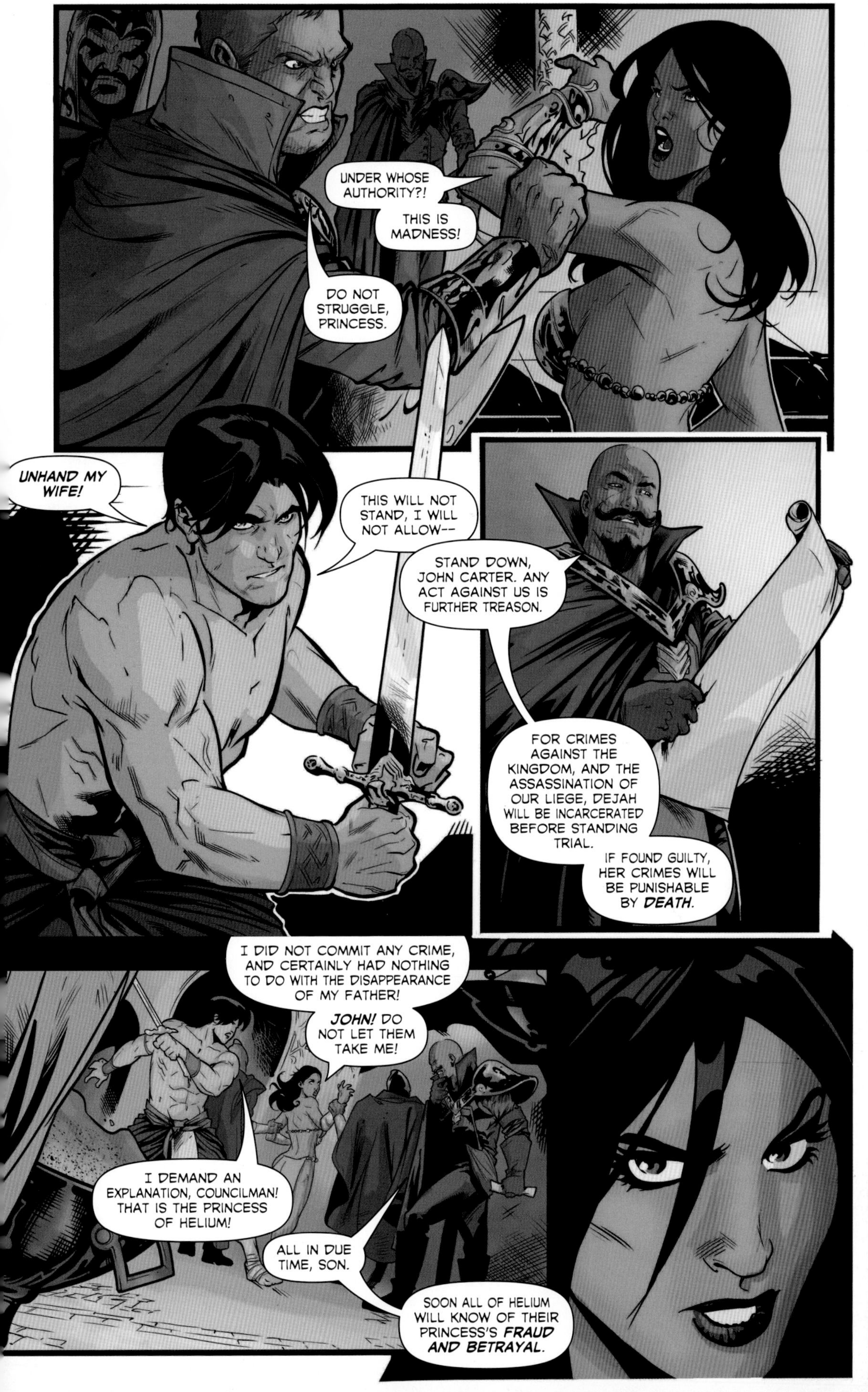
UNDER WHOSE AUTHORITY?!
THIS IS MADNESS!
DO NOT STRUGGLE, PRINCESS.
UNHAND MY WIFE!
THIS WILL NOT STAND, I WILL NOT ALLOW--
STAND DOWN, JOHN CARTER. ANY ACT AGAINST US IS FURTHER TREASON.
FOR CRIMES AGAINST THE KINGDOM, AND THE ASSASSINATION OF OUR LIEGE, DEJAH WILL BE INCARCERATED BEFORE STANDING TRIAL.
IF FOUND GUILTY, HER CRIMES WILL BE PUNISHABLE BY DEATH.
I DID NOT COMMIT ANY CRIME, AND CERTAINLY HAD NOTHING TO DO WITH THE DISAPPEARANCE OF MY FATHER!
JOHN! DO NOT LET THEM TAKE ME!
I DEMAND AN EXPLANATION, COUNCILMAN! THAT IS THE PRINCESS OF HELIUM!
ALL IN DUE TIME, SON.
SOON ALL OF HELIUM WILL KNOW OF THEIR PRINCESS'S FRAUD AND BETRAYAL.

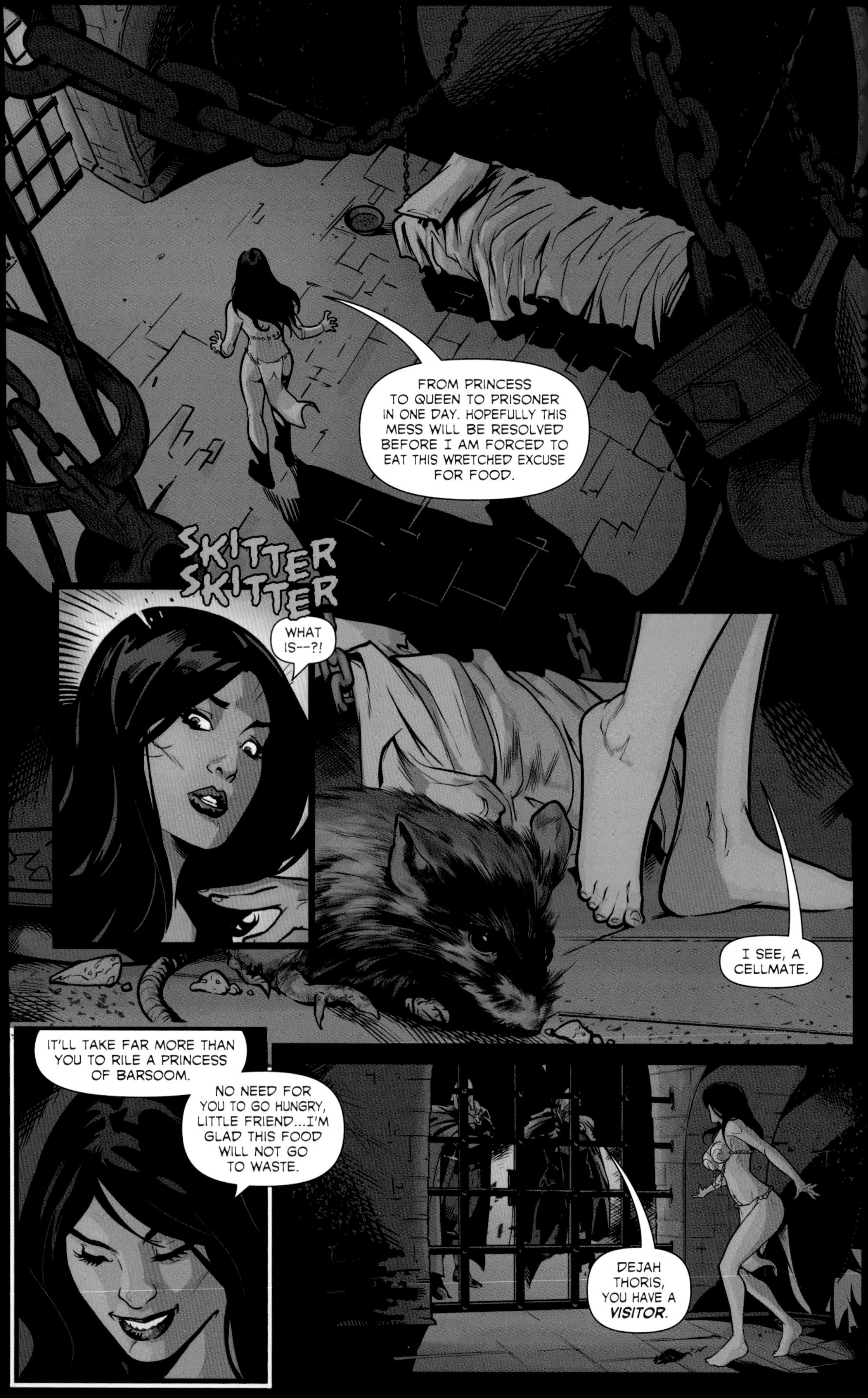
FROM PRINCESS TO QUEEN TO PRISONER IN ONE DAY. HOPEFULLY THIS MESS WILL BE RESOLVED BEFORE I AM FORCED TO EAT THIS WRETCHED EXCUSE FOR FOOD.
SKITTER SKITTER
WHAT IS--?!
I SEE, A CELLMATE.
IT'LL TAKE FAR MORE THAN YOU TO RILE A PRINCESS OF BARSOOM.
NO NEED FOR YOU TO GO HUNGRY, LITTLE FRIEND...I'M GLAD THIS FOOD WILL NOT GO TO WASTE.
DEJAH THORIS, YOU HAVE A VISITOR.

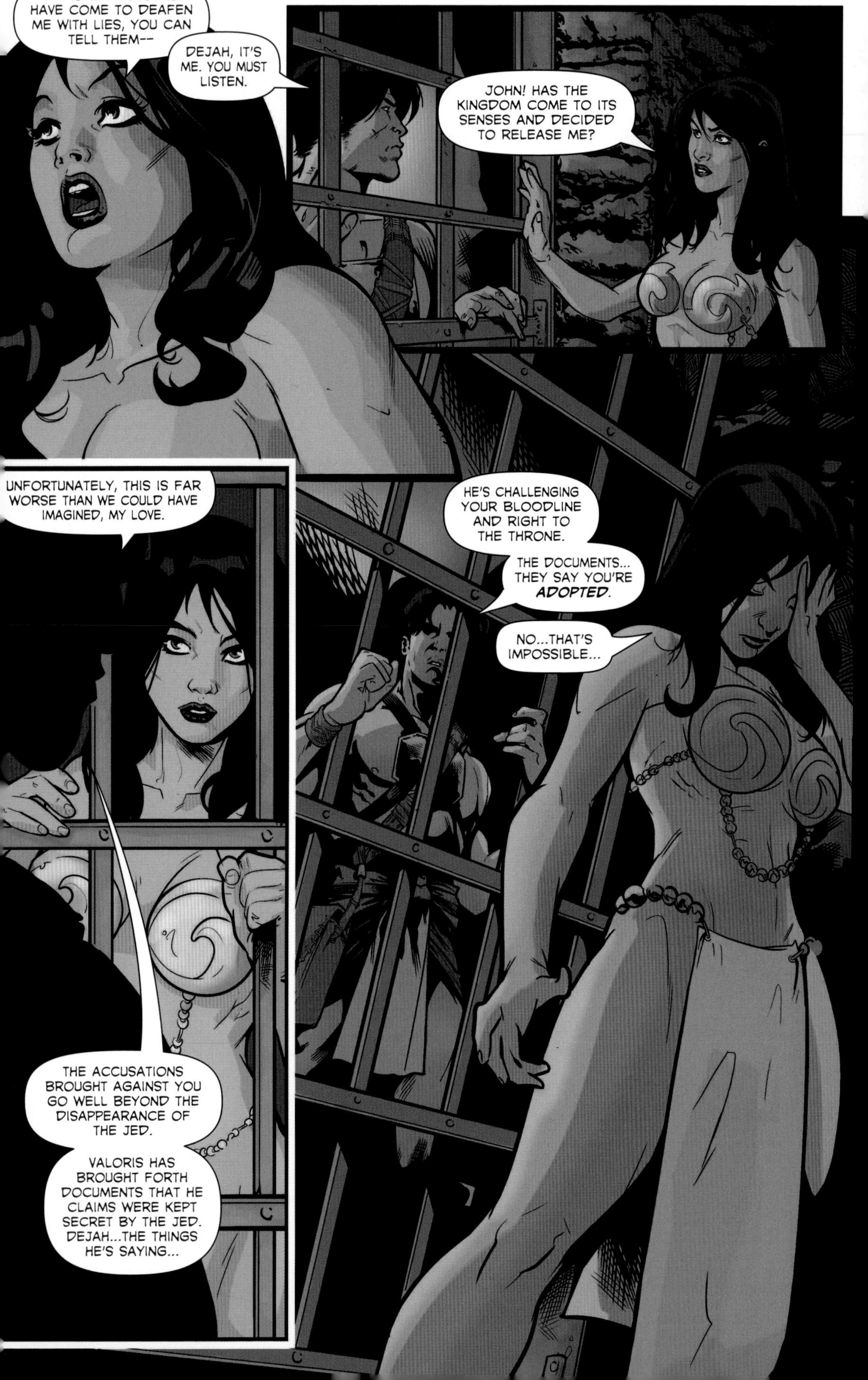
IF MORE ACCUSERS HAVE COME TO DEAFEN ME WITH LIES, YOU CAN TELL THEM--
DEJAH, IT'S ME. YOU MUST LISTEN.
JOHN! HAS THE KINGDOM COME TO ITS SENSES AND DECIDED TO RELEASE ME?
UNFORTUNATELY, THIS IS FAR WORSE THAN WE COULD HAVE IMAGINED, MY LOVE.
THE ACCUSATIONS BROUGHT AGAINST YOU GO WELL BEYOND THE DISAPPEARANCE OF THE JED.
VALORIS HAS BROUGHT FORTH DOCUMENTS THAT HE CLAIMS WERE KEPT SECRET BY THE JED. DEJAH...THE THINGS HE'S SAYING...
HE'S CHALLENGING YOUR BLOODLINE AND RIGHT TO THE THRONE.
THE DOCUMENTS... THEY SAY YOU'RE *ADOPTED*.
NO...THAT'S IMPOSSIBLE...

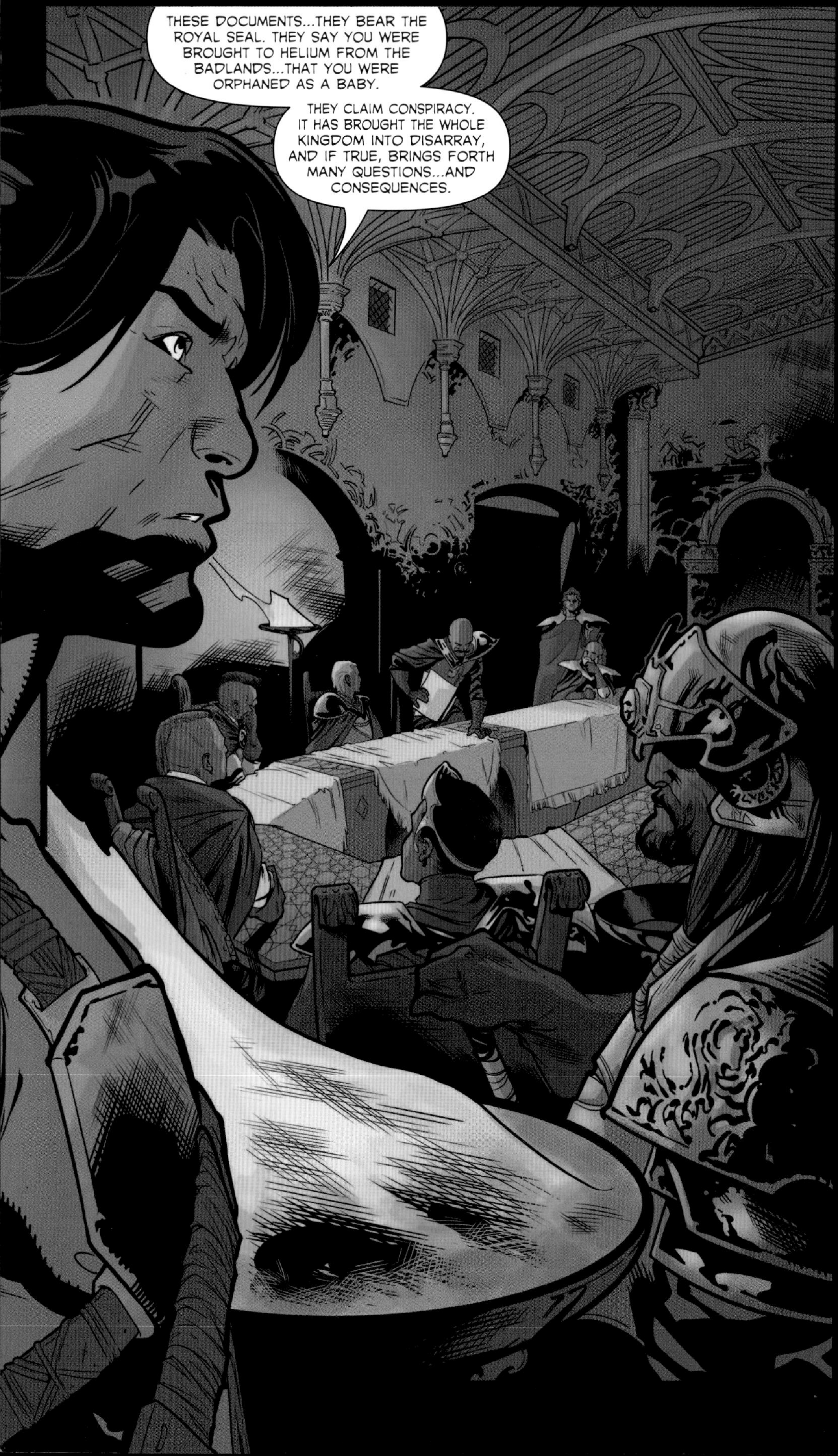
THESE DOCUMENTS...THEY BEAR THE ROYAL SEAL. THEY SAY YOU WERE BROUGHT TO HELIUM FROM THE BADLANDS...THAT YOU WERE ORPHANED AS A BABY.
THEY CLAIM CONSPIRACY. IT HAS BROUGHT THE WHOLE KINGDOM INTO DISARRAY, AND IF TRUE, BRINGS FORTH MANY QUESTIONS...AND CONSEQUENCES.

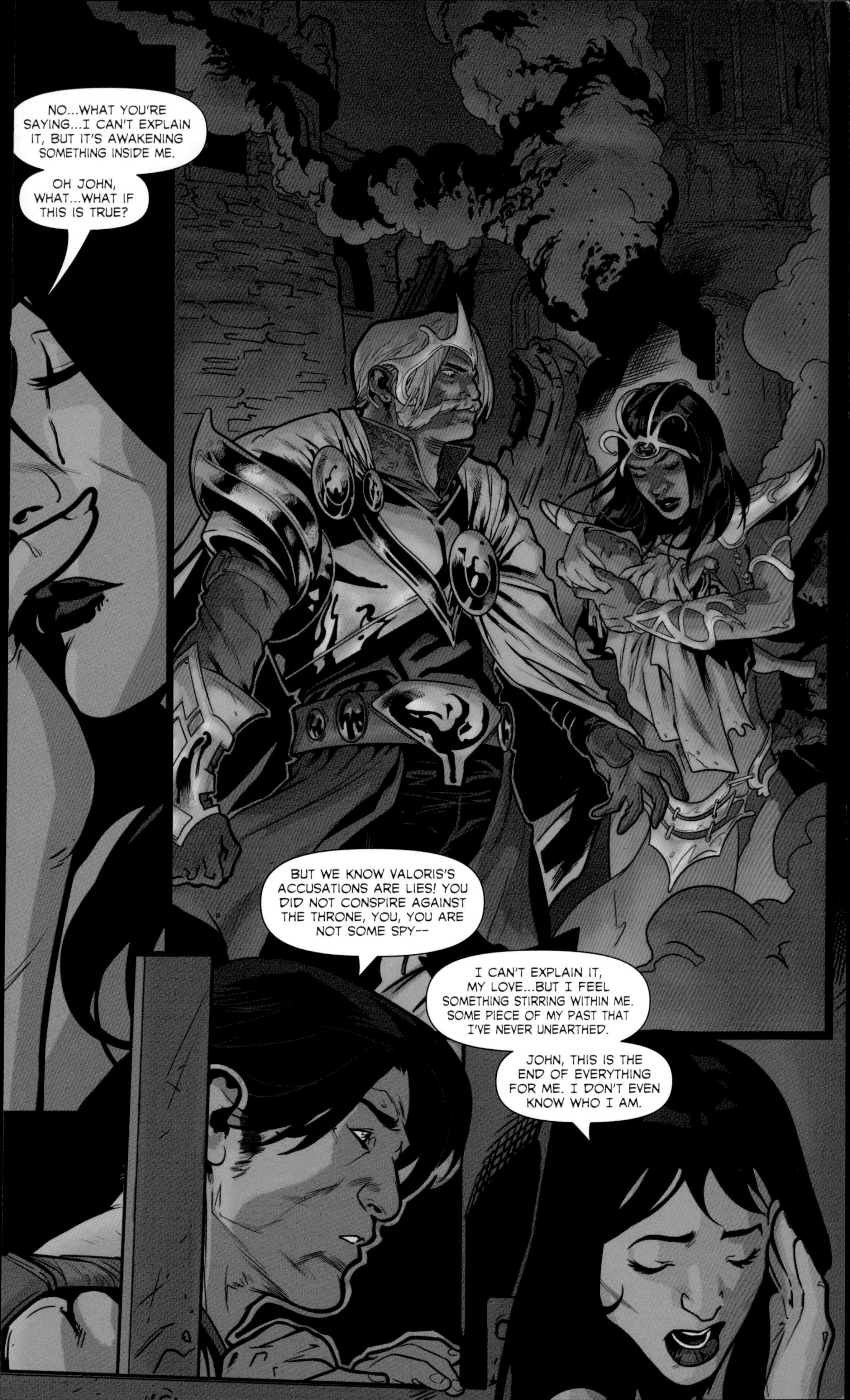
NO...WHAT YOU'RE SAYING...I CAN'T EXPLAIN IT, BUT IT'S AWAKENING SOMETHING INSIDE ME.
OH JOHN, WHAT...WHAT IF THIS IS TRUE?
BUT WE KNOW VALORIS'S ACCUSATIONS ARE LIES! YOU DID NOT CONSPIRE AGAINST THE THRONE, YOU, YOU ARE NOT SOME SPY--
I CAN'T EXPLAIN IT, MY LOVE...BUT I FEEL SOMETHING STIRRING WITHIN ME. SOME PIECE OF MY PAST THAT I'VE NEVER UNEARTHED.
JOHN, THIS IS THE END OF EVERYTHING FOR ME. I DON'T EVEN KNOW WHO I AM.

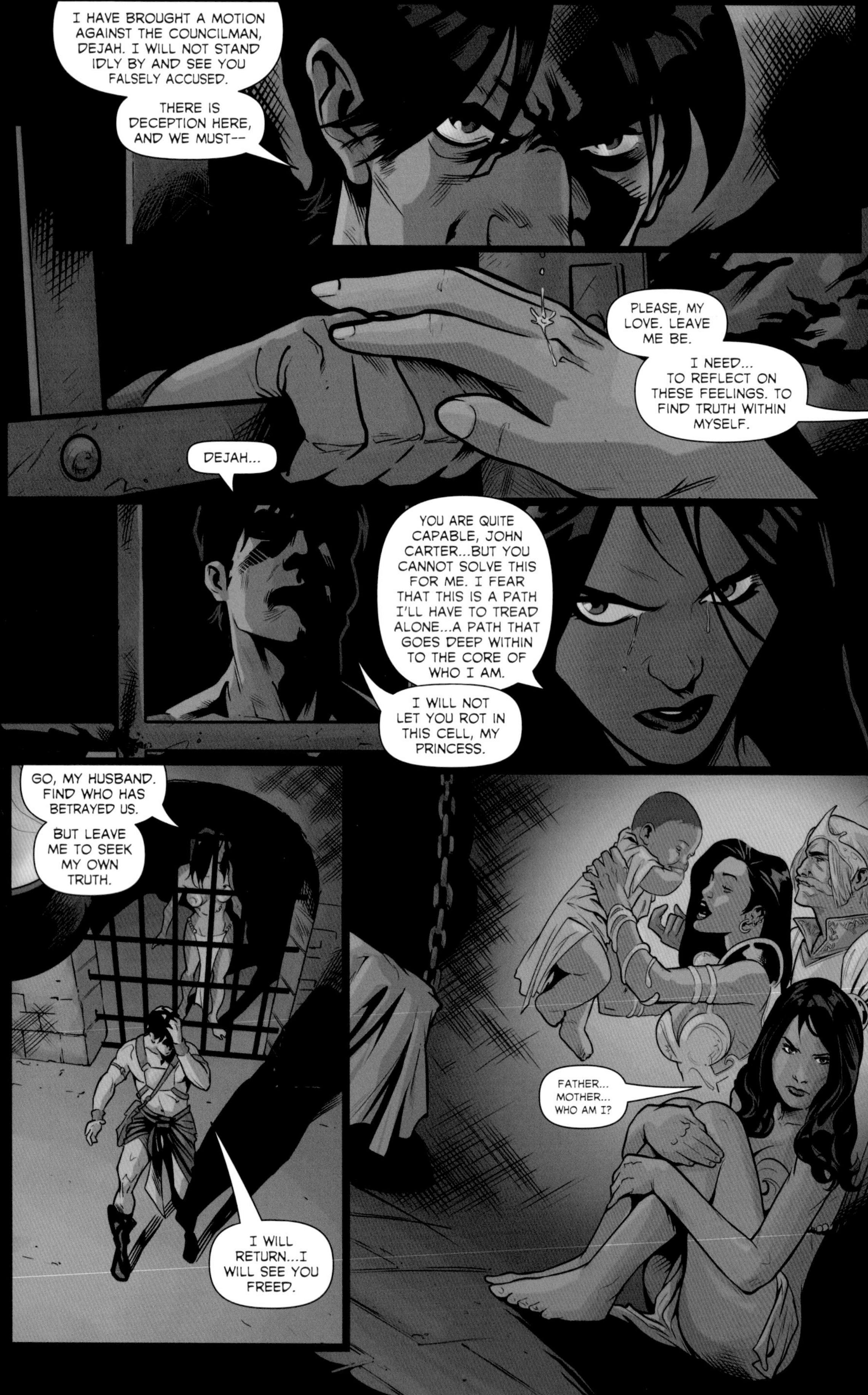
I HAVE BROUGHT A MOTION AGAINST THE COUNCILMAN, DEJAH. I WILL NOT STAND IDLY BY AND SEE YOU FALSELY ACCUSED.
THERE IS DECEPTION HERE, AND WE MUST--
PLEASE, MY LOVE. LEAVE ME BE.
I NEED... TO REFLECT ON THESE FEELINGS. TO FIND TRUTH WITHIN MYSELF.
DEJAH...
YOU ARE QUITE CAPABLE, JOHN CARTER...BUT YOU CANNOT SOLVE THIS FOR ME. I FEAR THAT THIS IS A PATH I'LL HAVE TO TREAD ALONE...A PATH THAT GOES DEEP WITHIN TO THE CORE OF WHO I AM.
I WILL NOT LET YOU ROT IN THIS CELL, MY PRINCESS.
GO, MY HUSBAND. FIND WHO HAS BETRAYED US.
BUT LEAVE ME TO SEEK MY OWN TRUTH.
I WILL RETURN...I WILL SEE YOU FREED.
FATHER... MOTHER... WHO AM I?

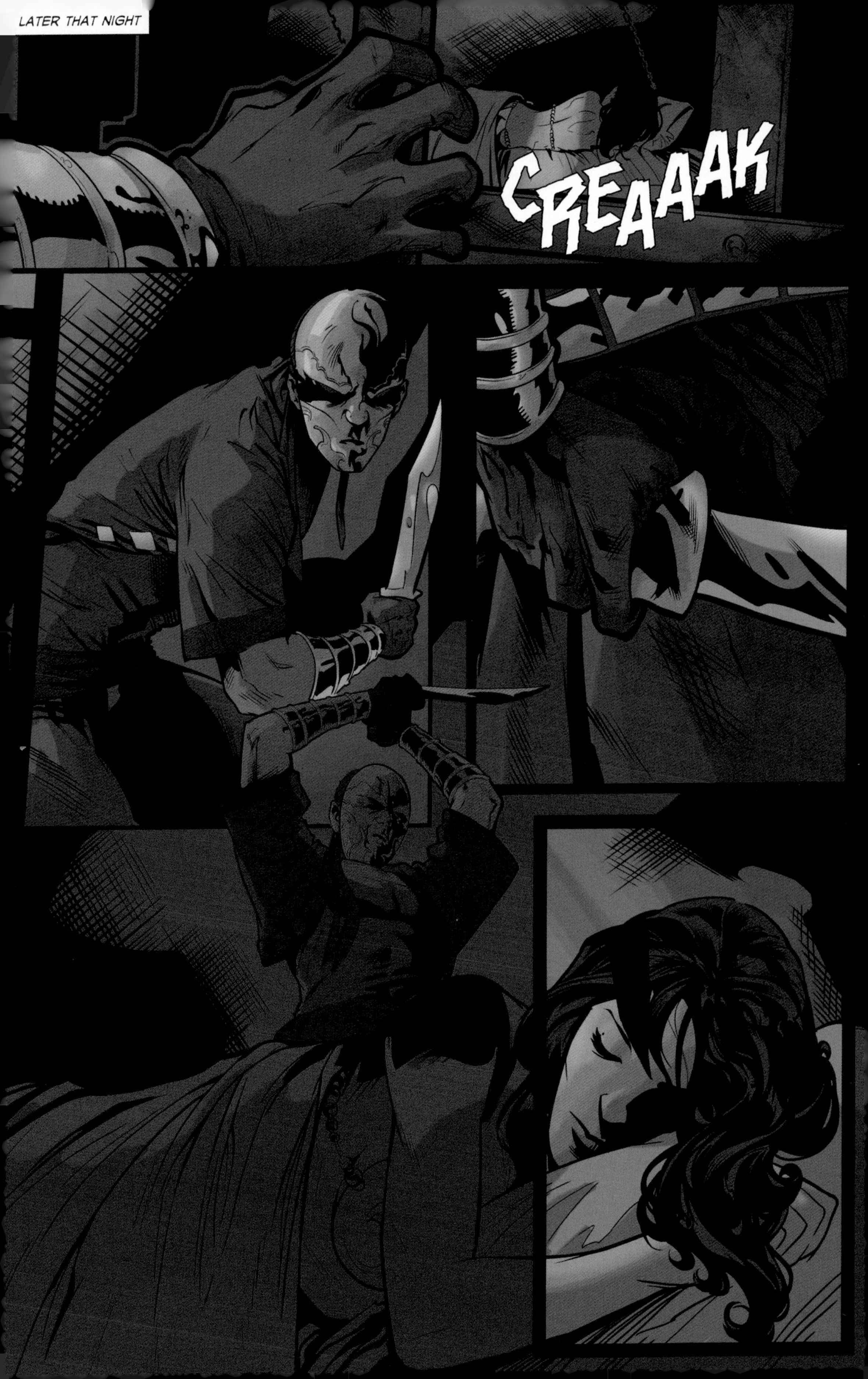

LATER THAT NIGHT
CREAAAK

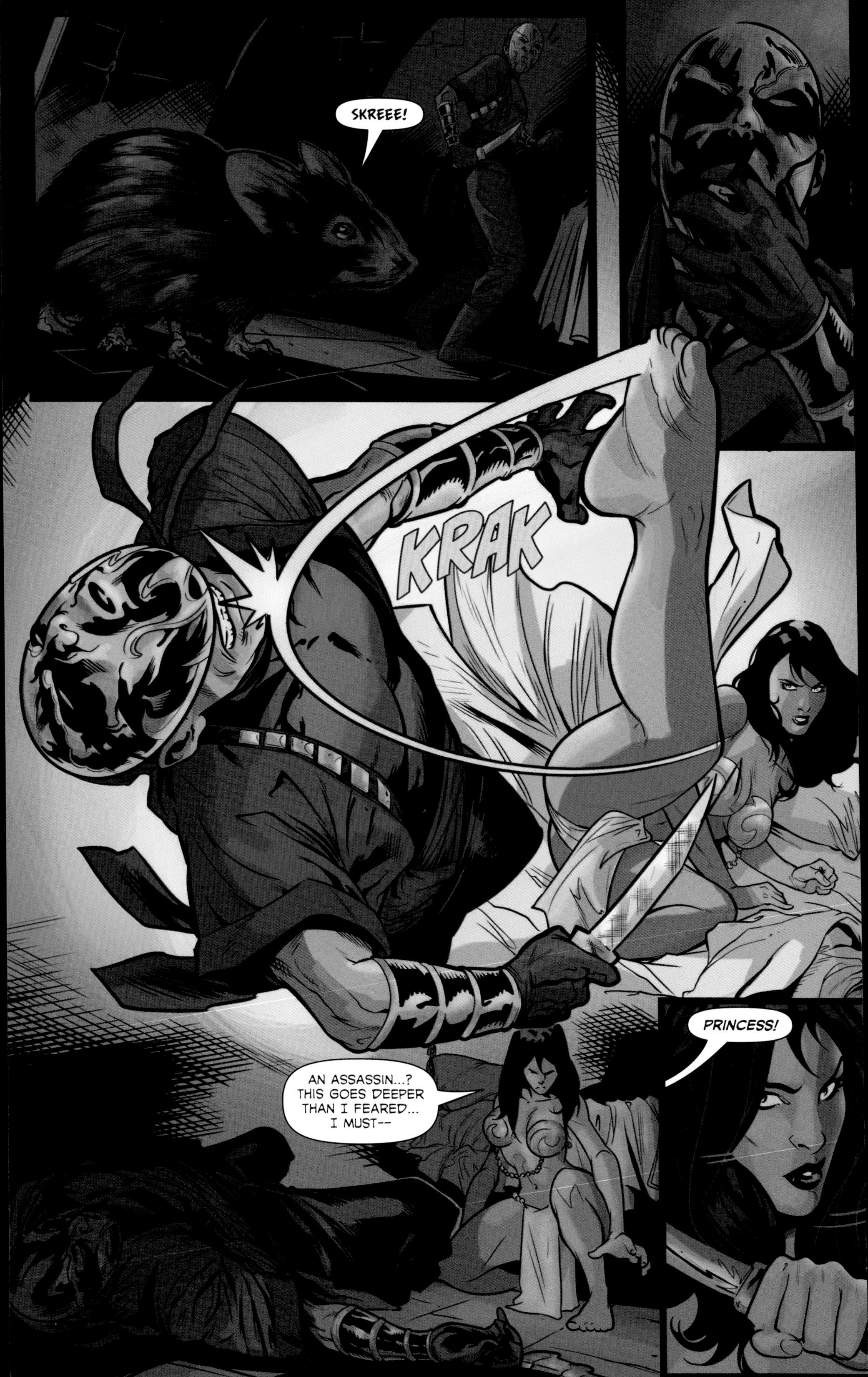
SKREEE!
KRAK
PRINCESS!
AN ASSASSIN...? THIS GOES DEEPER THAN I FEARED... I MUST--

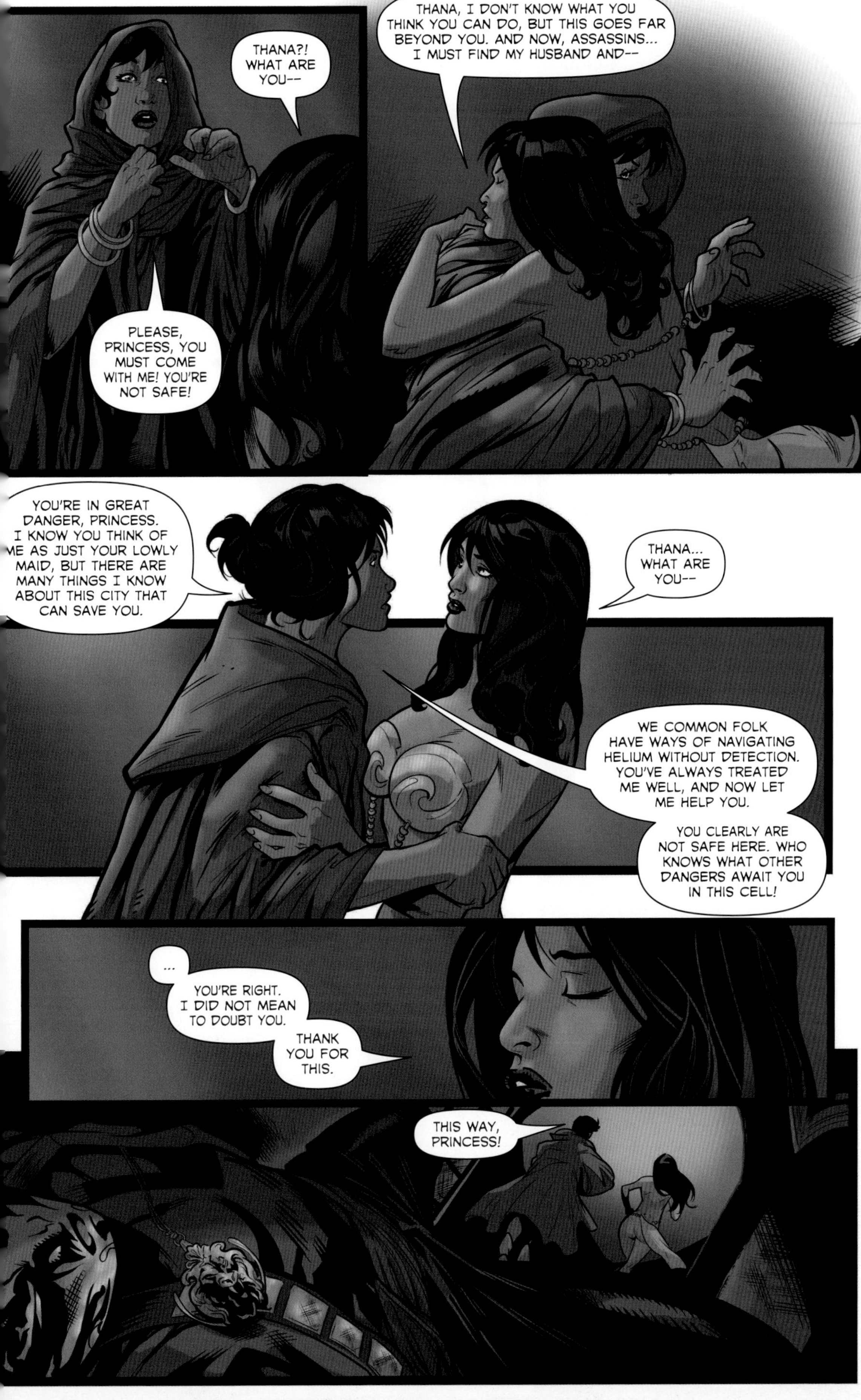
THANA?! WHAT ARE YOU--
PLEASE, PRINCESS, YOU MUST COME WITH ME! YOU'RE NOT SAFE!
THANA, I DON'T KNOW WHAT YOU THINK YOU CAN DO, BUT THIS GOES FAR BEYOND YOU. AND NOW, ASSASSINS... I MUST FIND MY HUSBAND AND--
YOU'RE IN GREAT DANGER, PRINCESS. I KNOW YOU THINK OF ME AS JUST YOUR LOWLY MAID, BUT THERE ARE MANY THINGS I KNOW ABOUT THIS CITY THAT CAN SAVE YOU.
THANA... WHAT ARE YOU--
WE COMMON FOLK HAVE WAYS OF NAVIGATING HELIUM WITHOUT DETECTION. YOU'VE ALWAYS TREATED ME WELL, AND NOW LET ME HELP YOU.
YOU CLEARLY ARE NOT SAFE HERE. WHO KNOWS WHAT OTHER DANGERS AWAIT YOU IN THIS CELL!
...
YOU'RE RIGHT. I DID NOT MEAN TO DOUBT YOU.
THANK YOU FOR THIS.
THIS WAY, PRINCESS!

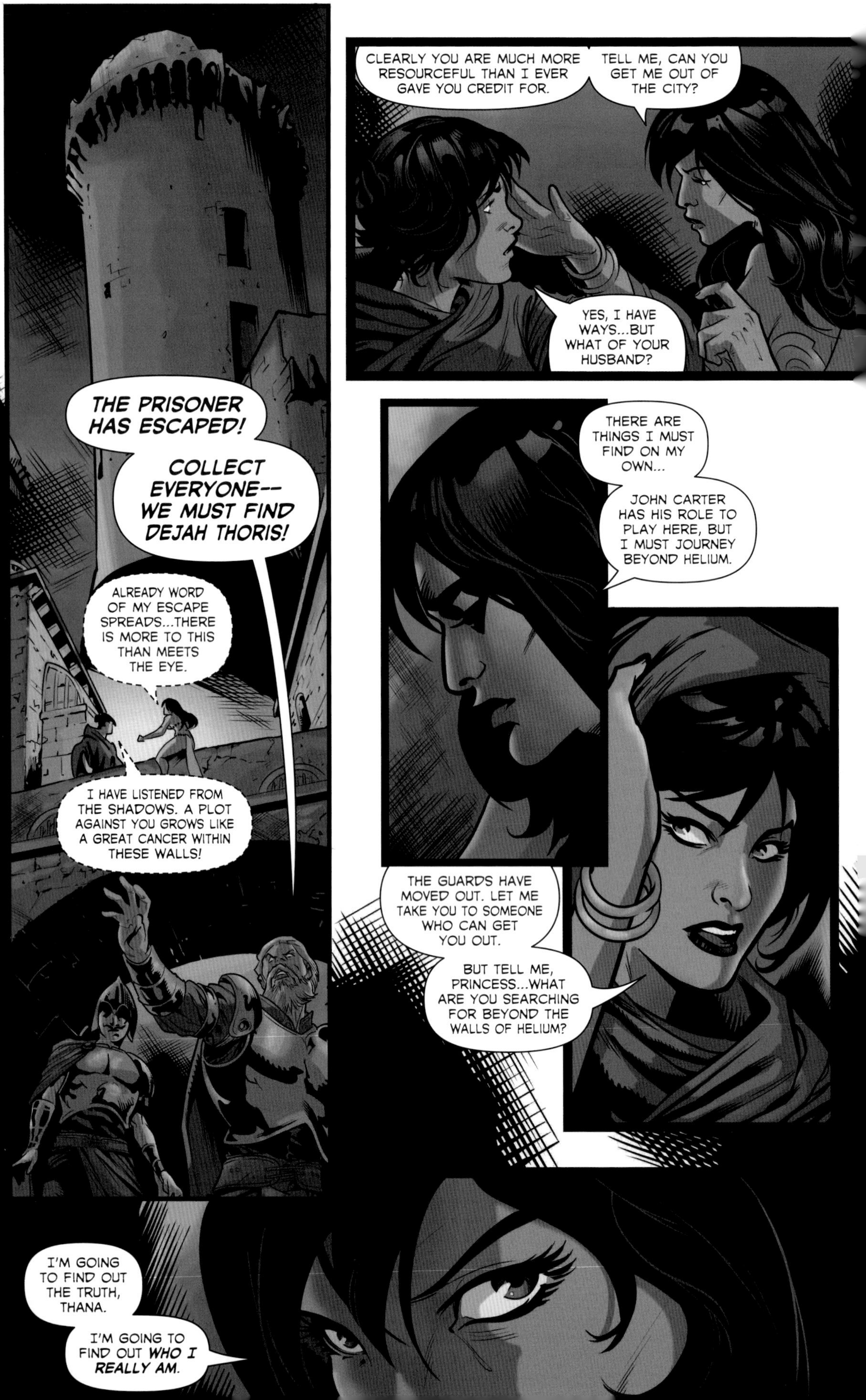
THE PRISONER HAS ESCAPED!
COLLECT EVERYONE-- WE MUST FIND DEJAH THORIS!
ALREADY WORD OF MY ESCAPE SPREADS...THERE IS MORE TO THIS THAN MEETS THE EYE.
I HAVE LISTENED FROM THE SHADOWS. A PLOT AGAINST YOU GROWS LIKE A GREAT CANCER WITHIN THESE WALLS!
CLEARLY YOU ARE MUCH MORE RESOURCEFUL THAN I EVER GAVE YOU CREDIT FOR.
TELL ME, CAN YOU GET ME OUT OF THE CITY?
YES, I HAVE WAYS...BUT WHAT OF YOUR HUSBAND?
THERE ARE THINGS I MUST FIND ON MY OWN...
JOHN CARTER HAS HIS ROLE TO PLAY HERE, BUT I MUST JOURNEY BEYOND HELIUM.
THE GUARDS HAVE MOVED OUT. LET ME TAKE YOU TO SOMEONE WHO CAN GET YOU OUT.
BUT TELL ME, PRINCESS...WHAT ARE YOU SEARCHING FOR BEYOND THE WALLS OF HELIUM?
I'M GOING TO FIND OUT THE TRUTH, THANA.
I'M GOING TO FIND OUT WHO I REALLY AM.

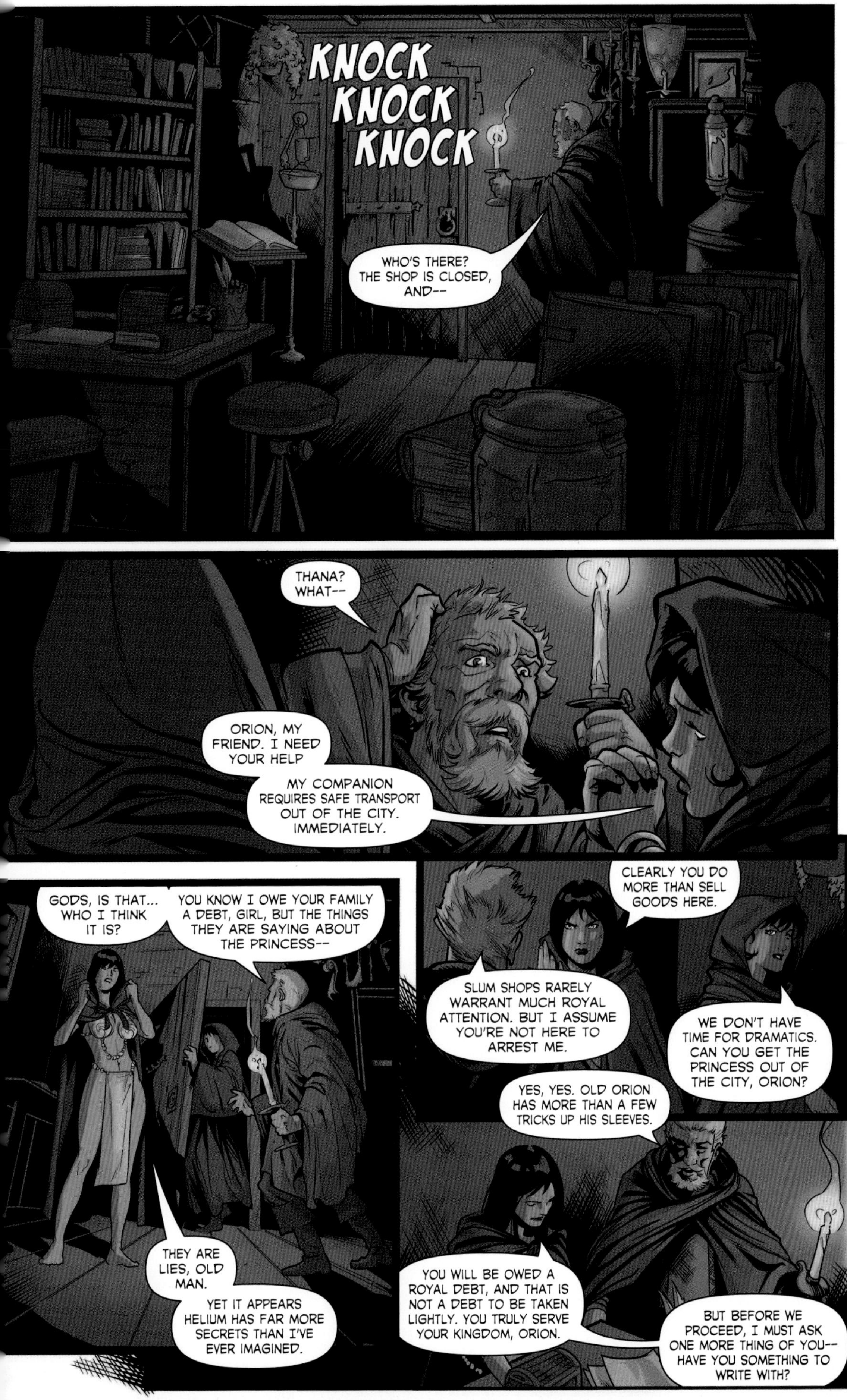
KNOCK KNOCK KNOCK
WHO'S THERE? THE SHOP IS CLOSED, AND--
THANA? WHAT--
ORION, MY FRIEND. I NEED YOUR HELP
MY COMPANION REQUIRES SAFE TRANSPORT OUT OF THE CITY. IMMEDIATELY.
GODS, IS THAT... WHO I THINK IT IS?
YOU KNOW I OWE YOUR FAMILY A DEBT, GIRL, BUT THE THINGS THEY ARE SAYING ABOUT THE PRINCESS--
THEY ARE LIES, OLD MAN.
YET IT APPEARS HELIUM HAS FAR MORE SECRETS THAN I'VE EVER IMAGINED.
CLEARLY YOU DO MORE THAN SELL GOODS HERE.
SLUM SHOPS RARELY WARRANT MUCH ROYAL ATTENTION. BUT I ASSUME YOU'RE NOT HERE TO ARREST ME.
WE DON'T HAVE TIME FOR DRAMATICS. CAN YOU GET THE PRINCESS OUT OF THE CITY, ORION?
YES, YES. OLD ORION HAS MORE THAN A FEW TRICKS UP HIS SLEEVES.
YOU WILL BE OWED A ROYAL DEBT, AND THAT IS NOT A DEBT TO BE TAKEN LIGHTLY. YOU TRULY SERVE YOUR KINGDOM, ORION.
BUT BEFORE WE PROCEED, I MUST ASK ONE MORE THING OF YOU-- HAVE YOU SOMETHING TO WRITE WITH?

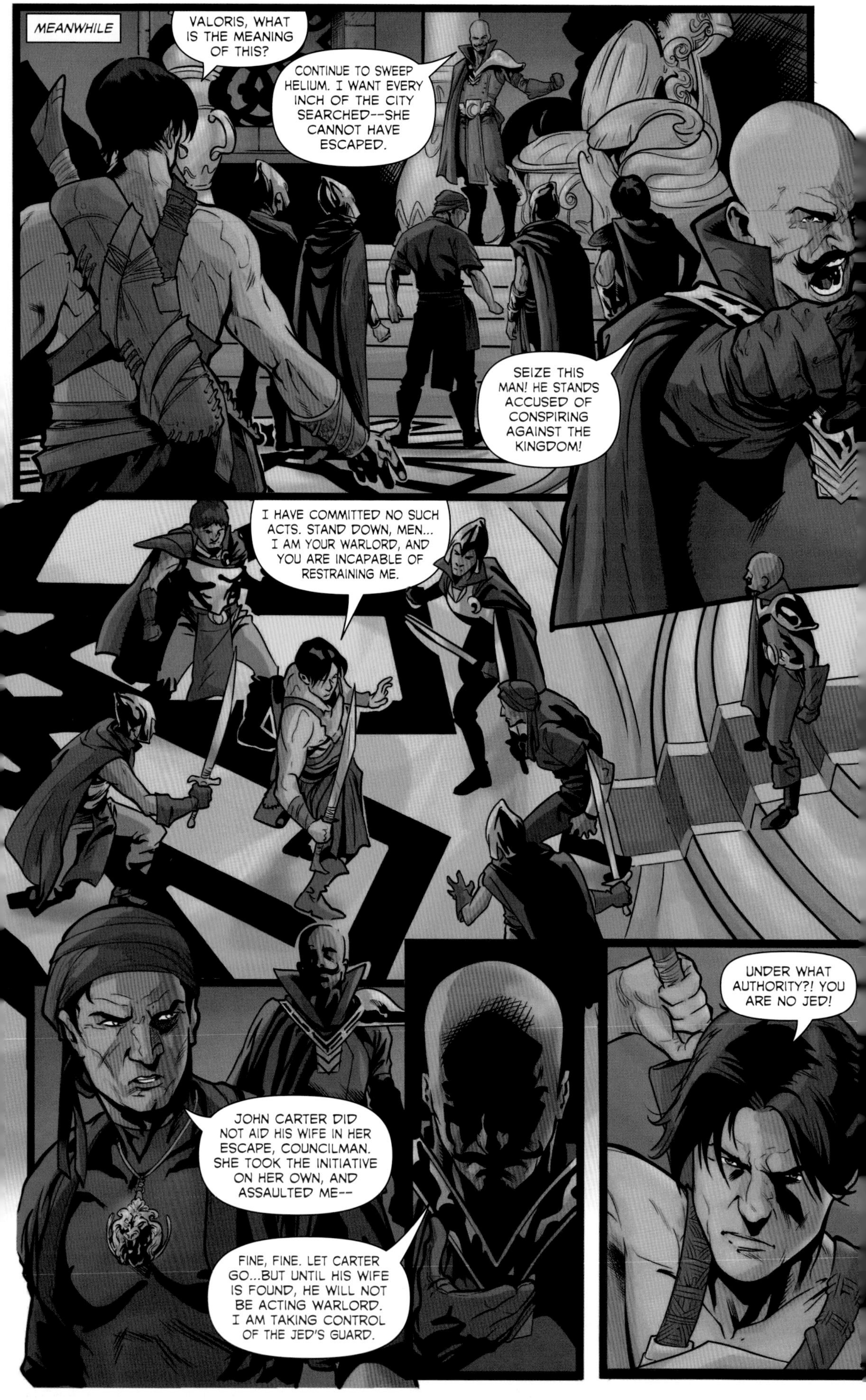
MEANWHILE
VALORIS, WHAT IS THE MEANING OF THIS?
CONTINUE TO SWEEP HELIUM. I WANT EVERY INCH OF THE CITY SEARCHED--SHE CANNOT HAVE ESCAPED.
SEIZE THIS MAN! HE STANDS ACCUSED OF CONSPIRING AGAINST THE KINGDOM!
I HAVE COMMITTED NO SUCH ACTS. STAND DOWN, MEN... I AM YOUR WARLORD, AND YOU ARE INCAPABLE OF RESTRAINING ME.
JOHN CARTER DID NOT AID HIS WIFE IN HER ESCAPE, COUNCILMAN. SHE TOOK THE INITIATIVE ON HER OWN, AND ASSAULTED ME--
FINE, FINE. LET CARTER GO...BUT UNTIL HIS WIFE IS FOUND, HE WILL NOT BE ACTING WARLORD. I AM TAKING CONTROL OF THE JED'S GUARD.
UNDER WHAT AUTHORITY?! YOU ARE NO JED!

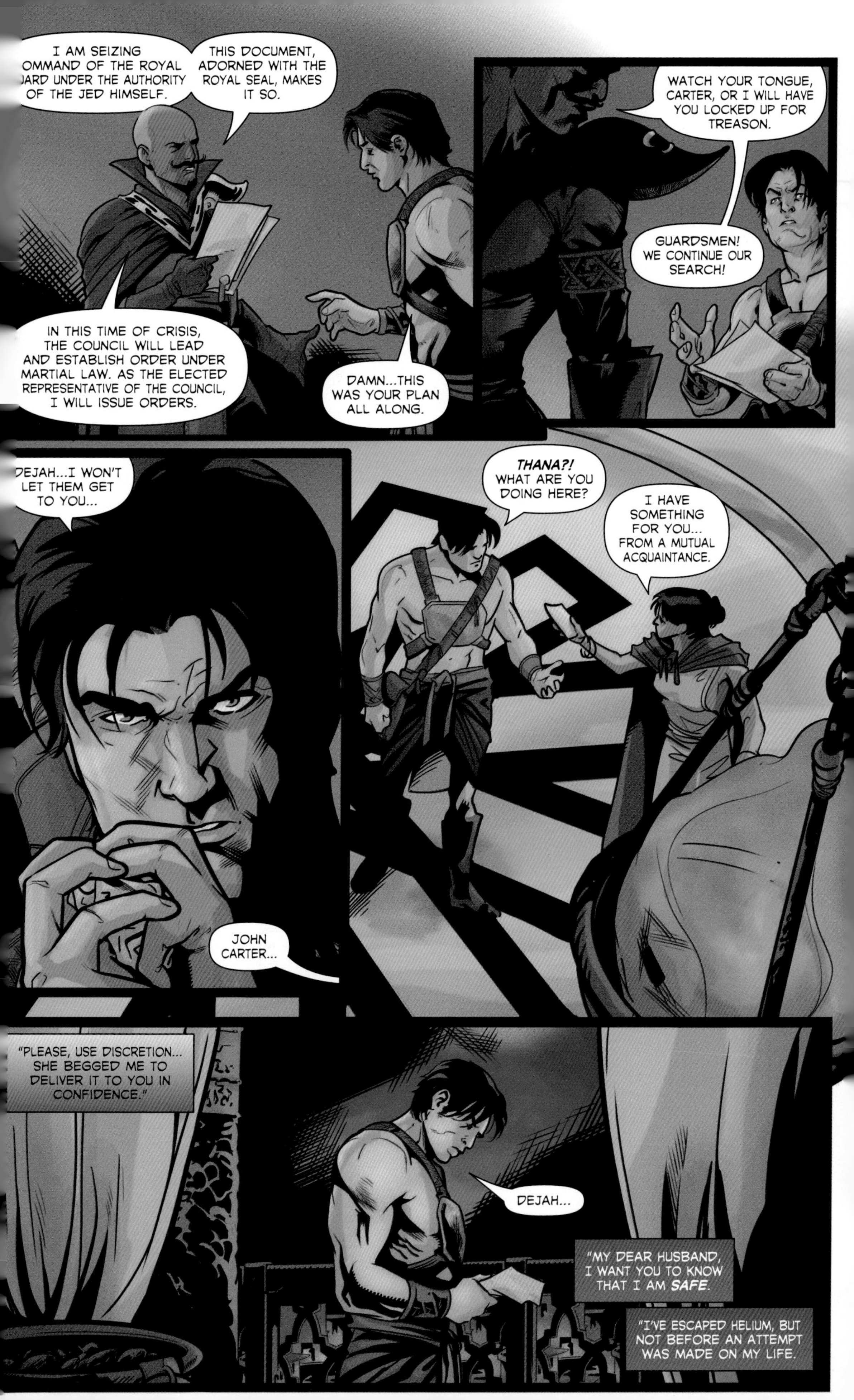
I AM SEIZING OMMAND OF THE ROYAL JARD UNDER THE AUTHORITY OF THE JED HIMSELF.
THIS DOCUMENT, ADORNED WITH THE ROYAL SEAL, MAKES IT SO.
IN THIS TIME OF CRISIS, THE COUNCIL WILL LEAD AND ESTABLISH ORDER UNDER MARTIAL LAW. AS THE ELECTED REPRESENTATIVE OF THE COUNCIL, I WILL ISSUE ORDERS.
DAMN...THIS WAS YOUR PLAN ALL ALONG.
WATCH YOUR TONGUE, CARTER, OR I WILL HAVE YOU LOCKED UP FOR TREASON.
GUARDSMEN! WE CONTINUE OUR SEARCH!
DEJAH...I WON'T LET THEM GET TO YOU...
JOHN CARTER...
THANA?! WHAT ARE YOU DOING HERE?
I HAVE SOMETHING FOR YOU... FROM A MUTUAL ACQUAINTANCE.
"PLEASE, USE DISCRETION... SHE BEGGED ME TO DELIVER IT TO YOU IN CONFIDENCE."
DEJAH...
"MY DEAR HUSBAND, I WANT YOU TO KNOW THAT I AM SAFE.
"I'VE ESCAPED HELIUM, BUT NOT BEFORE AN ATTEMPT WAS MADE ON MY LIFE.

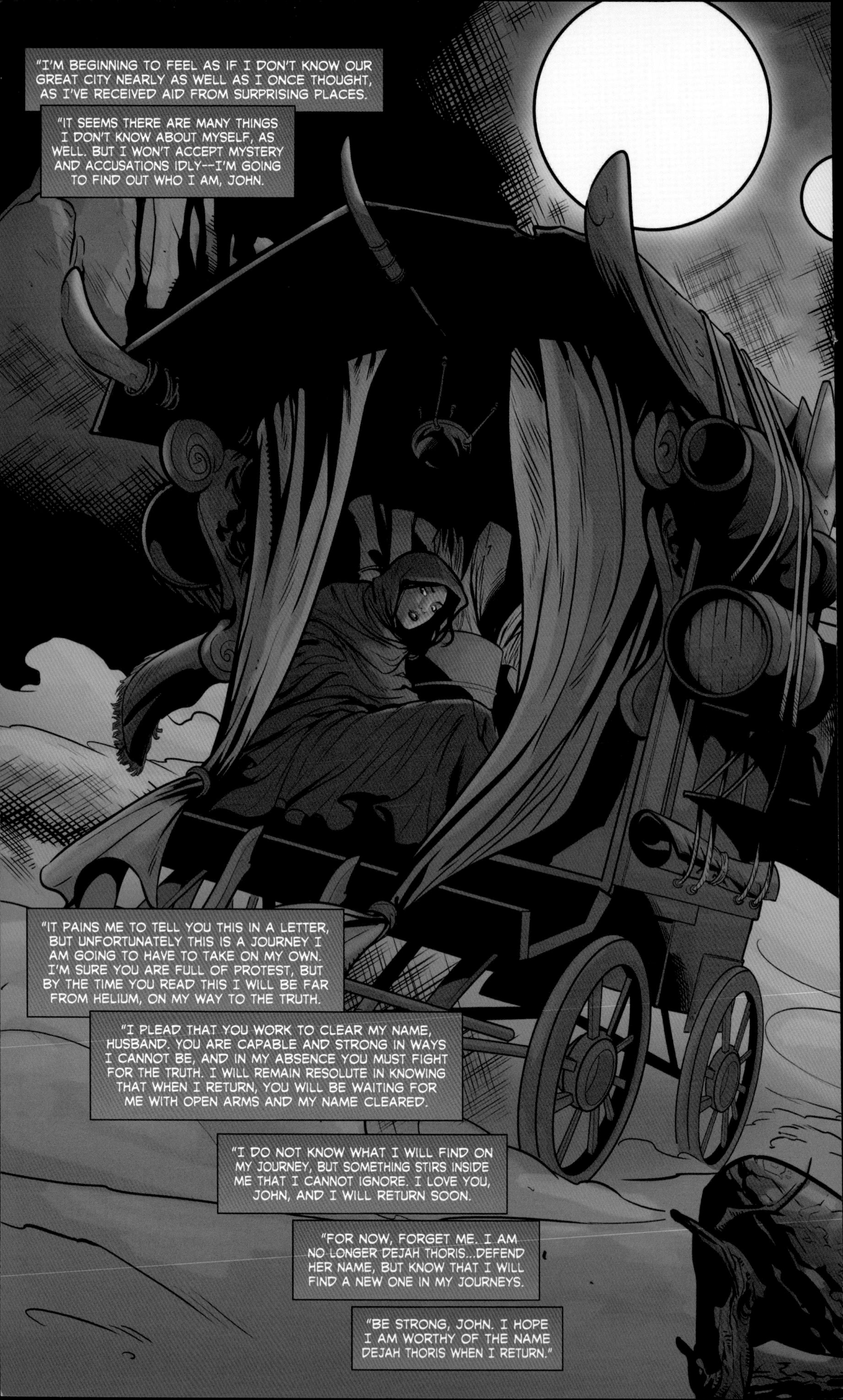
"I'M BEGINNING TO FEEL AS IF I DON'T KNOW OUR GREAT CITY NEARLY AS WELL AS I ONCE THOUGHT, AS I'VE RECEIVED AID FROM SURPRISING PLACES.
"IT SEEMS THERE ARE MANY THINGS I DON'T KNOW ABOUT MYSELF, AS WELL. BUT I WON'T ACCEPT MYSTERY AND ACCUSATIONS IDLY--I'M GOING TO FIND OUT WHO I AM, JOHN.
"IT PAINS ME TO TELL YOU THIS IN A LETTER, BUT UNFORTUNATELY THIS IS A JOURNEY I AM GOING TO HAVE TO TAKE ON MY OWN. I'M SURE YOU ARE FULL OF PROTEST, BUT BY THE TIME YOU READ THIS I WILL BE FAR FROM HELIUM, ON MY WAY TO THE TRUTH.
"I PLEAD THAT YOU WORK TO CLEAR MY NAME, HUSBAND. YOU ARE CAPABLE AND STRONG IN WAYS I CANNOT BE, AND IN MY ABSENCE YOU MUST FIGHT FOR THE TRUTH. I WILL REMAIN RESOLUTE IN KNOWING THAT WHEN I RETURN, YOU WILL BE WAITING FOR ME WITH OPEN ARMS AND MY NAME CLEARED.
"I DO NOT KNOW WHAT I WILL FIND ON MY JOURNEY, BUT SOMETHING STIRS INSIDE ME THAT I CANNOT IGNORE. I LOVE YOU, JOHN, AND I WILL RETURN SOON.
"FOR NOW, FORGET ME. I AM NO LONGER DEJAH THORIS...DEFEND HER NAME, BUT KNOW THAT I WILL FIND A NEW ONE IN MY JOURNEYS.
"BE STRONG, JOHN. I HOPE I AM WORTHY OF THE NAME DEJAH THORIS WHEN I RETURN."

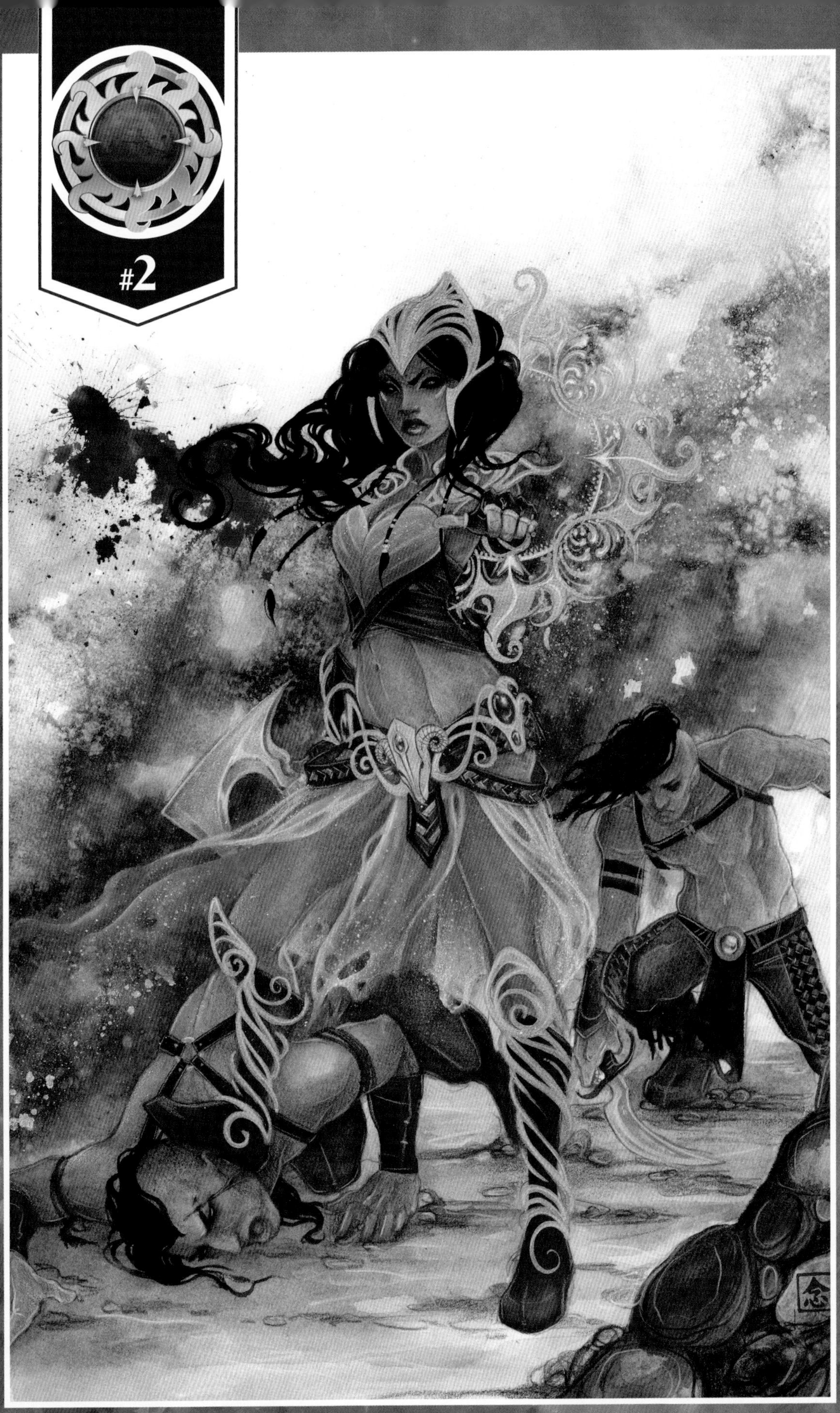
#2

cover by NEN CHANG

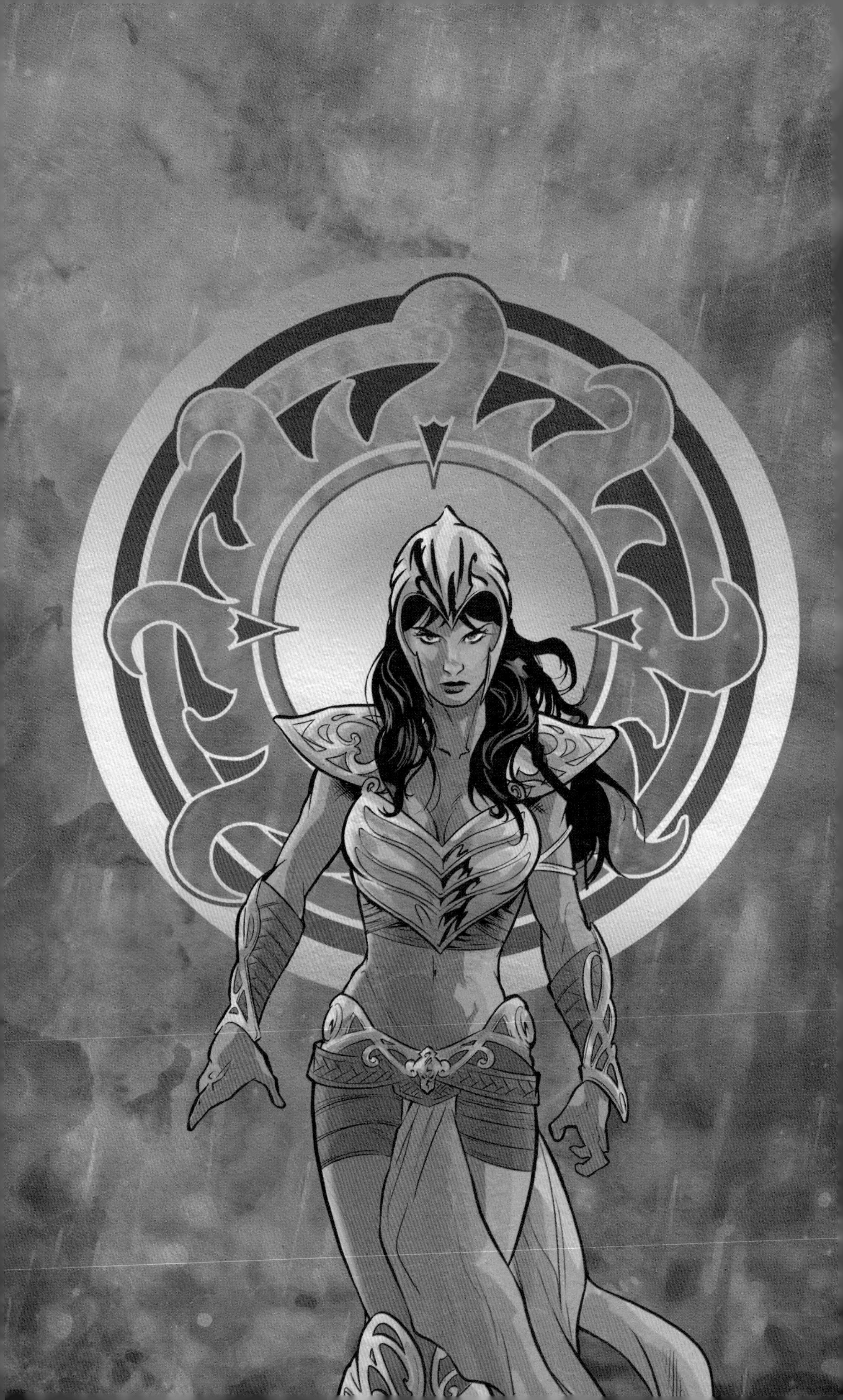

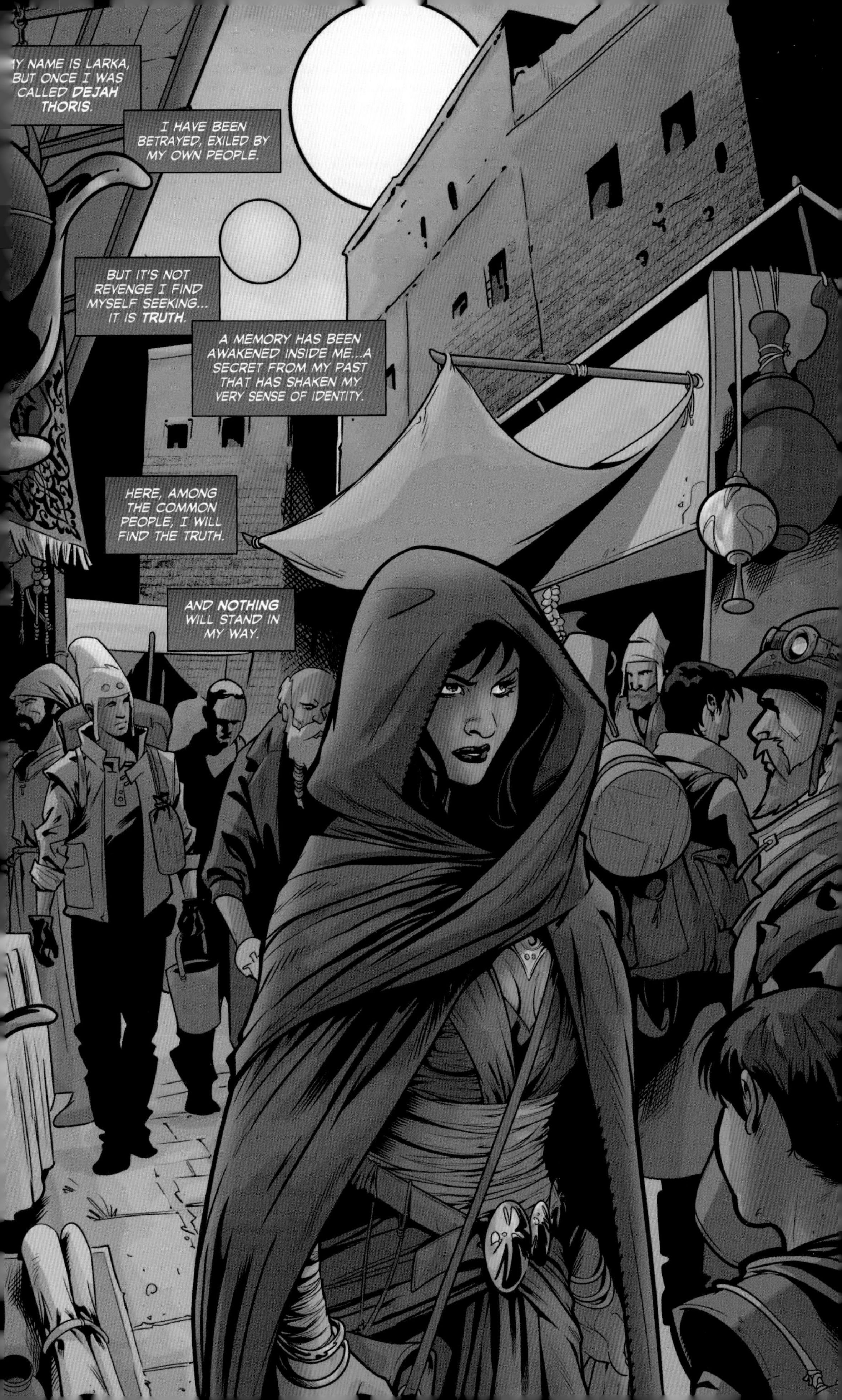
MY NAME IS LARKA, BUT ONCE I WAS CALLED DEJAH THORIS.
I HAVE BEEN BETRAYED, EXILED BY MY OWN PEOPLE.
BUT IT'S NOT REVENGE I FIND MYSELF SEEKING... IT IS TRUTH.
A MEMORY HAS BEEN AWAKENED INSIDE ME...A SECRET FROM MY PAST THAT HAS SHAKEN MY VERY SENSE OF IDENTITY.
HERE, AMONG THE COMMON PEOPLE, I WILL FIND THE TRUTH.
AND NOTHING WILL STAND IN MY WAY.

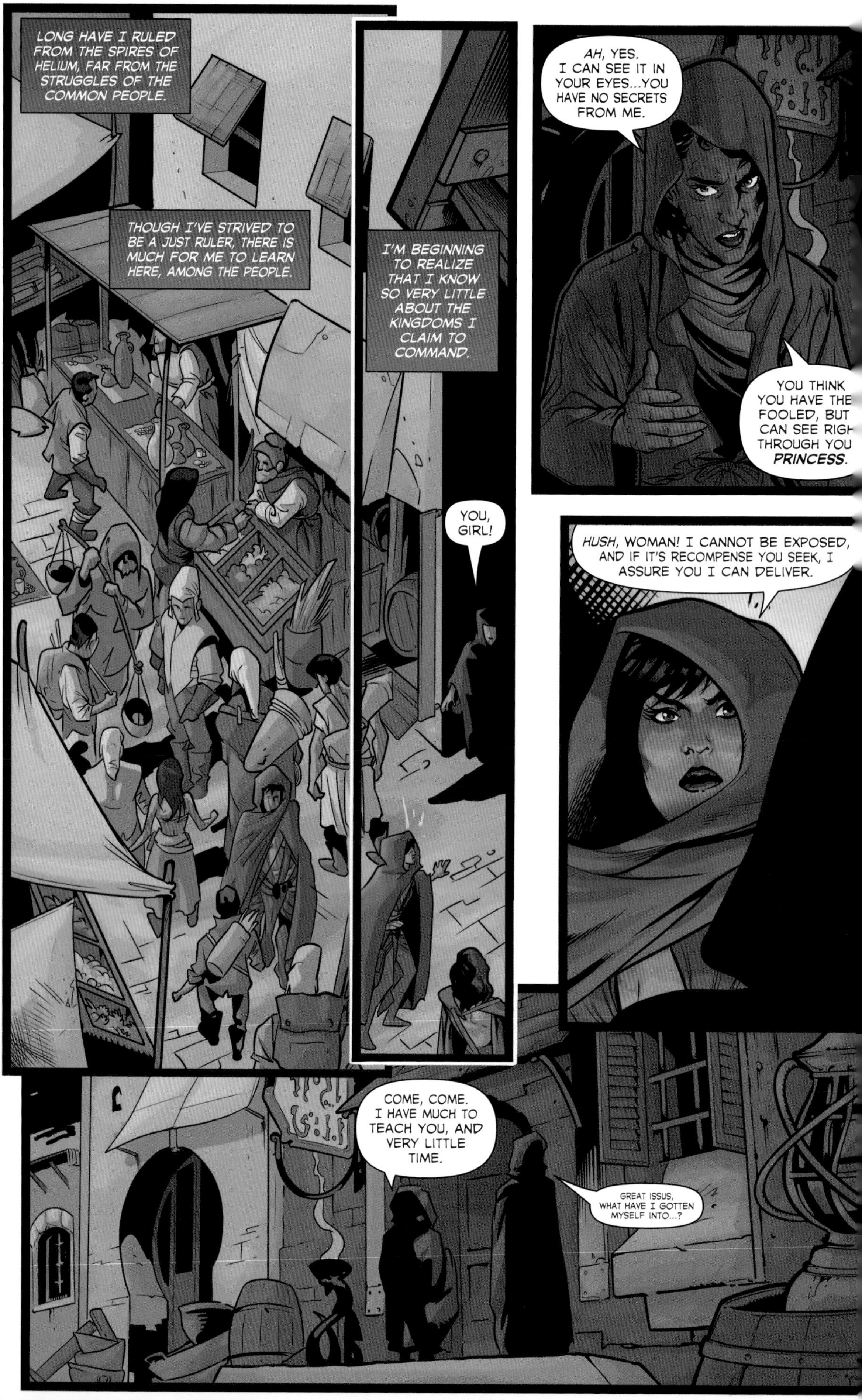
LONG HAVE I RULED FROM THE SPIRES OF HELIUM, FAR FROM THE STRUGGLES OF THE COMMON PEOPLE.
THOUGH I'VE STRIVED TO BE A JUST RULER, THERE IS MUCH FOR ME TO LEARN HERE, AMONG THE PEOPLE.
I'M BEGINNING TO REALIZE THAT I KNOW SO VERY LITTLE ABOUT THE KINGDOMS I CLAIM TO COMMAND.
YOU, GIRL!
AH, YES. I CAN SEE IT IN YOUR EYES...YOU HAVE NO SECRETS FROM ME.
YOU THINK YOU HAVE THE FOOLED, BUT CAN SEE RIGH THROUGH YOU PRINCESS.
HUSH, WOMAN! I CANNOT BE EXPOSED, AND IF IT'S RECOMPENSE YOU SEEK, I ASSURE YOU I CAN DELIVER.
COME, COME. I HAVE MUCH TO TEACH YOU, AND VERY LITTLE TIME.
GREAT ISSUS, WHAT HAVE I GOTTEN MYSELF INTO...?

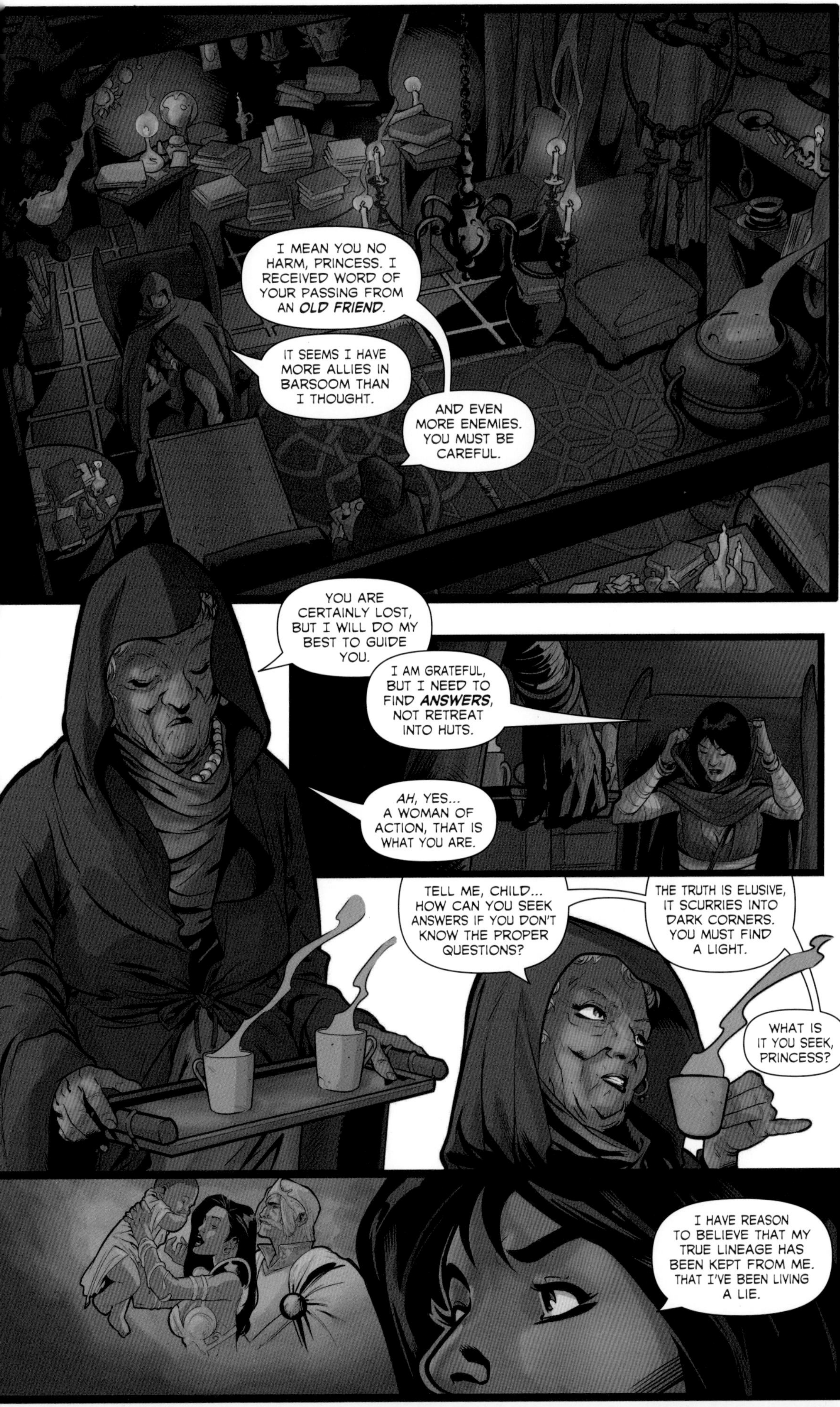
I MEAN YOU NO HARM, PRINCESS. I RECEIVED WORD OF YOUR PASSING FROM AN *OLD FRIEND*.
IT SEEMS I HAVE MORE ALLIES IN BARSOOM THAN I THOUGHT.
AND EVEN MORE ENEMIES. YOU MUST BE CAREFUL.
YOU ARE CERTAINLY LOST, BUT I WILL DO MY BEST TO GUIDE YOU.
I AM GRATEFUL, BUT I NEED TO FIND ***ANSWERS***, NOT RETREAT INTO HUTS.
AH, YES... A WOMAN OF ACTION, THAT IS WHAT YOU ARE.
TELL ME, CHILD... HOW CAN YOU SEEK ANSWERS IF YOU DON'T KNOW THE PROPER QUESTIONS?
THE TRUTH IS ELUSIVE, IT SCURRIES INTO DARK CORNERS. YOU MUST FIND A LIGHT.
WHAT IS IT YOU SEEK, PRINCESS?
I HAVE REASON TO BELIEVE THAT MY TRUE LINEAGE HAS BEEN KEPT FROM ME. THAT I'VE BEEN LIVING A LIE.

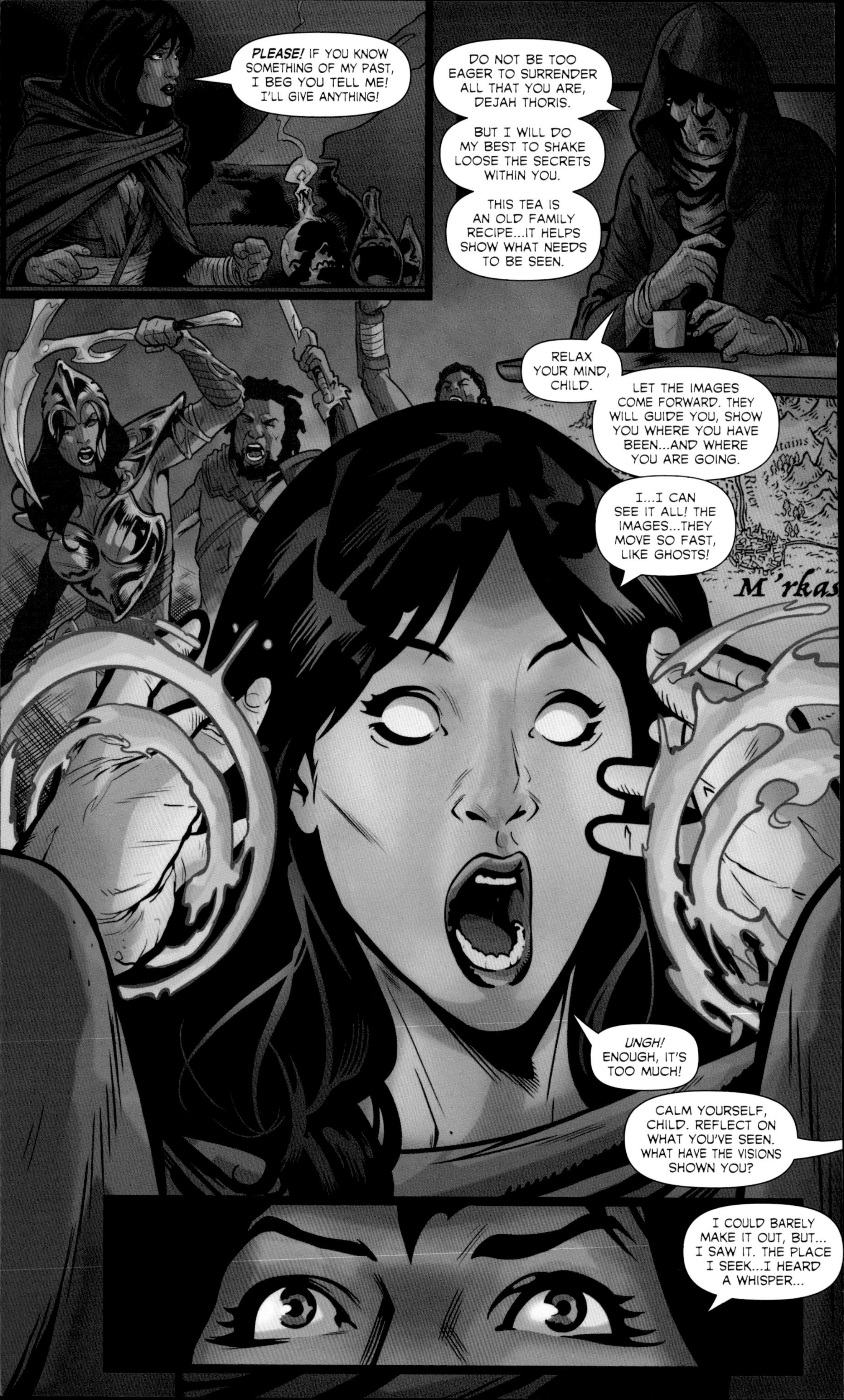
PLEASE! IF YOU KNOW SOMETHING OF MY PAST, I BEG YOU TELL ME! I'LL GIVE ANYTHING!
DO NOT BE TOO EAGER TO SURRENDER ALL THAT YOU ARE, DEJAH THORIS.
BUT I WILL DO MY BEST TO SHAKE LOOSE THE SECRETS WITHIN YOU.
THIS TEA IS AN OLD FAMILY RECIPE...IT HELPS SHOW WHAT NEEDS TO BE SEEN.
RELAX YOUR MIND, CHILD.
LET THE IMAGES COME FORWARD. THEY WILL GUIDE YOU, SHOW YOU WHERE YOU HAVE BEEN...AND WHERE YOU ARE GOING.
I...I CAN SEE IT ALL! THE IMAGES...THEY MOVE SO FAST, LIKE GHOSTS!
M'rkas
River
UNGH! ENOUGH, IT'S TOO MUCH!
CALM YOURSELF, CHILD. REFLECT ON WHAT YOU'VE SEEN. WHAT HAVE THE VISIONS SHOWN YOU?
I COULD BARELY MAKE IT OUT, BUT... I SAW IT. THE PLACE I SEEK...I HEARD A WHISPER...

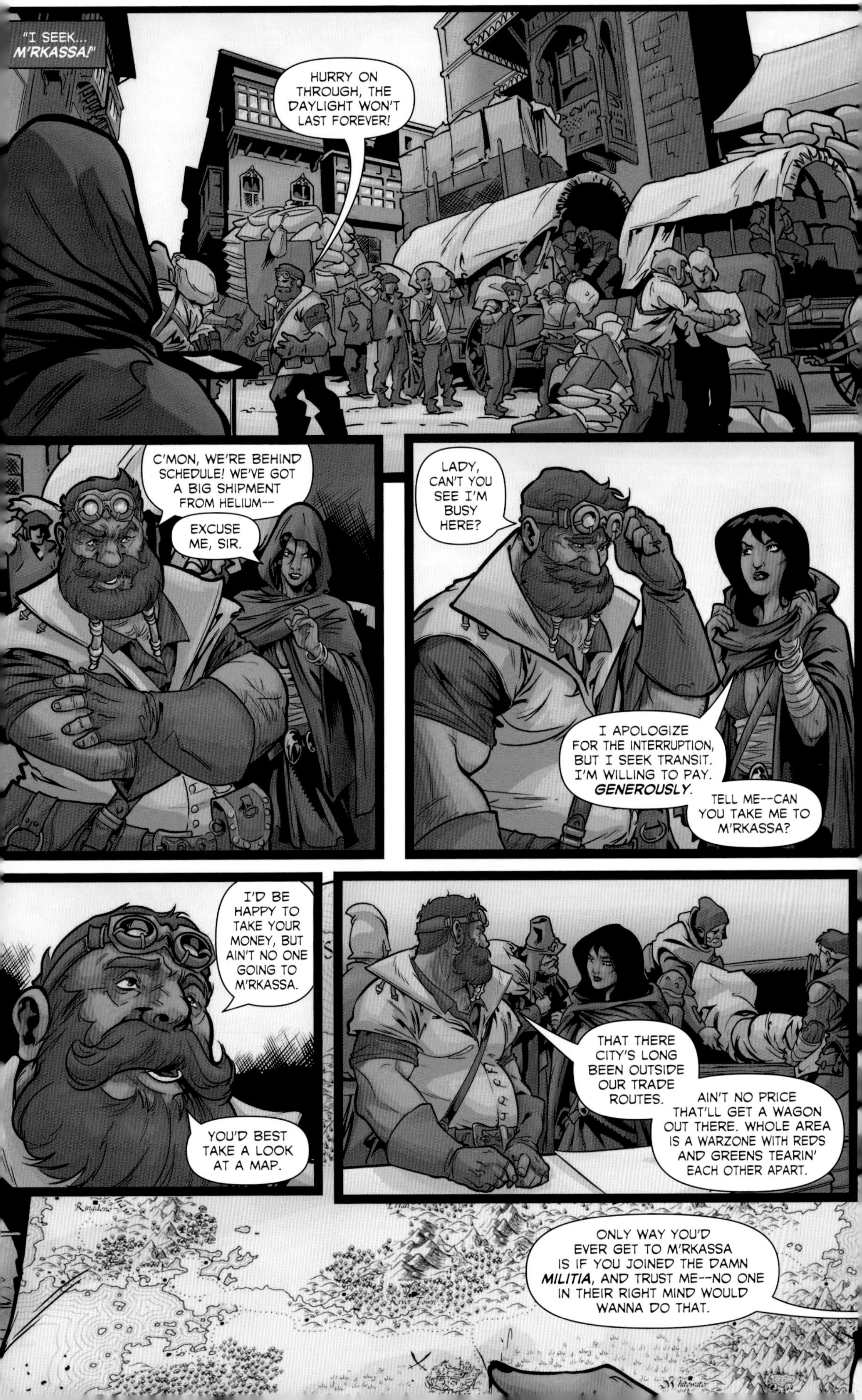
"I SEEK... M'RKASSA!"
HURRY ON THROUGH, THE DAYLIGHT WON'T LAST FOREVER!
C'MON, WE'RE BEHIND SCHEDULE! WE'VE GOT A BIG SHIPMENT FROM HELIUM--
EXCUSE ME, SIR.
LADY, CAN'T YOU SEE I'M BUSY HERE?
I APOLOGIZE FOR THE INTERRUPTION, BUT I SEEK TRANSIT. I'M WILLING TO PAY. GENEROUSLY.
TELL ME--CAN YOU TAKE ME TO M'RKASSA?
I'D BE HAPPY TO TAKE YOUR MONEY, BUT AIN'T NO ONE GOING TO M'RKASSA.
YOU'D BEST TAKE A LOOK AT A MAP.
THAT THERE CITY'S LONG BEEN OUTSIDE OUR TRADE ROUTES.
AIN'T NO PRICE THAT'LL GET A WAGON OUT THERE. WHOLE AREA IS A WARZONE WITH REDS AND GREENS TEARIN' EACH OTHER APART.
ONLY WAY YOU'D EVER GET TO M'RKASSA IS IF YOU JOINED THE DAMN MILITIA, AND TRUST ME--NO ONE IN THEIR RIGHT MIND WOULD WANNA DO THAT.

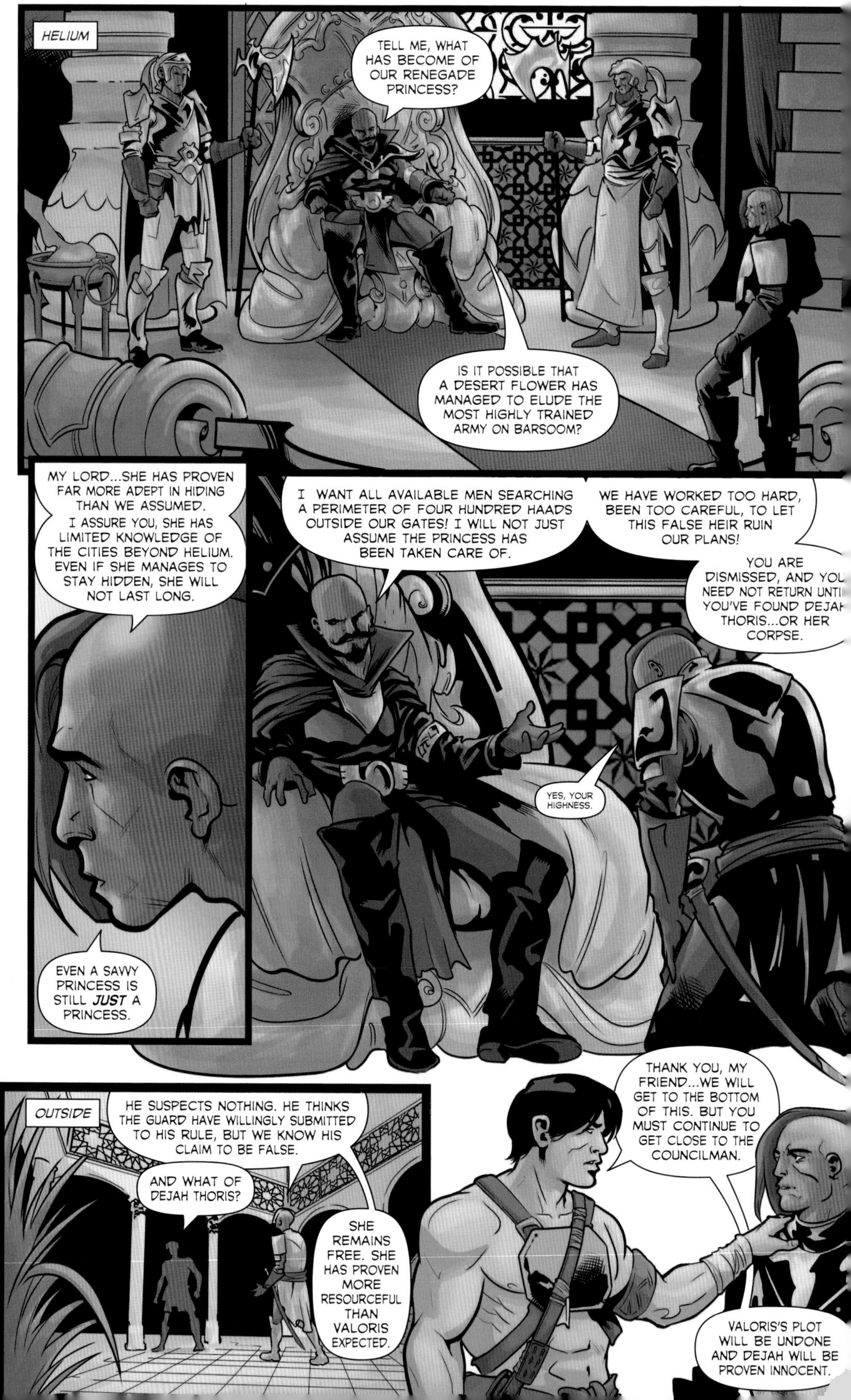
HELIUM
TELL ME, WHAT HAS BECOME OF OUR RENEGADE PRINCESS?
IS IT POSSIBLE THAT A DESERT FLOWER HAS MANAGED TO ELUDE THE MOST HIGHLY TRAINED ARMY ON BARSOOM?
MY LORD...SHE HAS PROVEN FAR MORE ADEPT IN HIDING THAN WE ASSUMED.
I ASSURE YOU, SHE HAS LIMITED KNOWLEDGE OF THE CITIES BEYOND HELIUM. EVEN IF SHE MANAGES TO STAY HIDDEN, SHE WILL NOT LAST LONG.
EVEN A SAVVY PRINCESS IS STILL *JUST* A PRINCESS.
I WANT ALL AVAILABLE MEN SEARCHING A PERIMETER OF FOUR HUNDRED HAADS OUTSIDE OUR GATES! I WILL NOT JUST ASSUME THE PRINCESS HAS BEEN TAKEN CARE OF.
WE HAVE WORKED TOO HARD, BEEN TOO CAREFUL, TO LET THIS FALSE HEIR RUIN OUR PLANS!
YOU ARE DISMISSED, AND YOU NEED NOT RETURN UNTIL YOU'VE FOUND DEJAH THORIS...OR HER CORPSE.
YES, YOUR HIGHNESS.
OUTSIDE
HE SUSPECTS NOTHING. HE THINKS THE GUARD HAVE WILLINGLY SUBMITTED TO HIS RULE, BUT WE KNOW HIS CLAIM TO BE FALSE.
AND WHAT OF DEJAH THORIS?
SHE REMAINS FREE. SHE HAS PROVEN MORE RESOURCEFUL THAN VALORIS EXPECTED.
THANK YOU, MY FRIEND...WE WILL GET TO THE BOTTOM OF THIS. BUT YOU MUST CONTINUE TO GET CLOSE TO THE COUNCILMAN.
VALORIS'S PLOT WILL BE UNDONE AND DEJAH WILL BE PROVEN INNOCENT.

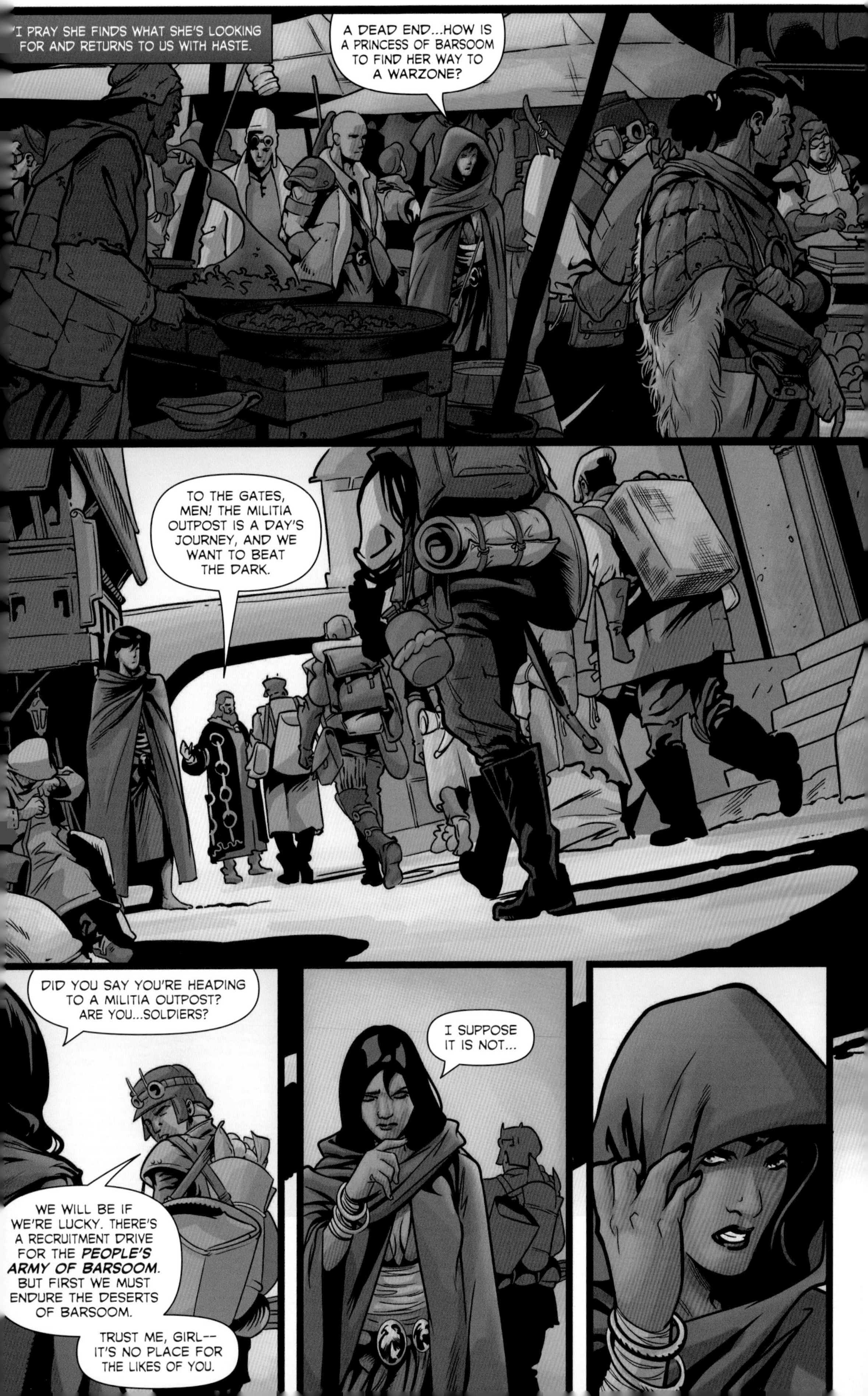
I PRAY SHE FINDS WHAT SHE'S LOOKING FOR AND RETURNS TO US WITH HASTE.
A DEAD END...HOW IS A PRINCESS OF BARSOOM TO FIND HER WAY TO A WARZONE?
TO THE GATES, MEN! THE MILITIA OUTPOST IS A DAY'S JOURNEY, AND WE WANT TO BEAT THE DARK.
DID YOU SAY YOU'RE HEADING TO A MILITIA OUTPOST? ARE YOU...SOLDIERS?
WE WILL BE IF WE'RE LUCKY. THERE'S A RECRUITMENT DRIVE FOR THE PEOPLE'S ARMY OF BARSOOM. BUT FIRST WE MUST ENDURE THE DESERTS OF BARSOOM.
TRUST ME, GIRL-- IT'S NO PLACE FOR THE LIKES OF YOU.
I SUPPOSE IT IS NOT...

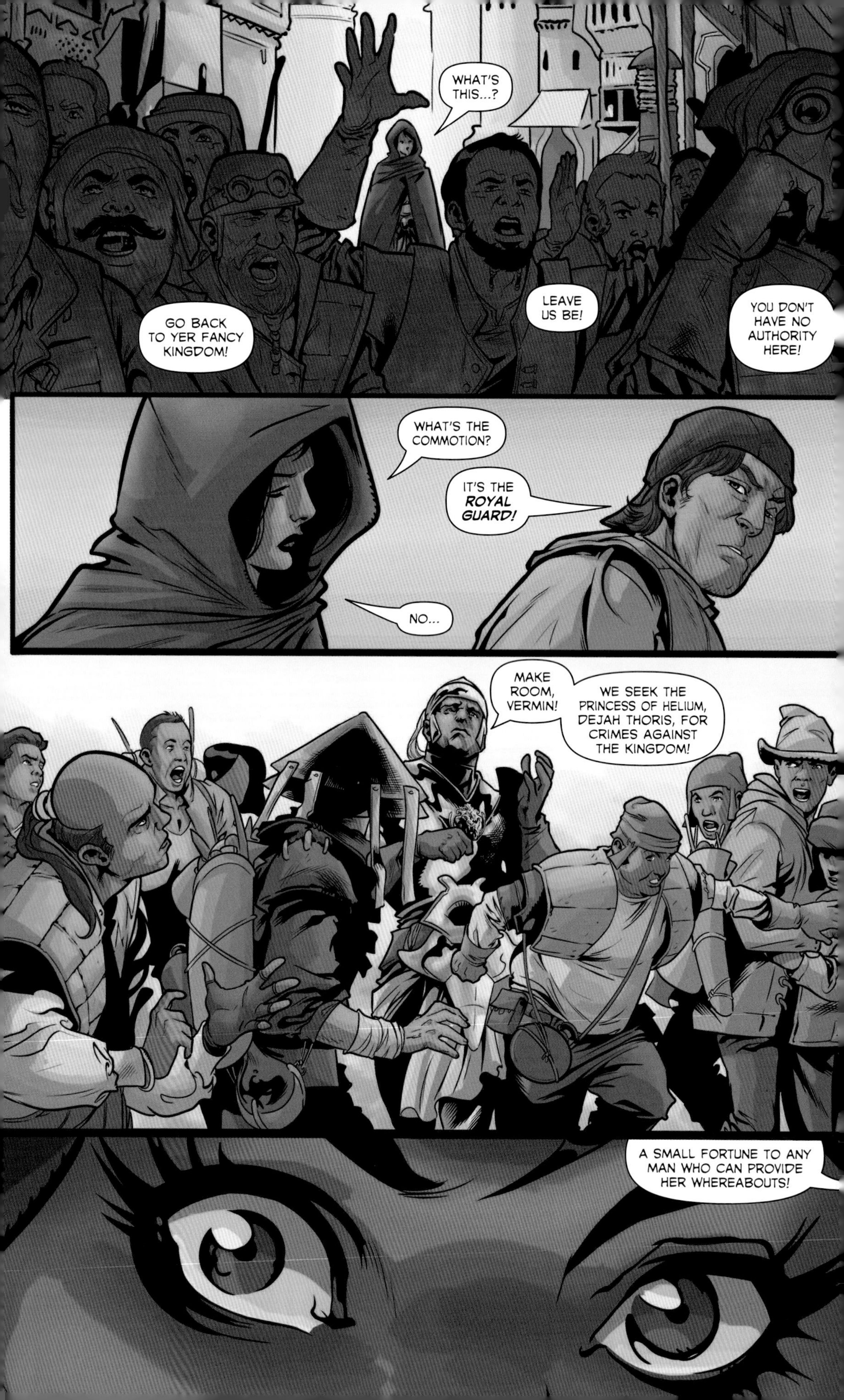
WHAT'S THIS...?
GO BACK TO YER FANCY KINGDOM!
LEAVE US BE!
YOU DON'T HAVE NO AUTHORITY HERE!
WHAT'S THE COMMOTION?
IT'S THE ROYAL GUARD!
NO...
MAKE ROOM, VERMIN!
WE SEEK THE PRINCESS OF HELIUM, DEJAH THORIS, FOR CRIMES AGAINST THE KINGDOM!
A SMALL FORTUNE TO ANY MAN WHO CAN PROVIDE HER WHEREABOUTS!

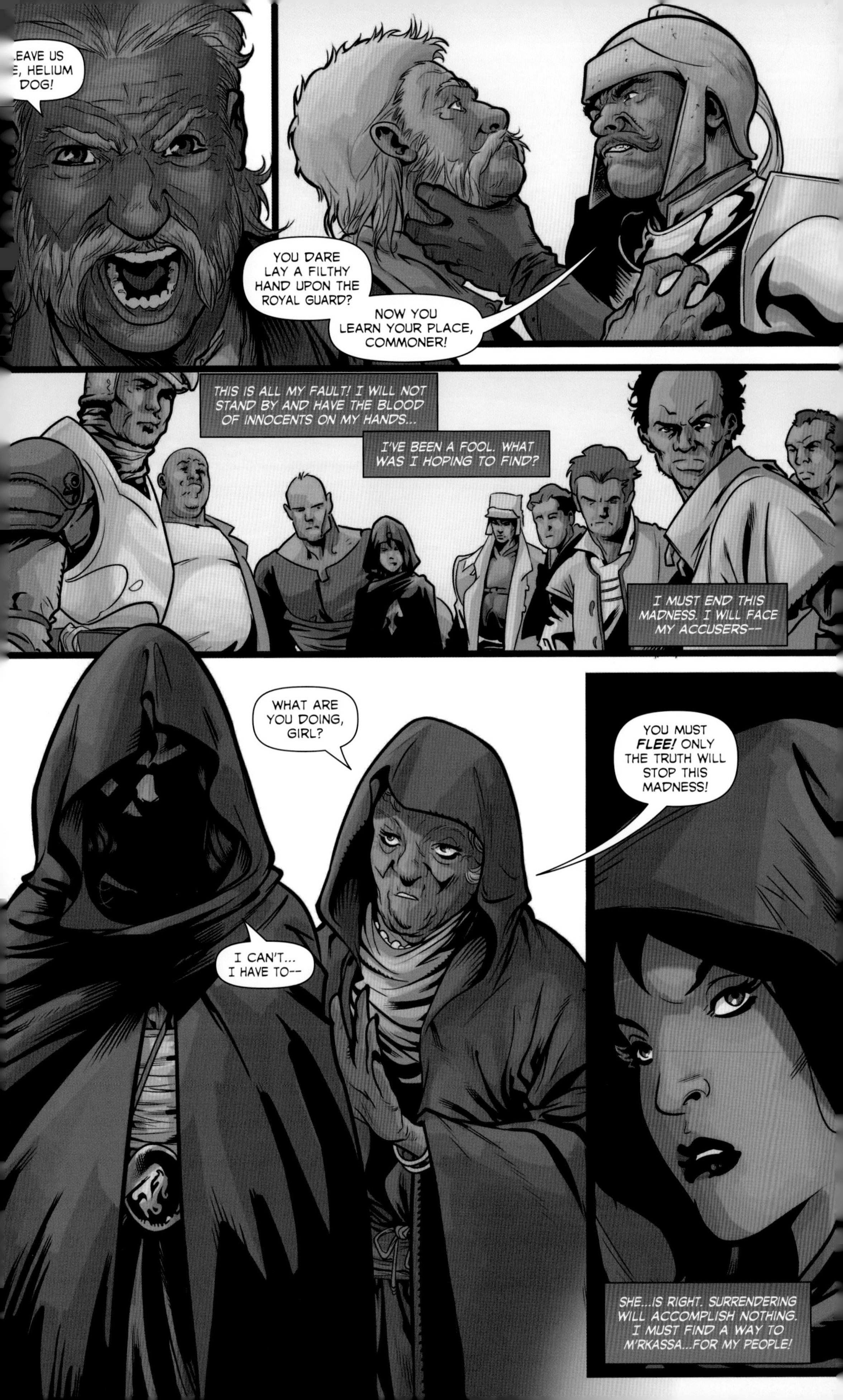
EAVE US
E, HELIUM
DOG!
YOU DARE LAY A FILTHY HAND UPON THE ROYAL GUARD?
NOW YOU LEARN YOUR PLACE, COMMONER!
THIS IS ALL MY FAULT! I WILL NOT STAND BY AND HAVE THE BLOOD OF INNOCENTS ON MY HANDS...
I'VE BEEN A FOOL. WHAT WAS I HOPING TO FIND?
I MUST END THIS MADNESS. I WILL FACE MY ACCUSERS--
WHAT ARE YOU DOING, GIRL?
I CAN'T... I HAVE TO--
YOU MUST FLEE! ONLY THE TRUTH WILL STOP THIS MADNESS!
SHE...IS RIGHT. SURRENDERING WILL ACCOMPLISH NOTHING. I MUST FIND A WAY TO M'RKASSA...FOR MY PEOPLE!

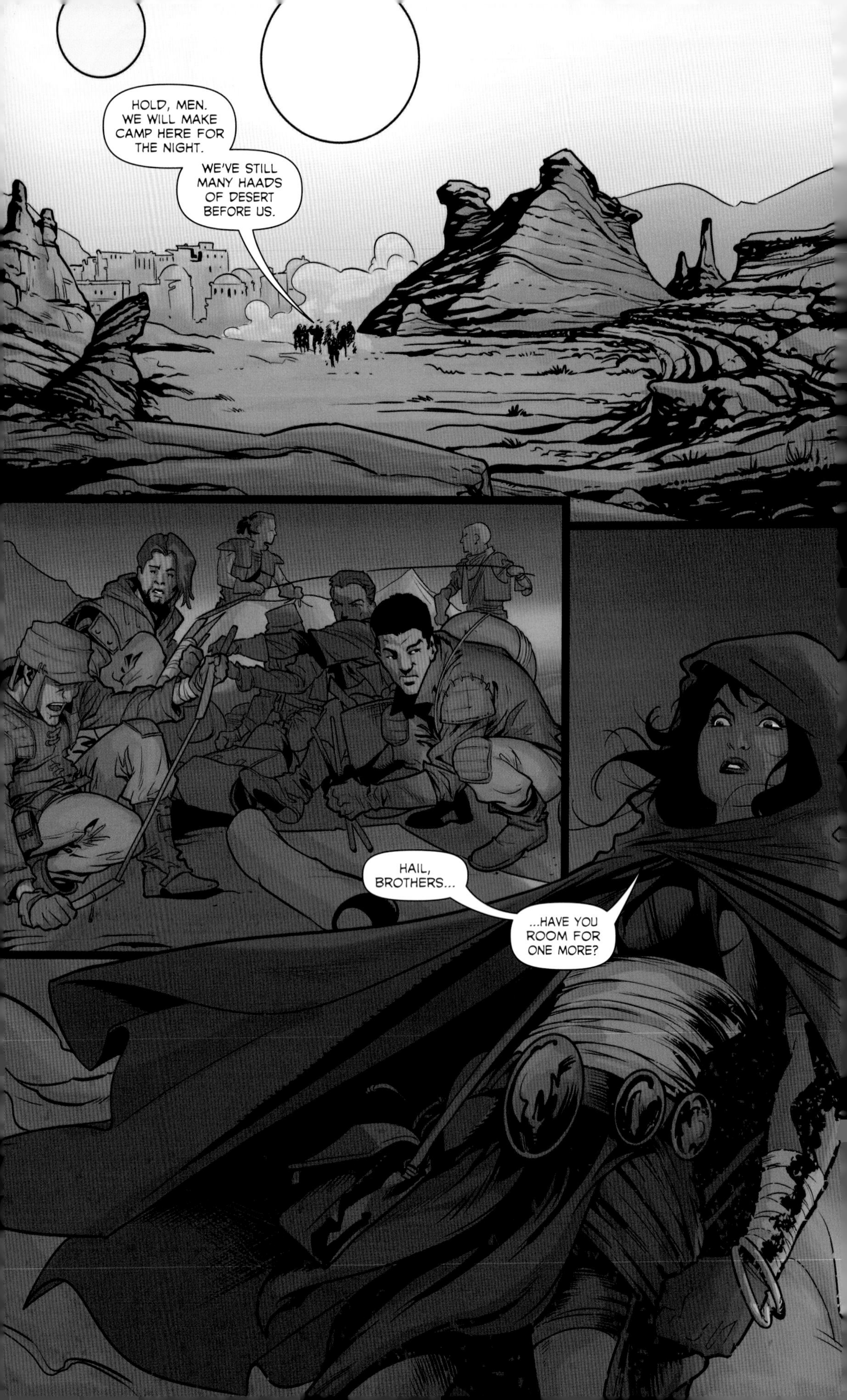

HOLD, MEN. WE WILL MAKE CAMP HERE FOR THE NIGHT.
WE'VE STILL MANY HAADS OF DESERT BEFORE US.
HAIL, BROTHERS...
...HAVE YOU ROOM FOR ONE MORE?

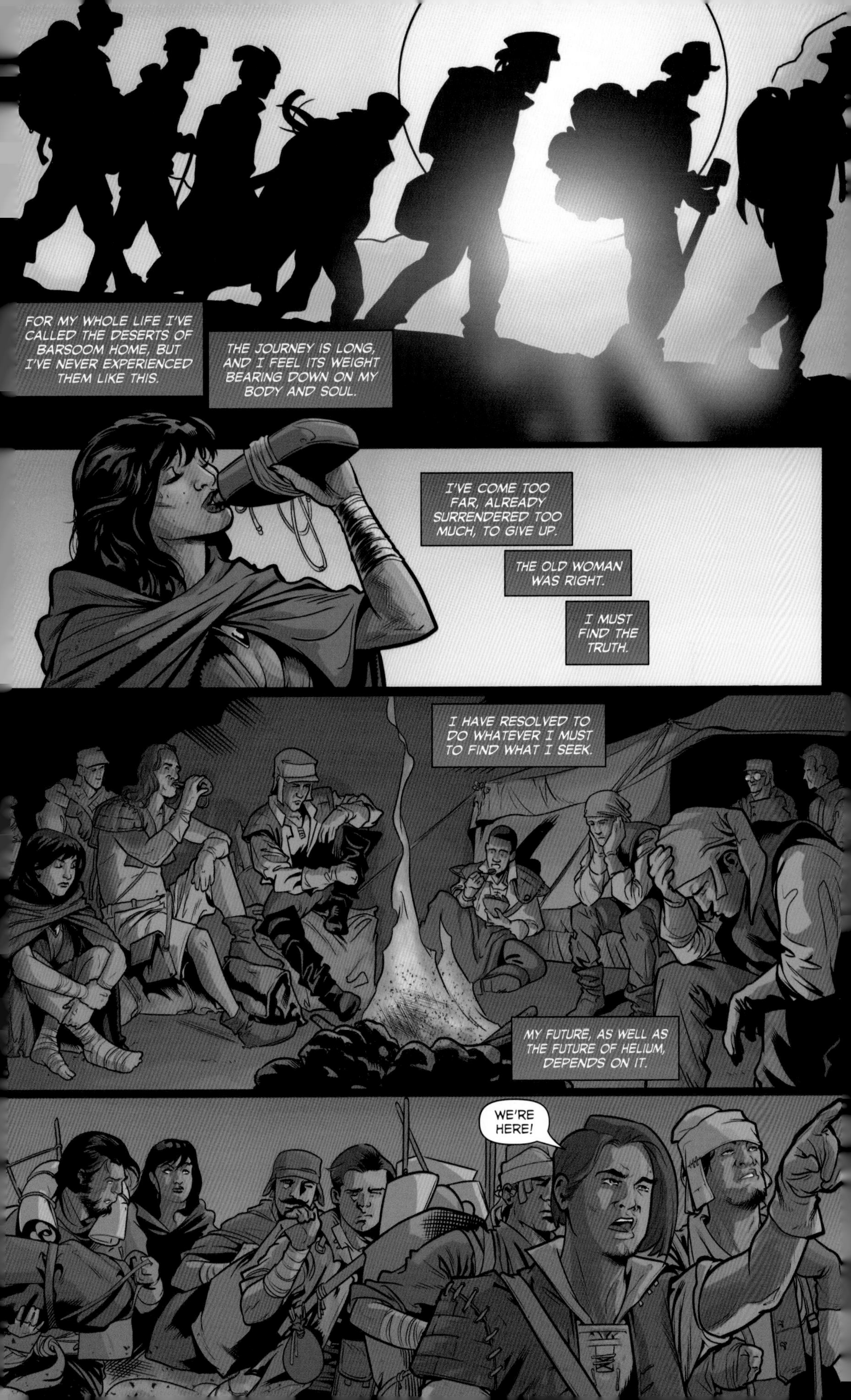

FOR MY WHOLE LIFE I'VE CALLED THE DESERTS OF BARSOOM HOME, BUT I'VE NEVER EXPERIENCED THEM LIKE THIS.
THE JOURNEY IS LONG, AND I FEEL ITS WEIGHT BEARING DOWN ON MY BODY AND SOUL.
I'VE COME TOO FAR, ALREADY SURRENDERED TOO MUCH, TO GIVE UP.
THE OLD WOMAN WAS RIGHT.
I MUST FIND THE TRUTH.
I HAVE RESOLVED TO DO WHATEVER I MUST TO FIND WHAT I SEEK.
MY FUTURE, AS WELL AS THE FUTURE OF HELIUM, DEPENDS ON IT.
WE'RE HERE!

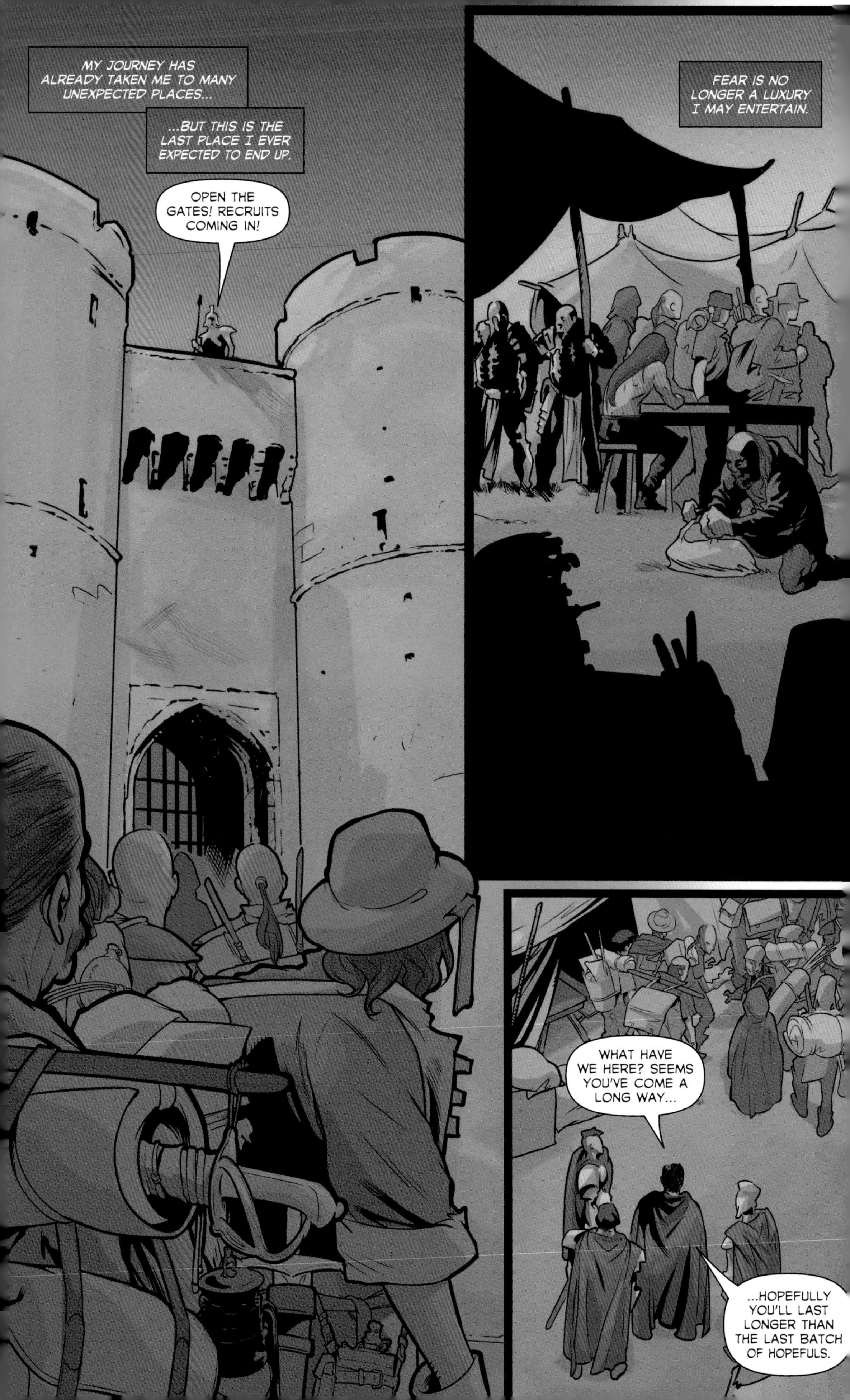
MY JOURNEY HAS ALREADY TAKEN ME TO MANY UNEXPECTED PLACES...
...BUT THIS IS THE LAST PLACE I EVER EXPECTED TO END UP.
OPEN THE GATES! RECRUITS COMING IN!
FEAR IS NO LONGER A LUXURY I MAY ENTERTAIN.
WHAT HAVE WE HERE? SEEMS YOU'VE COME A LONG WAY...
...HOPEFULLY YOU'LL LAST LONGER THAN THE LAST BATCH OF HOPEFULS.

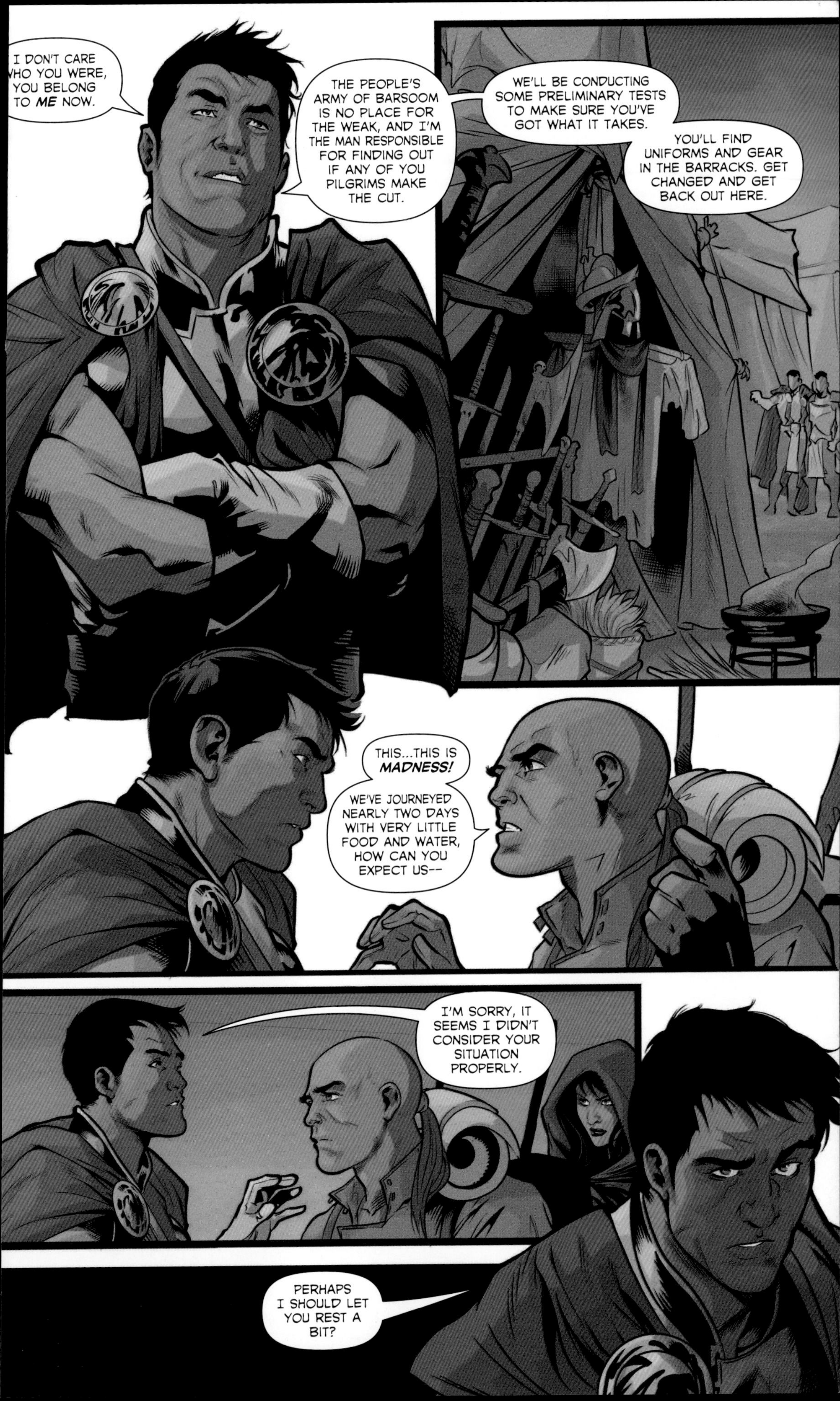
I DON'T CARE WHO YOU WERE, YOU BELONG TO *ME* NOW.
THE PEOPLE'S ARMY OF BARSOOM IS NO PLACE FOR THE WEAK, AND I'M THE MAN RESPONSIBLE FOR FINDING OUT IF ANY OF YOU PILGRIMS MAKE THE CUT.
WE'LL BE CONDUCTING SOME PRELIMINARY TESTS TO MAKE SURE YOU'VE GOT WHAT IT TAKES.
YOU'LL FIND UNIFORMS AND GEAR IN THE BARRACKS. GET CHANGED AND GET BACK OUT HERE.
THIS...THIS IS *MADNESS!*
WE'VE JOURNEYED NEARLY TWO DAYS WITH VERY LITTLE FOOD AND WATER, HOW CAN YOU EXPECT US--
I'M SORRY, IT SEEMS I DIDN'T CONSIDER YOUR SITUATION PROPERLY.
PERHAPS I SHOULD LET YOU REST A BIT?

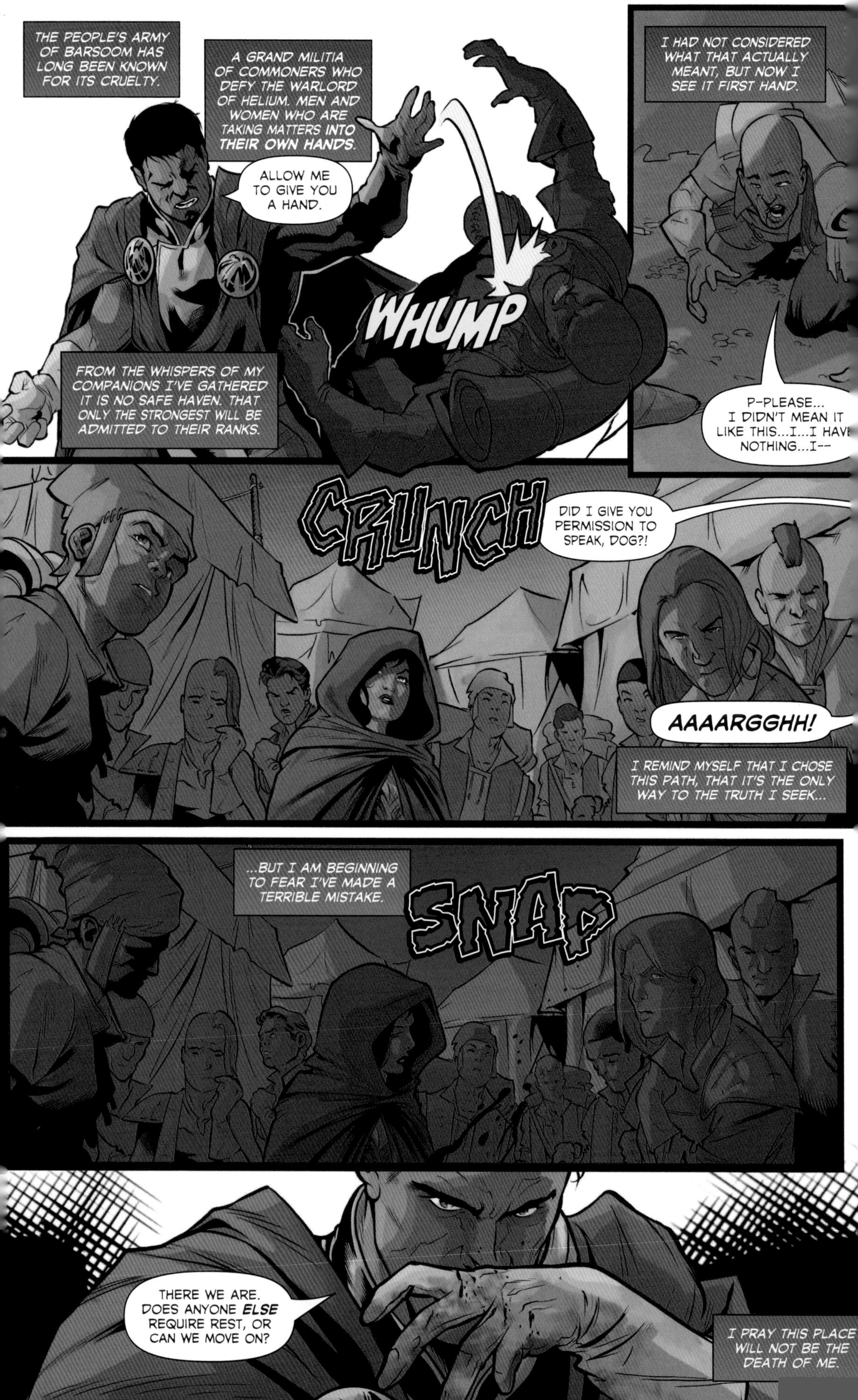
THE PEOPLE'S ARMY OF BARSOOM HAS LONG BEEN KNOWN FOR ITS CRUELTY.
A GRAND MILITIA OF COMMONERS WHO DEFY THE WARLORD OF HELIUM. MEN AND WOMEN WHO ARE TAKING MATTERS INTO THEIR OWN HANDS.
ALLOW ME TO GIVE YOU A HAND.
WHUMP
FROM THE WHISPERS OF MY COMPANIONS I'VE GATHERED IT IS NO SAFE HAVEN. THAT ONLY THE STRONGEST WILL BE ADMITTED TO THEIR RANKS.
I HAD NOT CONSIDERED WHAT THAT ACTUALLY MEANT, BUT NOW I SEE IT FIRST HAND.
P-PLEASE... I DIDN'T MEAN IT LIKE THIS...I...I HAVE NOTHING...I--
CRUNCH
DID I GIVE YOU PERMISSION TO SPEAK, DOG?!
AAAARGGHH!
I REMIND MYSELF THAT I CHOSE THIS PATH, THAT IT'S THE ONLY WAY TO THE TRUTH I SEEK...
...BUT I AM BEGINNING TO FEAR I'VE MADE A TERRIBLE MISTAKE.
SNAP
THERE WE ARE. DOES ANYONE ELSE REQUIRE REST, OR CAN WE MOVE ON?
I PRAY THIS PLACE WILL NOT BE THE DEATH OF ME.

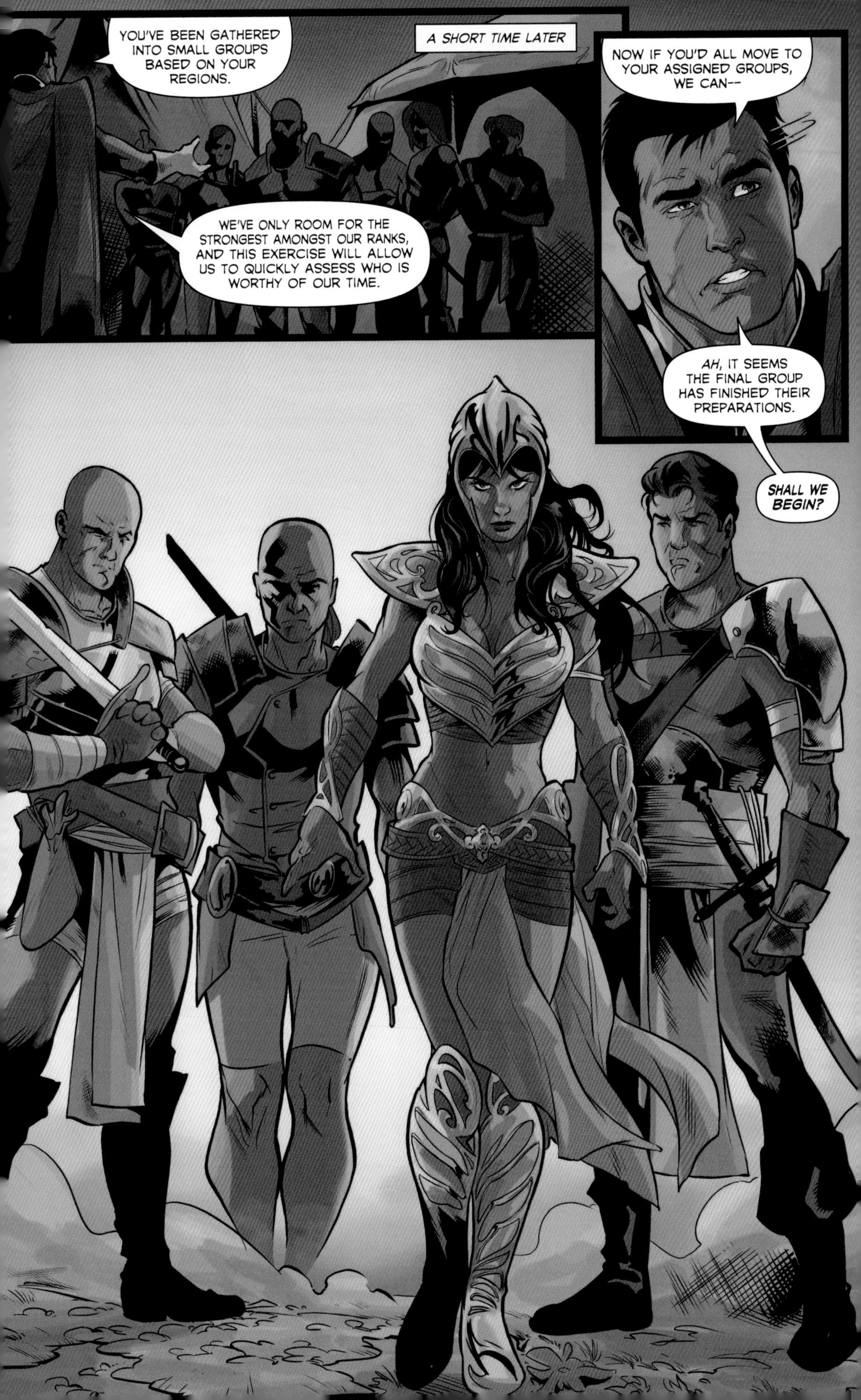
YOU'VE BEEN GATHERED INTO SMALL GROUPS BASED ON YOUR REGIONS.
A SHORT TIME LATER
WE'VE ONLY ROOM FOR THE STRONGEST AMONGST OUR RANKS, AND THIS EXERCISE WILL ALLOW US TO QUICKLY ASSESS WHO IS WORTHY OF OUR TIME.
NOW IF YOU'D ALL MOVE TO YOUR ASSIGNED GROUPS, WE CAN--
AH, IT SEEMS THE FINAL GROUP HAS FINISHED THEIR PREPARATIONS.
SHALL WE BEGIN?

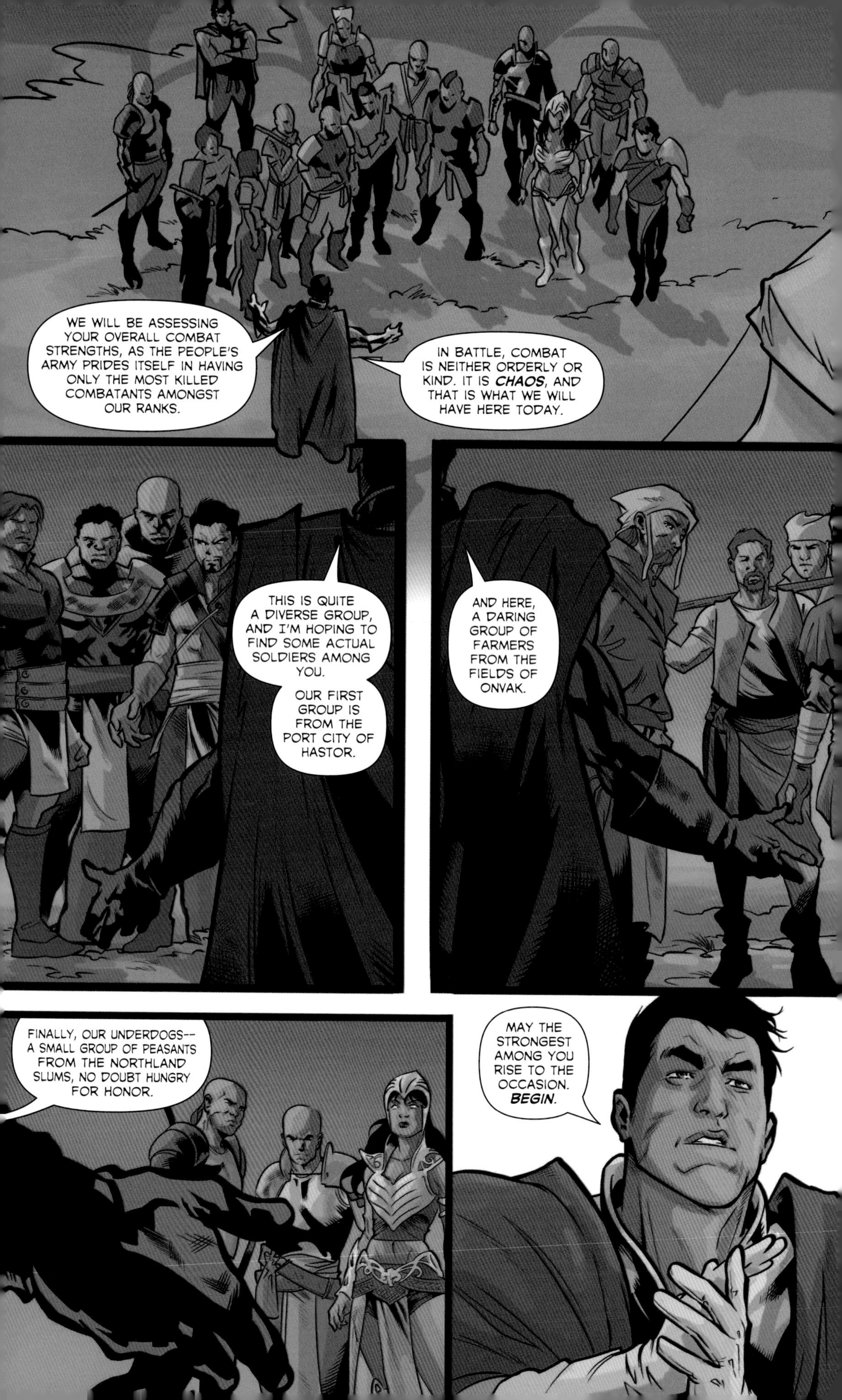
WE WILL BE ASSESSING YOUR OVERALL COMBAT STRENGTHS, AS THE PEOPLE'S ARMY PRIDES ITSELF IN HAVING ONLY THE MOST KILLED COMBATANTS AMONGST OUR RANKS.
IN BATTLE, COMBAT IS NEITHER ORDERLY OR KIND. IT IS *CHAOS*, AND THAT IS WHAT WE WILL HAVE HERE TODAY.
THIS IS QUITE A DIVERSE GROUP, AND I'M HOPING TO FIND SOME ACTUAL SOLDIERS AMONG YOU.
OUR FIRST GROUP IS FROM THE PORT CITY OF HASTOR.
AND HERE, A DARING GROUP OF FARMERS FROM THE FIELDS OF ONVAK.
FINALLY, OUR UNDERDOGS-- A SMALL GROUP OF PEASANTS FROM THE NORTHLAND SLUMS, NO DOUBT HUNGRY FOR HONOR.
MAY THE STRONGEST AMONG YOU RISE TO THE OCCASION. *BEGIN*.

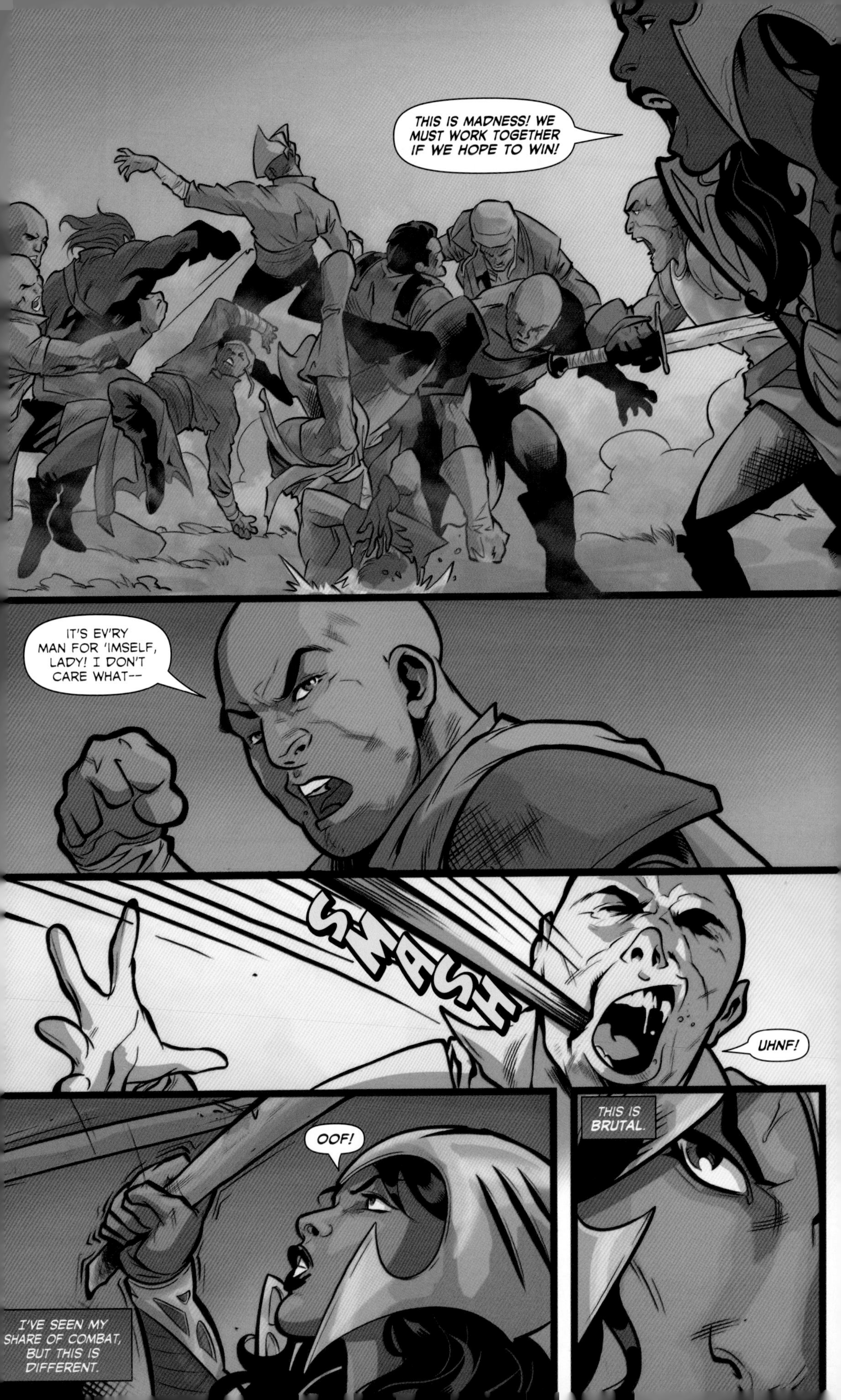
THIS IS MADNESS! WE MUST WORK TOGETHER IF WE HOPE TO WIN!
IT'S EV'RY MAN FOR 'IMSELF, LADY! I DON'T CARE WHAT--
SMASH
UHNF!
OOF!
I'VE SEEN MY SHARE OF COMBAT, BUT THIS IS DIFFERENT.
THIS IS BRUTAL.

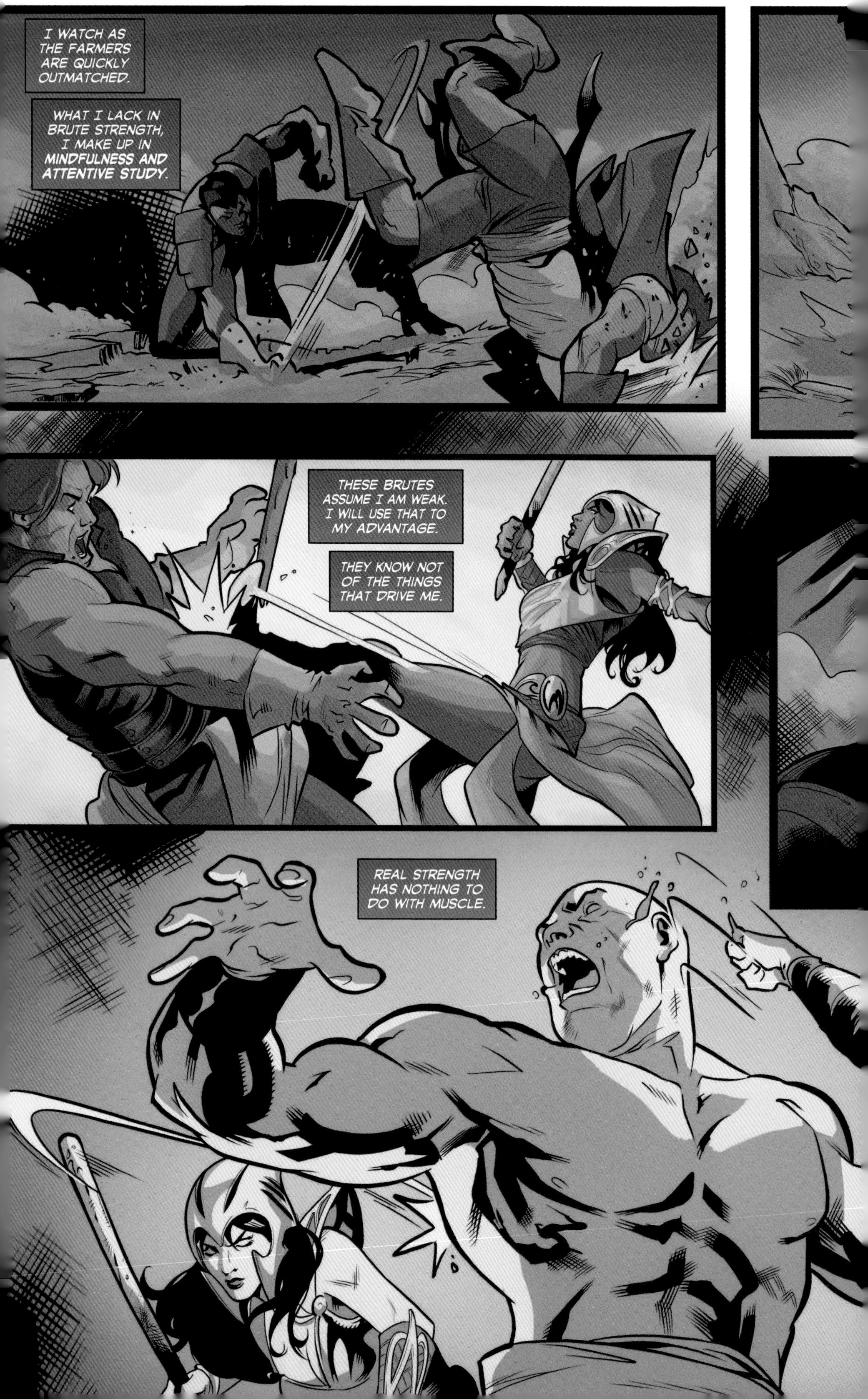
I WATCH AS THE FARMERS ARE QUICKLY OUTMATCHED.
WHAT I LACK IN BRUTE STRENGTH, I MAKE UP IN **MINDFULNESS AND ATTENTIVE STUDY**.
THESE BRUTES ASSUME I AM WEAK. I WILL USE THAT TO MY ADVANTAGE.
THEY KNOW NOT OF THE THINGS THAT DRIVE ME.
REAL STRENGTH HAS NOTHING TO DO WITH MUSCLE.

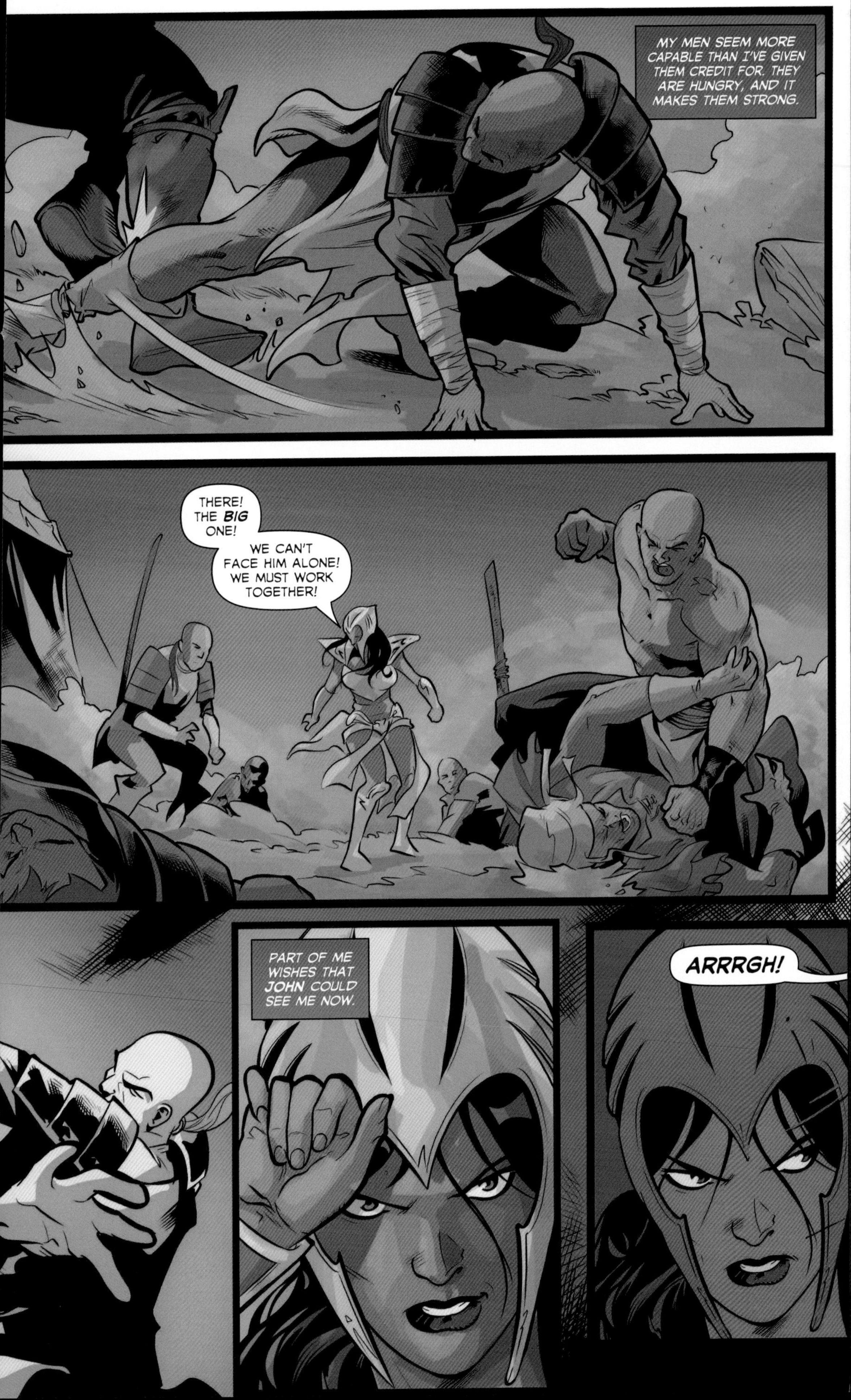

MY MEN SEEM MORE CAPABLE THAN I'VE GIVEN THEM CREDIT FOR. THEY ARE HUNGRY, AND IT MAKES THEM STRONG.
THERE! THE BIG ONE!
WE CAN'T FACE HIM ALONE! WE MUST WORK TOGETHER!
PART OF ME WISHES THAT JOHN COULD SEE ME NOW.
ARRRGH!

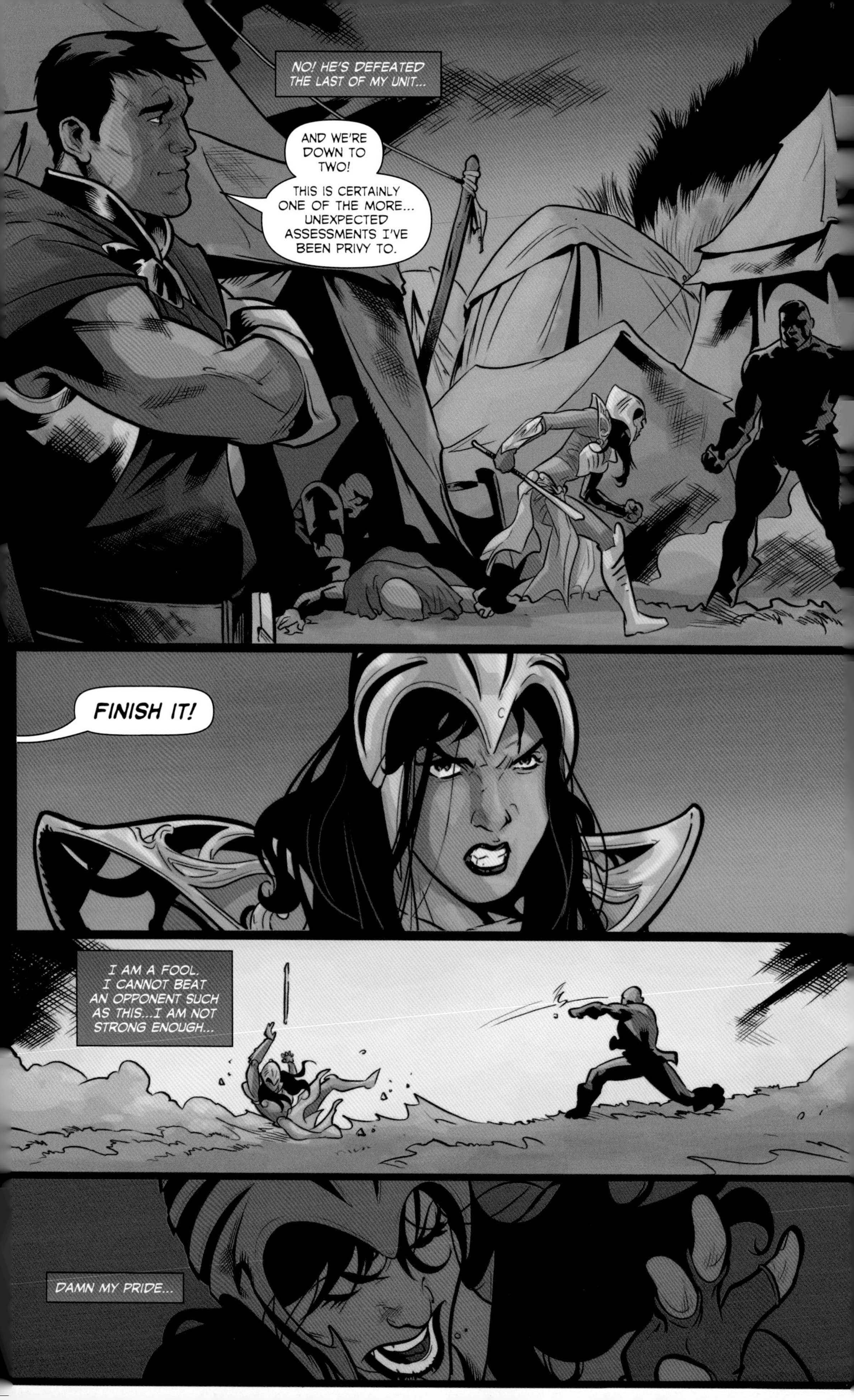

NO! HE'S DEFEATED THE LAST OF MY UNIT...
AND WE'RE DOWN TO TWO!
THIS IS CERTAINLY ONE OF THE MORE... UNEXPECTED ASSESSMENTS I'VE BEEN PRIVY TO.
FINISH IT!
I AM A FOOL. I CANNOT BEAT AN OPPONENT SUCH AS THIS...I AM NOT STRONG ENOUGH...
DAMN MY PRIDE...

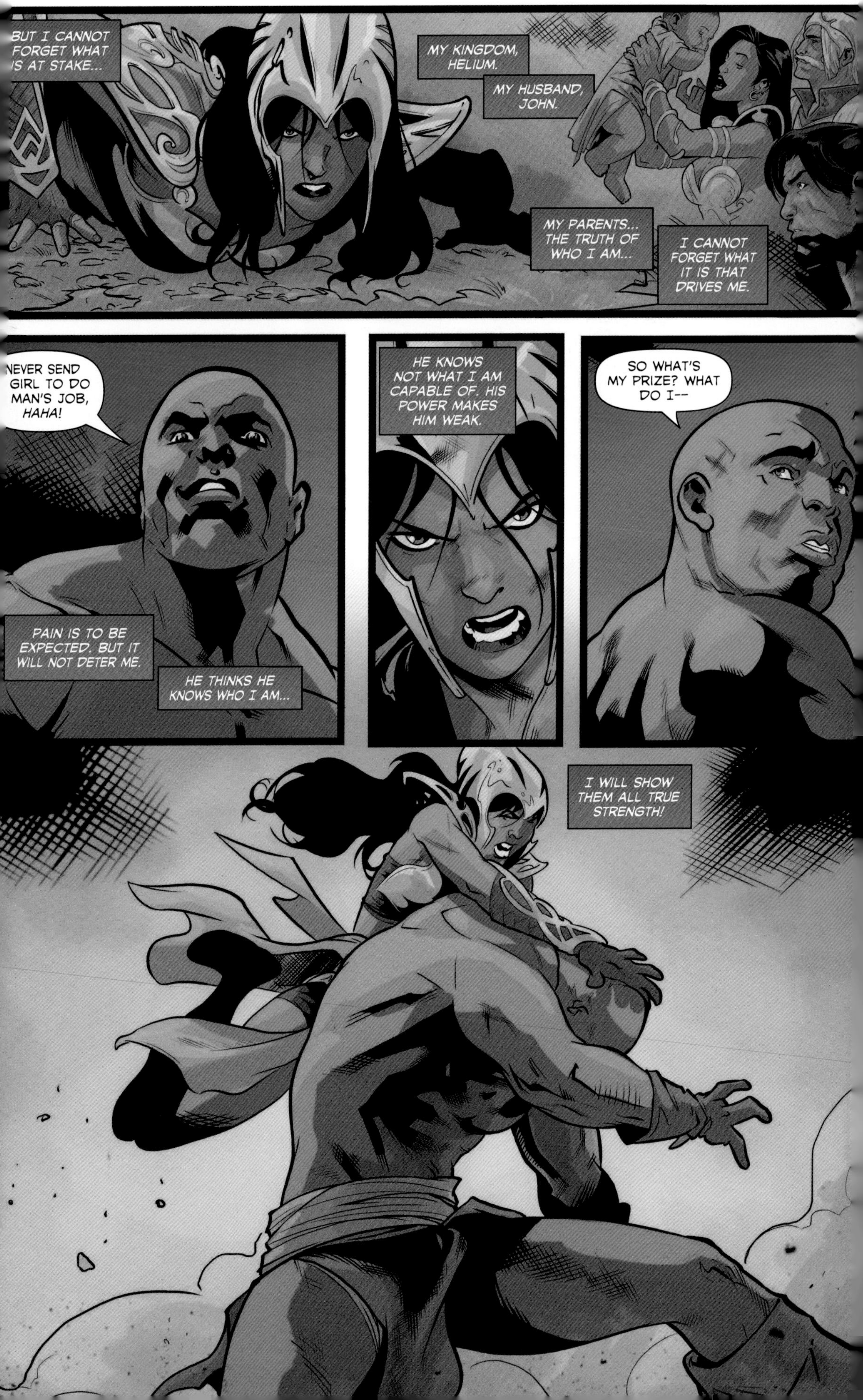
BUT I CANNOT FORGET WHAT IS AT STAKE...
MY KINGDOM, HELIUM.
MY HUSBAND, JOHN.
MY PARENTS... THE TRUTH OF WHO I AM...
I CANNOT FORGET WHAT IT IS THAT DRIVES ME.
NEVER SEND GIRL TO DO MAN'S JOB, HAHA!
PAIN IS TO BE EXPECTED. BUT IT WILL NOT DETER ME.
HE THINKS HE KNOWS WHO I AM...
HE KNOWS NOT WHAT I AM CAPABLE OF. HIS POWER MAKES HIM WEAK.
SO WHAT'S MY PRIZE? WHAT DO I--
I WILL SHOW THEM ALL TRUE STRENGTH!

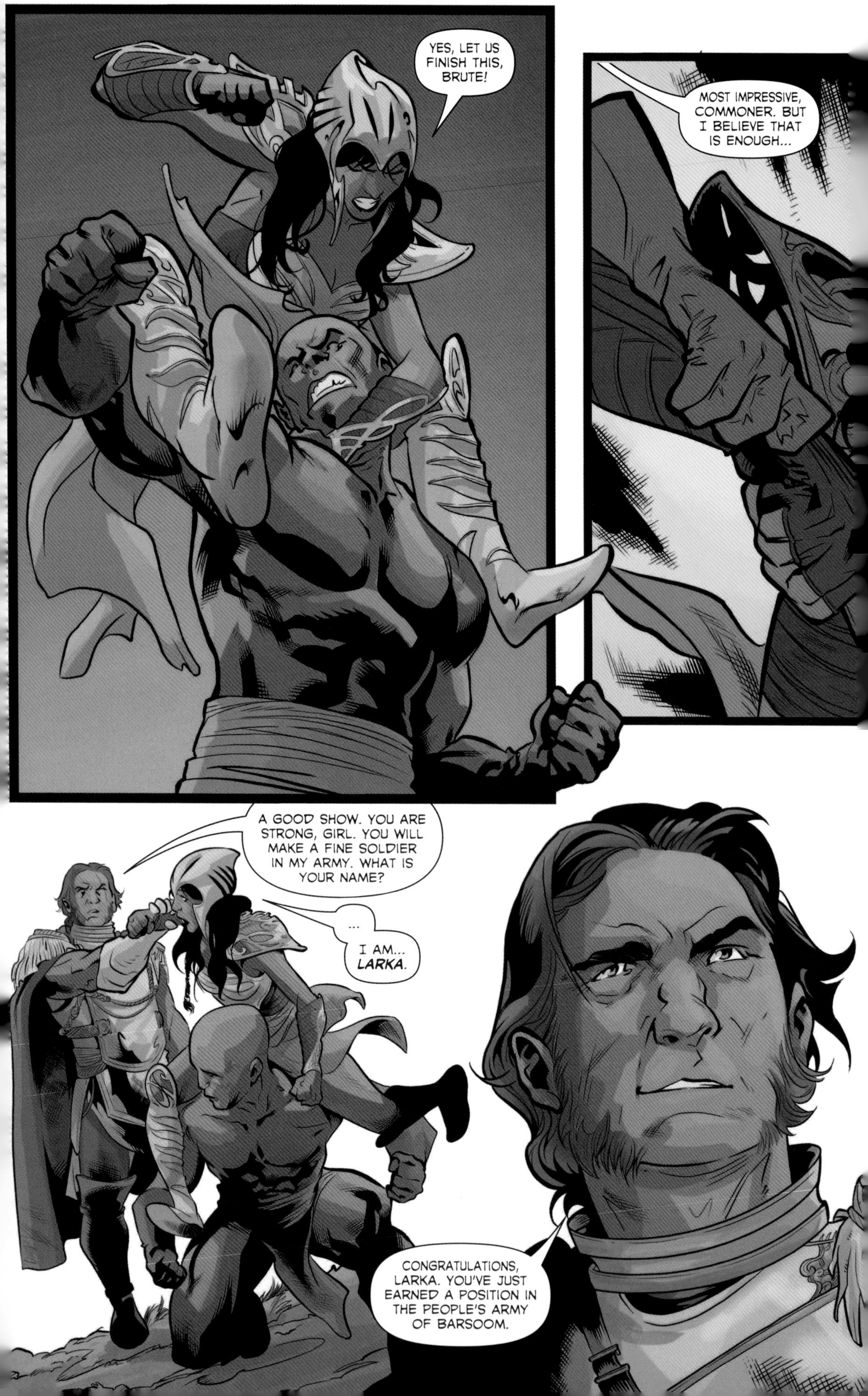
YES, LET US FINISH THIS, BRUTE!
MOST IMPRESSIVE, COMMONER. BUT I BELIEVE THAT IS ENOUGH...
A GOOD SHOW. YOU ARE STRONG, GIRL. YOU WILL MAKE A FINE SOLDIER IN MY ARMY. WHAT IS YOUR NAME?
...
I AM... *LARKA*.
CONGRATULATIONS, LARKA. YOU'VE JUST EARNED A POSITION IN THE PEOPLE'S ARMY OF BARSOOM.

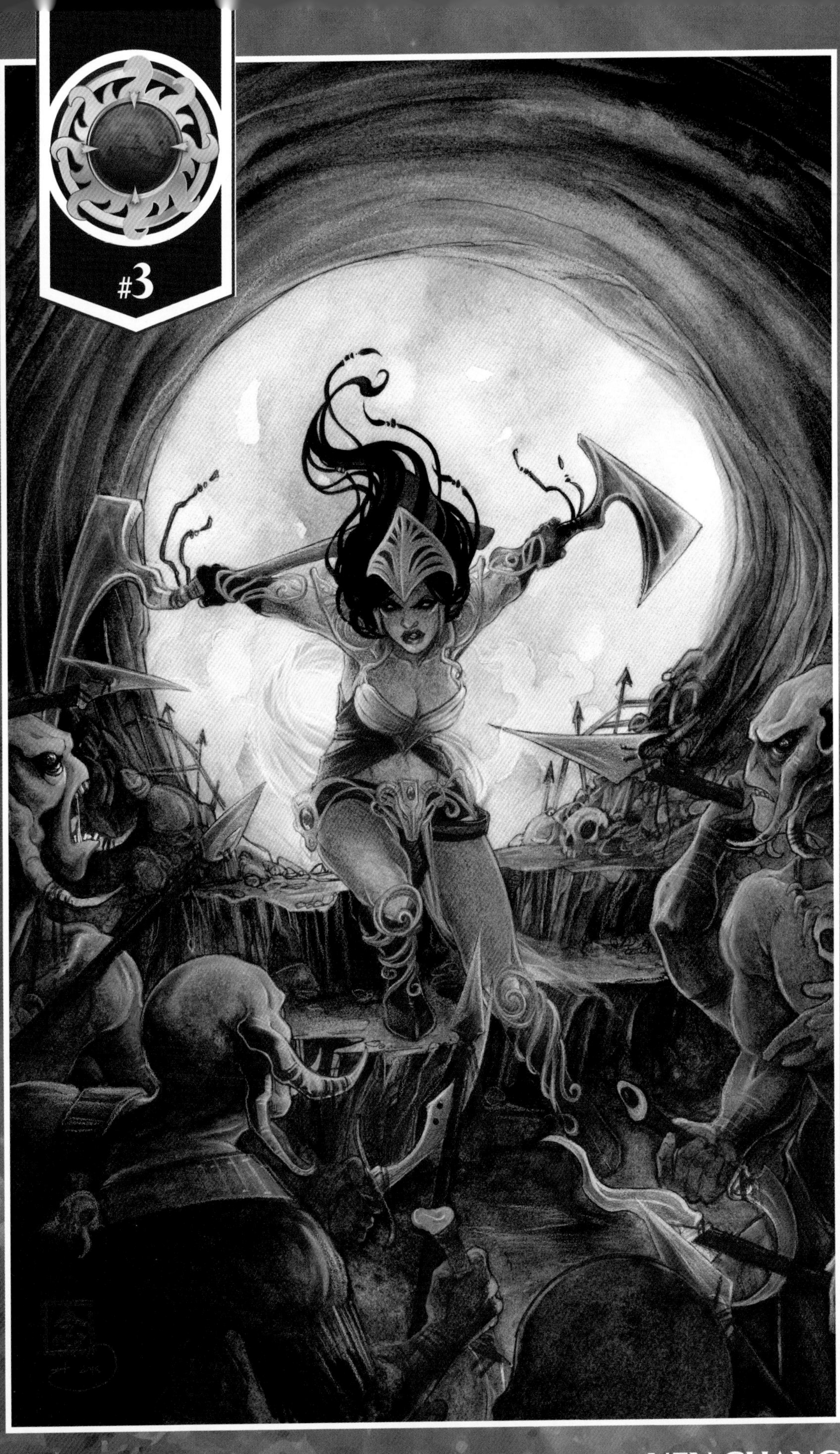
#3

cover by **NEN CHANG**

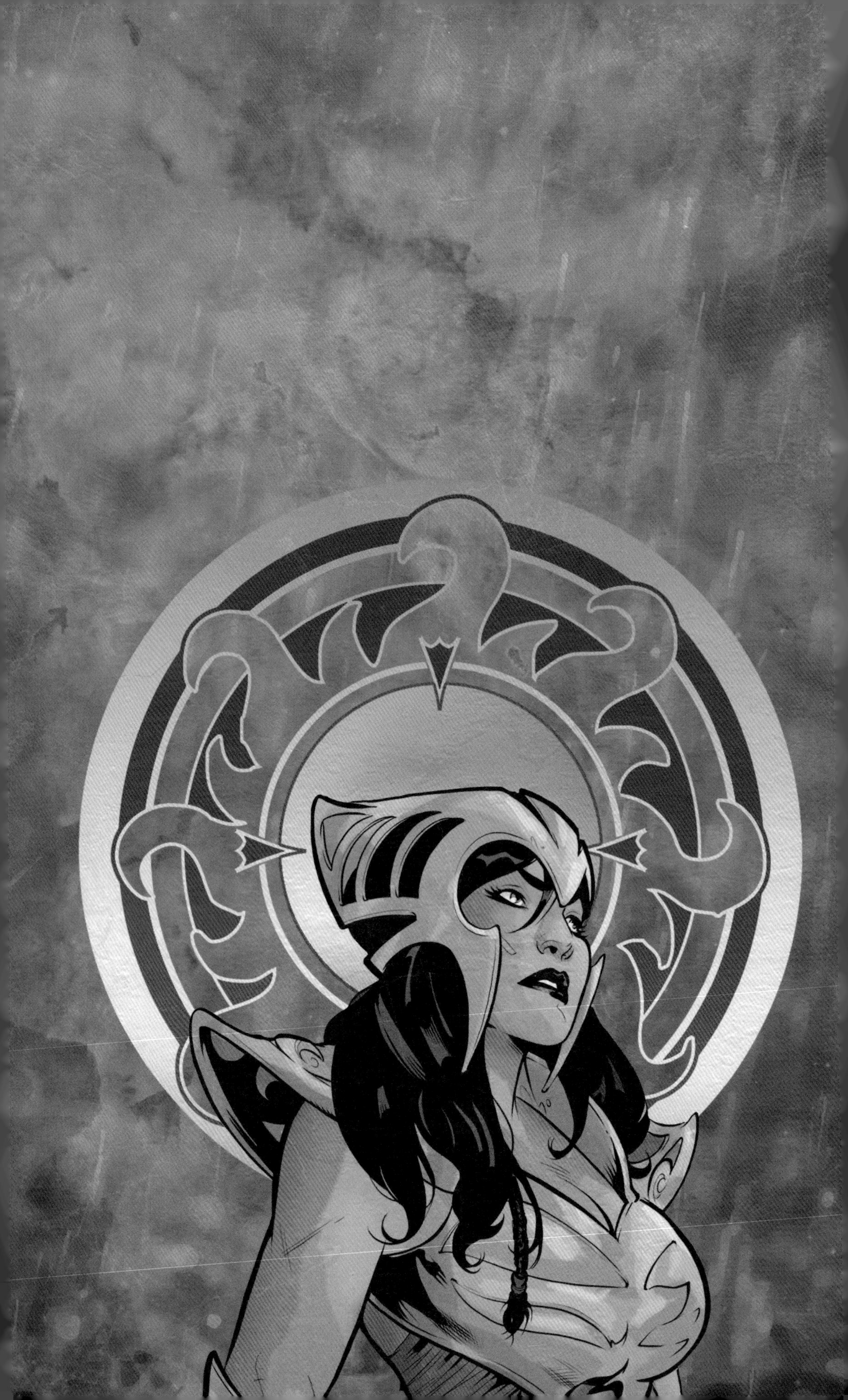

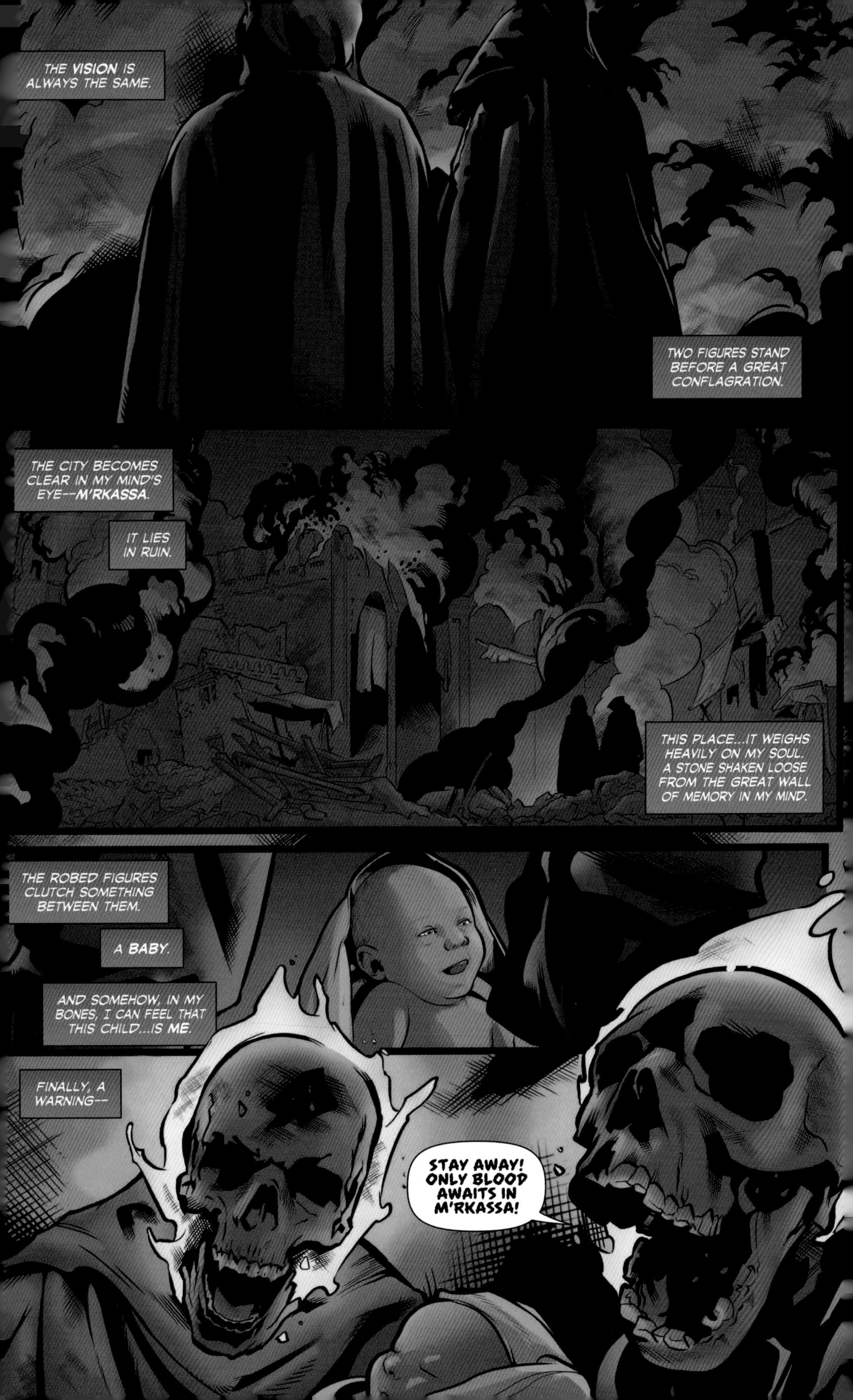
THE VISION IS ALWAYS THE SAME.
TWO FIGURES STAND BEFORE A GREAT CONFLAGRATION.
THE CITY BECOMES CLEAR IN MY MIND'S EYE--M'RKASSA.
IT LIES IN RUIN.
THIS PLACE...IT WEIGHS HEAVILY ON MY SOUL. A STONE SHAKEN LOOSE FROM THE GREAT WALL OF MEMORY IN MY MIND.
THE ROBED FIGURES CLUTCH SOMETHING BETWEEN THEM.
A BABY.
AND SOMEHOW, IN MY BONES, I CAN FEEL THAT THIS CHILD...IS ME.
FINALLY, A WARNING--
STAY AWAY! ONLY BLOOD AWAITS IN M'RKASSA!

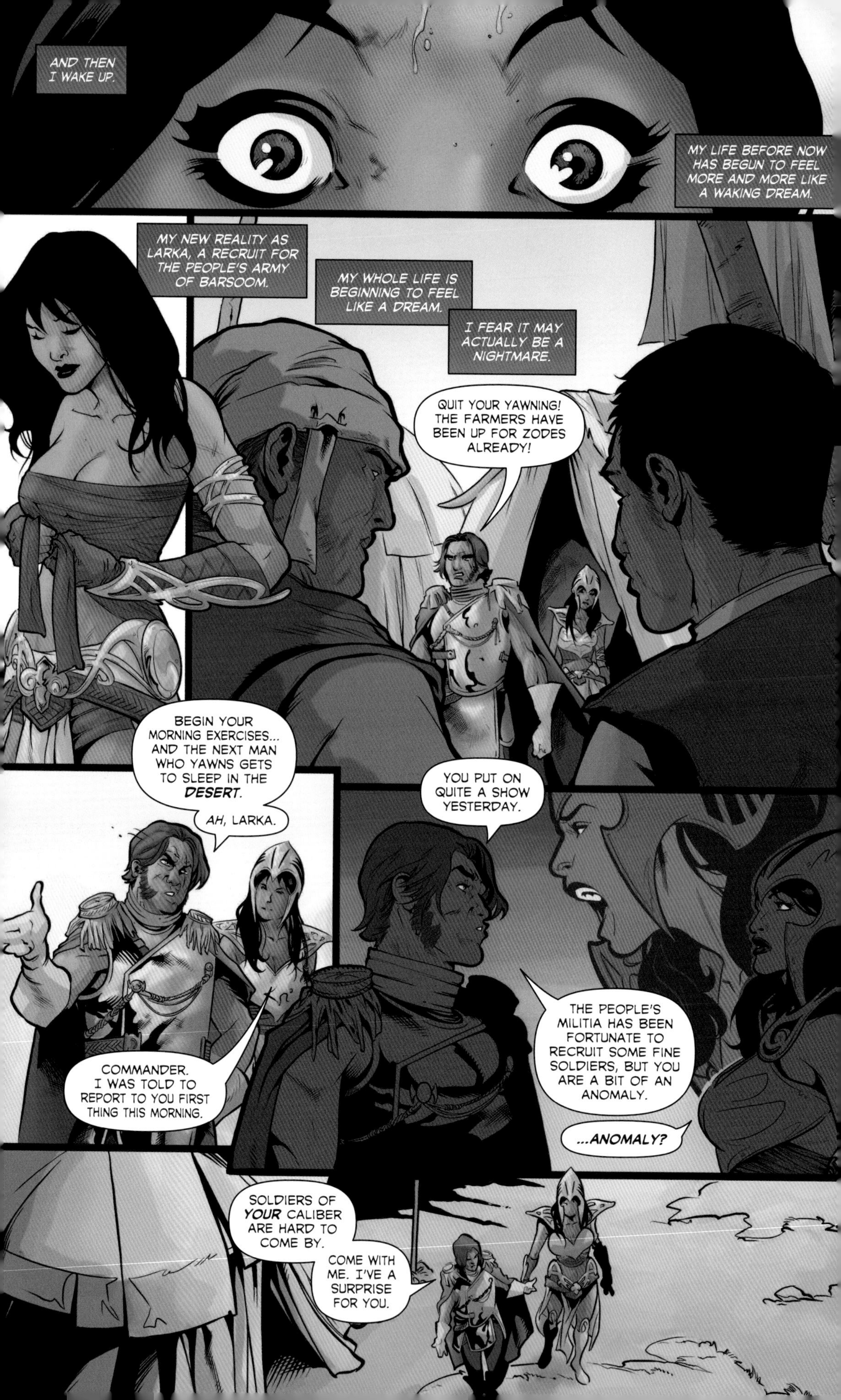
AND THEN I WAKE UP.
MY LIFE BEFORE NOW HAS BEGUN TO FEEL MORE AND MORE LIKE A WAKING DREAM.
MY NEW REALITY AS LARKA, A RECRUIT FOR THE PEOPLE'S ARMY OF BARSOOM.
MY WHOLE LIFE IS BEGINNING TO FEEL LIKE A DREAM.
I FEAR IT MAY ACTUALLY BE A NIGHTMARE.
QUIT YOUR YAWNING! THE FARMERS HAVE BEEN UP FOR ZODES ALREADY!
BEGIN YOUR MORNING EXERCISES... AND THE NEXT MAN WHO YAWNS GETS TO SLEEP IN THE DESERT.
AH, LARKA.
COMMANDER. I WAS TOLD TO REPORT TO YOU FIRST THING THIS MORNING.
YOU PUT ON QUITE A SHOW YESTERDAY.
THE PEOPLE'S MILITIA HAS BEEN FORTUNATE TO RECRUIT SOME FINE SOLDIERS, BUT YOU ARE A BIT OF AN ANOMALY.
...ANOMALY?
SOLDIERS OF YOUR CALIBER ARE HARD TO COME BY.
COME WITH ME. I'VE A SURPRISE FOR YOU.

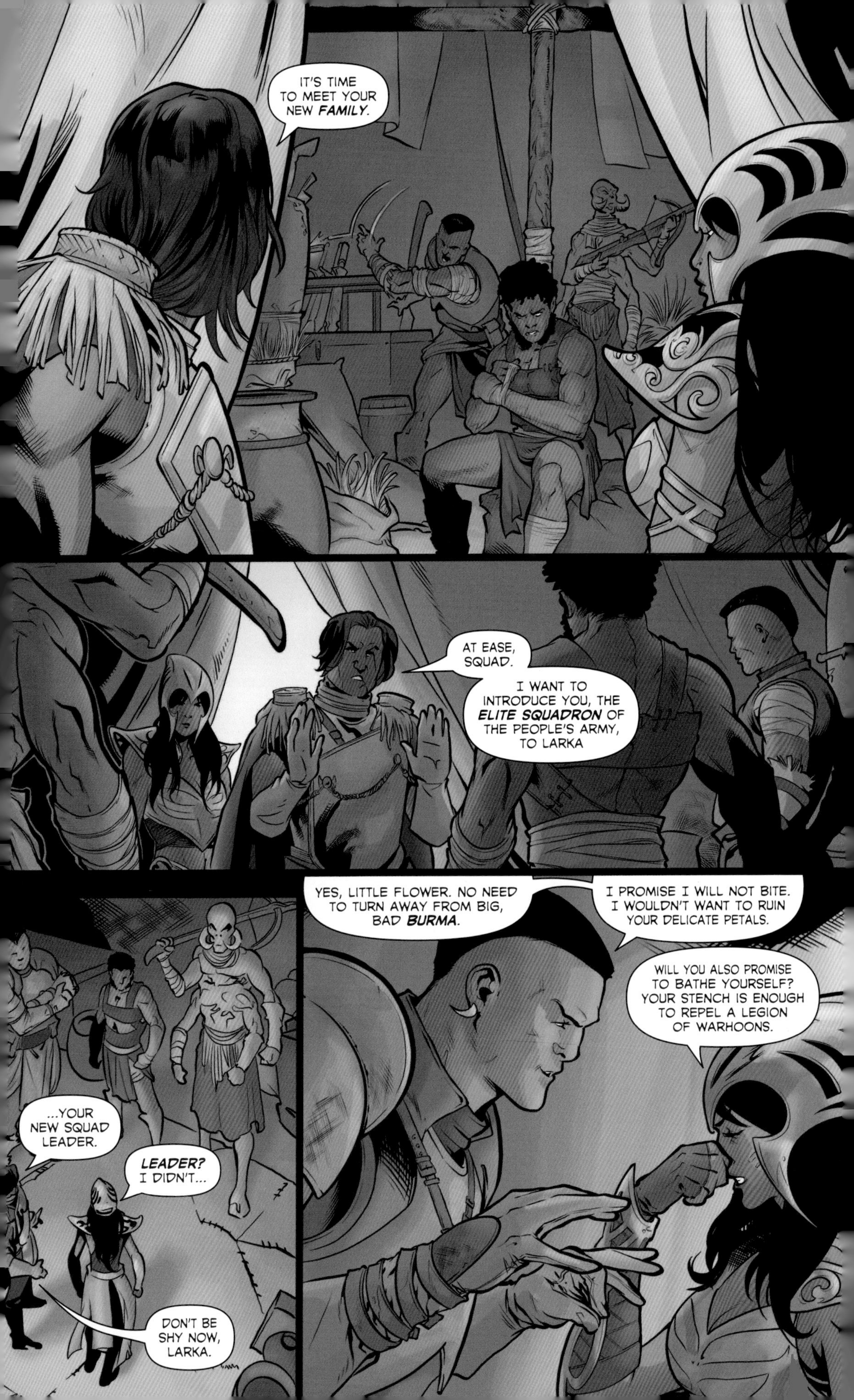
IT'S TIME TO MEET YOUR NEW *FAMILY*.
AT EASE, SQUAD.
I WANT TO INTRODUCE YOU, THE ***ELITE SQUADRON*** OF THE PEOPLE'S ARMY, TO LARKA
...YOUR NEW SQUAD LEADER.
LEADER? I DIDN'T...
DON'T BE SHY NOW, LARKA.
YES, LITTLE FLOWER. NO NEED TO TURN AWAY FROM BIG, BAD ***BURMA***.
I PROMISE I WILL NOT BITE. I WOULDN'T WANT TO RUIN YOUR DELICATE PETALS.
WILL YOU ALSO PROMISE TO BATHE YOURSELF? YOUR STENCH IS ENOUGH TO REPEL A LEGION OF WARHOONS.

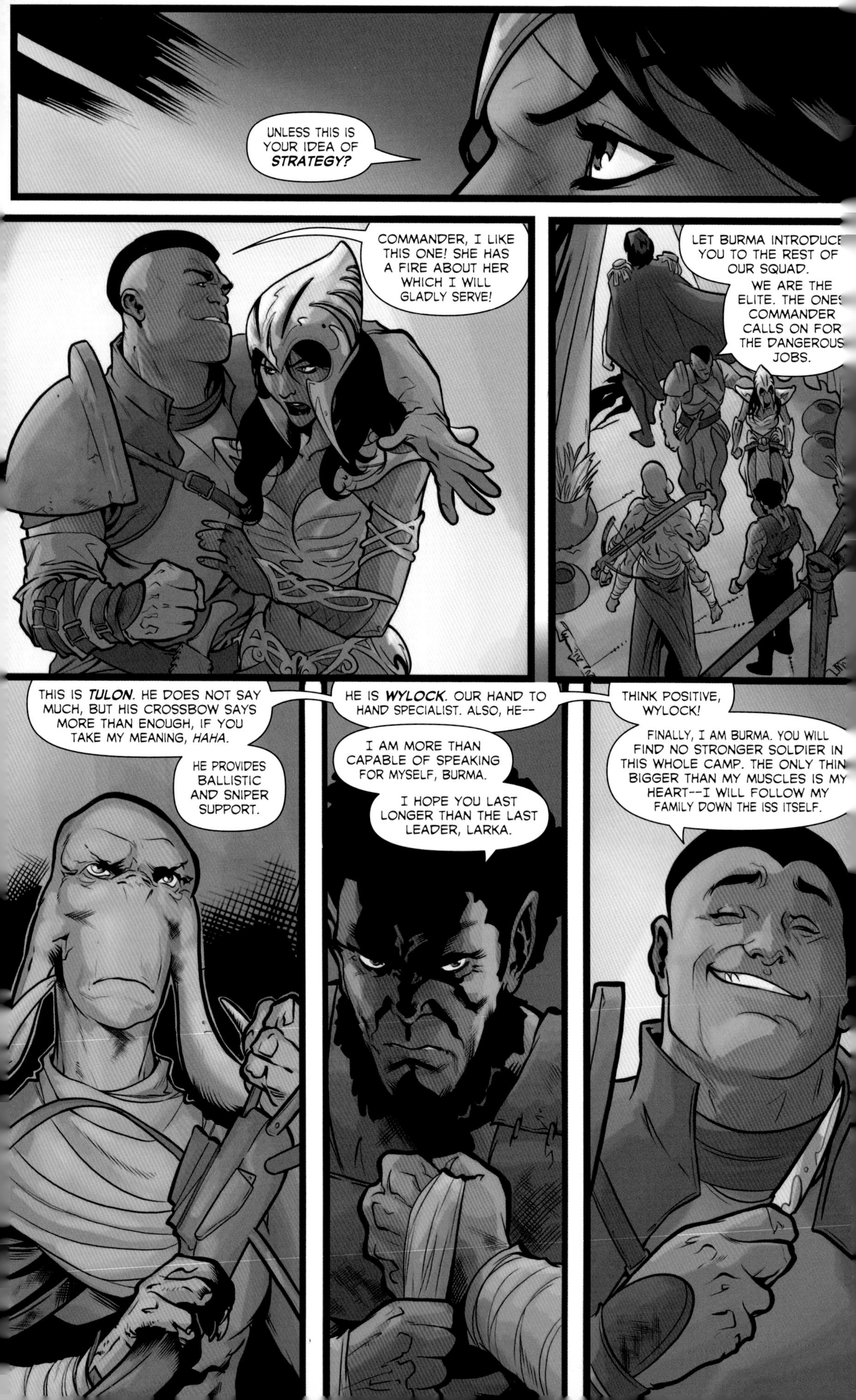

UNLESS THIS IS YOUR IDEA OF **STRATEGY?**
COMMANDER, I LIKE THIS ONE! SHE HAS A FIRE ABOUT HER WHICH I WILL GLADLY SERVE!
LET BURMA INTRODUCE YOU TO THE REST OF OUR SQUAD.
WE ARE THE ELITE. THE ONES COMMANDER CALLS ON FOR THE DANGEROUS JOBS.
THIS IS **TULON**. HE DOES NOT SAY MUCH, BUT HIS CROSSBOW SAYS MORE THAN ENOUGH, IF YOU TAKE MY MEANING, *HAHA*.
HE PROVIDES BALLISTIC AND SNIPER SUPPORT.
HE IS **WYLOCK**. OUR HAND TO HAND SPECIALIST. ALSO, HE--
I AM MORE THAN CAPABLE OF SPEAKING FOR MYSELF, BURMA.
I HOPE YOU LAST LONGER THAN THE LAST LEADER, LARKA.
THINK POSITIVE, WYLOCK!
FINALLY, I AM BURMA. YOU WILL FIND NO STRONGER SOLDIER IN THIS WHOLE CAMP. THE ONLY THING BIGGER THAN MY MUSCLES IS MY HEART--I WILL FOLLOW MY FAMILY DOWN THE ISS ITSELF.

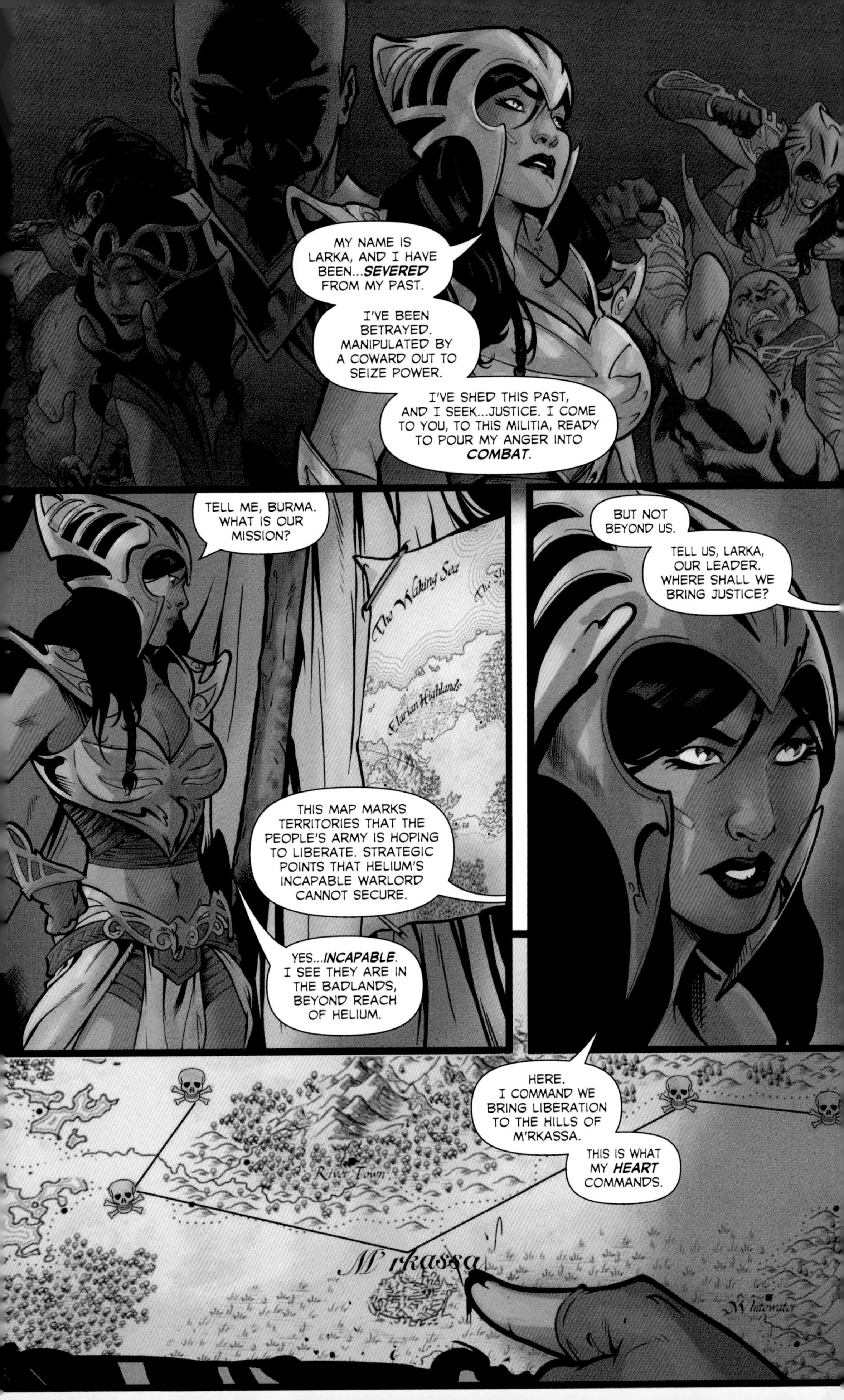
MY NAME IS LARKA, AND I HAVE BEEN...SEVERED FROM MY PAST.
I'VE BEEN BETRAYED. MANIPULATED BY A COWARD OUT TO SEIZE POWER.
I'VE SHED THIS PAST, AND I SEEK...JUSTICE. I COME TO YOU, TO THIS MILITIA, READY TO POUR MY ANGER INTO COMBAT.
TELL ME, BURMA. WHAT IS OUR MISSION?
The Waking Sea
Elarian Highlands
THIS MAP MARKS TERRITORIES THAT THE PEOPLE'S ARMY IS HOPING TO LIBERATE. STRATEGIC POINTS THAT HELIUM'S INCAPABLE WARLORD CANNOT SECURE.
YES...INCAPABLE. I SEE THEY ARE IN THE BADLANDS, BEYOND REACH OF HELIUM.
BUT NOT BEYOND US.
TELL US, LARKA, OUR LEADER. WHERE SHALL WE BRING JUSTICE?
HERE. I COMMAND WE BRING LIBERATION TO THE HILLS OF M'RKASSA.
THIS IS WHAT MY HEART COMMANDS.
River Town
M'rkassa
Whitewater

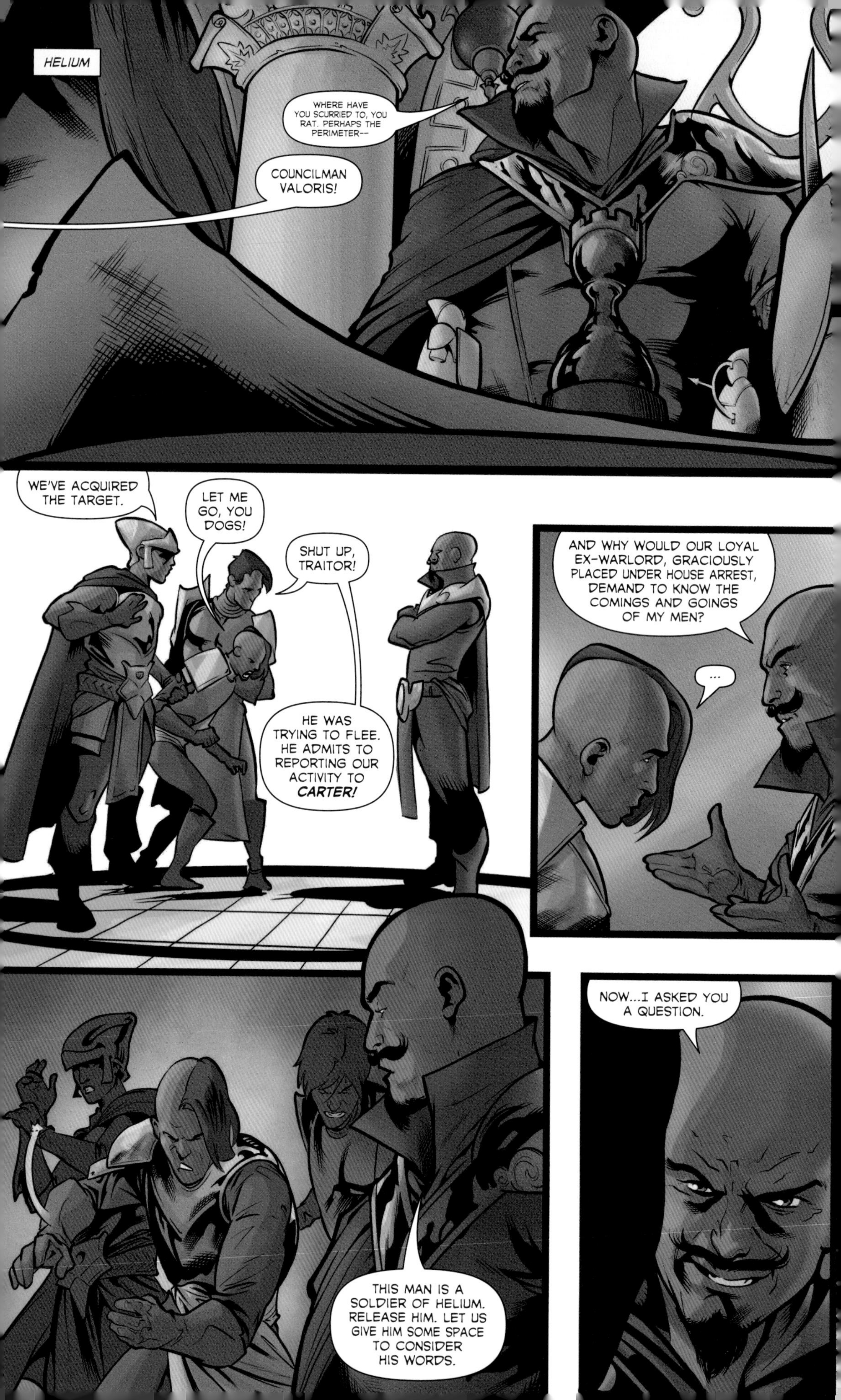
HELIUM
WHERE HAVE YOU SCURRIED TO, YOU RAT. PERHAPS THE PERIMETER--
COUNCILMAN VALORIS!
WE'VE ACQUIRED THE TARGET.
LET ME GO, YOU DOGS!
SHUT UP, TRAITOR!
HE WAS TRYING TO FLEE. HE ADMITS TO REPORTING OUR ACTIVITY TO *CARTER!*
AND WHY WOULD OUR LOYAL EX-WARLORD, GRACIOUSLY PLACED UNDER HOUSE ARREST, DEMAND TO KNOW THE COMINGS AND GOINGS OF MY MEN?
...
THIS MAN IS A SOLDIER OF HELIUM. RELEASE HIM. LET US GIVE HIM SOME SPACE TO CONSIDER HIS WORDS.
NOW...I ASKED YOU A QUESTION.

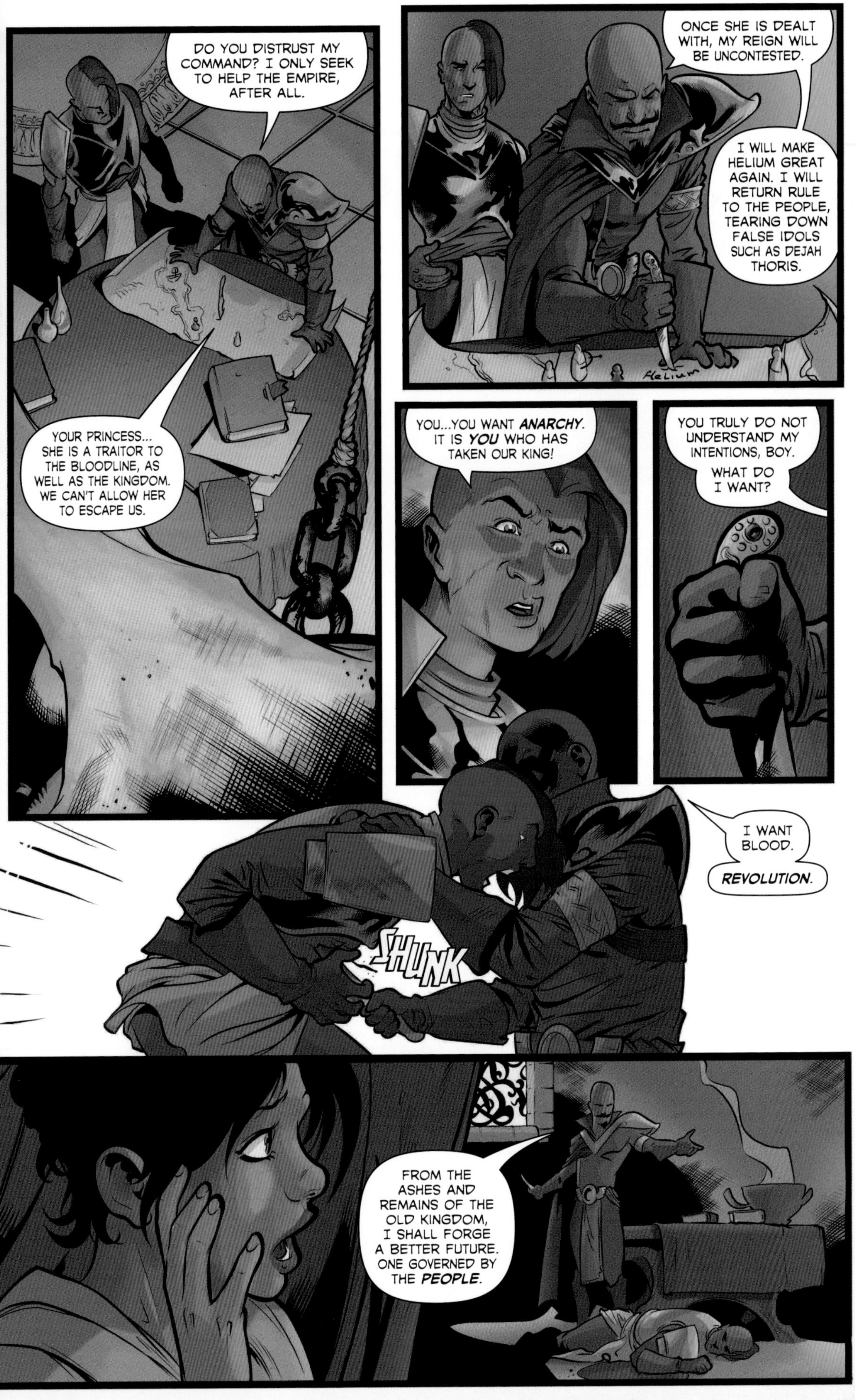
DO YOU DISTRUST MY COMMAND? I ONLY SEEK TO HELP THE EMPIRE, AFTER ALL.
YOUR PRINCESS... SHE IS A TRAITOR TO THE BLOODLINE, AS WELL AS THE KINGDOM. WE CAN'T ALLOW HER TO ESCAPE US.
ONCE SHE IS DEALT WITH, MY REIGN WILL BE UNCONTESTED.
I WILL MAKE HELIUM GREAT AGAIN. I WILL RETURN RULE TO THE PEOPLE, TEARING DOWN FALSE IDOLS SUCH AS DEJAH THORIS.
Helium
YOU...YOU WANT ***ANARCHY***. IT IS ***YOU*** WHO HAS TAKEN OUR KING!
YOU TRULY DO NOT UNDERSTAND MY INTENTIONS, BOY.
WHAT DO I WANT?
I WANT BLOOD.
REVOLUTION.
SHUNK
FROM THE ASHES AND REMAINS OF THE OLD KINGDOM, I SHALL FORGE A BETTER FUTURE. ONE GOVERNED BY THE ***PEOPLE***.

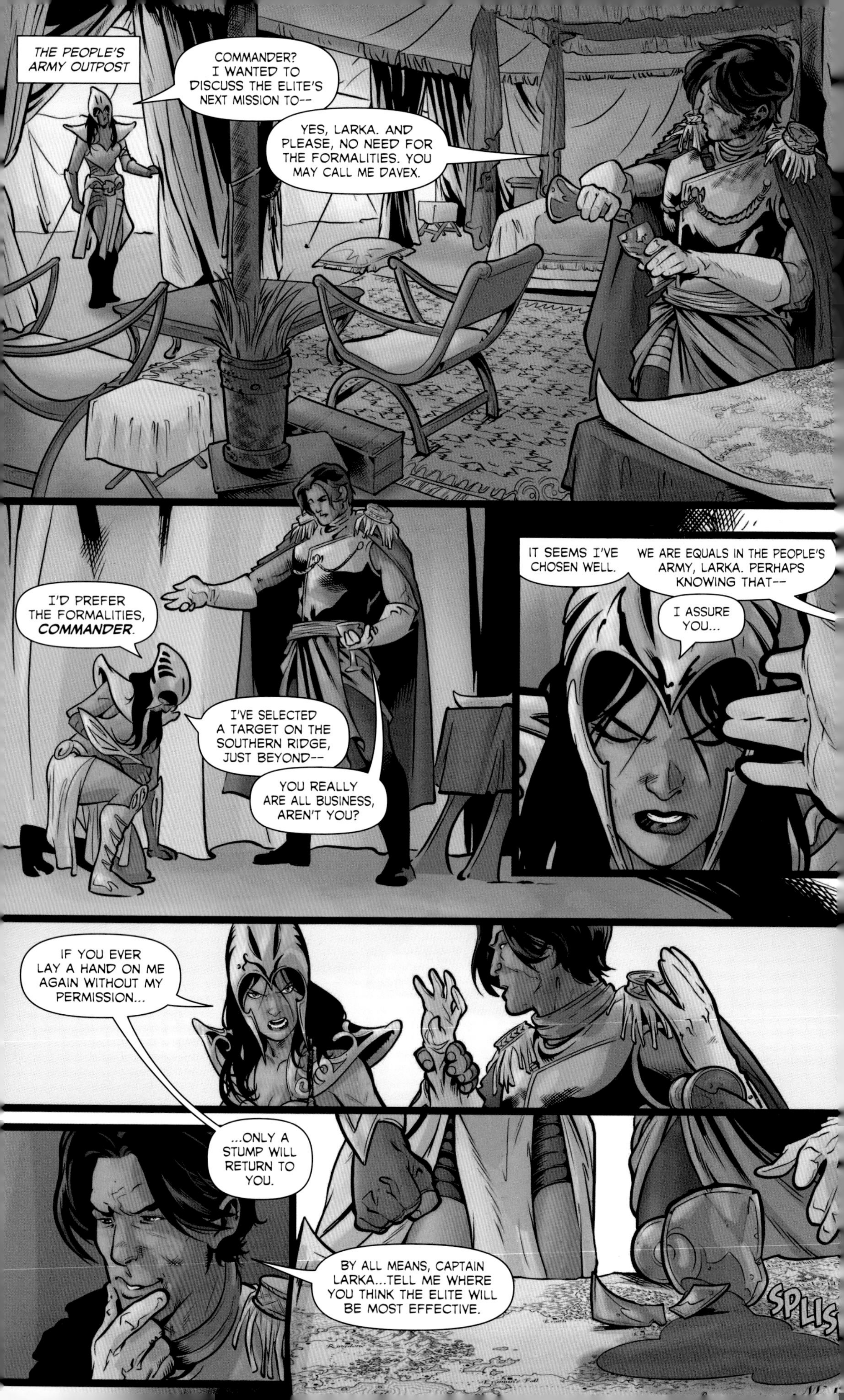
THE PEOPLE'S ARMY OUTPOST
COMMANDER? I WANTED TO DISCUSS THE ELITE'S NEXT MISSION TO--
YES, LARKA. AND PLEASE, NO NEED FOR THE FORMALITIES. YOU MAY CALL ME DAVEX.
I'D PREFER THE FORMALITIES, COMMANDER.
I'VE SELECTED A TARGET ON THE SOUTHERN RIDGE, JUST BEYOND--
YOU REALLY ARE ALL BUSINESS, AREN'T YOU?
IT SEEMS I'VE CHOSEN WELL.
WE ARE EQUALS IN THE PEOPLE'S ARMY, LARKA. PERHAPS KNOWING THAT--
I ASSURE YOU...
IF YOU EVER LAY A HAND ON ME AGAIN WITHOUT MY PERMISSION...
...ONLY A STUMP WILL RETURN TO YOU.
BY ALL MEANS, CAPTAIN LARKA...TELL ME WHERE YOU THINK THE ELITE WILL BE MOST EFFECTIVE.
SPLISH

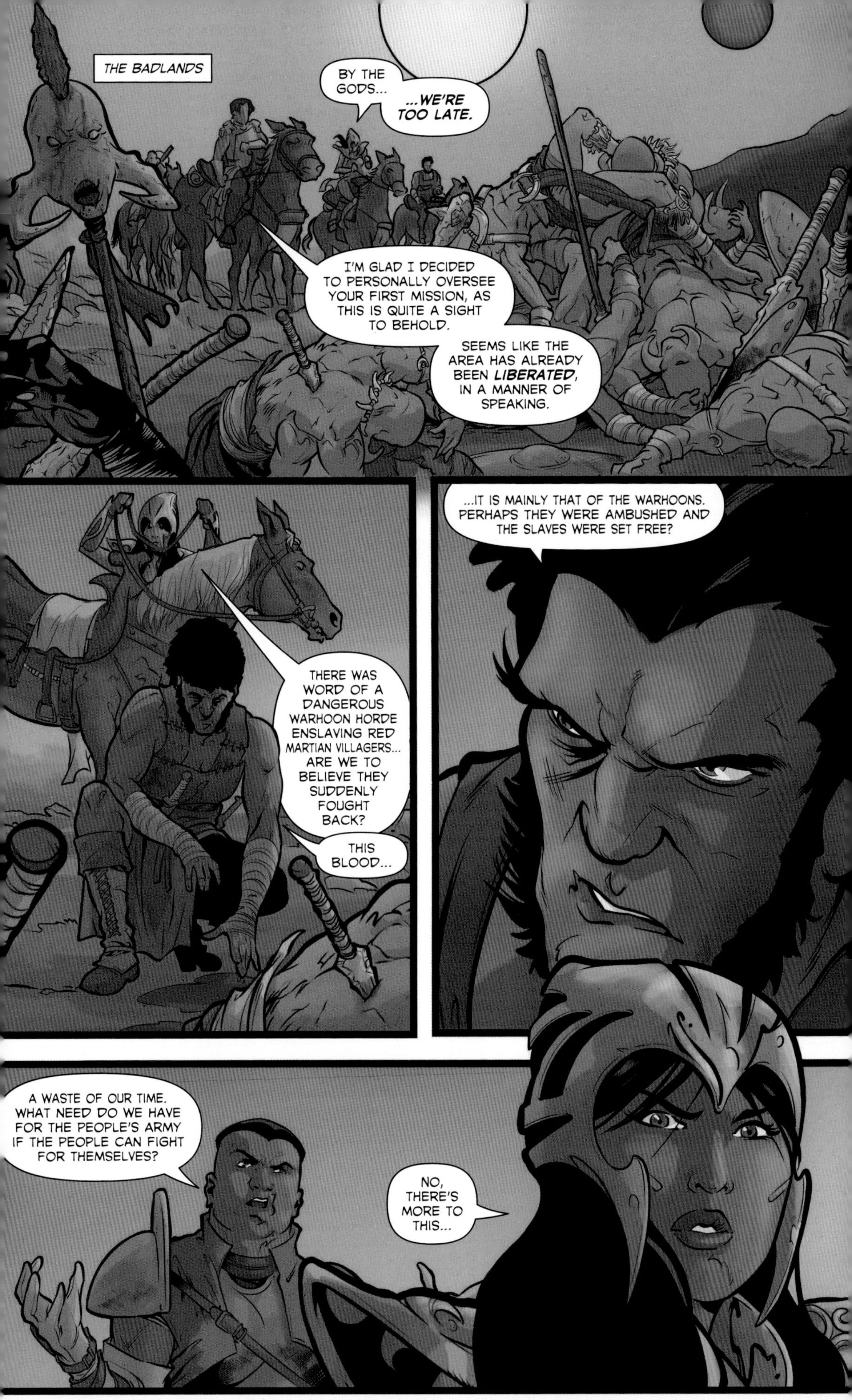
THE BADLANDS
BY THE GODS...
...WE'RE TOO LATE.
I'M GLAD I DECIDED TO PERSONALLY OVERSEE YOUR FIRST MISSION, AS THIS IS QUITE A SIGHT TO BEHOLD.
SEEMS LIKE THE AREA HAS ALREADY BEEN *LIBERATED*, IN A MANNER OF SPEAKING.
THERE WAS WORD OF A DANGEROUS WARHOON HORDE ENSLAVING RED MARTIAN VILLAGERS... ARE WE TO BELIEVE THEY SUDDENLY FOUGHT BACK?
THIS BLOOD...
...IT IS MAINLY THAT OF THE WARHOONS. PERHAPS THEY WERE AMBUSHED AND THE SLAVES WERE SET FREE?
A WASTE OF OUR TIME. WHAT NEED DO WE HAVE FOR THE PEOPLE'S ARMY IF THE PEOPLE CAN FIGHT FOR THEMSELVES?
NO, THERE'S MORE TO THIS...

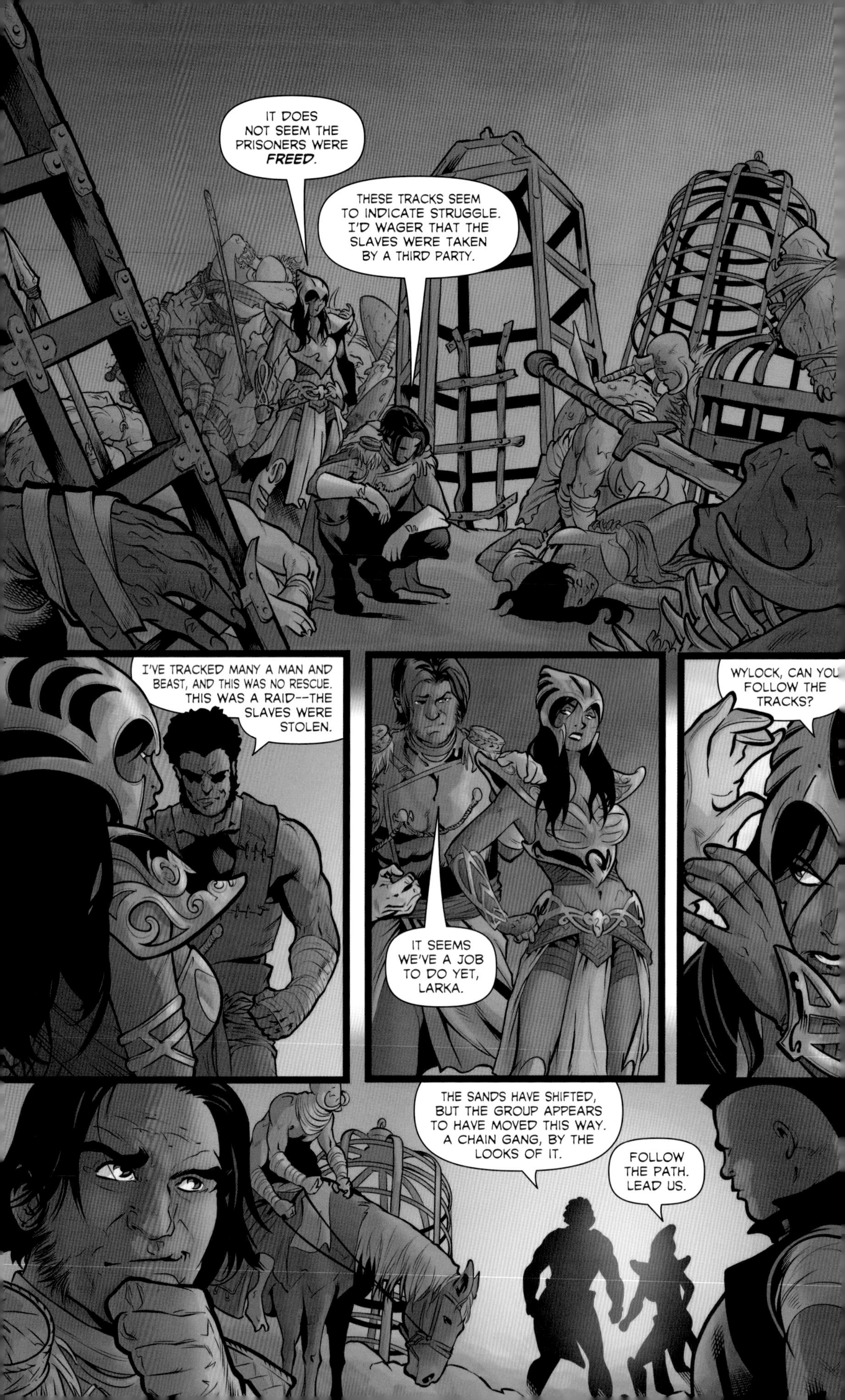
IT DOES NOT SEEM THE PRISONERS WERE *FREED*.
THESE TRACKS SEEM TO INDICATE STRUGGLE. I'D WAGER THAT THE SLAVES WERE TAKEN BY A THIRD PARTY.
I'VE TRACKED MANY A MAN AND BEAST, AND THIS WAS NO RESCUE. THIS WAS A RAID--THE SLAVES WERE STOLEN.
IT SEEMS WE'VE A JOB TO DO YET, LARKA.
WYLOCK, CAN YOU FOLLOW THE TRACKS?
THE SANDS HAVE SHIFTED, BUT THE GROUP APPEARS TO HAVE MOVED THIS WAY. A CHAIN GANG, BY THE LOOKS OF IT.
FOLLOW THE PATH. LEAD US.

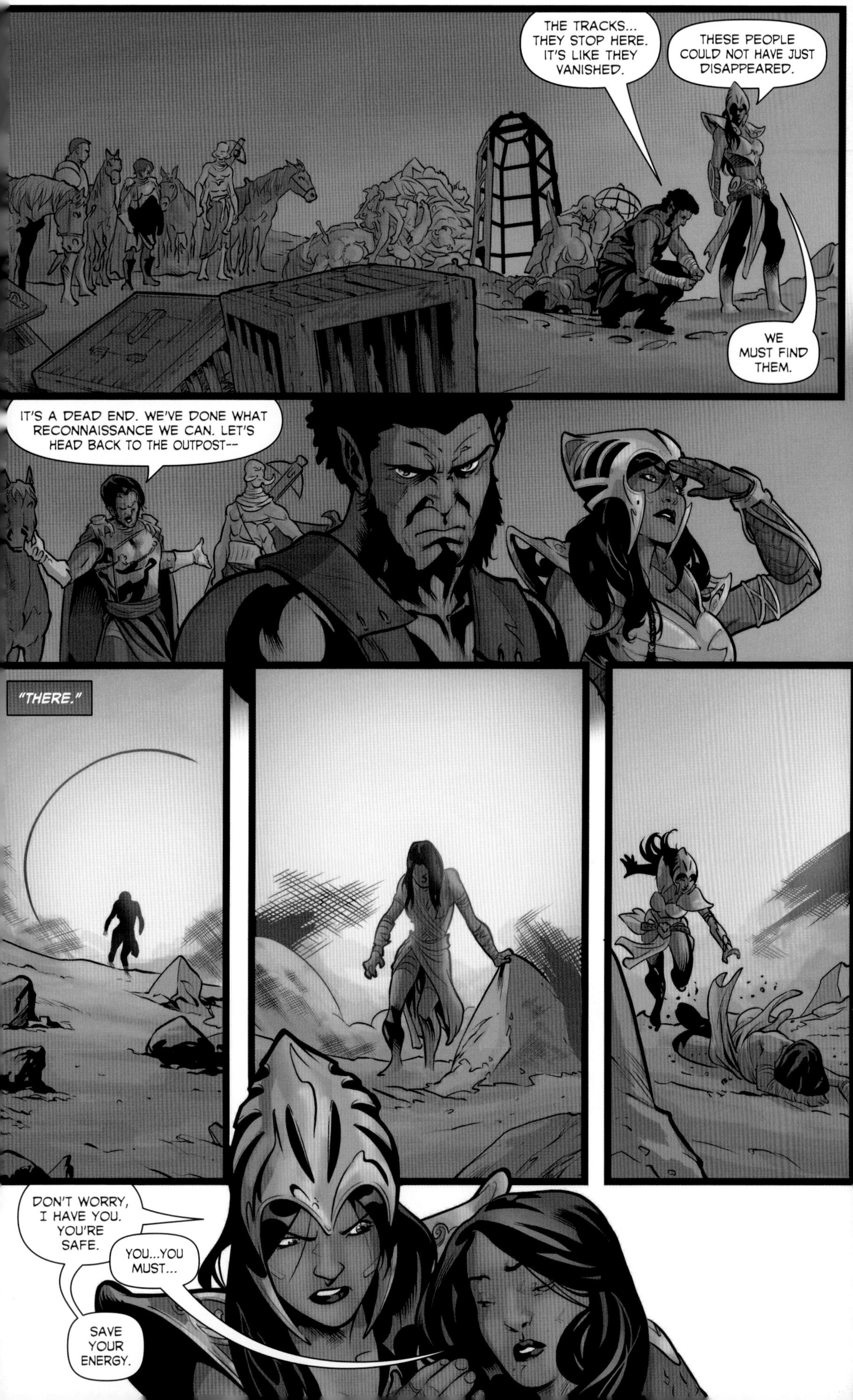
THE TRACKS... THEY STOP HERE. IT'S LIKE THEY VANISHED.
THESE PEOPLE COULD NOT HAVE JUST DISAPPEARED.
WE MUST FIND THEM.
IT'S A DEAD END. WE'VE DONE WHAT RECONNAISSANCE WE CAN. LET'S HEAD BACK TO THE OUTPOST--
"THERE."
DON'T WORRY, I HAVE YOU. YOU'RE SAFE.
YOU...YOU MUST...
SAVE YOUR ENERGY.

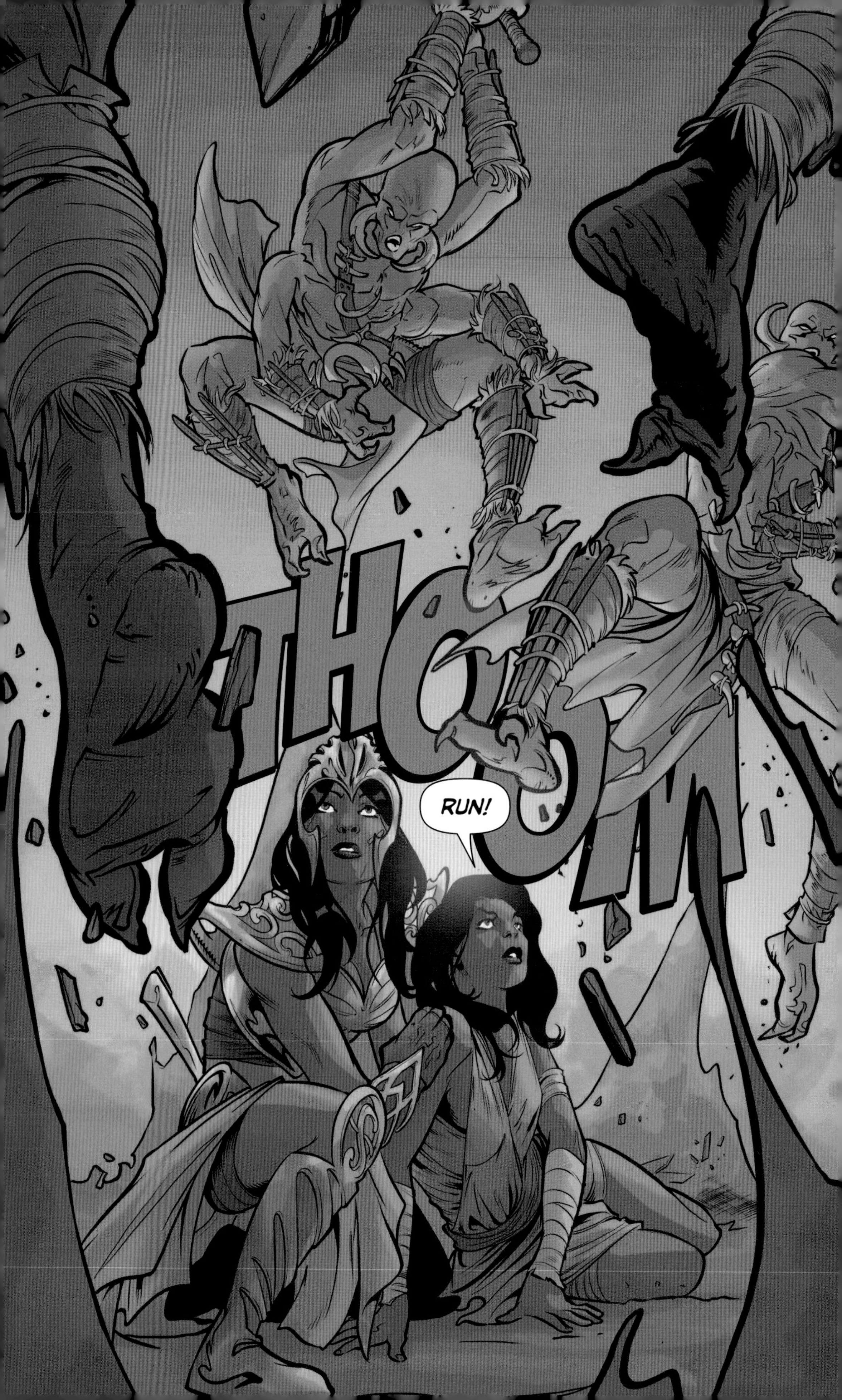
THOOM
RUN!

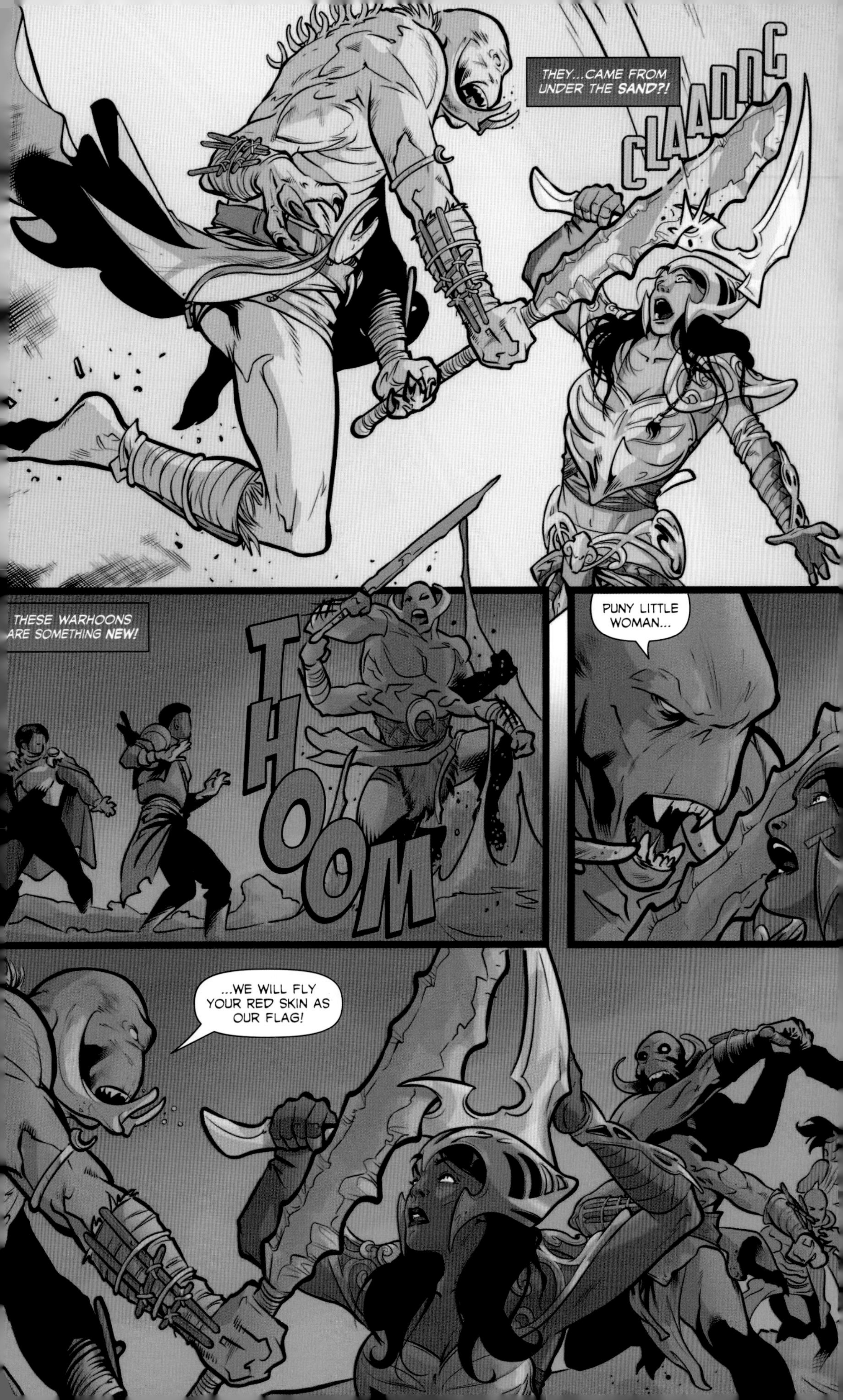
THEY...CAME FROM UNDER THE **SAND?!**
CLAANNG
THESE WARHOONS ARE SOMETHING **NEW!**
THOOOM
PUNY LITTLE WOMAN...
...WE WILL FLY YOUR RED SKIN AS OUR FLAG!

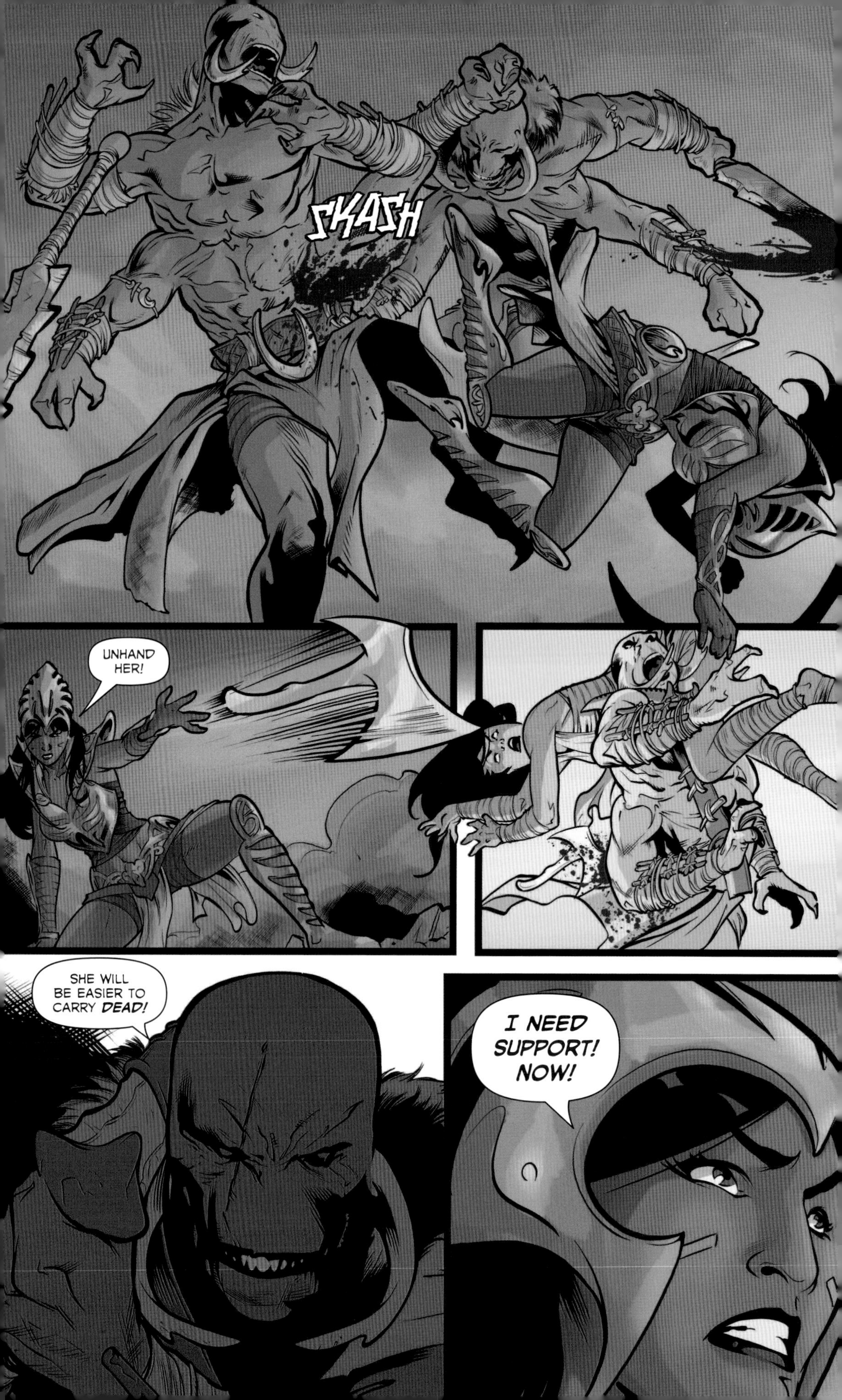
SKASH
UNHAND HER!
SHE WILL BE EASIER TO CARRY *DEAD!*
I NEED SUPPORT! NOW!

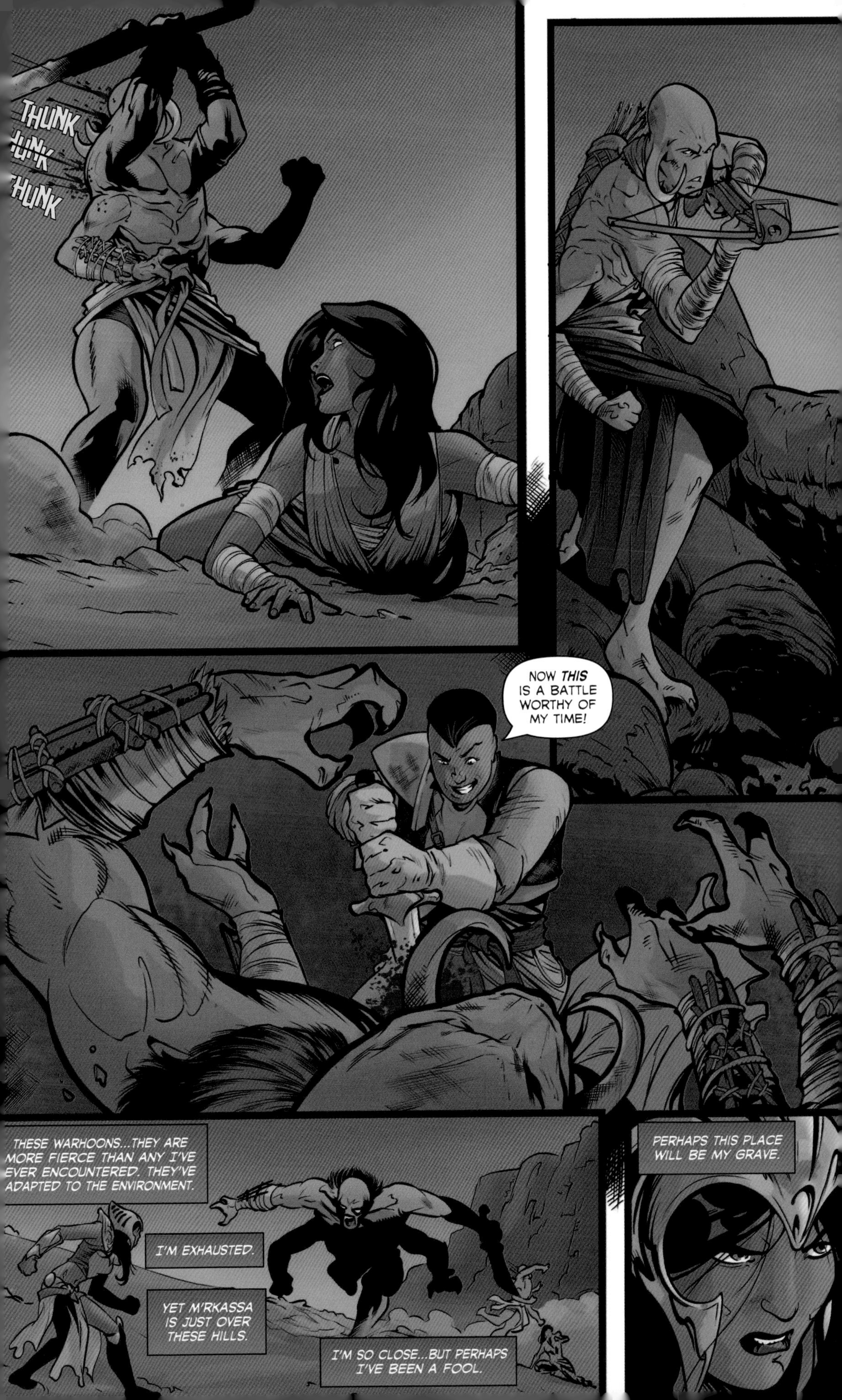
THUNK
THUNK
THUNK
NOW THIS IS A BATTLE WORTHY OF MY TIME!
THESE WARHOONS...THEY ARE MORE FIERCE THAN ANY I'VE EVER ENCOUNTERED. THEY'VE ADAPTED TO THE ENVIRONMENT.
I'M EXHAUSTED.
YET M'RKASSA IS JUST OVER THESE HILLS.
I'M SO CLOSE...BUT PERHAPS I'VE BEEN A FOOL.
PERHAPS THIS PLACE WILL BE MY GRAVE.

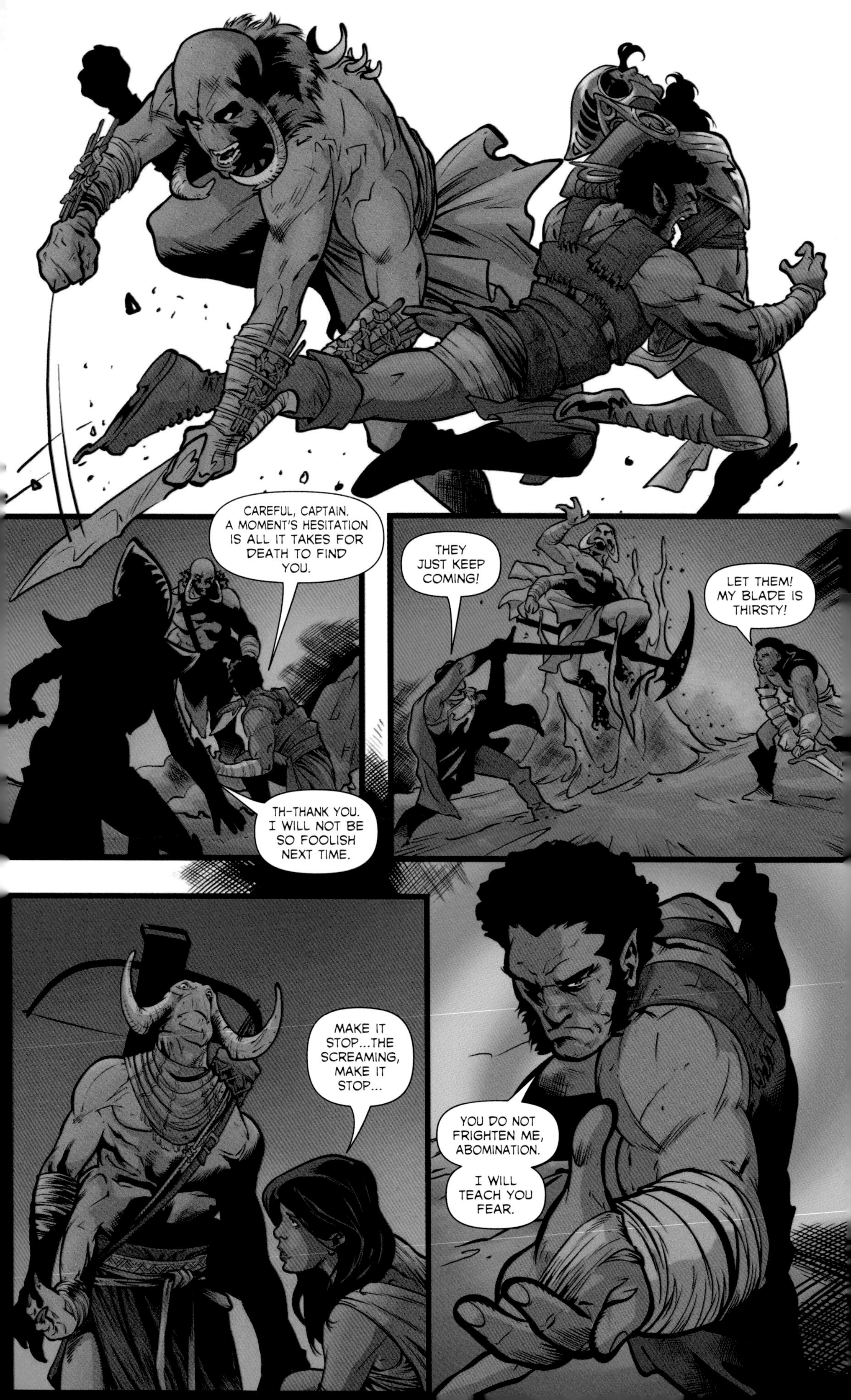
CAREFUL, CAPTAIN. A MOMENT'S HESITATION IS ALL IT TAKES FOR DEATH TO FIND YOU.
TH-THANK YOU. I WILL NOT BE SO FOOLISH NEXT TIME.
THEY JUST KEEP COMING!
LET THEM! MY BLADE IS THIRSTY!
MAKE IT STOP...THE SCREAMING, MAKE IT STOP...
YOU DO NOT FRIGHTEN ME, ABOMINATION.
I WILL TEACH YOU FEAR.

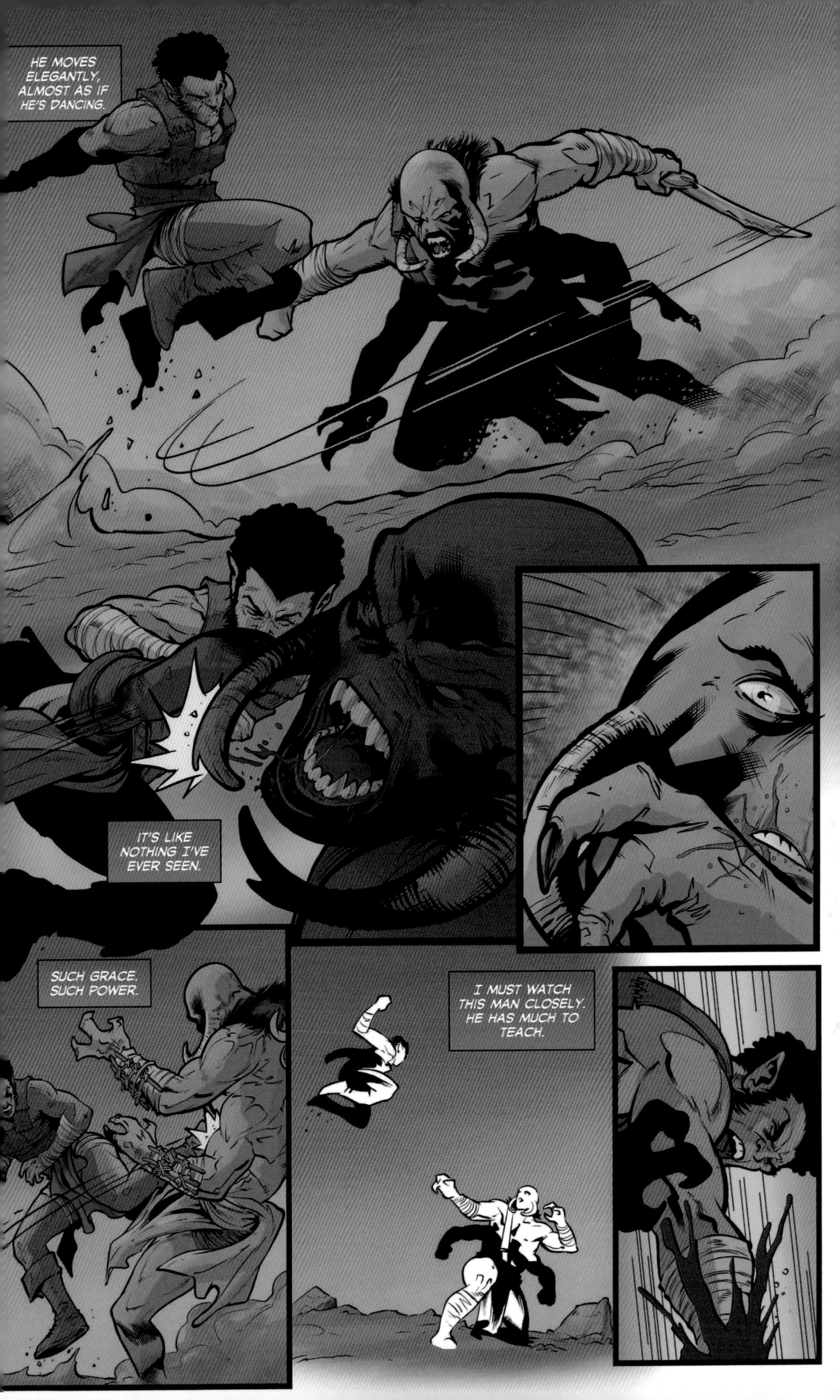
HE MOVES ELEGANTLY, ALMOST AS IF HE'S DANCING.
IT'S LIKE NOTHING I'VE EVER SEEN.
SUCH GRACE. SUCH POWER.
I MUST WATCH THIS MAN CLOSELY. HE HAS MUCH TO TEACH.

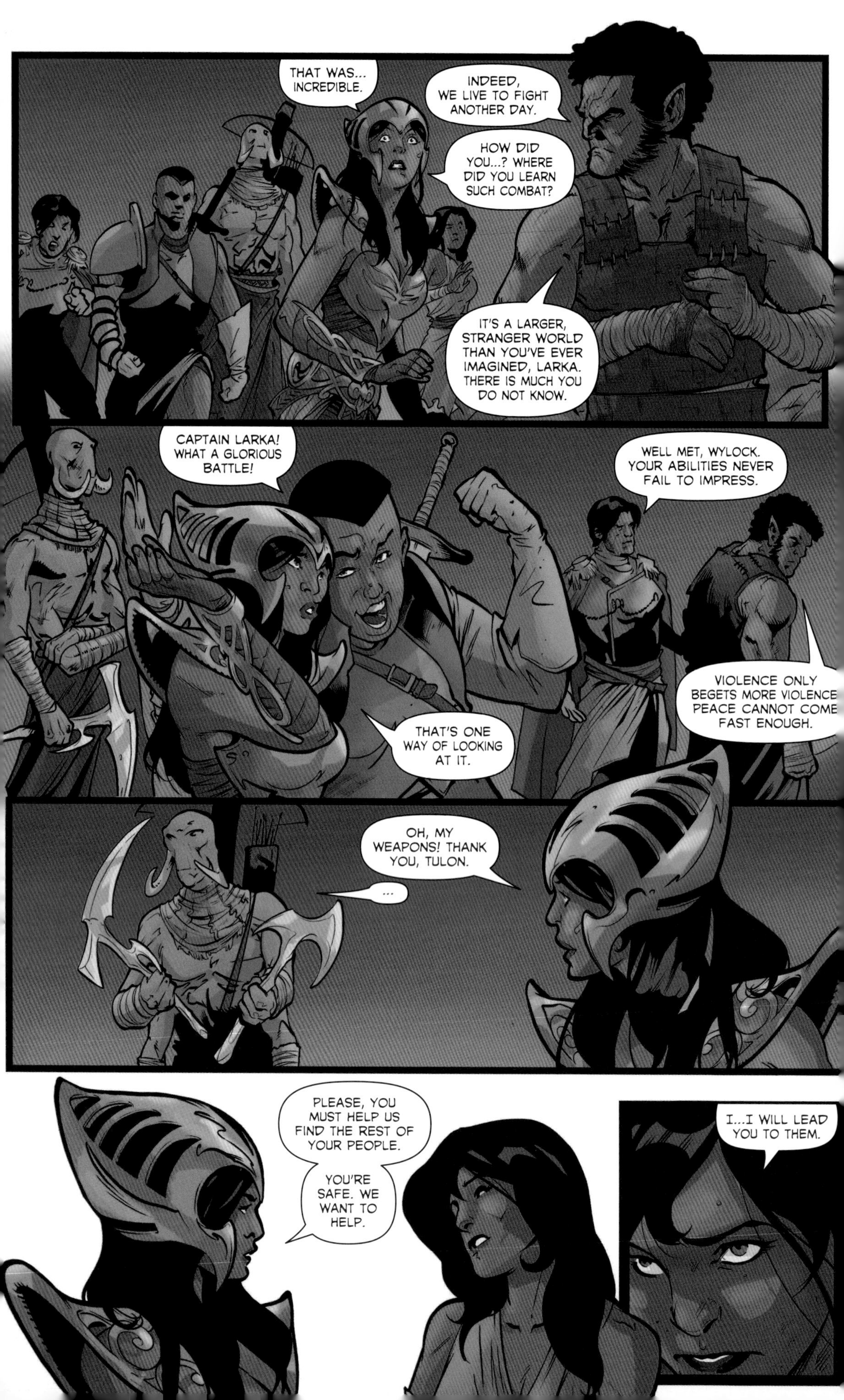
THAT WAS... INCREDIBLE.
INDEED, WE LIVE TO FIGHT ANOTHER DAY.
HOW DID YOU...? WHERE DID YOU LEARN SUCH COMBAT?
IT'S A LARGER, STRANGER WORLD THAN YOU'VE EVER IMAGINED, LARKA. THERE IS MUCH YOU DO NOT KNOW.
CAPTAIN LARKA! WHAT A GLORIOUS BATTLE!
THAT'S ONE WAY OF LOOKING AT IT.
WELL MET, WYLOCK. YOUR ABILITIES NEVER FAIL TO IMPRESS.
VIOLENCE ONLY BEGETS MORE VIOLENCE PEACE CANNOT COME FAST ENOUGH.
OH, MY WEAPONS! THANK YOU, TULON.
...
PLEASE, YOU MUST HELP US FIND THE REST OF YOUR PEOPLE.
YOU'RE SAFE. WE WANT TO HELP.
I...I WILL LEAD YOU TO THEM.

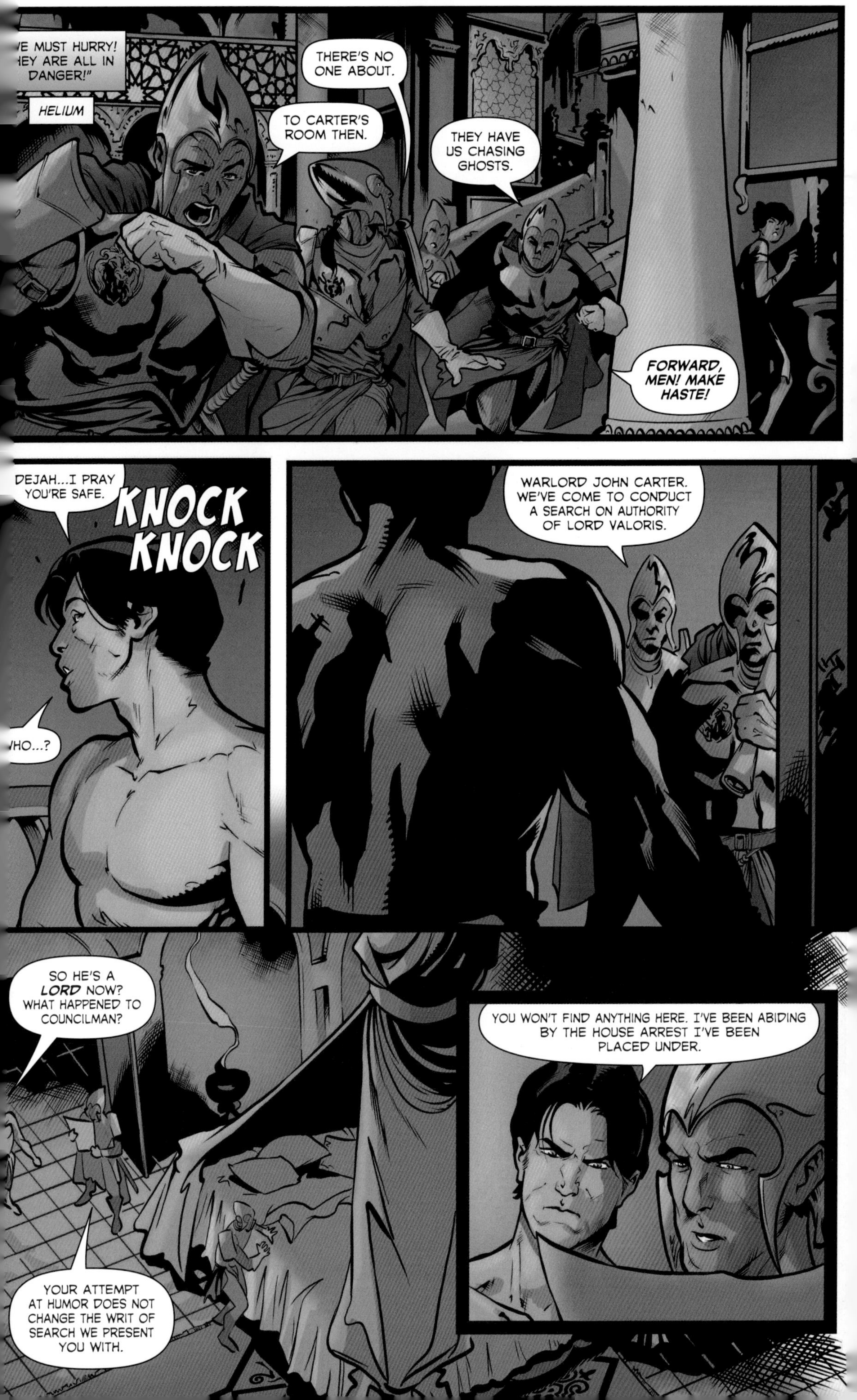

E MUST HURRY! HEY ARE ALL IN DANGER!"
HELIUM
THERE'S NO ONE ABOUT.
TO CARTER'S ROOM THEN.
THEY HAVE US CHASING GHOSTS.
FORWARD, MEN! MAKE HASTE!
DEJAH...I PRAY YOU'RE SAFE.
KNOCK KNOCK
HO...?
WARLORD JOHN CARTER. WE'VE COME TO CONDUCT A SEARCH ON AUTHORITY OF LORD VALORIS.
SO HE'S A LORD NOW? WHAT HAPPENED TO COUNCILMAN?
YOUR ATTEMPT AT HUMOR DOES NOT CHANGE THE WRIT OF SEARCH WE PRESENT YOU WITH.
YOU WON'T FIND ANYTHING HERE. I'VE BEEN ABIDING BY THE HOUSE ARREST I'VE BEEN PLACED UNDER.

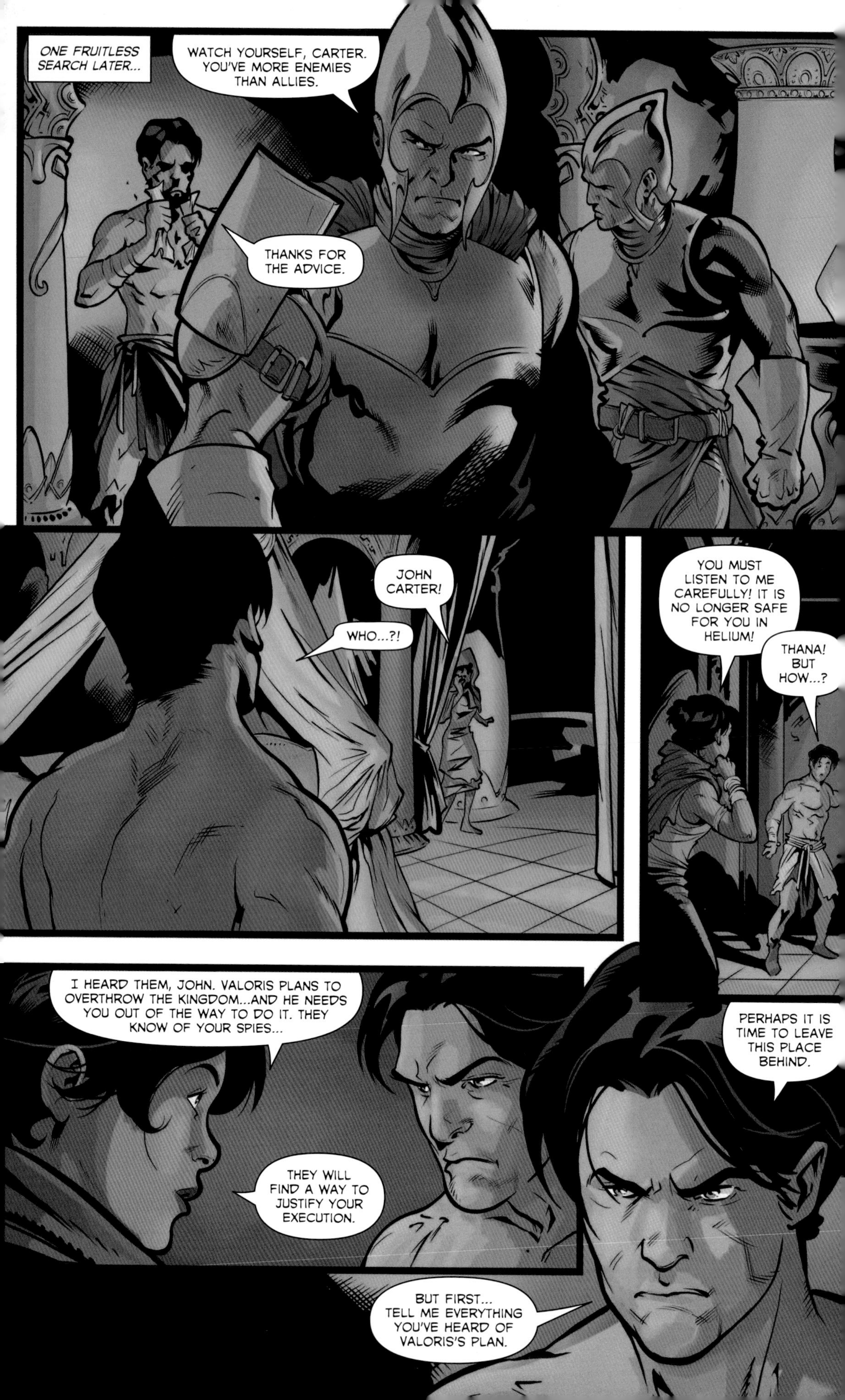
ONE FRUITLESS SEARCH LATER...
WATCH YOURSELF, CARTER. YOU'VE MORE ENEMIES THAN ALLIES.
THANKS FOR THE ADVICE.
JOHN CARTER!
WHO...?!
YOU MUST LISTEN TO ME CAREFULLY! IT IS NO LONGER SAFE FOR YOU IN HELIUM!
THANA! BUT HOW...?
I HEARD THEM, JOHN. VALORIS PLANS TO OVERTHROW THE KINGDOM...AND HE NEEDS YOU OUT OF THE WAY TO DO IT. THEY KNOW OF YOUR SPIES...
THEY WILL FIND A WAY TO JUSTIFY YOUR EXECUTION.
PERHAPS IT IS TIME TO LEAVE THIS PLACE BEHIND.
BUT FIRST... TELL ME EVERYTHING YOU'VE HEARD OF VALORIS'S PLAN.

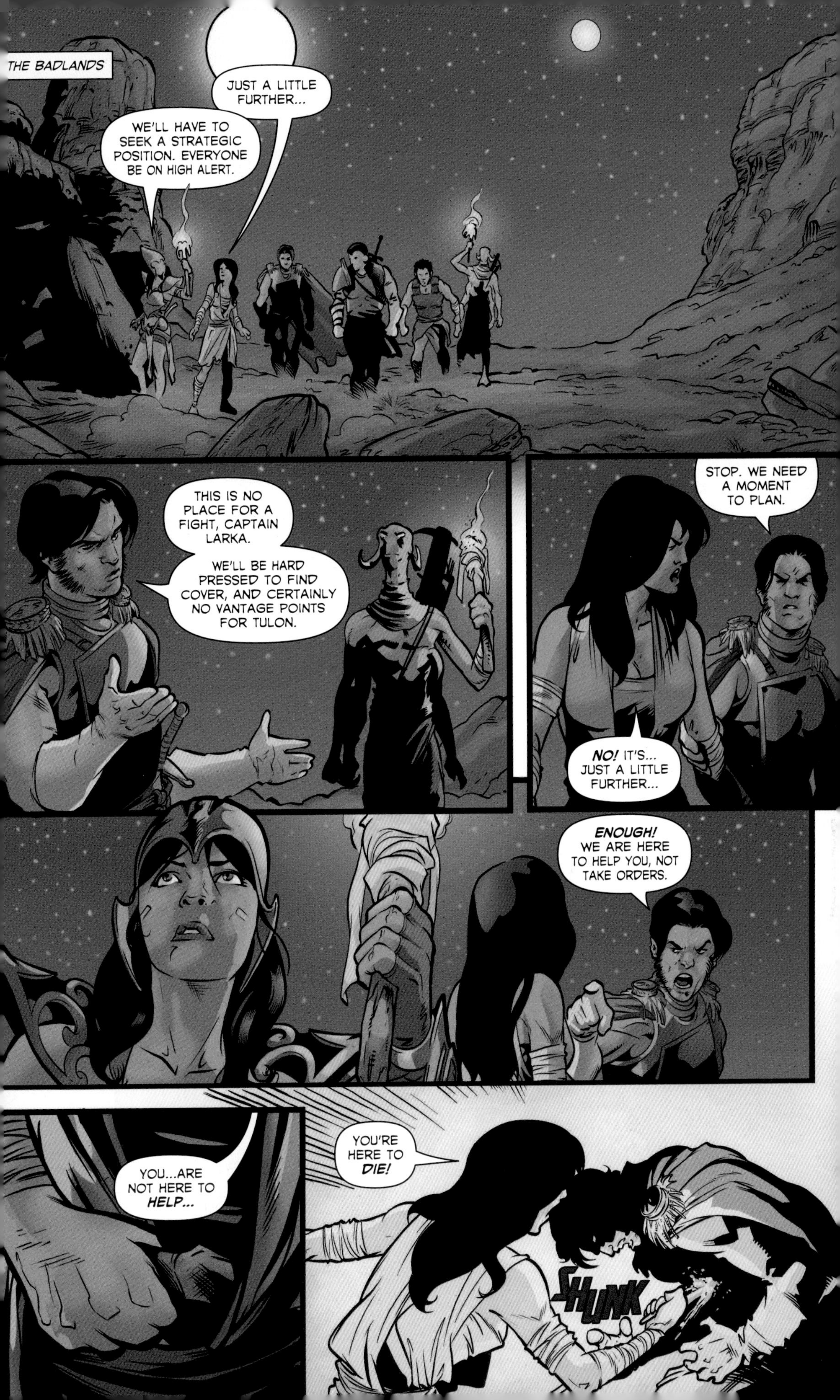
THE BADLANDS
JUST A LITTLE FURTHER...
WE'LL HAVE TO SEEK A STRATEGIC POSITION. EVERYONE BE ON HIGH ALERT.
THIS IS NO PLACE FOR A FIGHT, CAPTAIN LARKA.
WE'LL BE HARD PRESSED TO FIND COVER, AND CERTAINLY NO VANTAGE POINTS FOR TULON.
STOP. WE NEED A MOMENT TO PLAN.
NO! IT'S... JUST A LITTLE FURTHER...
ENOUGH! WE ARE HERE TO HELP YOU, NOT TAKE ORDERS.
YOU...ARE NOT HERE TO HELP...
YOU'RE HERE TO DIE!
SHUNK

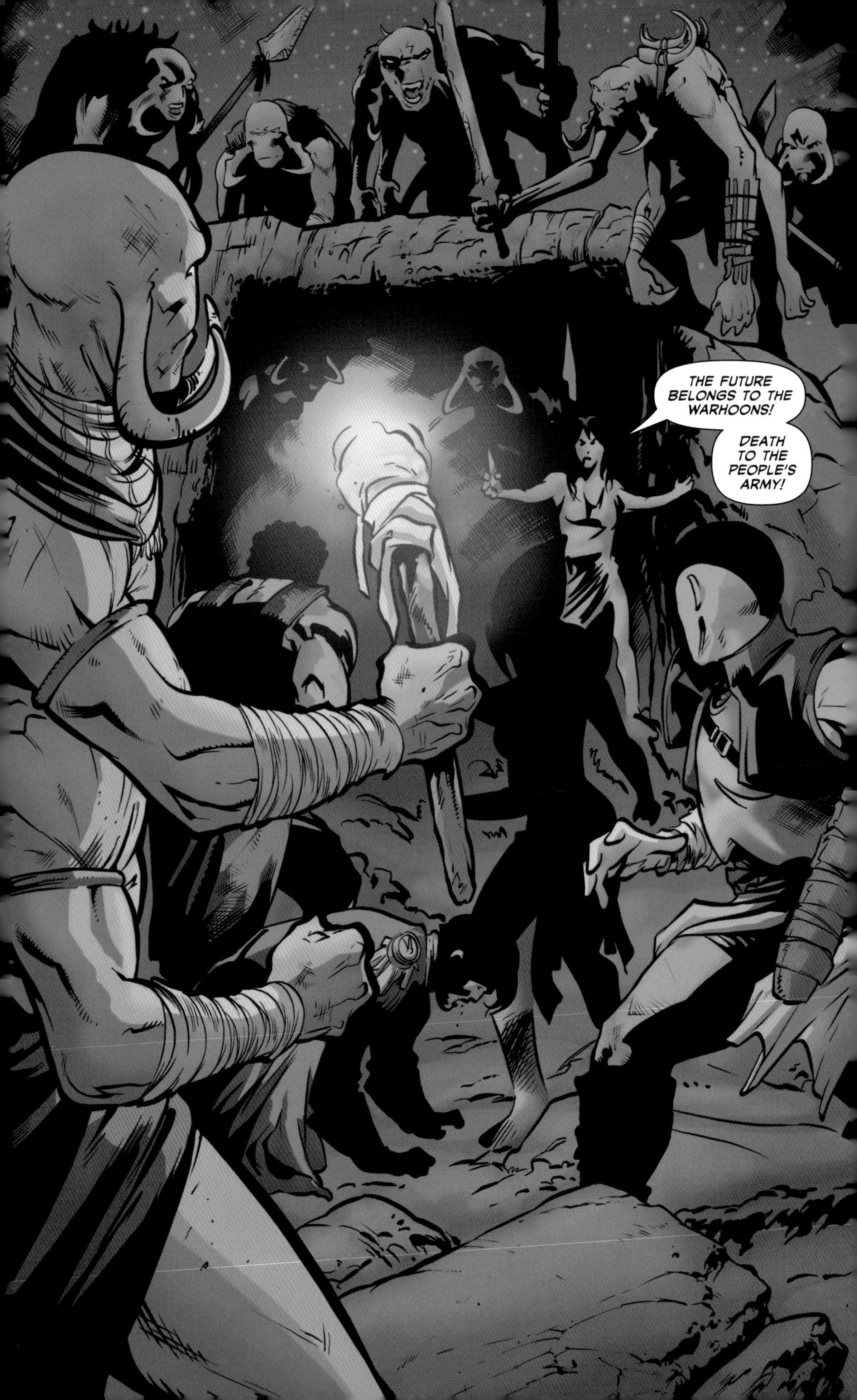
THE FUTURE BELONGS TO THE WARHOONS!
DEATH TO THE PEOPLE'S ARMY!

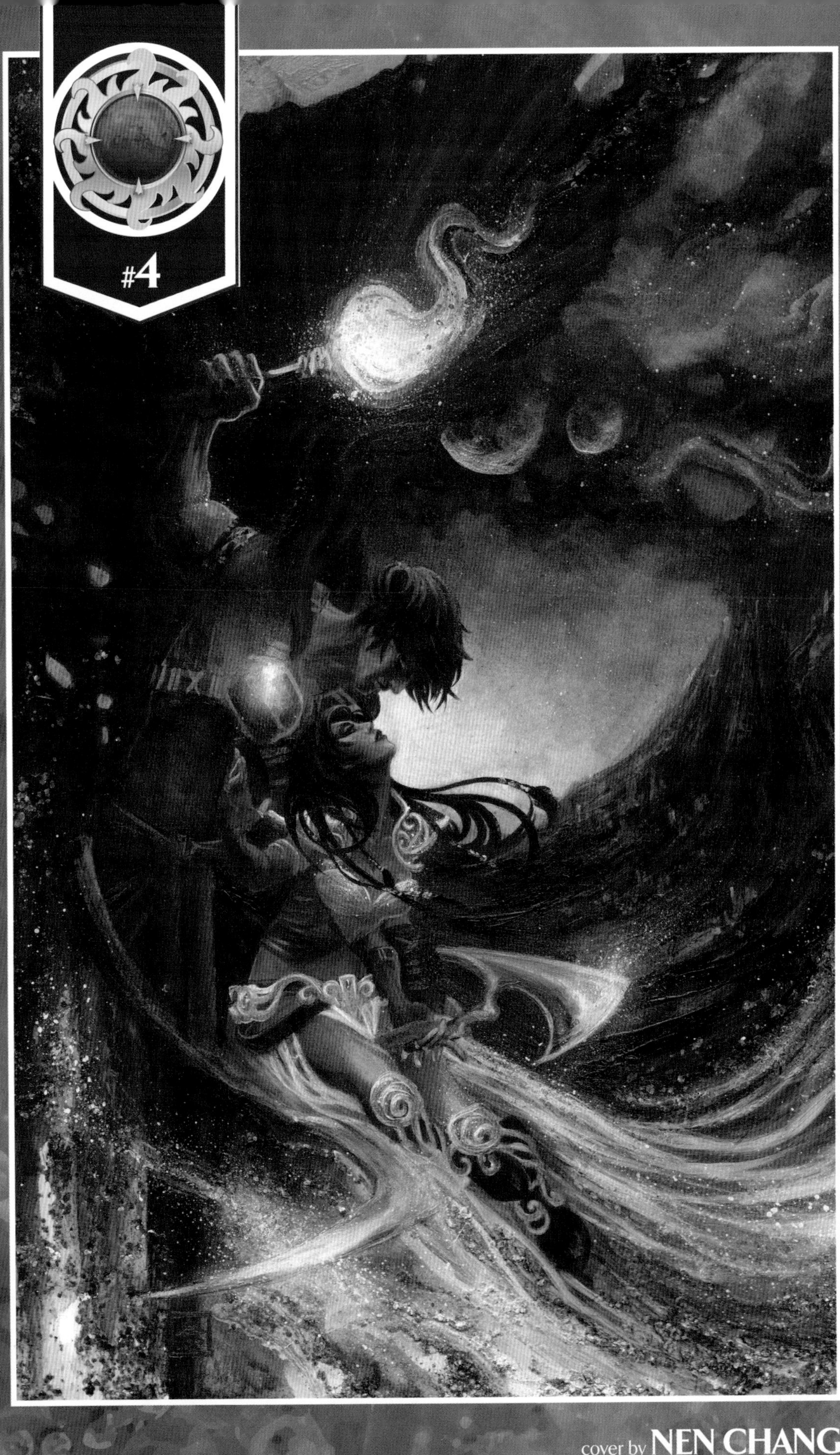

#4

cover by **NEN CHANG**

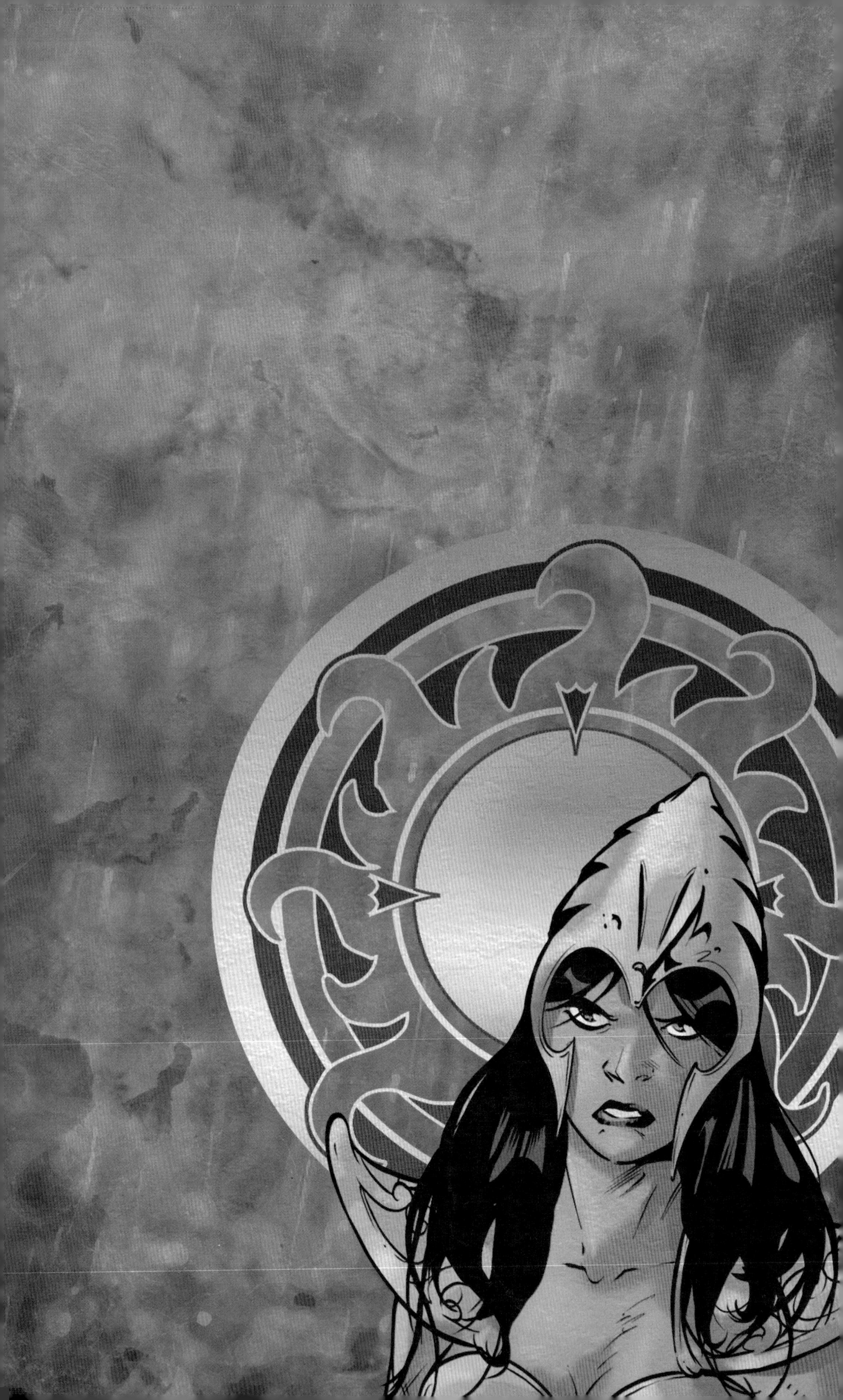

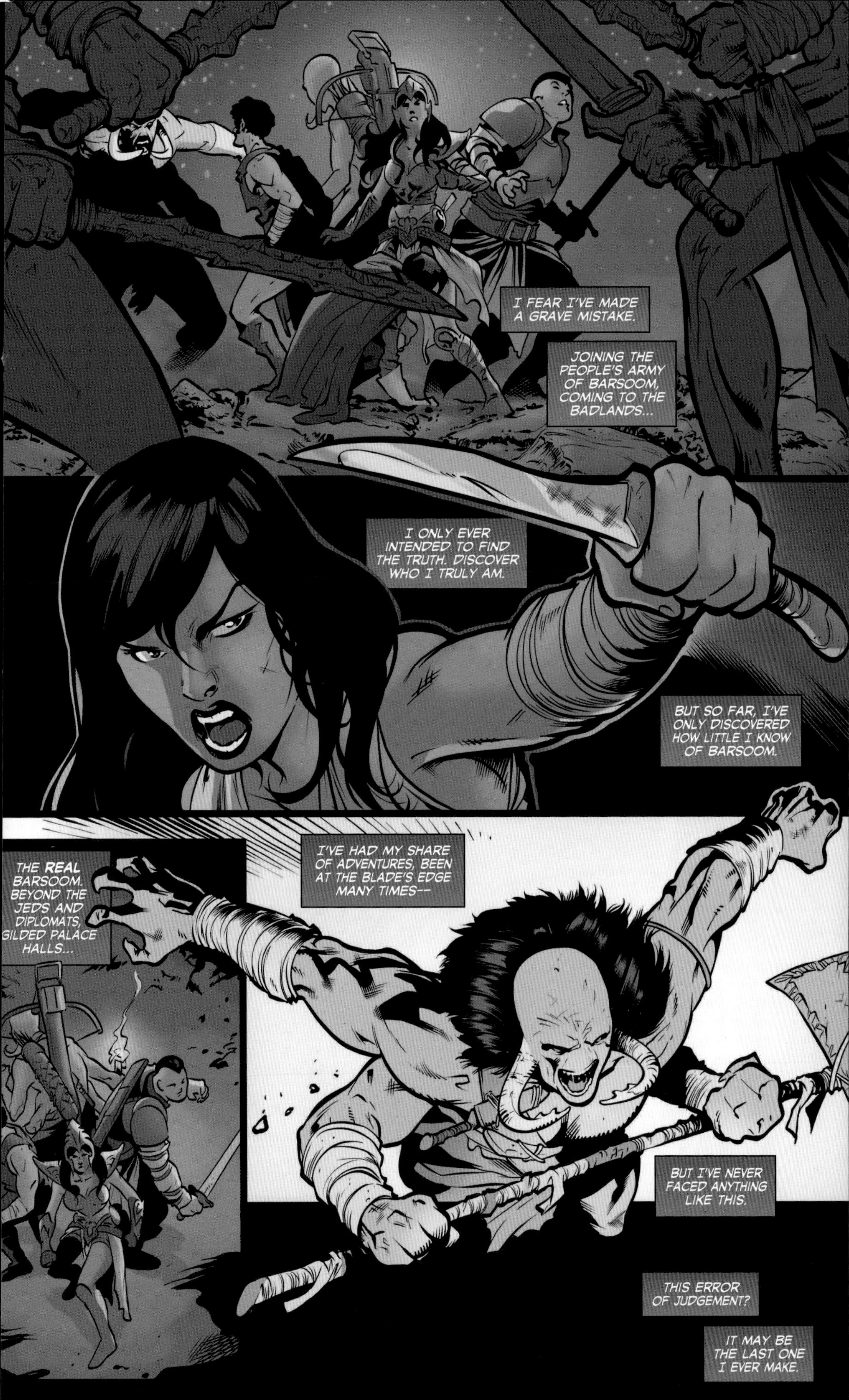
I FEAR I'VE MADE A GRAVE MISTAKE.
JOINING THE PEOPLE'S ARMY OF BARSOOM, COMING TO THE BADLANDS...
I ONLY EVER INTENDED TO FIND THE TRUTH. DISCOVER WHO I TRULY AM.
BUT SO FAR, I'VE ONLY DISCOVERED HOW LITTLE I KNOW OF BARSOOM.
THE REAL BARSOOM. BEYOND THE JEDS AND DIPLOMATS, GILDED PALACE HALLS...
I'VE HAD MY SHARE OF ADVENTURES, BEEN AT THE BLADE'S EDGE MANY TIMES--
BUT I'VE NEVER FACED ANYTHING LIKE THIS.
THIS ERROR OF JUDGEMENT?
IT MAY BE THE LAST ONE I EVER MAKE.

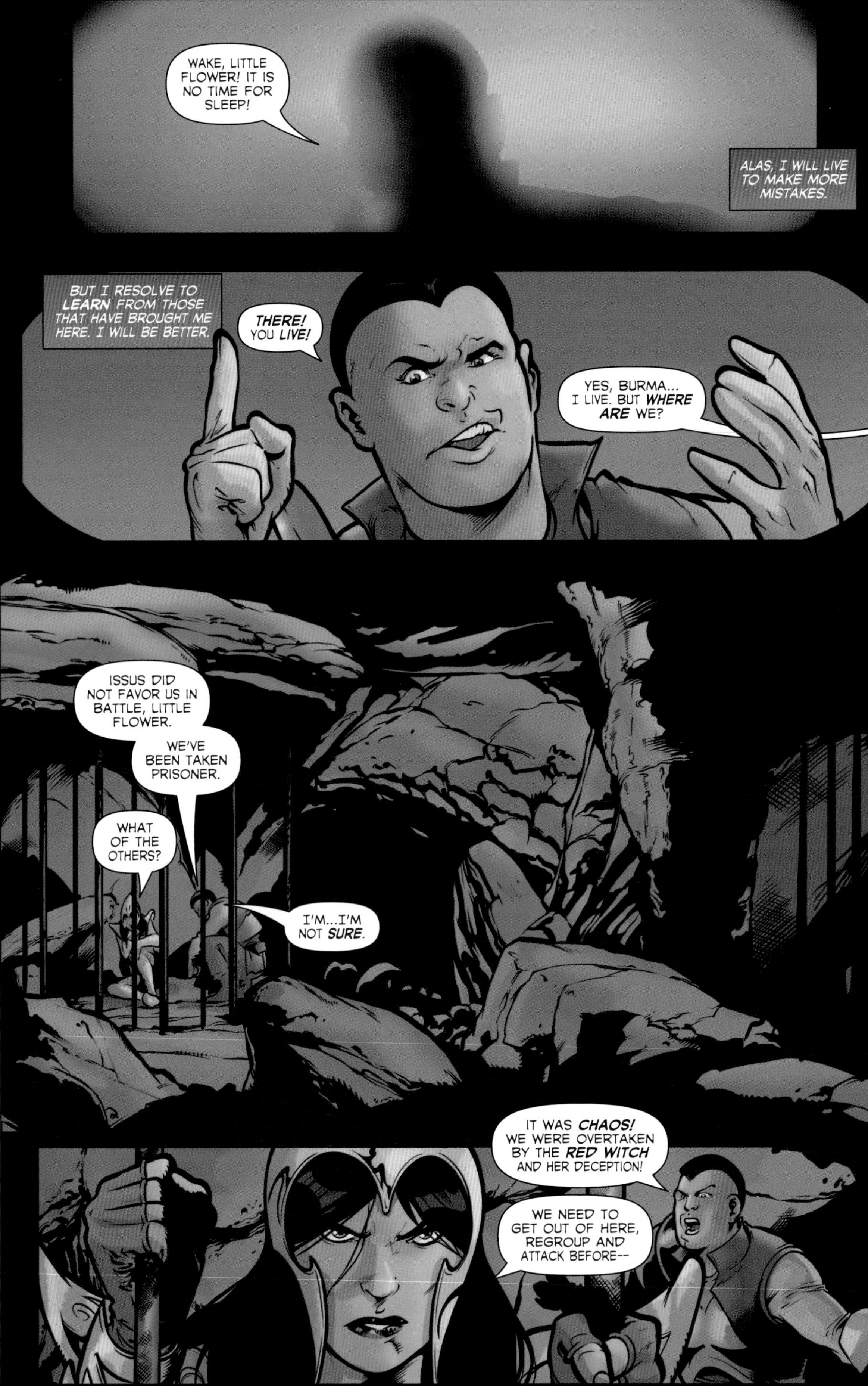
WAKE, LITTLE FLOWER! IT IS NO TIME FOR SLEEP!
ALAS, I WILL LIVE TO MAKE MORE MISTAKES.
BUT I RESOLVE TO LEARN FROM THOSE THAT HAVE BROUGHT ME HERE. I WILL BE BETTER.
THERE! YOU LIVE!
YES, BURMA... I LIVE. BUT WHERE ARE WE?
ISSUS DID NOT FAVOR US IN BATTLE, LITTLE FLOWER.
WE'VE BEEN TAKEN PRISONER.
WHAT OF THE OTHERS?
I'M...I'M NOT SURE.
IT WAS CHAOS! WE WERE OVERTAKEN BY THE RED WITCH AND HER DECEPTION!
WE NEED TO GET OUT OF HERE, REGROUP AND ATTACK BEFORE--

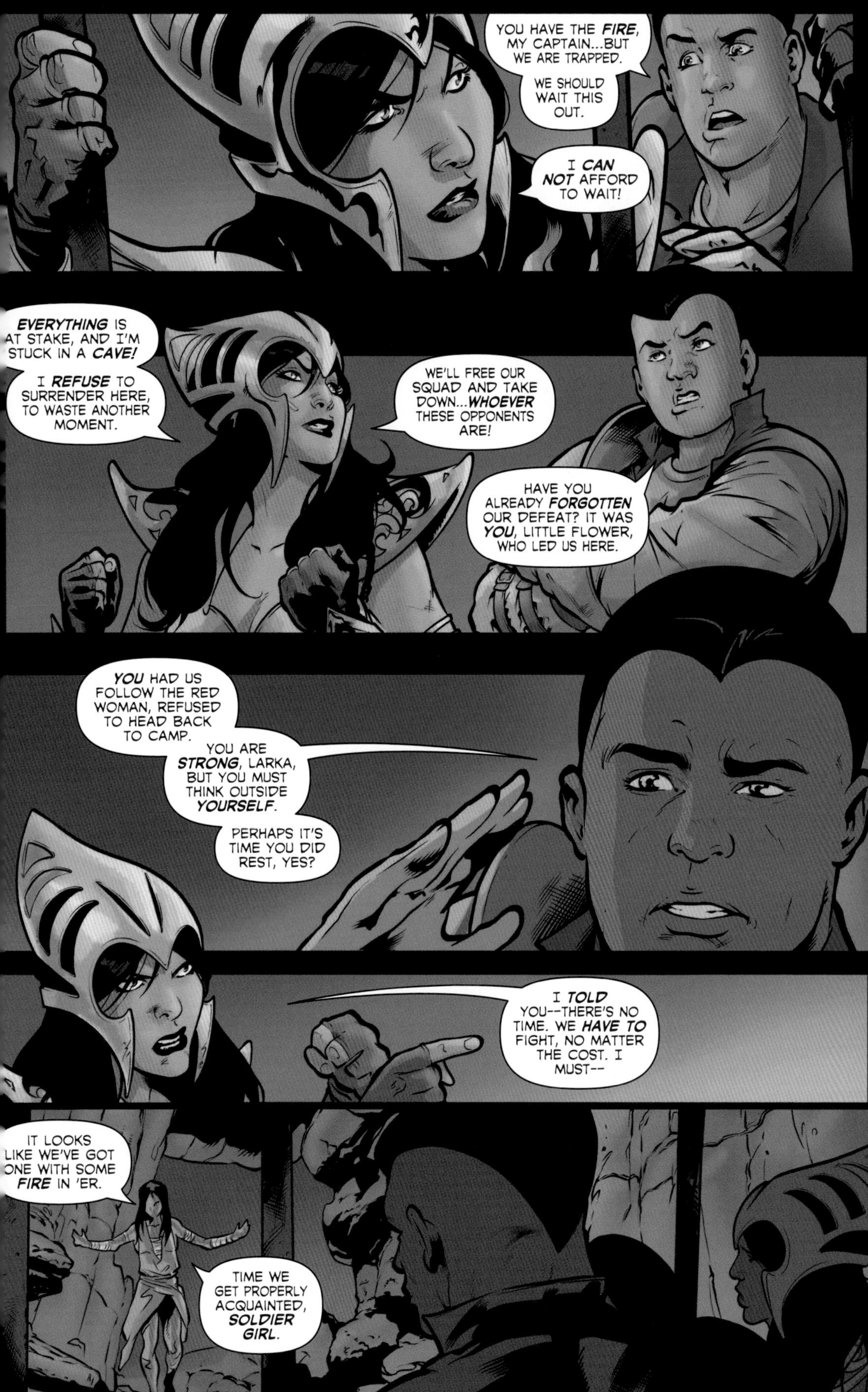
YOU HAVE THE *FIRE*, MY CAPTAIN...BUT WE ARE TRAPPED.
WE SHOULD WAIT THIS OUT.
I *CAN NOT* AFFORD TO WAIT!
EVERYTHING IS AT STAKE, AND I'M STUCK IN A *CAVE!*
I *REFUSE* TO SURRENDER HERE, TO WASTE ANOTHER MOMENT.
WE'LL FREE OUR SQUAD AND TAKE DOWN...*WHOEVER* THESE OPPONENTS ARE!
HAVE YOU ALREADY *FORGOTTEN* OUR DEFEAT? IT WAS *YOU*, LITTLE FLOWER, WHO LED US HERE.
YOU HAD US FOLLOW THE RED WOMAN, REFUSED TO HEAD BACK TO CAMP.
YOU ARE *STRONG*, LARKA, BUT YOU MUST THINK OUTSIDE *YOURSELF*.
PERHAPS IT'S TIME YOU DID REST, YES?
I *TOLD* YOU--THERE'S NO TIME. WE *HAVE TO* FIGHT, NO MATTER THE COST. I MUST--
IT LOOKS LIKE WE'VE GOT ONE WITH SOME *FIRE* IN 'ER.
TIME WE GET PROPERLY ACQUAINTED, *SOLDIER GIRL*.

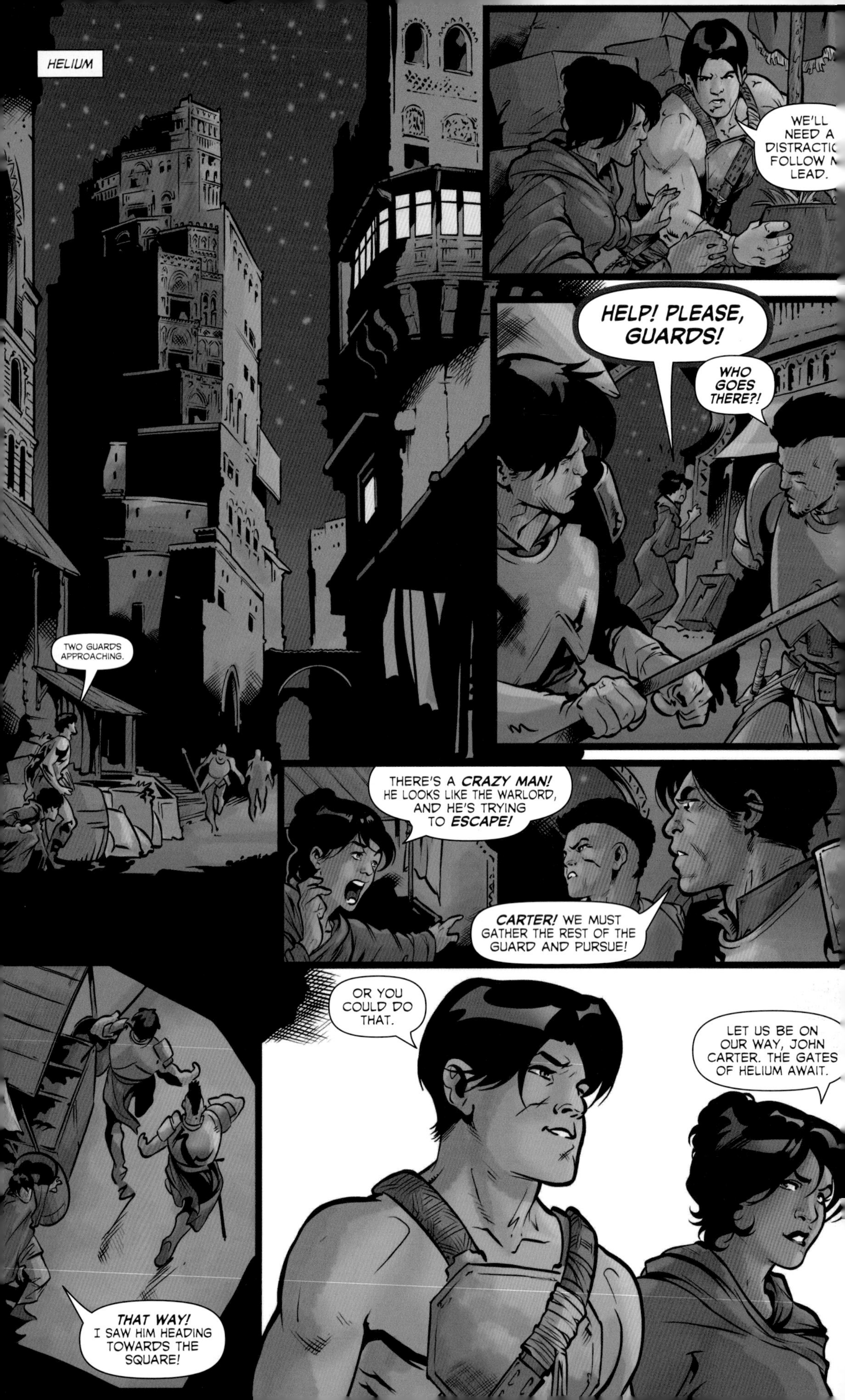
HELIUM
TWO GUARDS APPROACHING.
WE'LL NEED A DISTRACTIO FOLLOW M LEAD.
HELP! PLEASE, GUARDS!
WHO GOES THERE?!
THERE'S A CRAZY MAN! HE LOOKS LIKE THE WARLORD, AND HE'S TRYING TO ESCAPE!
CARTER! WE MUST GATHER THE REST OF THE GUARD AND PURSUE!
THAT WAY! I SAW HIM HEADING TOWARDS THE SQUARE!
OR YOU COULD DO THAT.
LET US BE ON OUR WAY, JOHN CARTER. THE GATES OF HELIUM AWAIT.

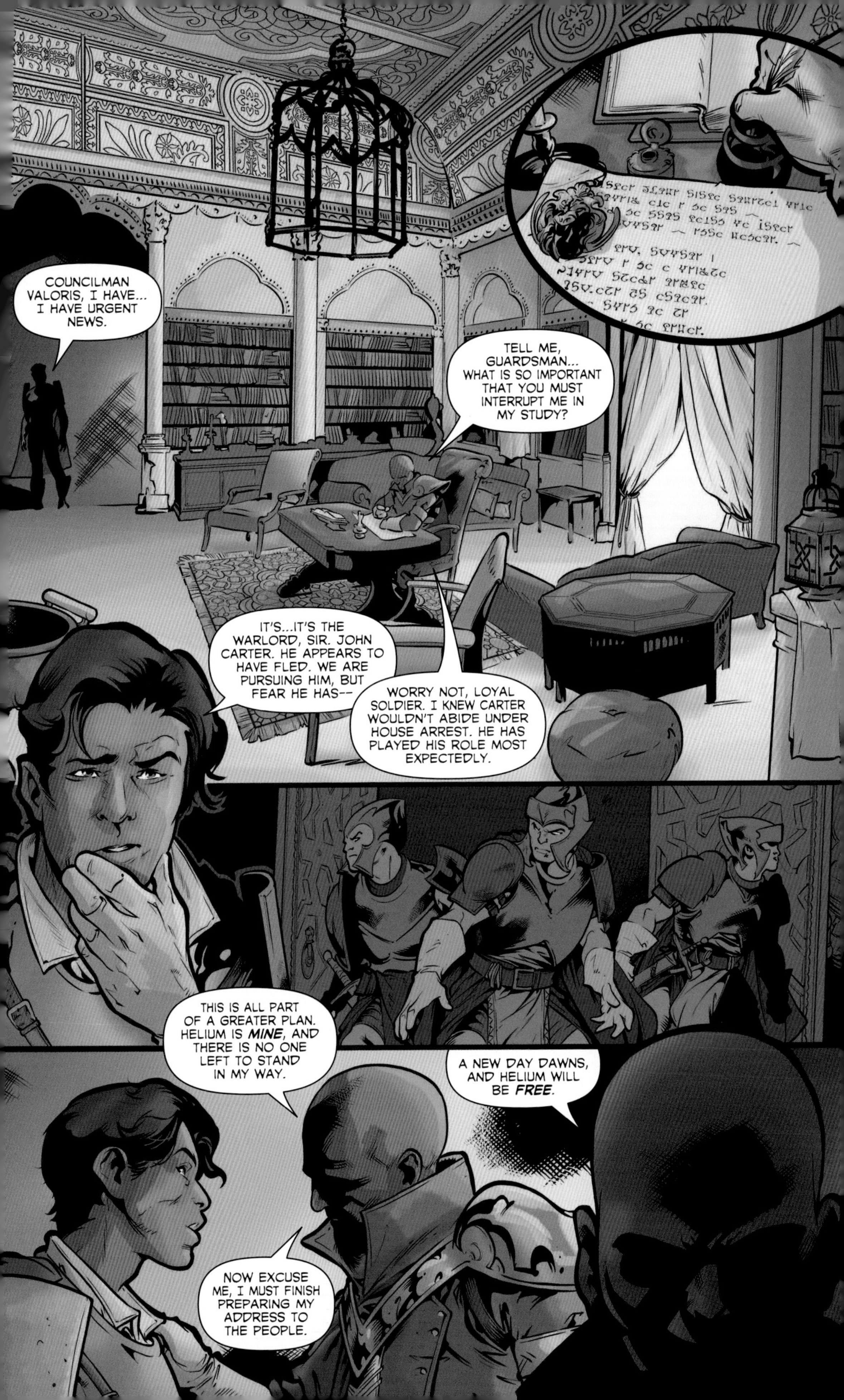
COUNCILMAN VALORIS, I HAVE... I HAVE URGENT NEWS.
TELL ME, GUARDSMAN... WHAT IS SO IMPORTANT THAT YOU MUST INTERRUPT ME IN MY STUDY?
IT'S...IT'S THE WARLORD, SIR. JOHN CARTER. HE APPEARS TO HAVE FLED. WE ARE PURSUING HIM, BUT FEAR HE HAS--
WORRY NOT, LOYAL SOLDIER. I KNEW CARTER WOULDN'T ABIDE UNDER HOUSE ARREST. HE HAS PLAYED HIS ROLE MOST EXPECTEDLY.
THIS IS ALL PART OF A GREATER PLAN. HELIUM IS MINE, AND THERE IS NO ONE LEFT TO STAND IN MY WAY.
A NEW DAY DAWNS, AND HELIUM WILL BE FREE.
NOW EXCUSE ME, I MUST FINISH PREPARING MY ADDRESS TO THE PEOPLE.

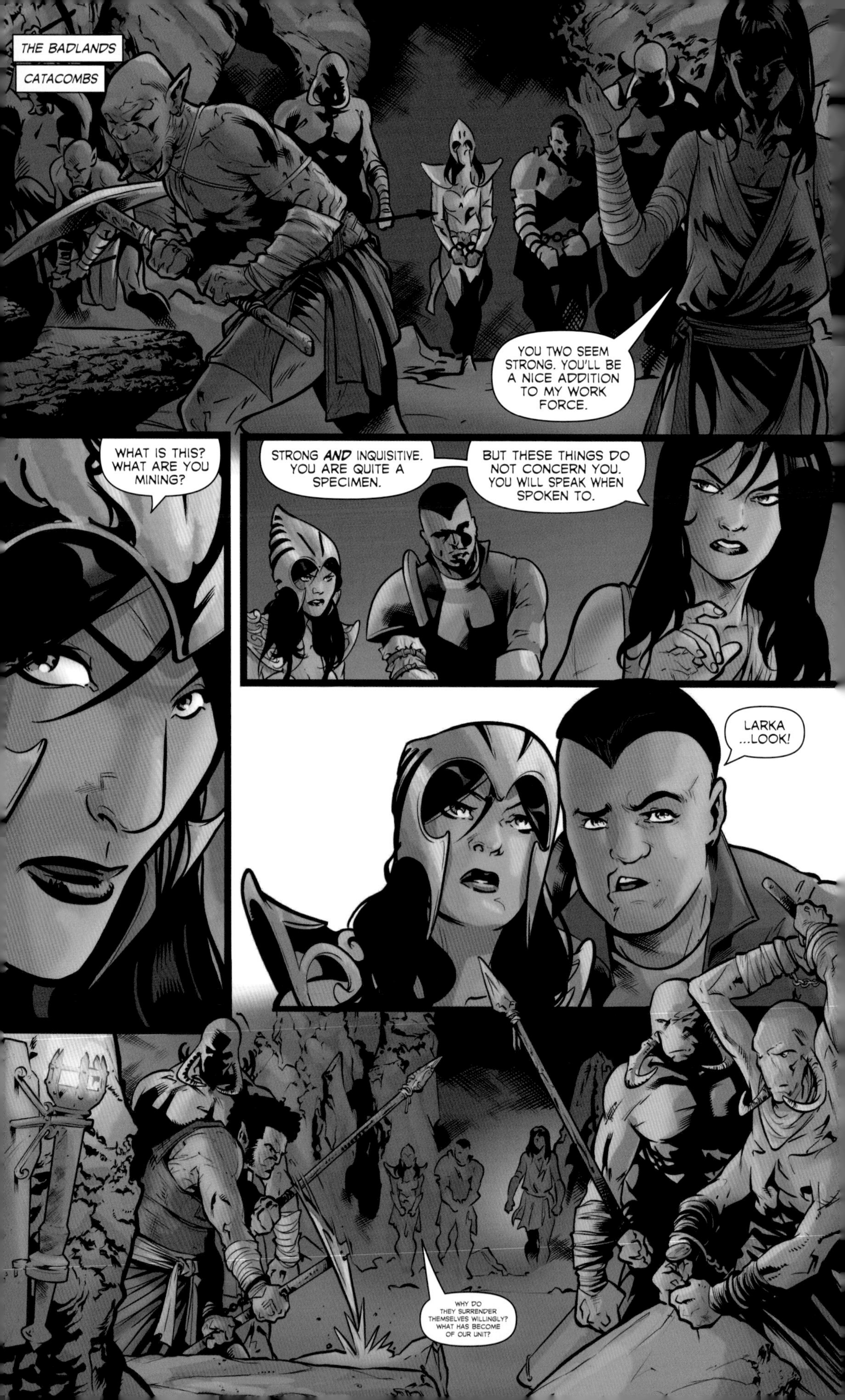
THE BADLANDS
CATACOMBS
YOU TWO SEEM STRONG. YOU'LL BE A NICE ADDITION TO MY WORK FORCE.
WHAT IS THIS? WHAT ARE YOU MINING?
STRONG AND INQUISITIVE. YOU ARE QUITE A SPECIMEN.
BUT THESE THINGS DO NOT CONCERN YOU. YOU WILL SPEAK WHEN SPOKEN TO.
LARKA ...LOOK!
WHY DO THEY SURRENDER THEMSELVES WILLINGLY? WHAT HAS BECOME OF OUR UNIT?

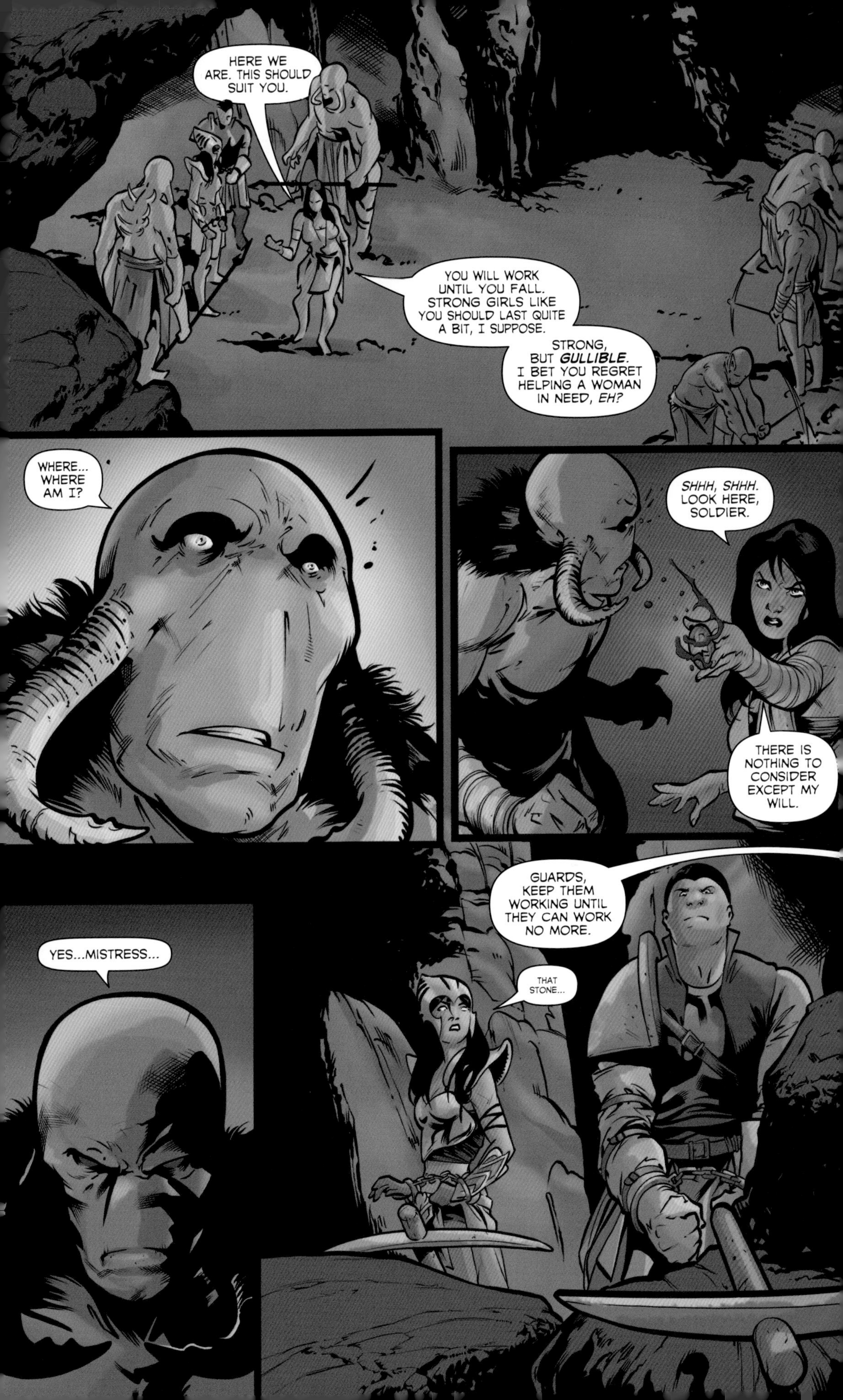
HERE WE ARE. THIS SHOULD SUIT YOU.
YOU WILL WORK UNTIL YOU FALL. STRONG GIRLS LIKE YOU SHOULD LAST QUITE A BIT, I SUPPOSE.
STRONG, BUT *GULLIBLE*. I BET YOU REGRET HELPING A WOMAN IN NEED, *EH?*
WHERE... WHERE AM I?
SHHH, SHHH. LOOK HERE, SOLDIER.
THERE IS NOTHING TO CONSIDER EXCEPT MY WILL.
YES...MISTRESS...
GUARDS, KEEP THEM WORKING UNTIL THEY CAN WORK NO MORE.
THAT STONE...

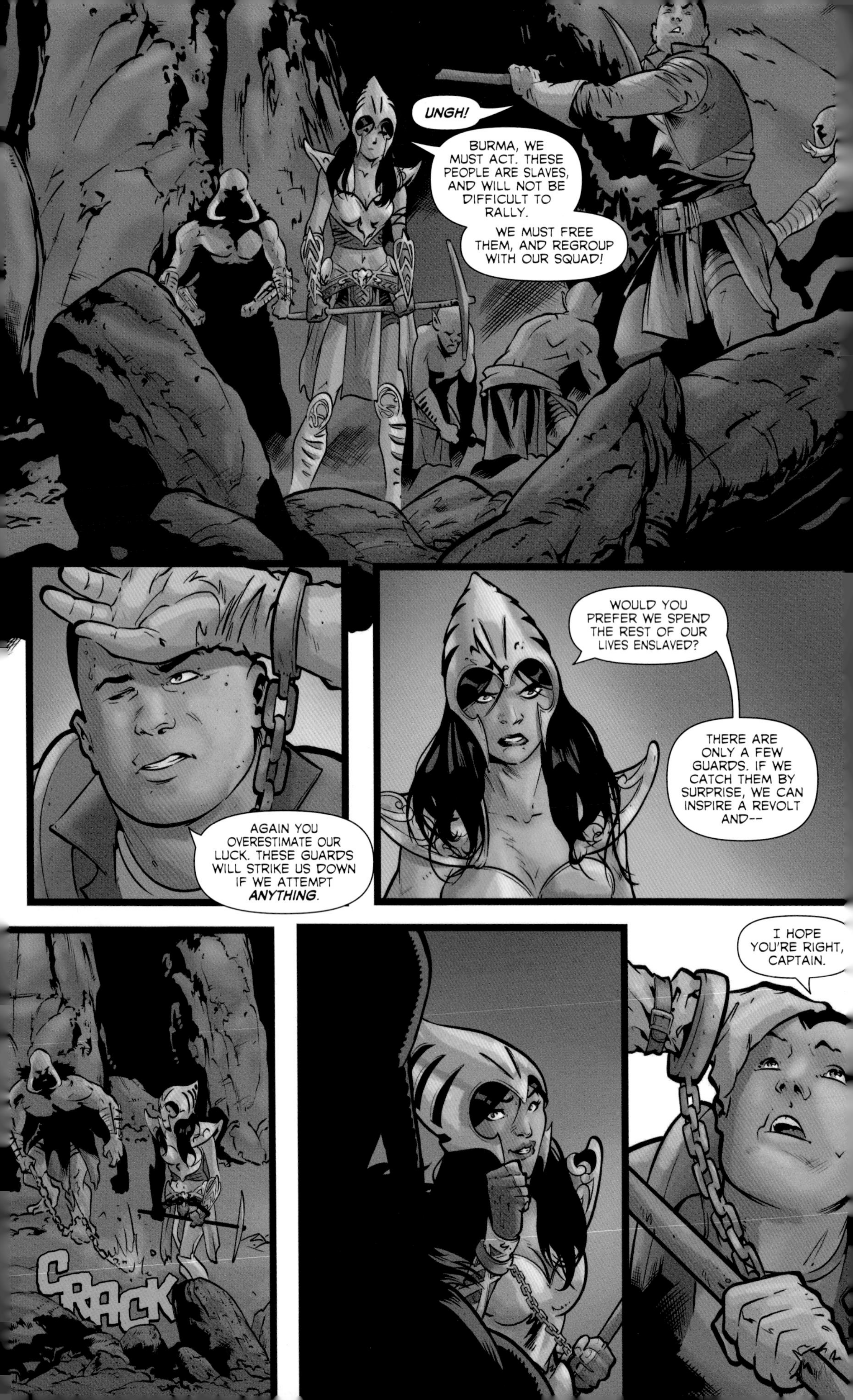
UNGH!
BURMA, WE MUST ACT. THESE PEOPLE ARE SLAVES, AND WILL NOT BE DIFFICULT TO RALLY.
WE MUST FREE THEM, AND REGROUP WITH OUR SQUAD!
AGAIN YOU OVERESTIMATE OUR LUCK. THESE GUARDS WILL STRIKE US DOWN IF WE ATTEMPT *ANYTHING*.
WOULD YOU PREFER WE SPEND THE REST OF OUR LIVES ENSLAVED?
THERE ARE ONLY A FEW GUARDS. IF WE CATCH THEM BY SURPRISE, WE CAN INSPIRE A REVOLT AND--
CRACK
I HOPE YOU'RE RIGHT, CAPTAIN.

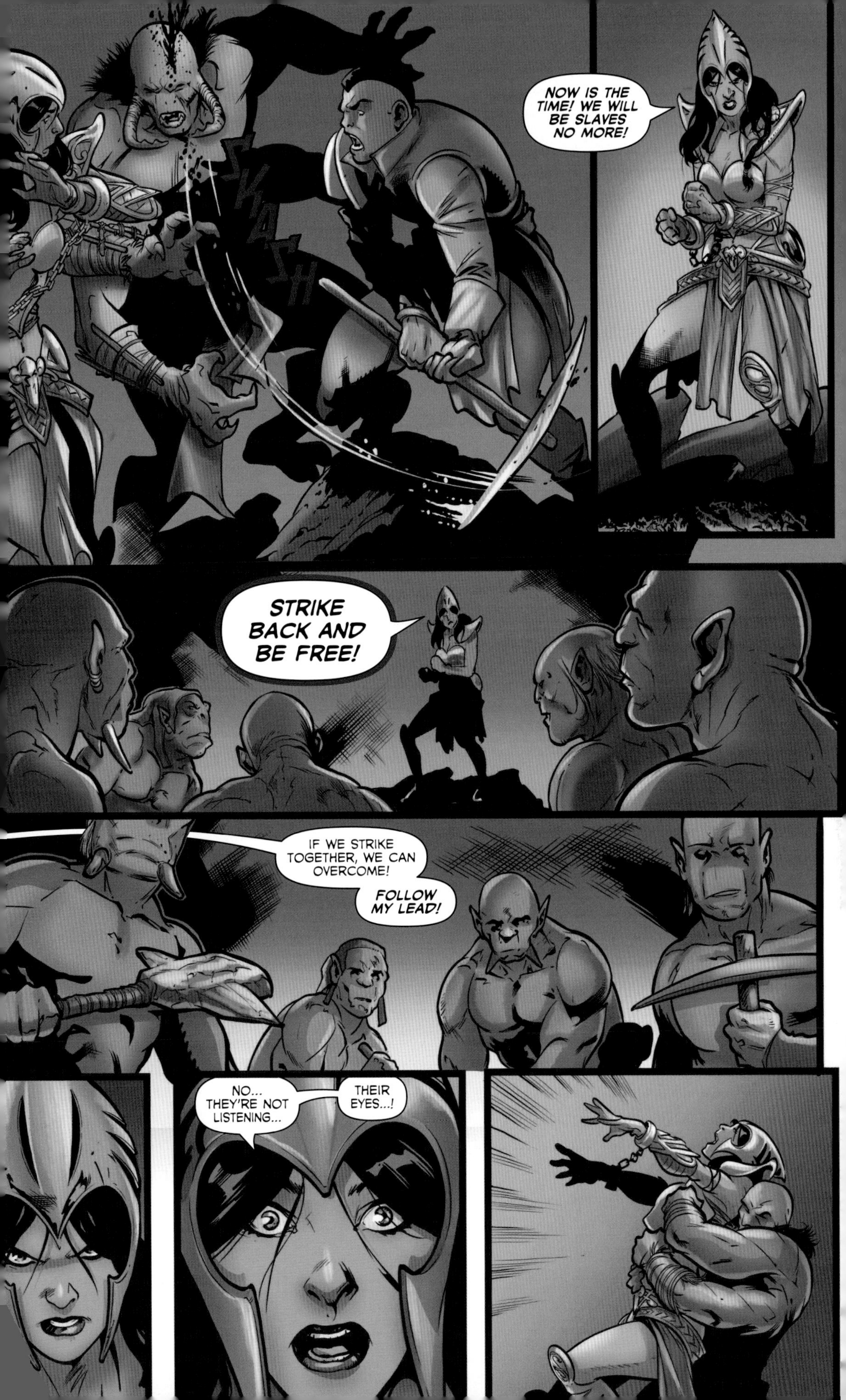
SHASH
NOW IS THE TIME! WE WILL BE SLAVES NO MORE!
STRIKE BACK AND BE FREE!
IF WE STRIKE TOGETHER, WE CAN OVERCOME!
FOLLOW MY LEAD!
NO... THEY'RE NOT LISTENING...
THEIR EYES...!

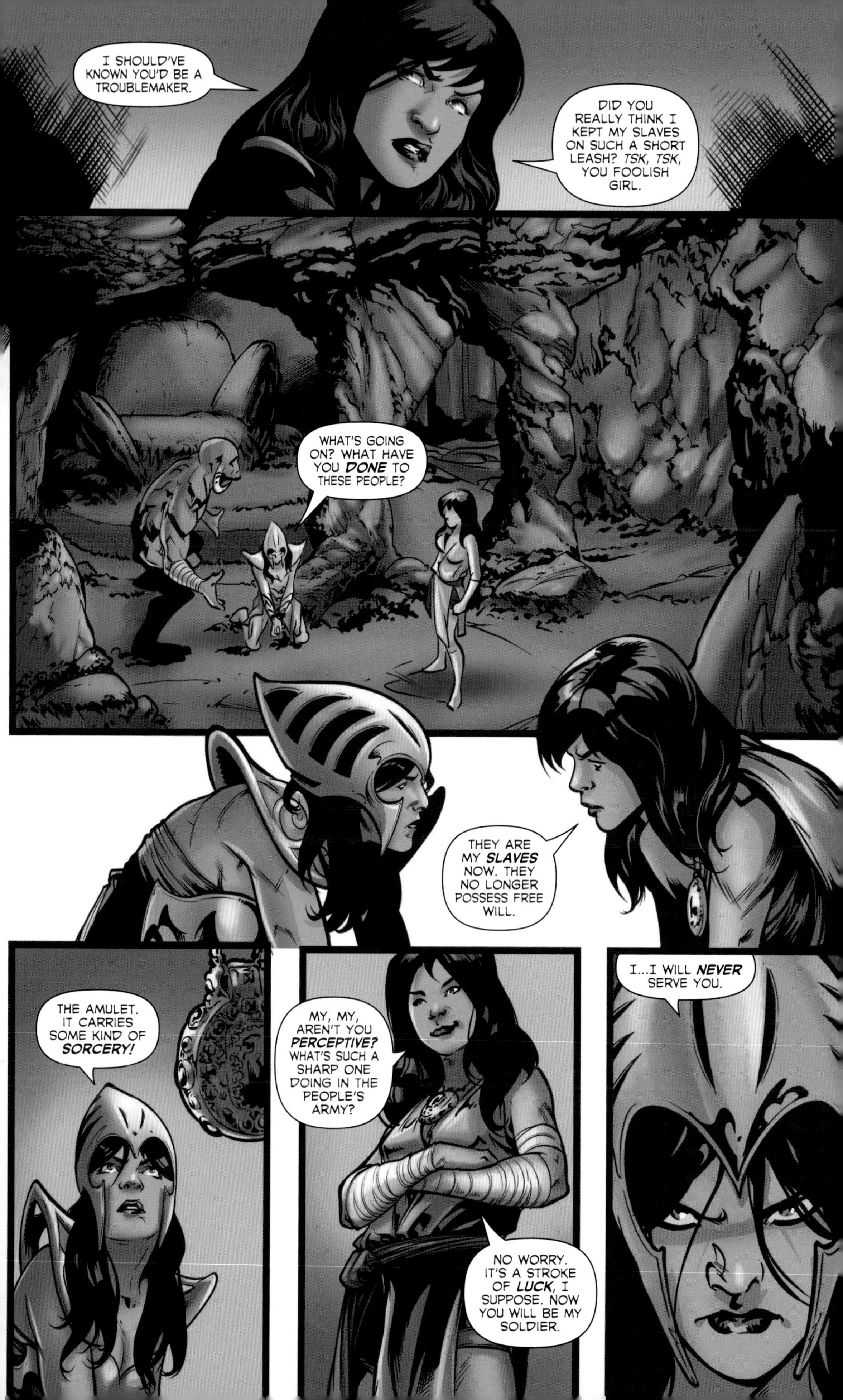
I SHOULD'VE KNOWN YOU'D BE A TROUBLEMAKER.
DID YOU REALLY THINK I KEPT MY SLAVES ON SUCH A SHORT LEASH? *TSK, TSK,* YOU FOOLISH GIRL.
WHAT'S GOING ON? WHAT HAVE YOU ***DONE*** TO THESE PEOPLE?
THEY ARE MY ***SLAVES*** NOW. THEY NO LONGER POSSESS FREE WILL.
THE AMULET. IT CARRIES SOME KIND OF ***SORCERY!***
MY, MY, AREN'T YOU ***PERCEPTIVE?*** WHAT'S SUCH A SHARP ONE DOING IN THE PEOPLE'S ARMY?
NO WORRY. IT'S A STROKE OF ***LUCK***, I SUPPOSE. NOW YOU WILL BE MY SOLDIER.
I...I WILL ***NEVER*** SERVE YOU.

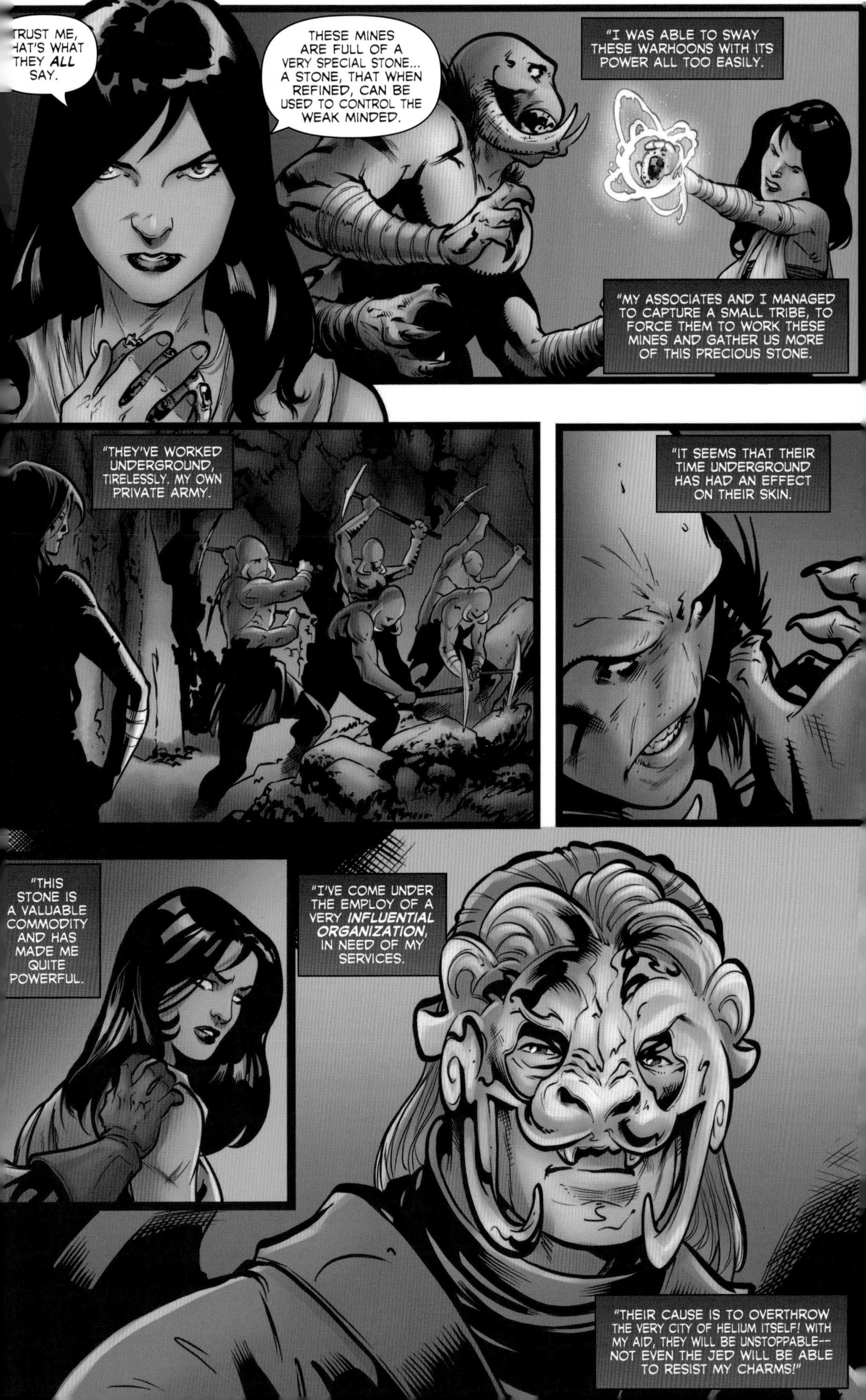
TRUST ME, THAT'S WHAT THEY *ALL* SAY.
THESE MINES ARE FULL OF A VERY SPECIAL STONE... A STONE, THAT WHEN REFINED, CAN BE USED TO CONTROL THE WEAK MINDED.
"I WAS ABLE TO SWAY THESE WARHOONS WITH ITS POWER ALL TOO EASILY.
"MY ASSOCIATES AND I MANAGED TO CAPTURE A SMALL TRIBE, TO FORCE THEM TO WORK THESE MINES AND GATHER US MORE OF THIS PRECIOUS STONE.
"THEY'VE WORKED UNDERGROUND, TIRELESSLY. MY OWN PRIVATE ARMY.
"IT SEEMS THAT THEIR TIME UNDERGROUND HAS HAD AN EFFECT ON THEIR SKIN.
"THIS STONE IS A VALUABLE COMMODITY AND HAS MADE ME QUITE POWERFUL.
"I'VE COME UNDER THE EMPLOY OF A VERY *INFLUENTIAL ORGANIZATION*, IN NEED OF MY SERVICES.
"THEIR CAUSE IS TO OVERTHROW THE VERY CITY OF HELIUM ITSELF! WITH MY AID, THEY WILL BE UNSTOPPABLE-- NOT EVEN THE JED WILL BE ABLE TO RESIST MY CHARMS!"

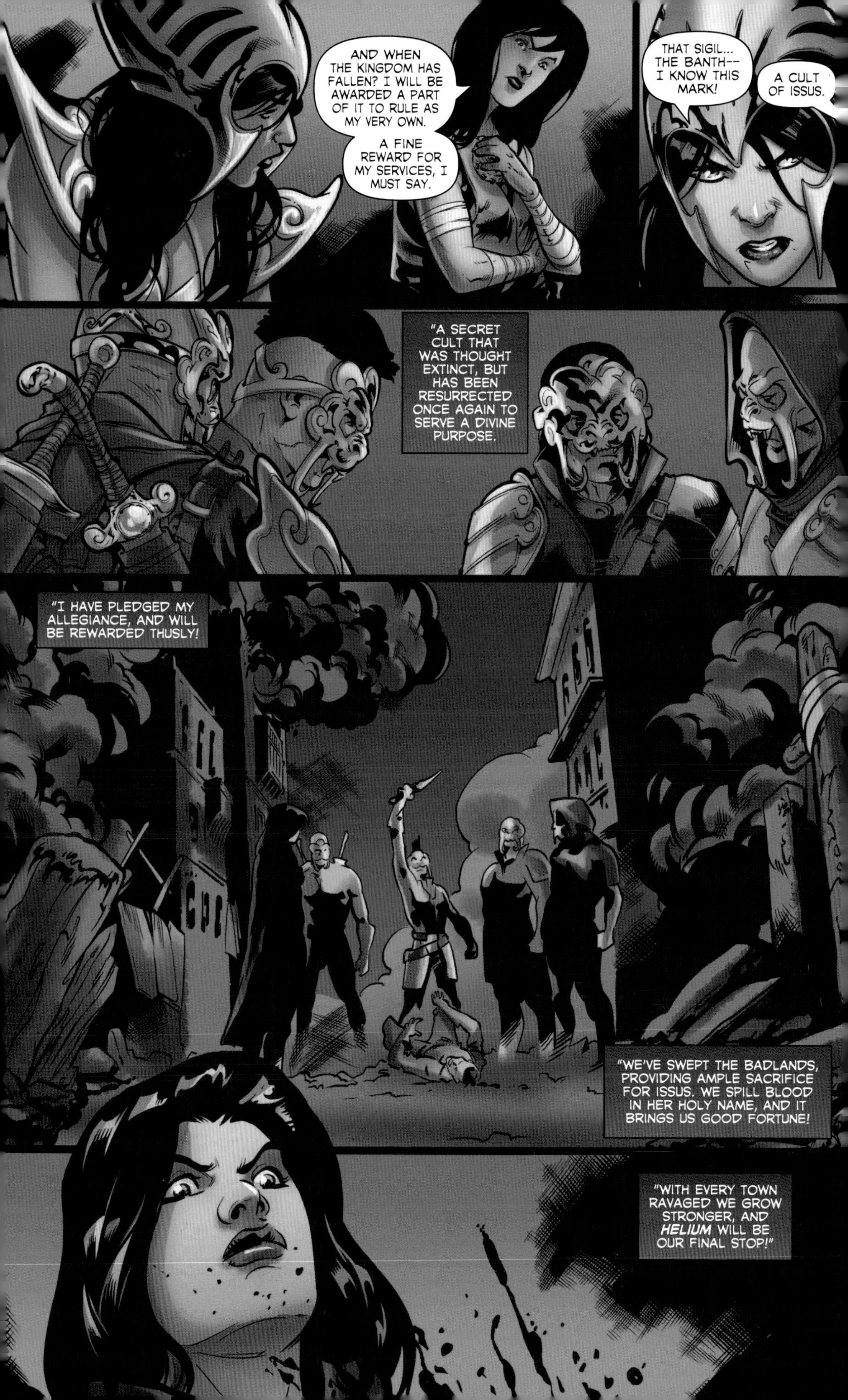
AND WHEN THE KINGDOM HAS FALLEN? I WILL BE AWARDED A PART OF IT TO RULE AS MY VERY OWN.
A FINE REWARD FOR MY SERVICES, I MUST SAY.
THAT SIGIL... THE BANTH-- I KNOW THIS MARK!
A CULT OF ISSUS.
"A SECRET CULT THAT WAS THOUGHT EXTINCT, BUT HAS BEEN RESURRECTED ONCE AGAIN TO SERVE A DIVINE PURPOSE.
"I HAVE PLEDGED MY ALLEGIANCE, AND WILL BE REWARDED THUSLY!
"WE'VE SWEPT THE BADLANDS, PROVIDING AMPLE SACRIFICE FOR ISSUS. WE SPILL BLOOD IN HER HOLY NAME, AND IT BRINGS US GOOD FORTUNE!
"WITH EVERY TOWN RAVAGED WE GROW STRONGER, AND HELIUM WILL BE OUR FINAL STOP!"

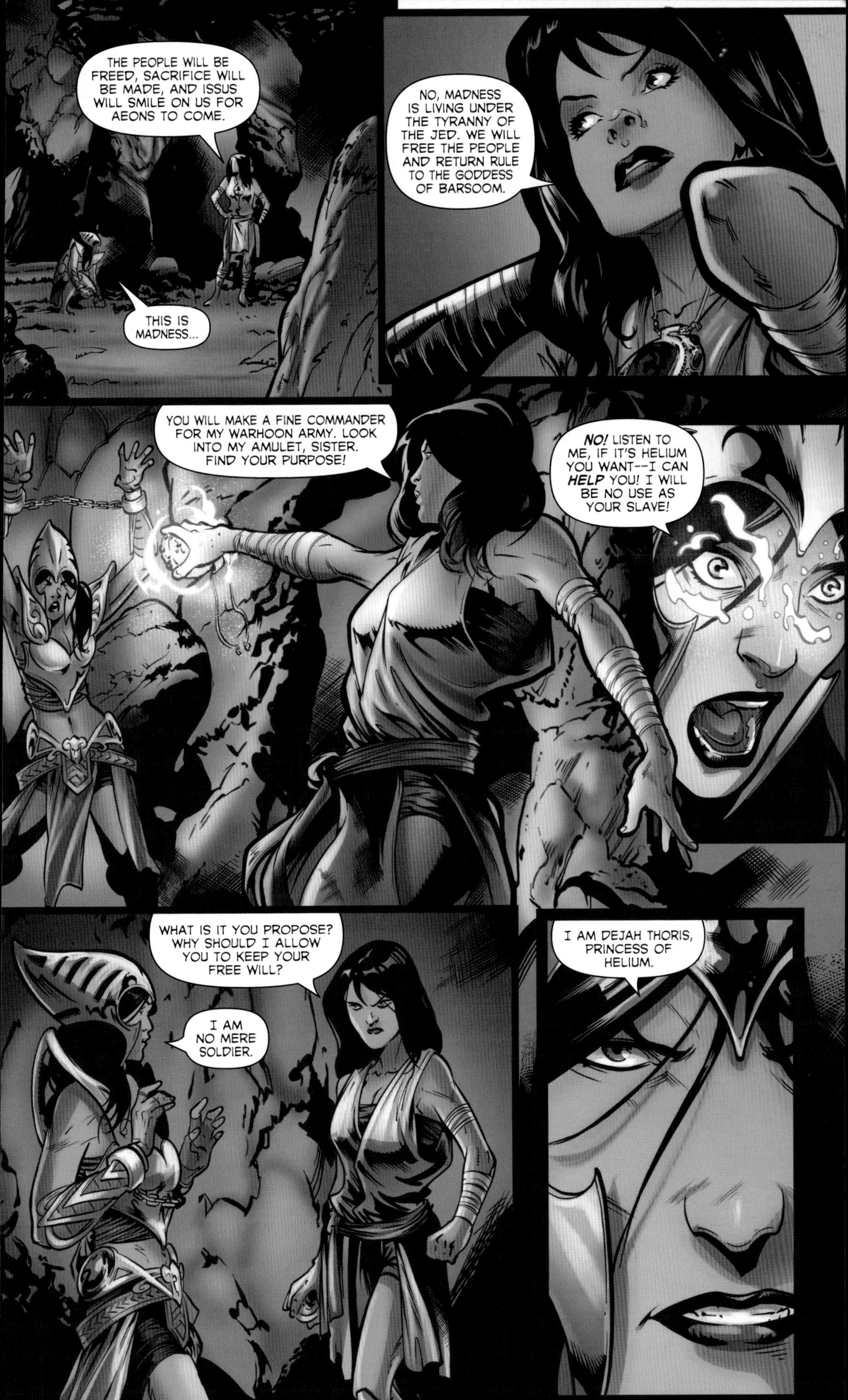
THE PEOPLE WILL BE FREED, SACRIFICE WILL BE MADE, AND ISSUS WILL SMILE ON US FOR AEONS TO COME.
THIS IS MADNESS...
NO, MADNESS IS LIVING UNDER THE TYRANNY OF THE JED. WE WILL FREE THE PEOPLE AND RETURN RULE TO THE GODDESS OF BARSOOM.
YOU WILL MAKE A FINE COMMANDER FOR MY WARHOON ARMY. LOOK INTO MY AMULET, SISTER. FIND YOUR PURPOSE!
NO! LISTEN TO ME, IF IT'S HELIUM YOU WANT--I CAN HELP YOU! I WILL BE NO USE AS YOUR SLAVE!
WHAT IS IT YOU PROPOSE? WHY SHOULD I ALLOW YOU TO KEEP YOUR FREE WILL?
I AM NO MERE SOLDIER.
I AM DEJAH THORIS, PRINCESS OF HELIUM.

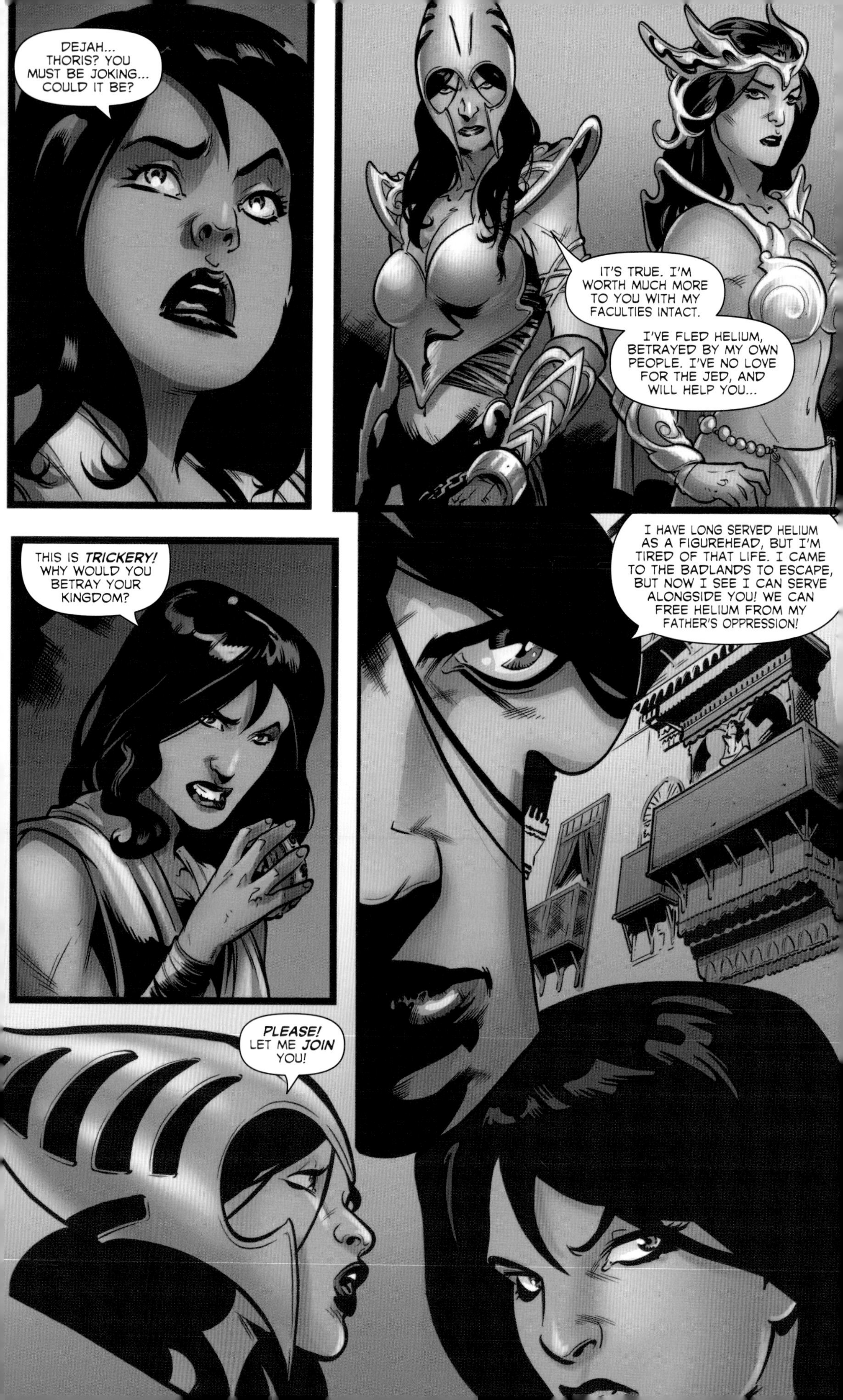
DEJAH... THORIS? YOU MUST BE JOKING... COULD IT BE?
IT'S TRUE. I'M WORTH MUCH MORE TO YOU WITH MY FACULTIES INTACT.
I'VE FLED HELIUM, BETRAYED BY MY OWN PEOPLE. I'VE NO LOVE FOR THE JED, AND WILL HELP YOU...
THIS IS TRICKERY! WHY WOULD YOU BETRAY YOUR KINGDOM?
I HAVE LONG SERVED HELIUM AS A FIGUREHEAD, BUT I'M TIRED OF THAT LIFE. I CAME TO THE BADLANDS TO ESCAPE, BUT NOW I SEE I CAN SERVE ALONGSIDE YOU! WE CAN FREE HELIUM FROM MY FATHER'S OPPRESSION!
PLEASE! LET ME JOIN YOU!

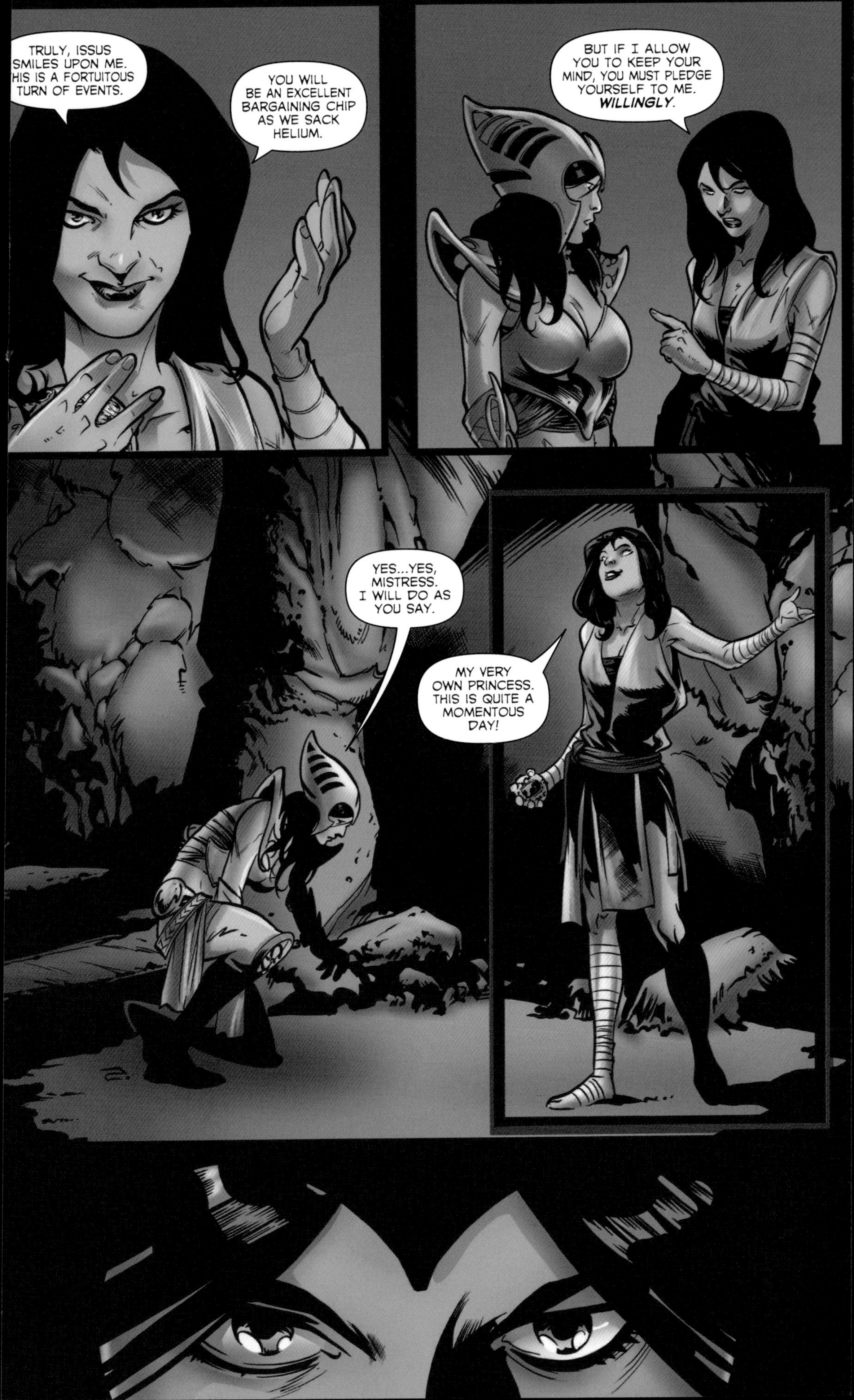
TRULY, ISSUS SMILES UPON ME. THIS IS A FORTUITOUS TURN OF EVENTS.
YOU WILL BE AN EXCELLENT BARGAINING CHIP AS WE SACK HELIUM.
BUT IF I ALLOW YOU TO KEEP YOUR MIND, YOU MUST PLEDGE YOURSELF TO ME. WILLINGLY.
YES...YES, MISTRESS. I WILL DO AS YOU SAY.
MY VERY OWN PRINCESS. THIS IS QUITE A MOMENTOUS DAY!

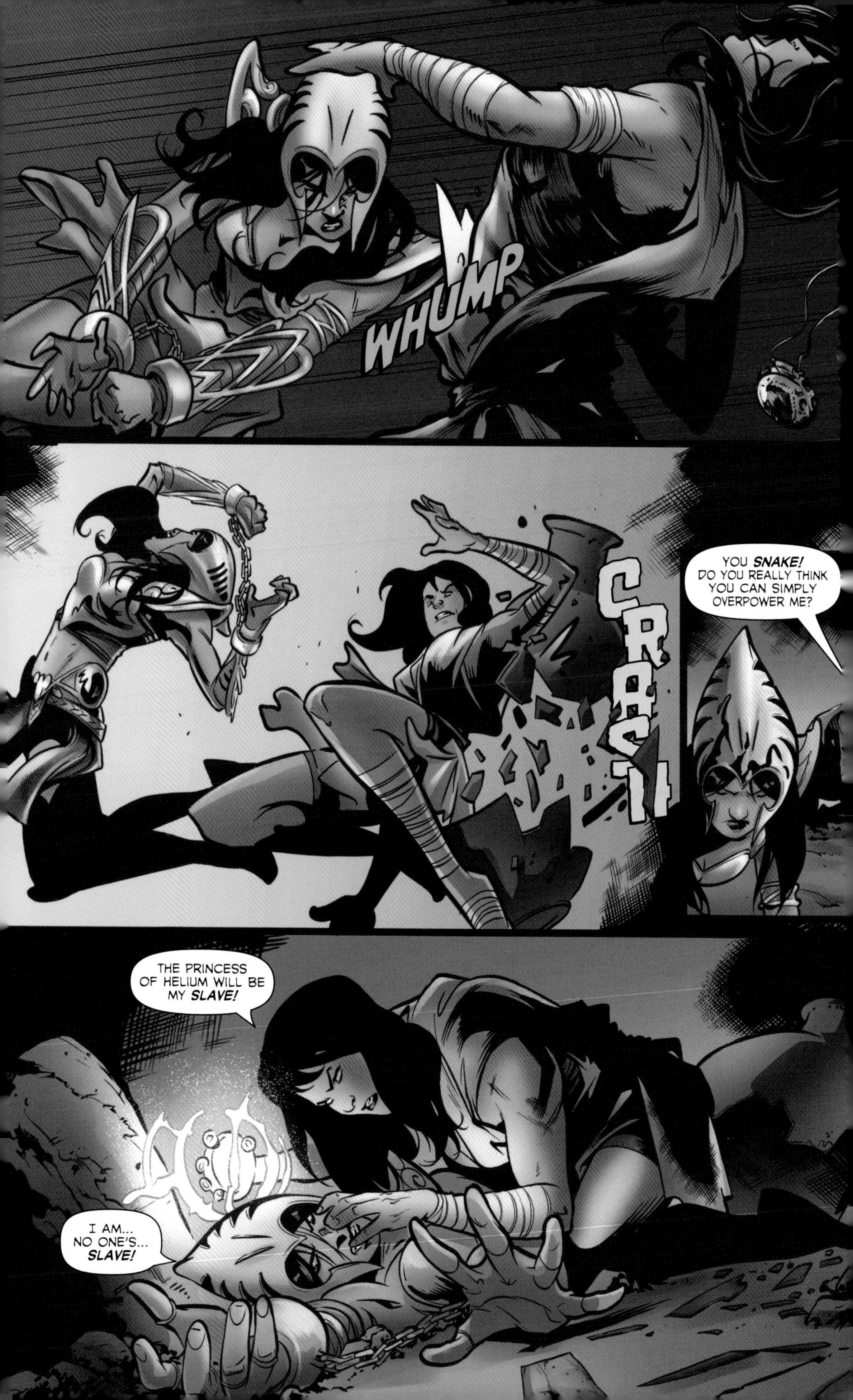
WHUMP
CRASH
YOU SNAKE! DO YOU REALLY THINK YOU CAN SIMPLY OVERPOWER ME?
THE PRINCESS OF HELIUM WILL BE MY SLAVE!
I AM... NO ONE'S... SLAVE!

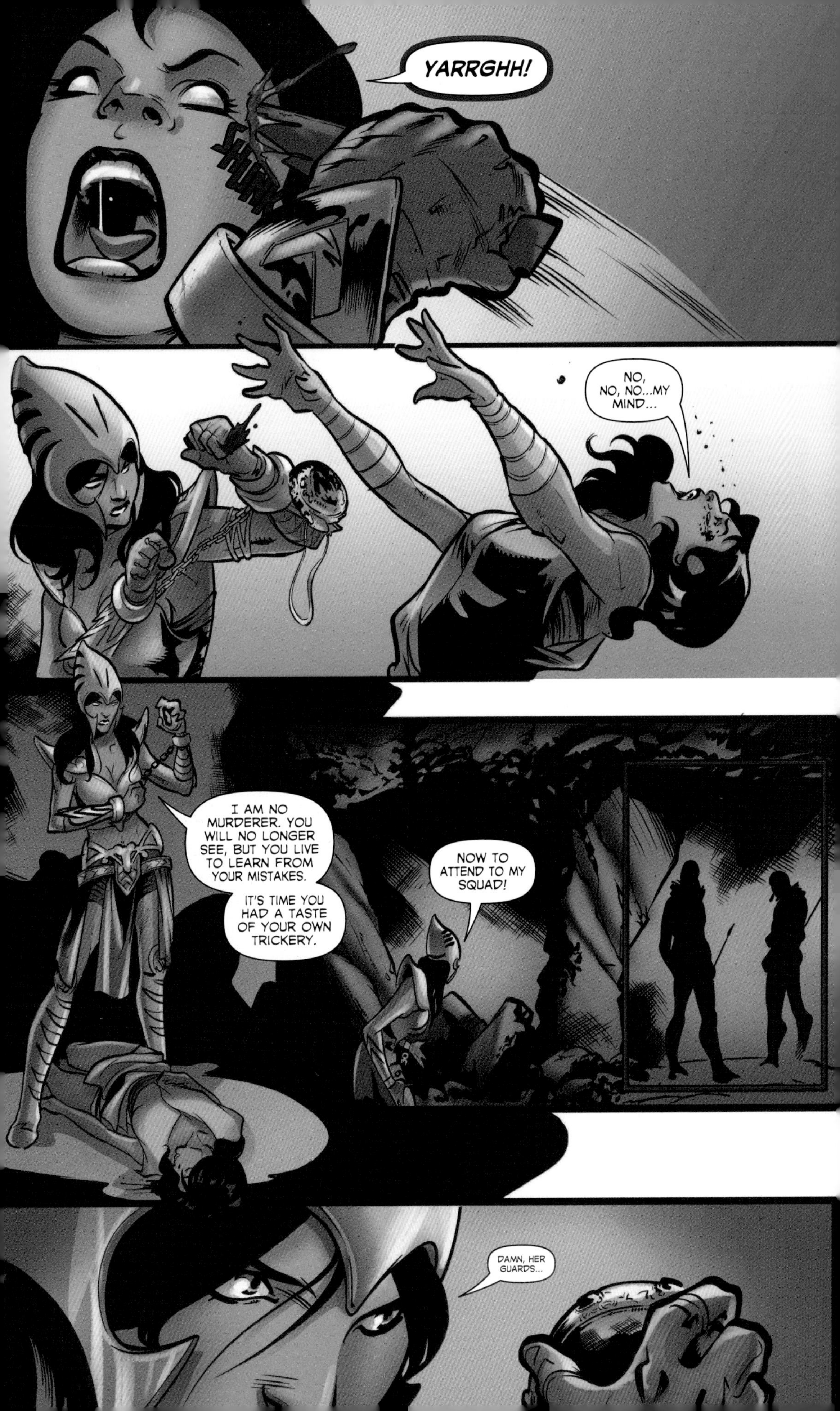

YARRGHH!
SHUNK
NO, NO, NO...MY MIND...
I AM NO MURDERER. YOU WILL NO LONGER SEE, BUT YOU LIVE TO LEARN FROM YOUR MISTAKES.
IT'S TIME YOU HAD A TASTE OF YOUR OWN TRICKERY.
NOW TO ATTEND TO MY SQUAD!
DAMN, HER GUARDS...

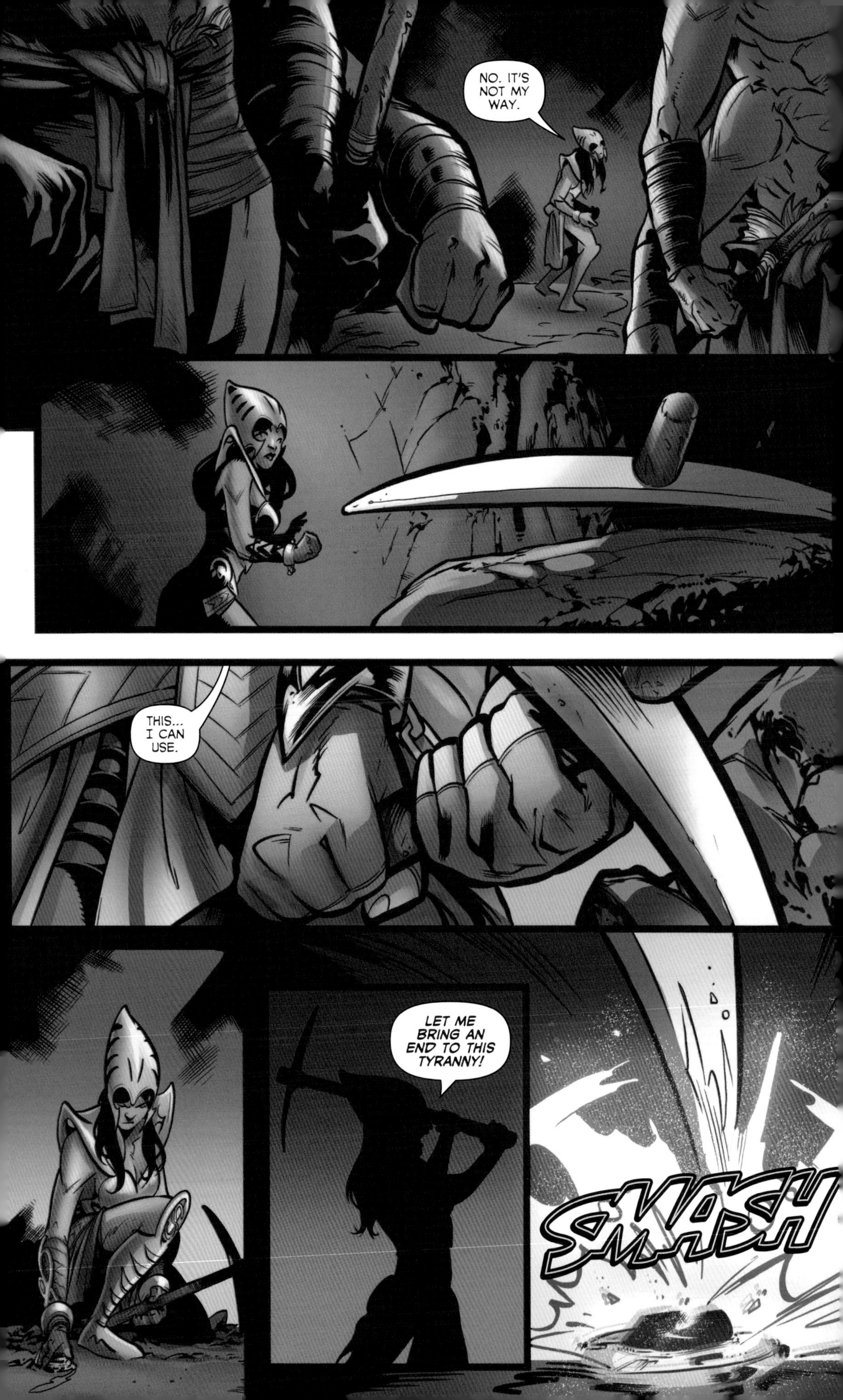
NO. IT'S NOT MY WAY.
THIS... I CAN USE.
LET ME BRING AN END TO THIS TYRANNY!
SMASH

MY MIND... IT'S *CLEARING!*

WE WERE UNDER SOME KIND OF SPELL...

IT SEEMS THAT THE LITTLE FLOWER HAS TURNED THE TIDE.

WE WERE FORCED TO WORK IN THESE MINES! WE HAVE NO QUARREL WITH YOU!

WE SEEK *JUSTICE!*

IT SEEMS EVERYONE HAS BEEN RESTORED TO THEIR RIGHT MIND.

THE WARHOONS DO NOT SEEM PLEASED... BUT PERHAPS I SHOULD STOP THEM BEFORE THEY REACH THE RED WOMAN.

PERHAPS NOT. JUSTICE WILL BE SERVED, HOWEVER CRUDELY.

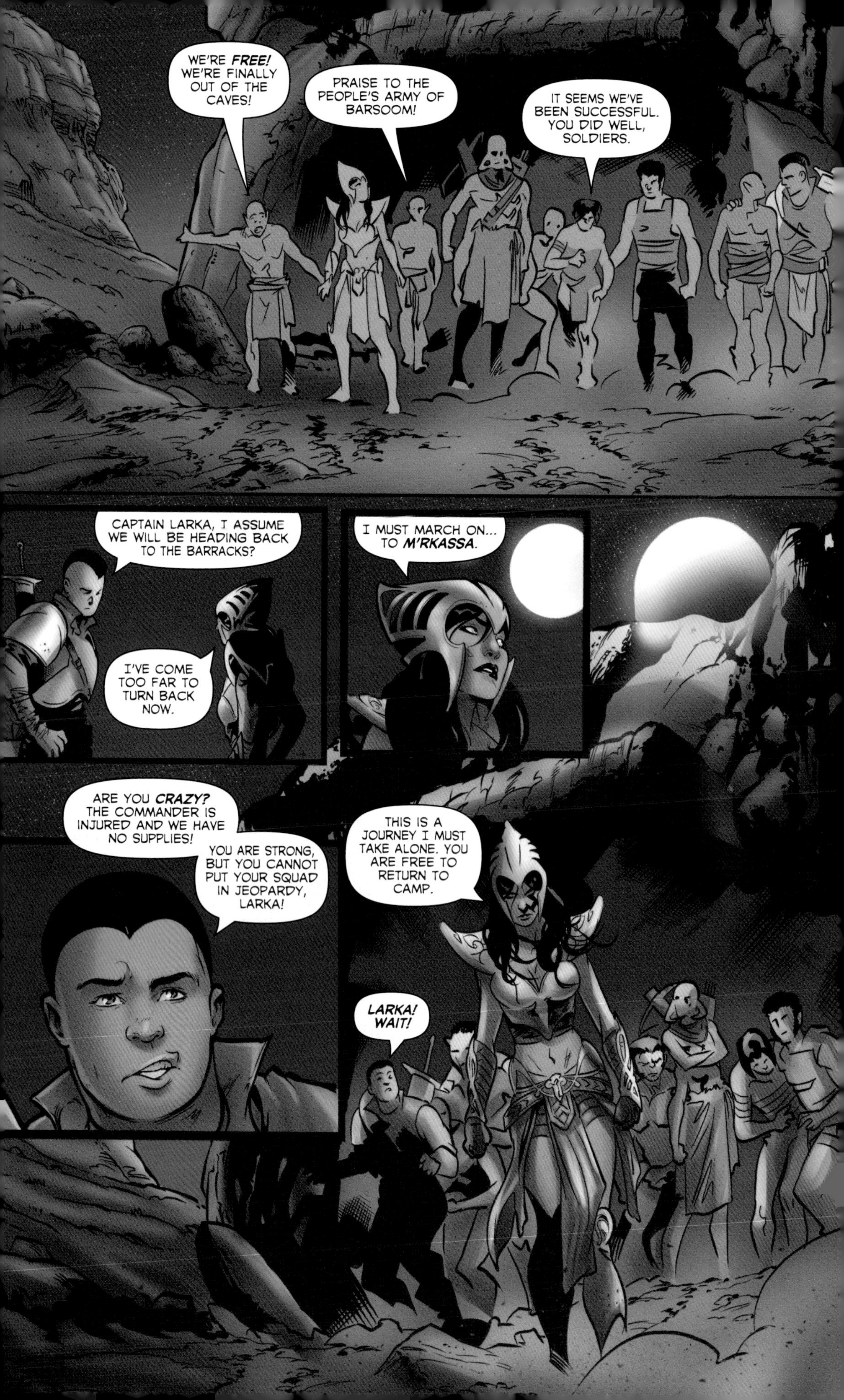
WE'RE FREE! WE'RE FINALLY OUT OF THE CAVES!
PRAISE TO THE PEOPLE'S ARMY OF BARSOOM!
IT SEEMS WE'VE BEEN SUCCESSFUL. YOU DID WELL, SOLDIERS.
CAPTAIN LARKA, I ASSUME WE WILL BE HEADING BACK TO THE BARRACKS?
I'VE COME TOO FAR TO TURN BACK NOW.
I MUST MARCH ON... TO M'RKASSA.
ARE YOU CRAZY? THE COMMANDER IS INJURED AND WE HAVE NO SUPPLIES!
YOU ARE STRONG, BUT YOU CANNOT PUT YOUR SQUAD IN JEOPARDY, LARKA!
THIS IS A JOURNEY I MUST TAKE ALONE. YOU ARE FREE TO RETURN TO CAMP.
LARKA! WAIT!

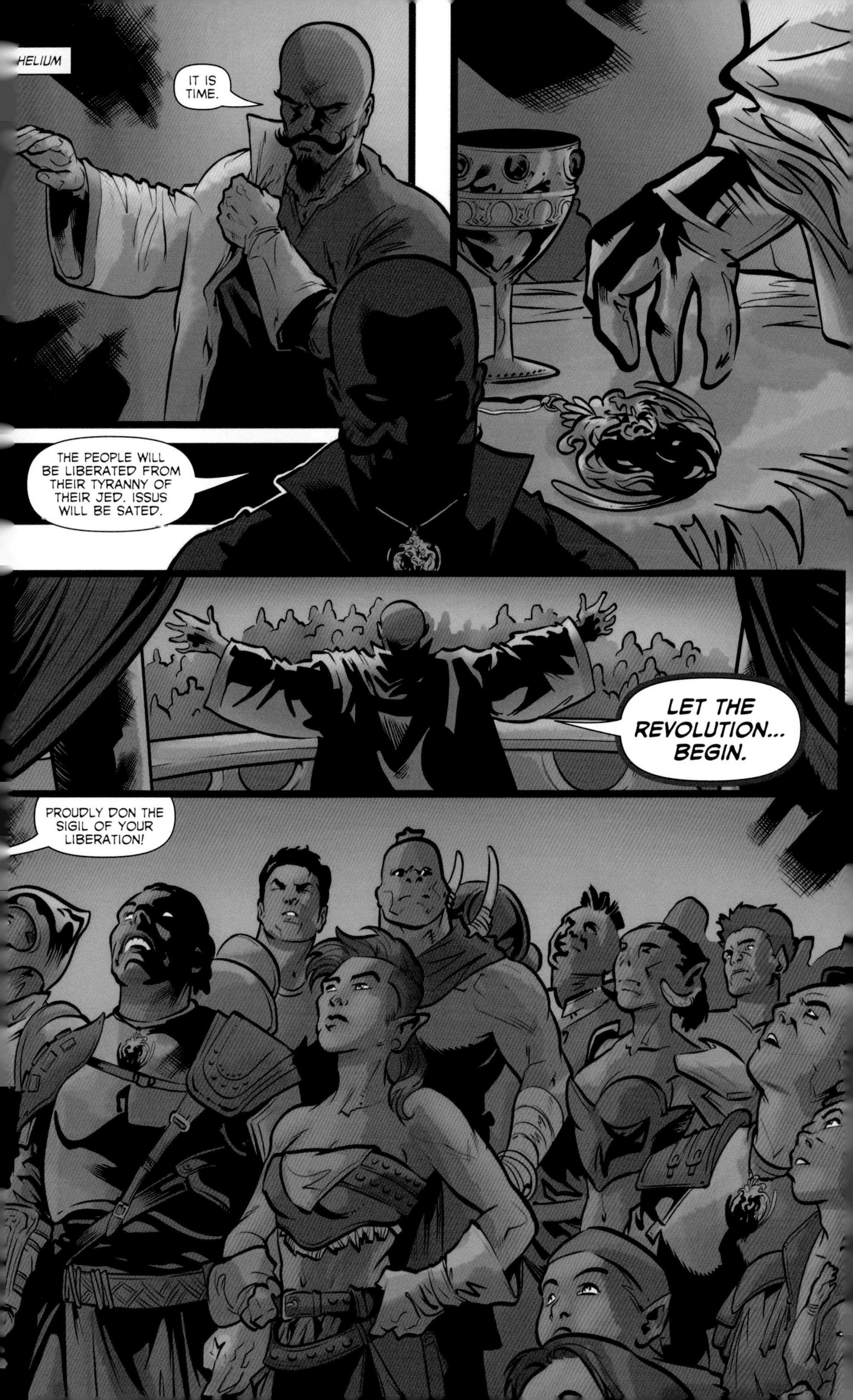
HELIUM
IT IS TIME.
THE PEOPLE WILL BE LIBERATED FROM THEIR TYRANNY OF THEIR JED. ISSUS WILL BE SATED.
LET THE REVOLUTION... BEGIN.
PROUDLY DON THE SIGIL OF YOUR LIBERATION!

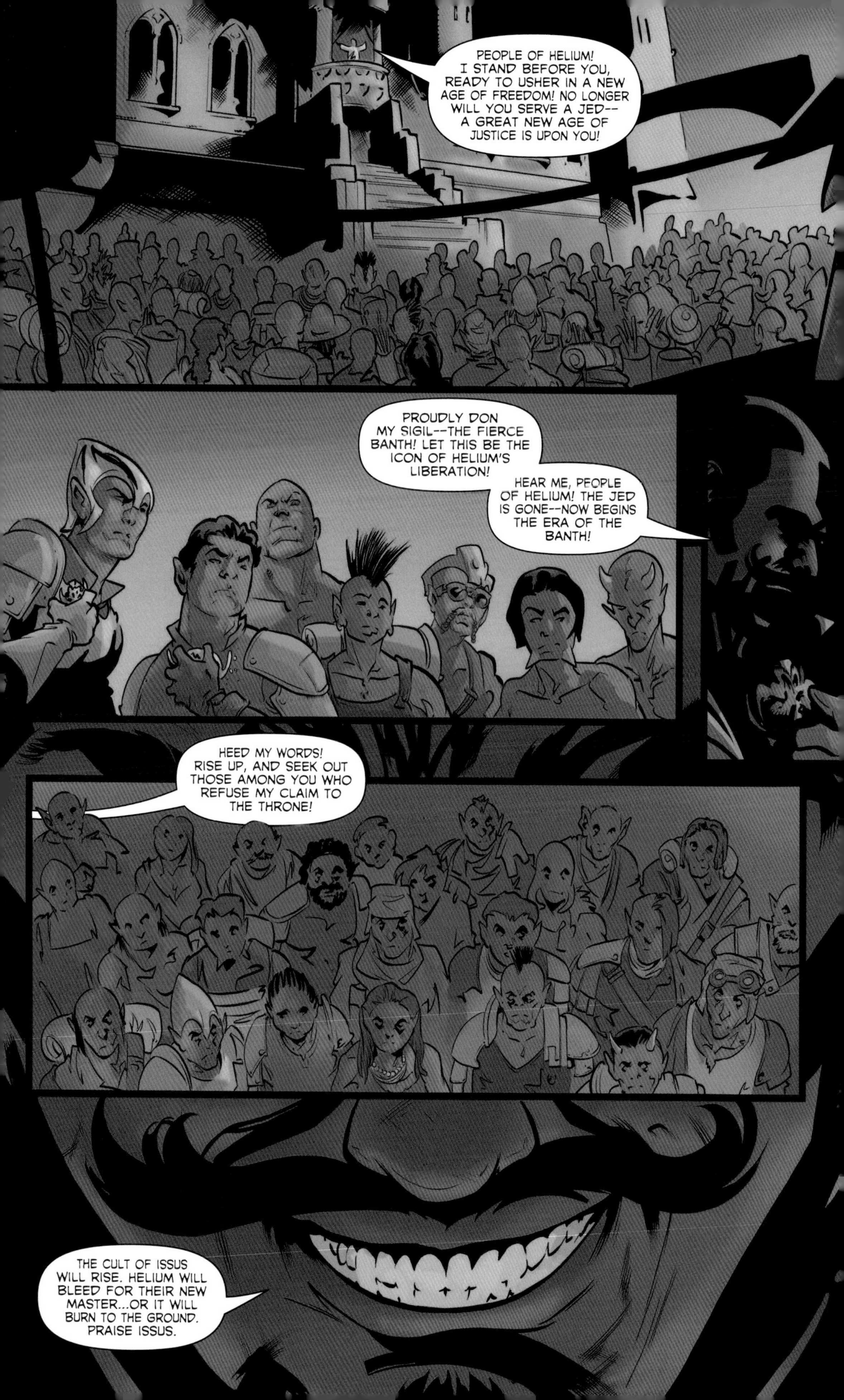

PEOPLE OF HELIUM! I STAND BEFORE YOU, READY TO USHER IN A NEW AGE OF FREEDOM! NO LONGER WILL YOU SERVE A JED-- A GREAT NEW AGE OF JUSTICE IS UPON YOU!
PROUDLY DON MY SIGIL--THE FIERCE BANTH! LET THIS BE THE ICON OF HELIUM'S LIBERATION!
HEAR ME, PEOPLE OF HELIUM! THE JED IS GONE--NOW BEGINS THE ERA OF THE BANTH!
HEED MY WORDS! RISE UP, AND SEEK OUT THOSE AMONG YOU WHO REFUSE MY CLAIM TO THE THRONE!
THE CULT OF ISSUS WILL RISE. HELIUM WILL BLEED FOR THEIR NEW MASTER...OR IT WILL BURN TO THE GROUND. PRAISE ISSUS.

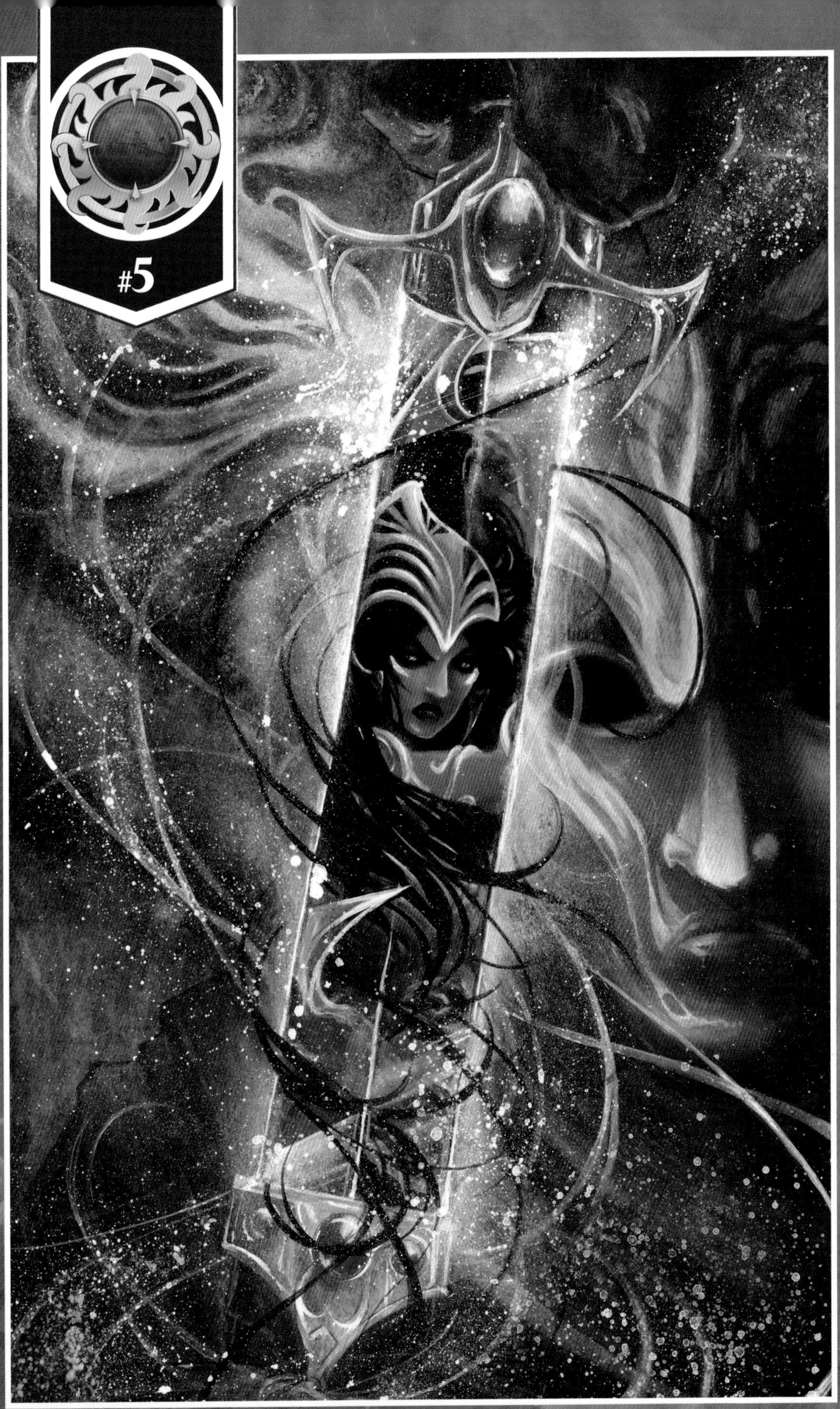
#5

cover by **NEN CHANG**

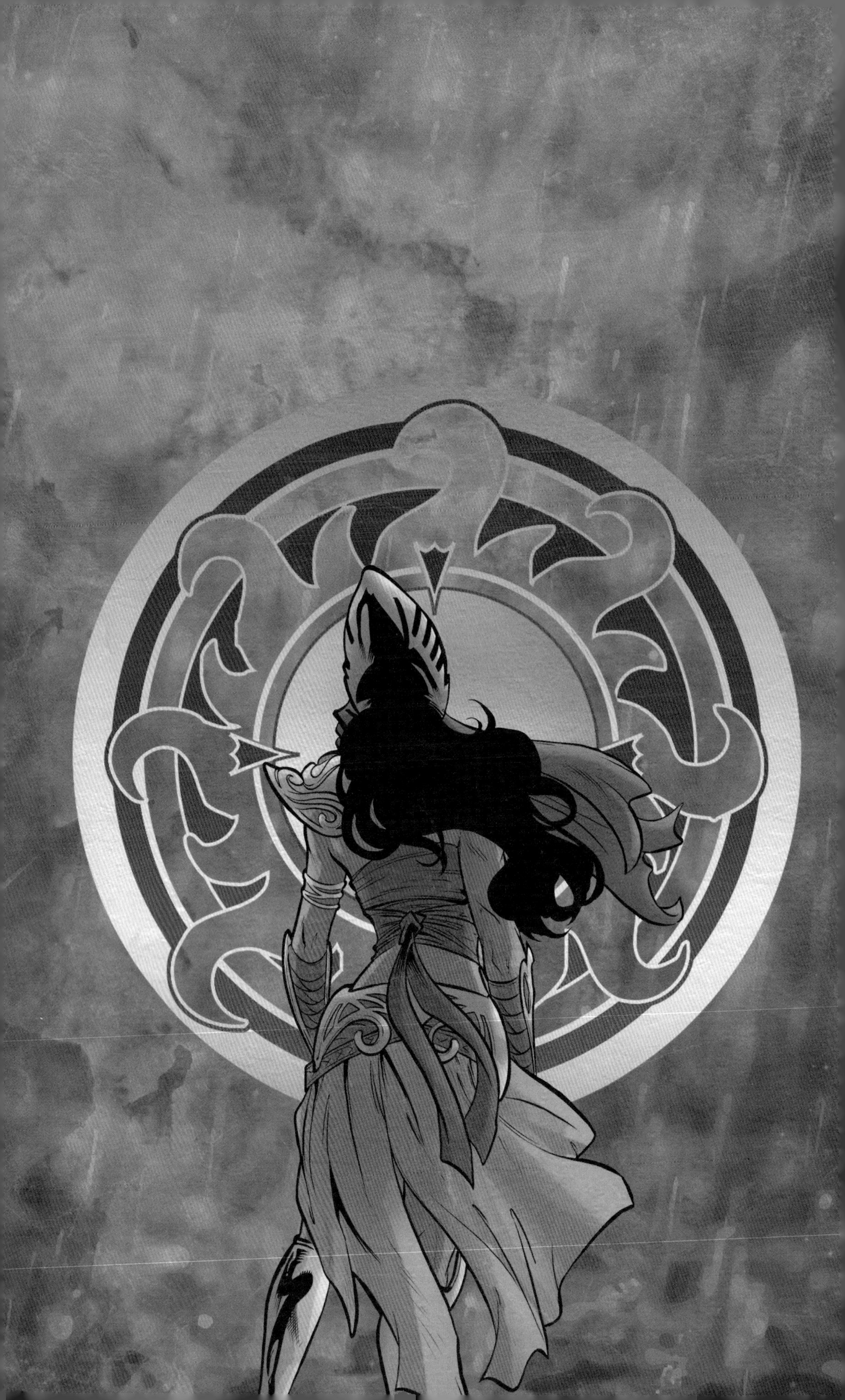

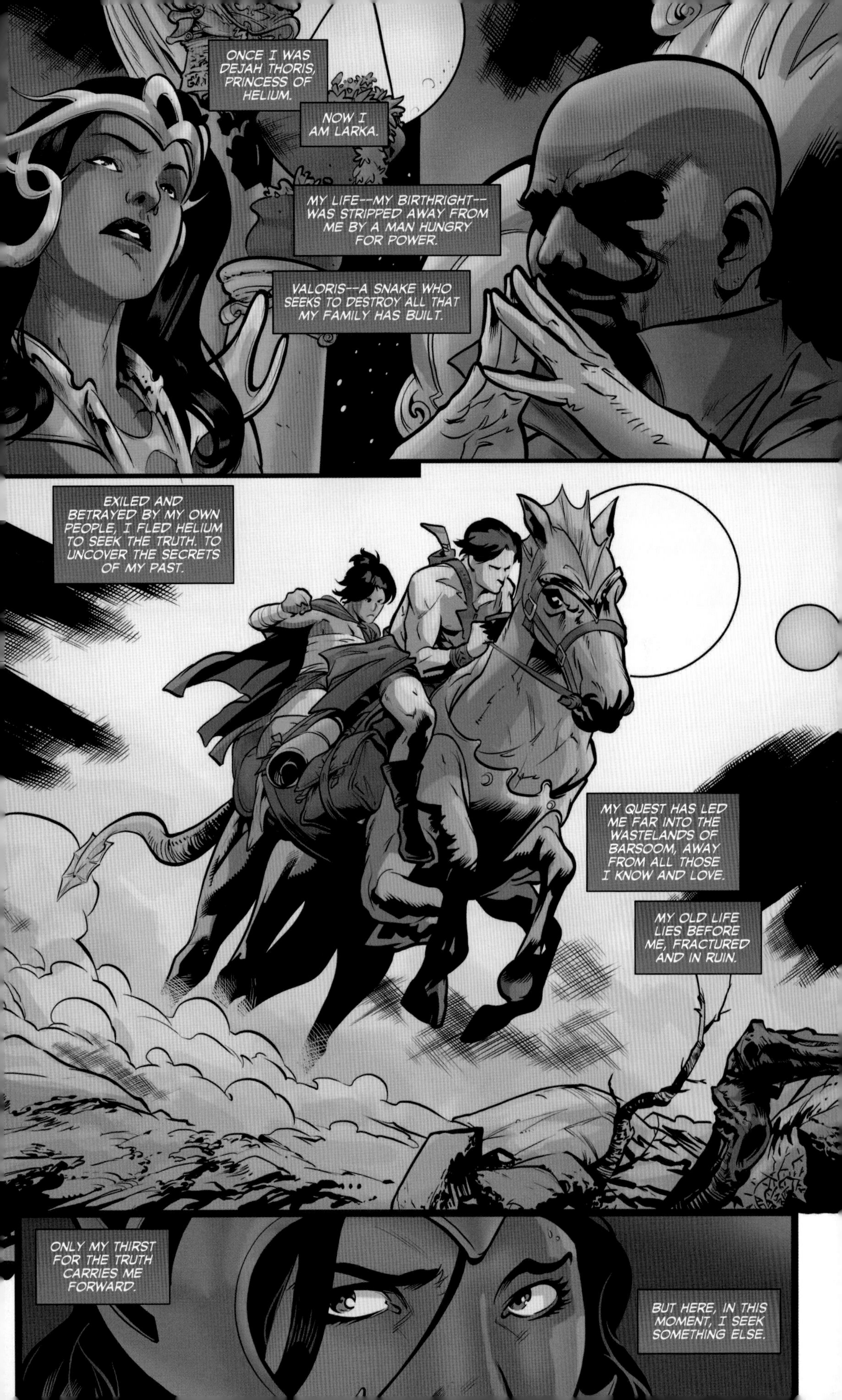

ONCE I WAS DEJAH THORIS, PRINCESS OF HELIUM.
NOW I AM LARKA.
MY LIFE--MY BIRTHRIGHT--WAS STRIPPED AWAY FROM ME BY A MAN HUNGRY FOR POWER.
VALORIS--A SNAKE WHO SEEKS TO DESTROY ALL THAT MY FAMILY HAS BUILT.
EXILED AND BETRAYED BY MY OWN PEOPLE, I FLED HELIUM TO SEEK THE TRUTH. TO UNCOVER THE SECRETS OF MY PAST.
MY QUEST HAS LED ME FAR INTO THE WASTELANDS OF BARSOOM, AWAY FROM ALL THOSE I KNOW AND LOVE.
MY OLD LIFE LIES BEFORE ME, FRACTURED AND IN RUIN.
ONLY MY THIRST FOR THE TRUTH CARRIES ME FORWARD.
BUT HERE, IN THIS MOMENT, I SEEK SOMETHING ELSE.

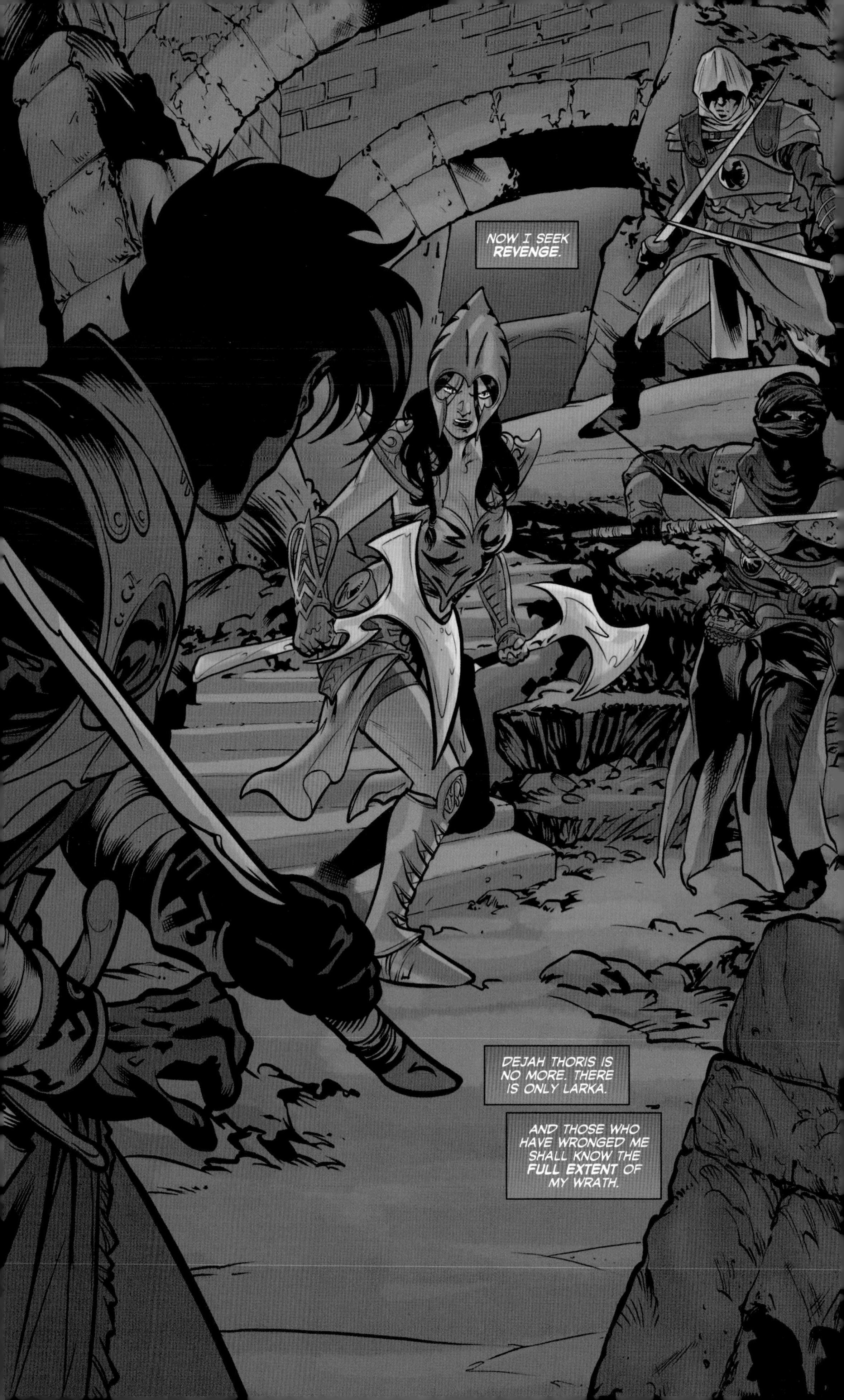
NOW I SEEK REVENGE.
DEJAH THORIS IS NO MORE. THERE IS ONLY LARKA.
AND THOSE WHO HAVE WRONGED ME SHALL KNOW THE FULL EXTENT OF MY WRATH.

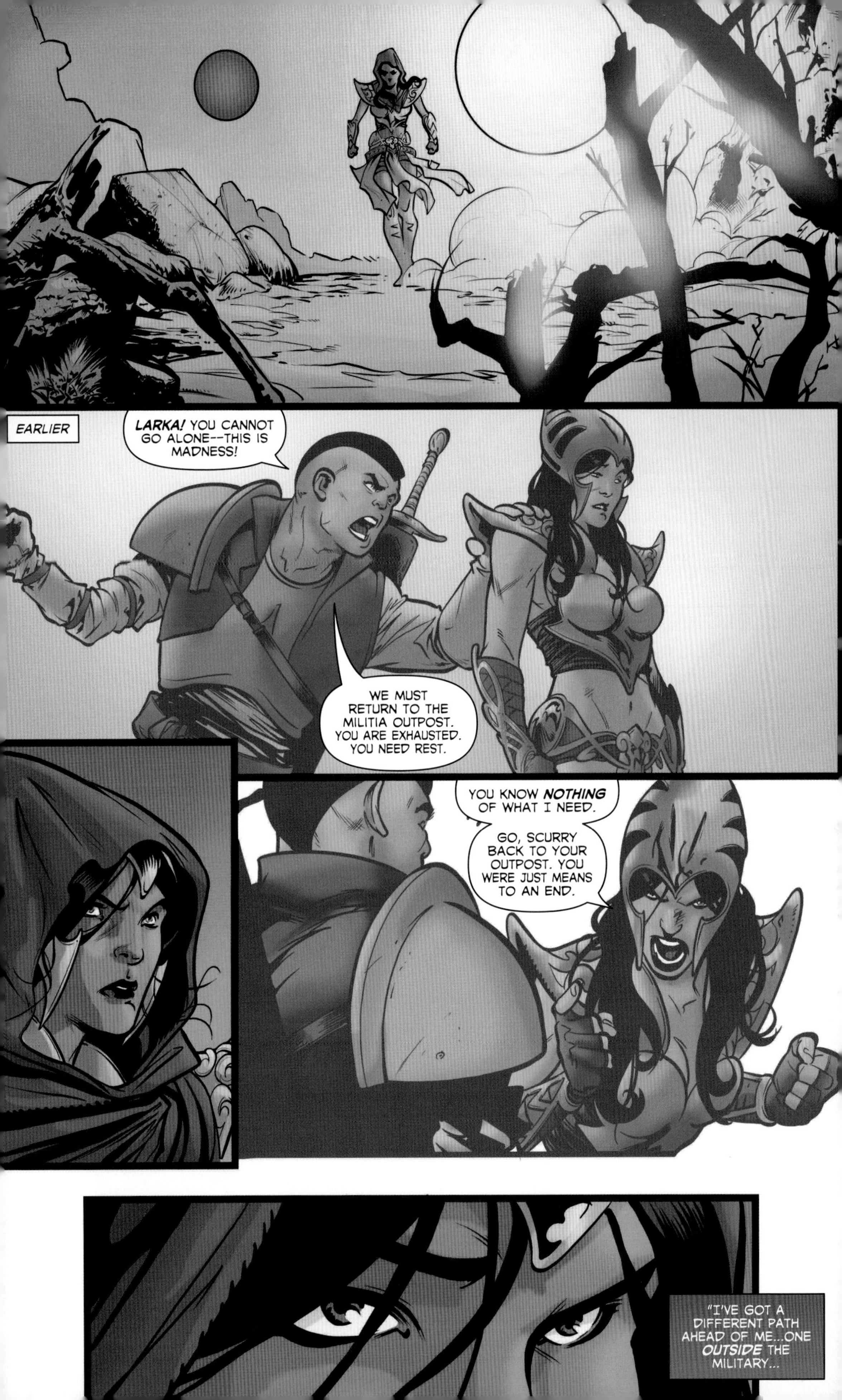
EARLIER
LARKA! YOU CANNOT GO ALONE--THIS IS MADNESS!
WE MUST RETURN TO THE MILITIA OUTPOST. YOU ARE EXHAUSTED. YOU NEED REST.
YOU KNOW NOTHING OF WHAT I NEED.
GO, SCURRY BACK TO YOUR OUTPOST. YOU WERE JUST MEANS TO AN END.
"I'VE GOT A DIFFERENT PATH AHEAD OF ME...ONE OUTSIDE THE MILITARY...

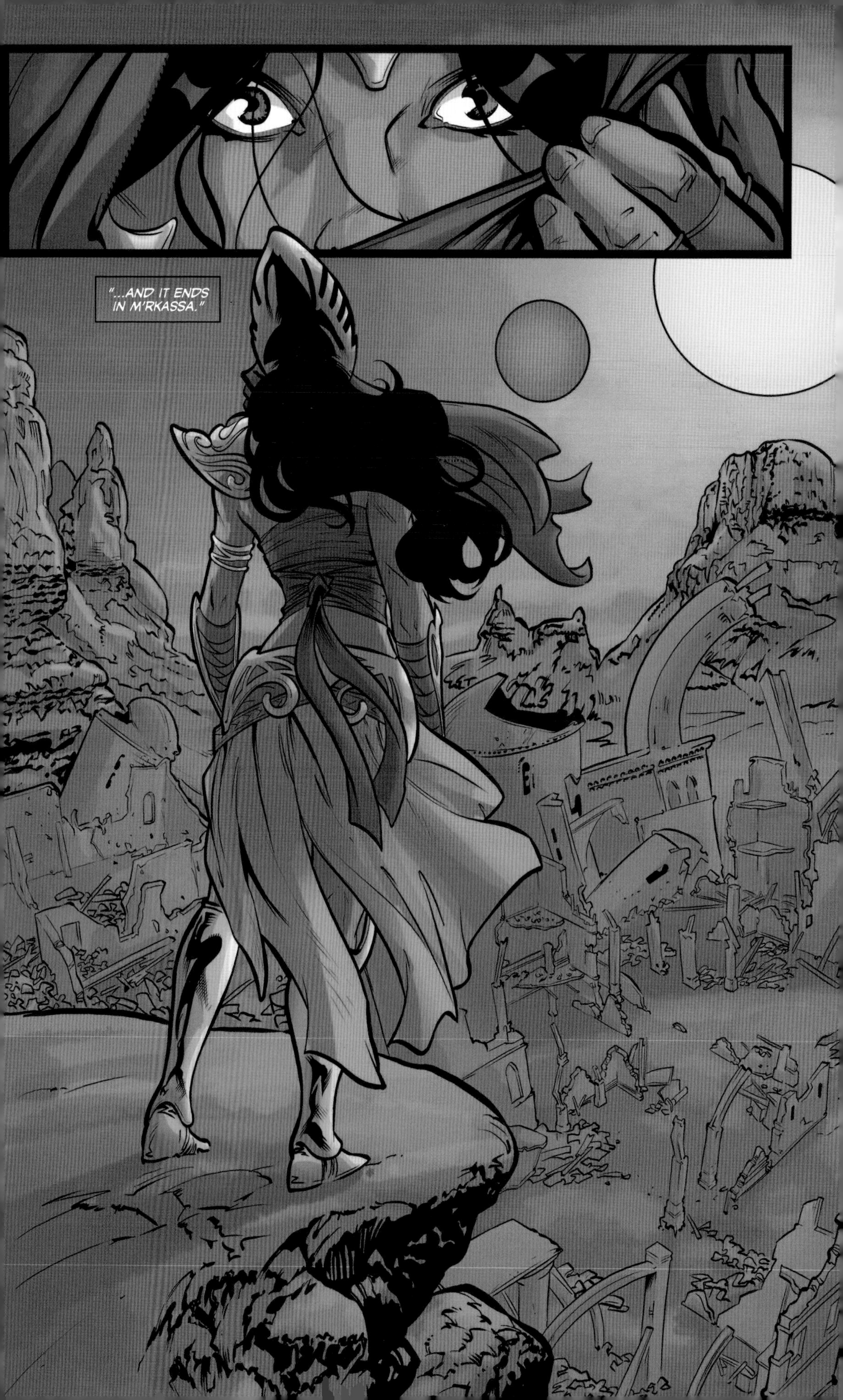
"...AND IT ENDS IN M'RKASSA."

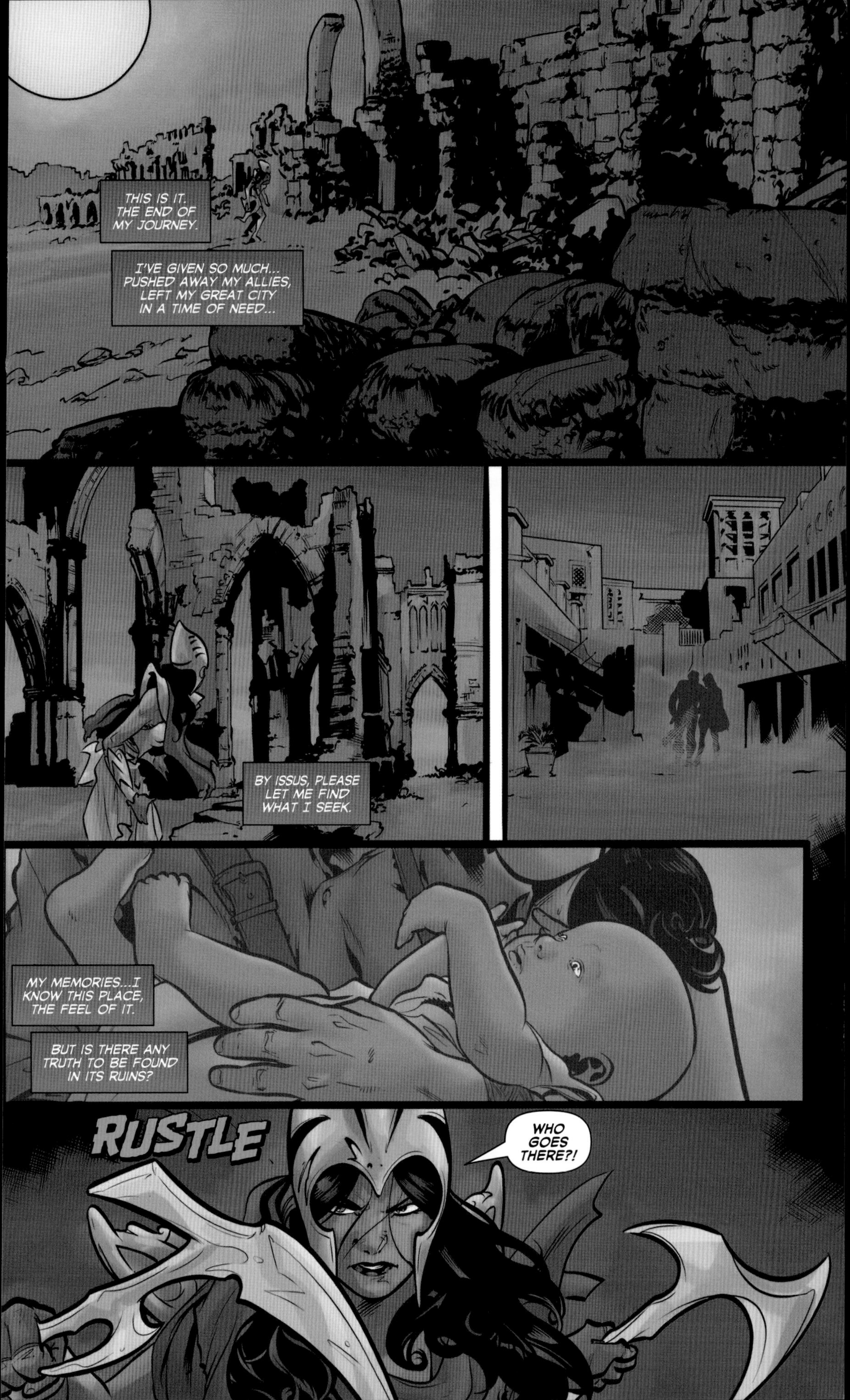
THIS IS IT. THE END OF MY JOURNEY.
I'VE GIVEN SO MUCH... PUSHED AWAY MY ALLIES, LEFT MY GREAT CITY IN A TIME OF NEED...
BY ISSUS, PLEASE LET ME FIND WHAT I SEEK.
MY MEMORIES...I KNOW THIS PLACE, THE FEEL OF IT.
BUT IS THERE ANY TRUTH TO BE FOUND IN ITS RUINS?
RUSTLE
WHO GOES THERE?!

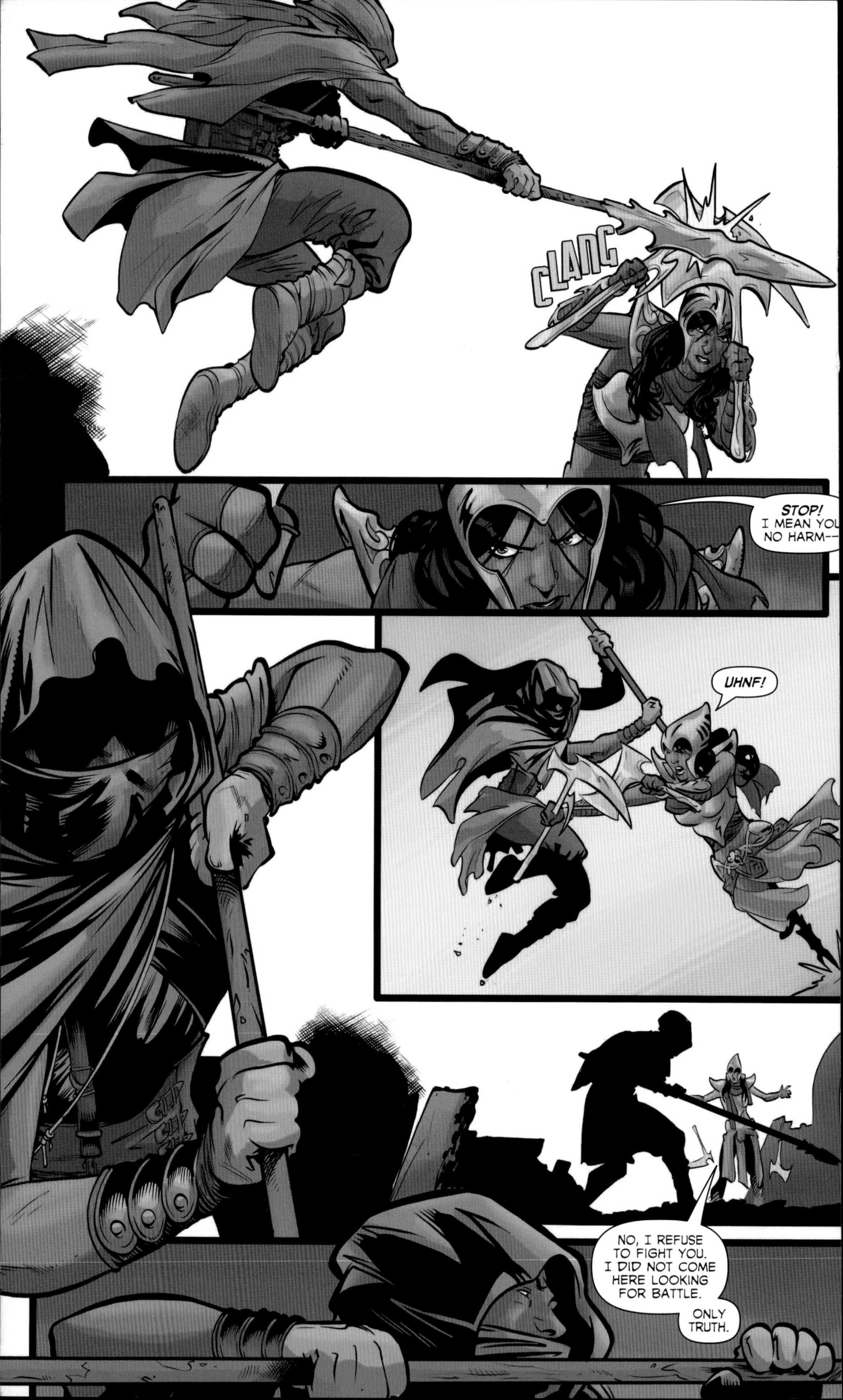

CLANG
STOP! I MEAN YOU NO HARM--
UHNF!
NO, I REFUSE TO FIGHT YOU. I DID NOT COME HERE LOOKING FOR BATTLE.
ONLY TRUTH.

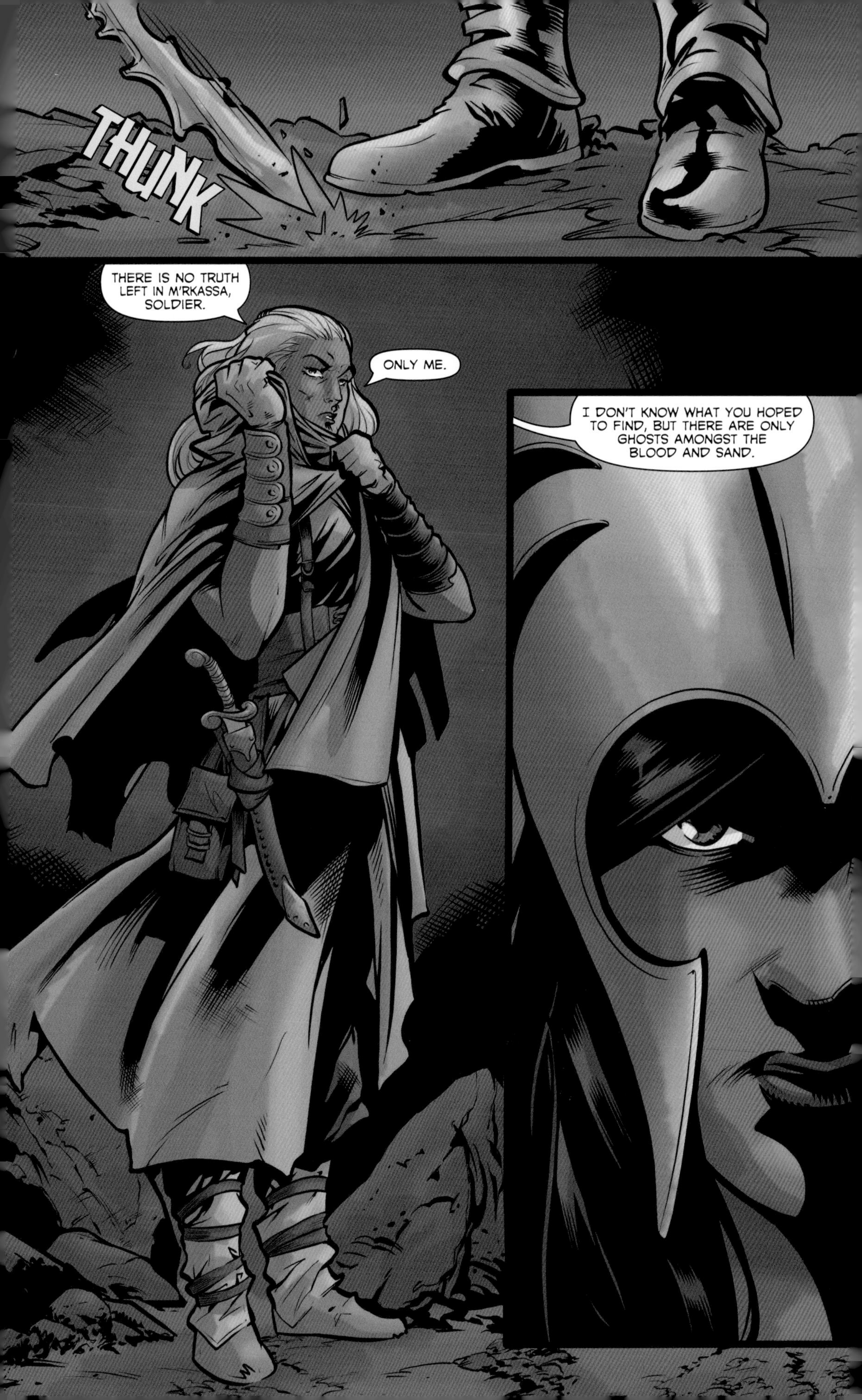
THUNK
THERE IS NO TRUTH LEFT IN M'RKASSA, SOLDIER.
ONLY ME.
I DON'T KNOW WHAT YOU HOPED TO FIND, BUT THERE ARE ONLY GHOSTS AMONGST THE BLOOD AND SAND.

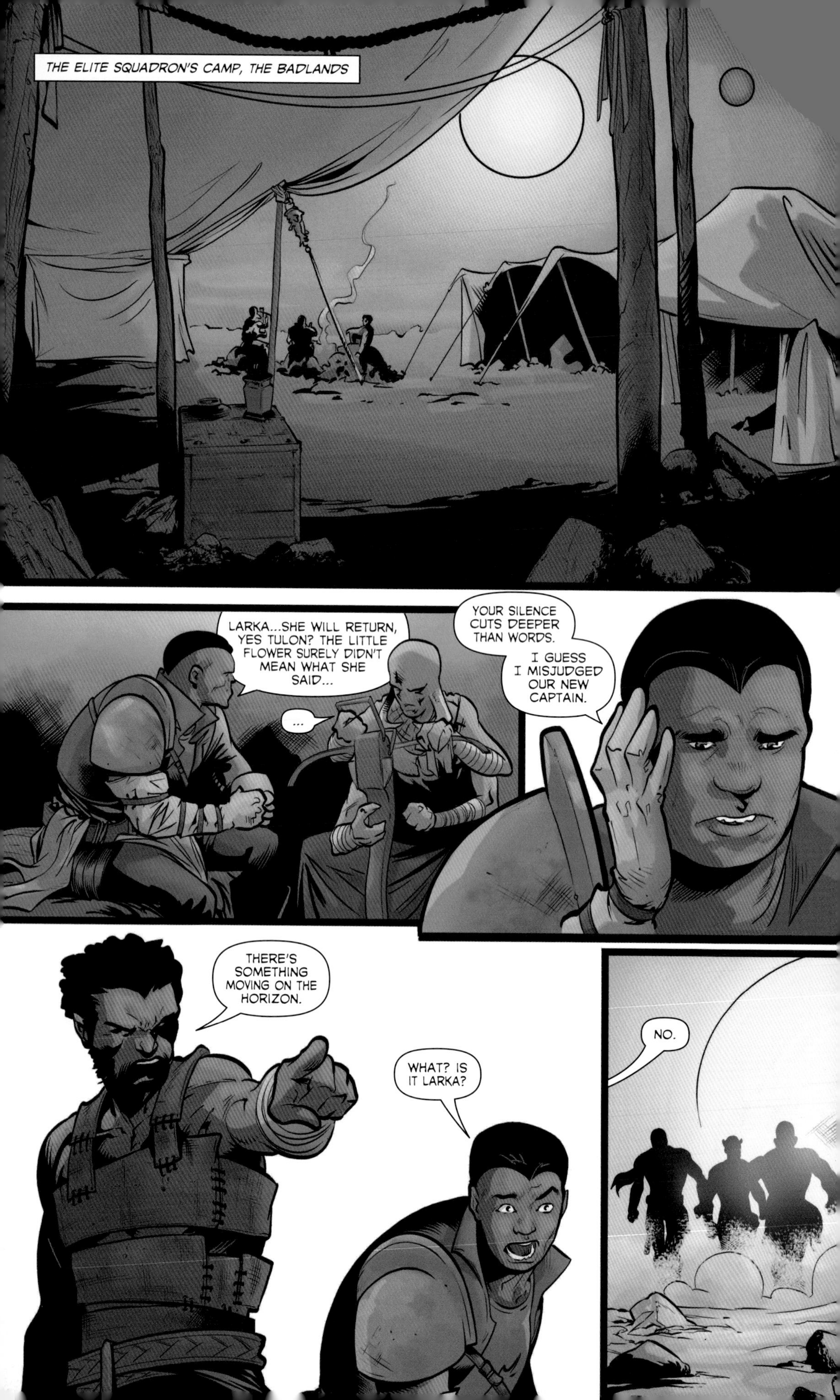
THE ELITE SQUADRON'S CAMP, THE BADLANDS
LARKA...SHE WILL RETURN, YES TULON? THE LITTLE FLOWER SURELY DIDN'T MEAN WHAT SHE SAID...
...
YOUR SILENCE CUTS DEEPER THAN WORDS.
I GUESS I MISJUDGED OUR NEW CAPTAIN.
THERE'S SOMETHING MOVING ON THE HORIZON.
WHAT? IS IT LARKA?
NO.

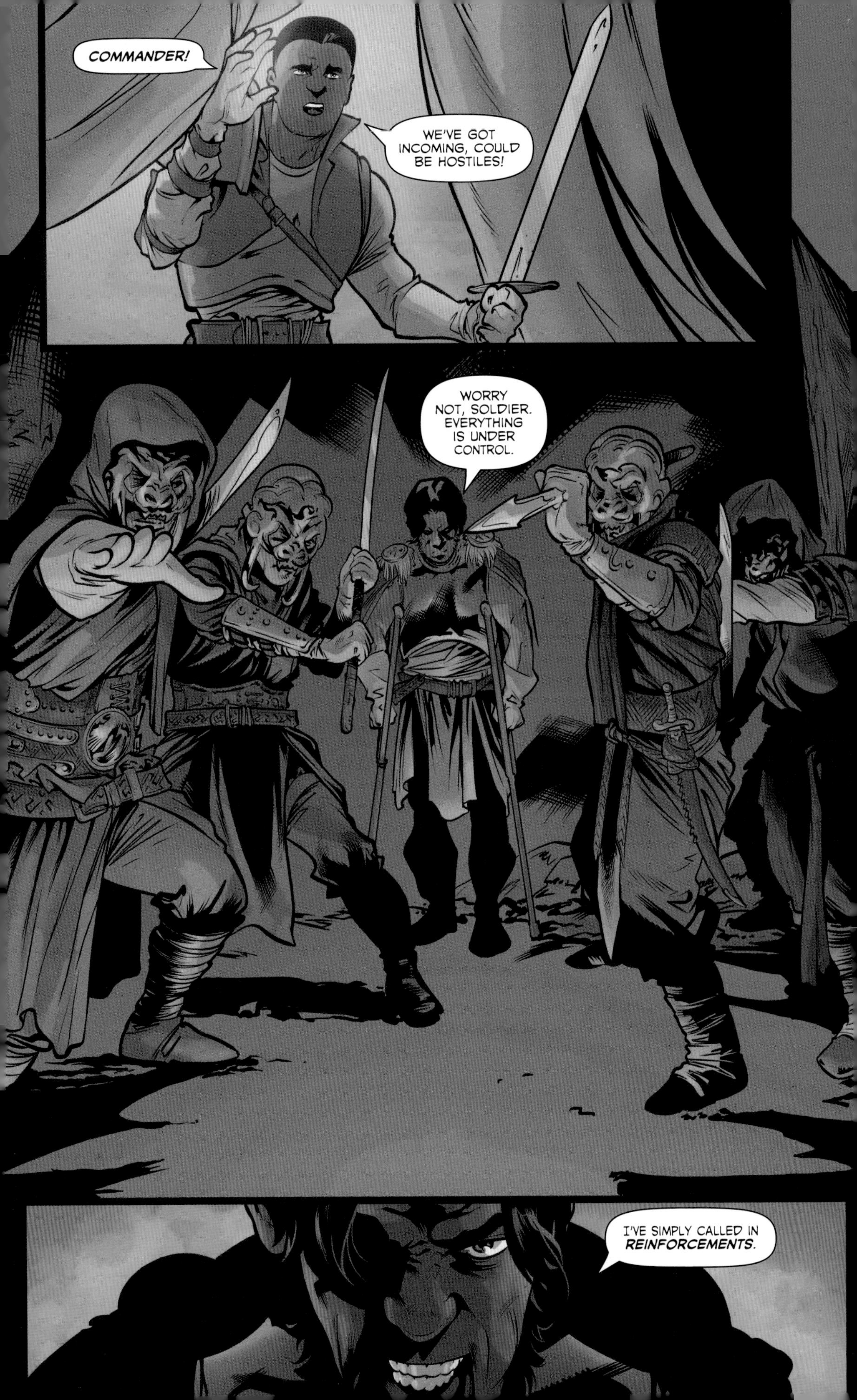
COMMANDER!
WE'VE GOT INCOMING, COULD BE HOSTILES!
WORRY NOT, SOLDIER. EVERYTHING IS UNDER CONTROL.
I'VE SIMPLY CALLED IN *REINFORCEMENTS*.

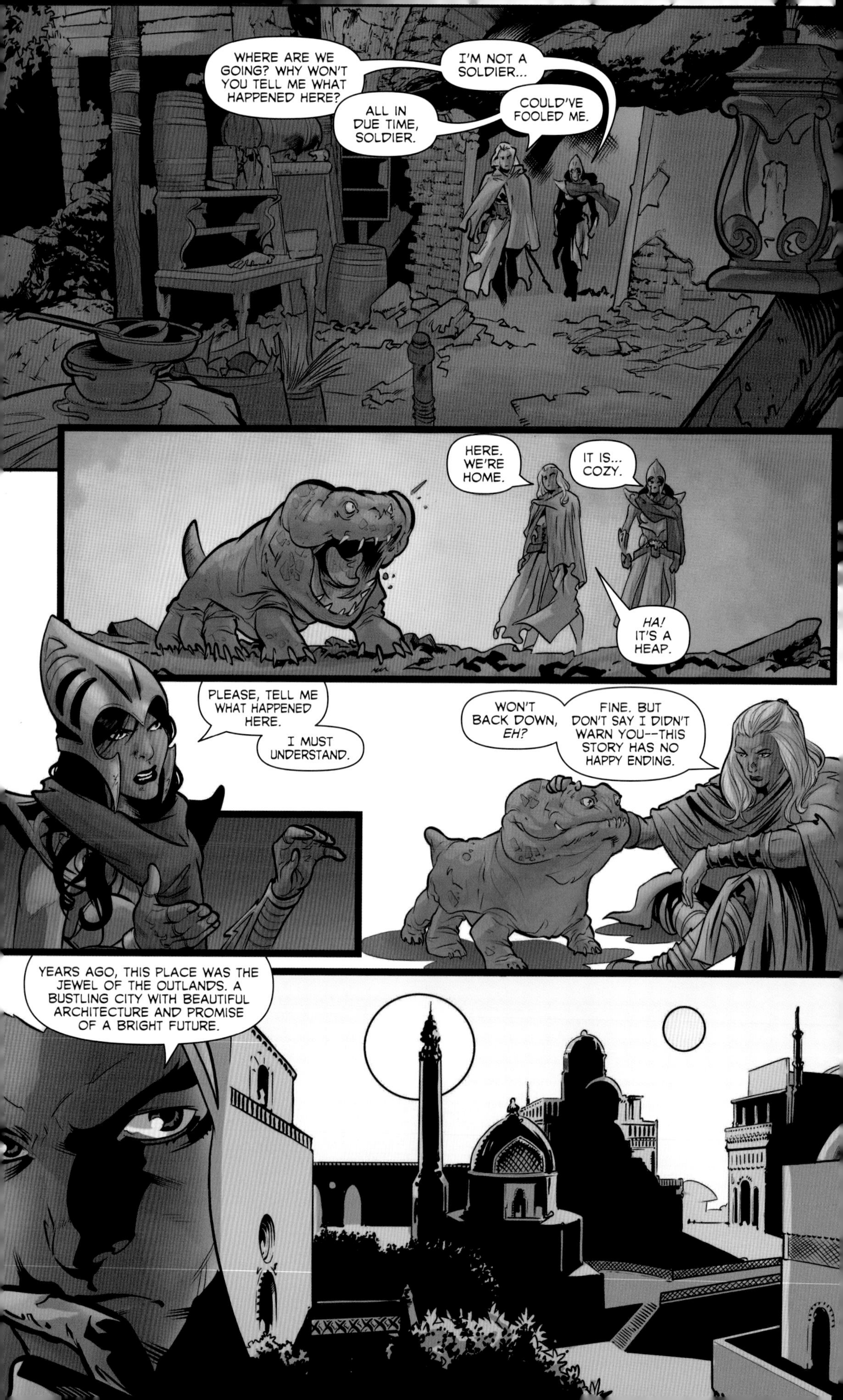
WHERE ARE WE GOING? WHY WON'T YOU TELL ME WHAT HAPPENED HERE?
ALL IN DUE TIME, SOLDIER.
I'M NOT A SOLDIER...
COULD'VE FOOLED ME.
HERE. WE'RE HOME.
IT IS... COZY.
HA! IT'S A HEAP.
PLEASE, TELL ME WHAT HAPPENED HERE.
I MUST UNDERSTAND.
WON'T BACK DOWN, EH?
FINE. BUT DON'T SAY I DIDN'T WARN YOU--THIS STORY HAS NO HAPPY ENDING.
YEARS AGO, THIS PLACE WAS THE JEWEL OF THE OUTLANDS. A BUSTLING CITY WITH BEAUTIFUL ARCHITECTURE AND PROMISE OF A BRIGHT FUTURE.

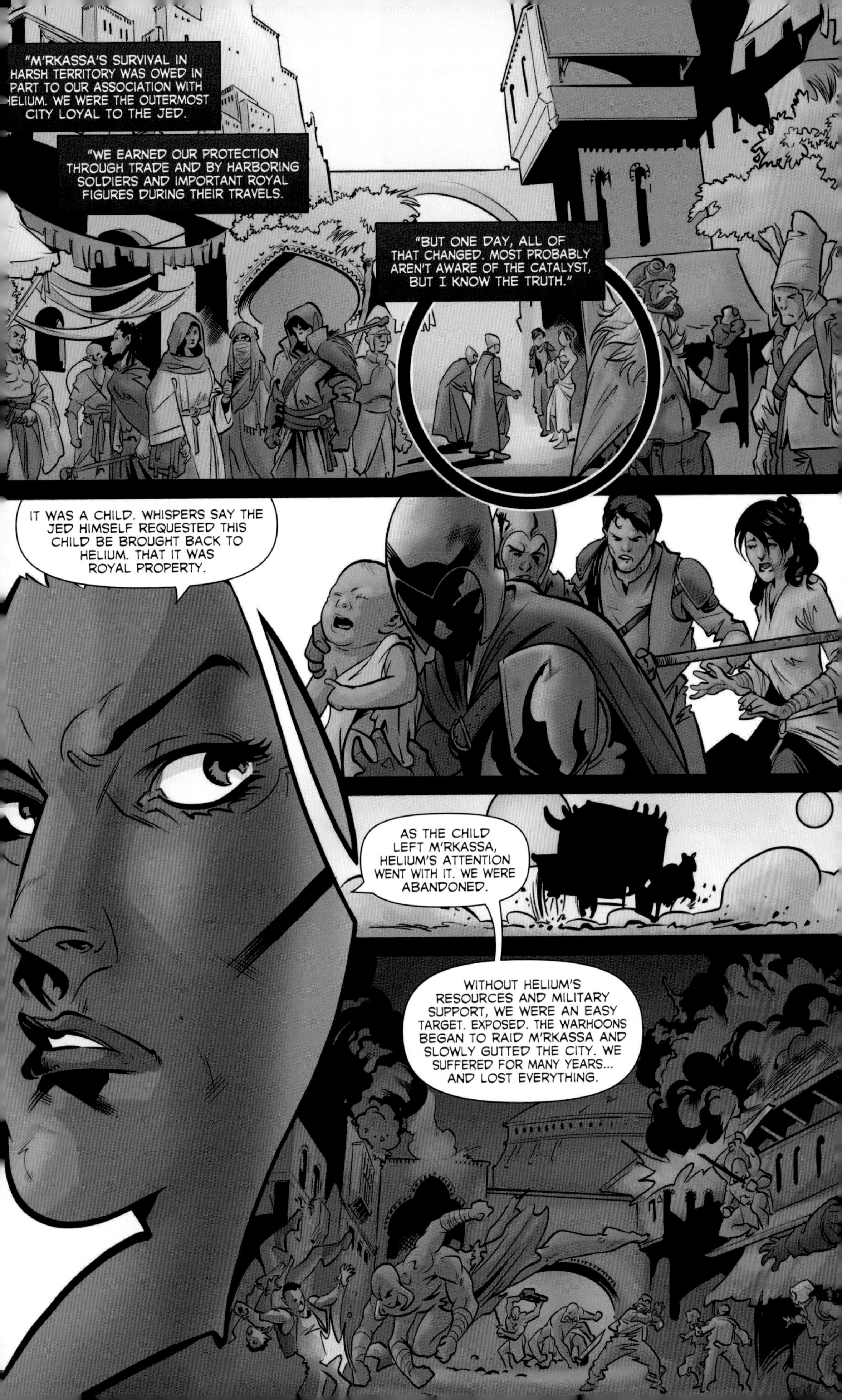
"M'RKASSA'S SURVIVAL IN HARSH TERRITORY WAS OWED IN PART TO OUR ASSOCIATION WITH HELIUM. WE WERE THE OUTERMOST CITY LOYAL TO THE JED.
"WE EARNED OUR PROTECTION THROUGH TRADE AND BY HARBORING SOLDIERS AND IMPORTANT ROYAL FIGURES DURING THEIR TRAVELS.
"BUT ONE DAY, ALL OF THAT CHANGED. MOST PROBABLY AREN'T AWARE OF THE CATALYST, BUT I KNOW THE TRUTH."
IT WAS A CHILD. WHISPERS SAY THE JED HIMSELF REQUESTED THIS CHILD BE BROUGHT BACK TO HELIUM. THAT IT WAS ROYAL PROPERTY.
AS THE CHILD LEFT M'RKASSA, HELIUM'S ATTENTION WENT WITH IT. WE WERE ABANDONED.
WITHOUT HELIUM'S RESOURCES AND MILITARY SUPPORT, WE WERE AN EASY TARGET. EXPOSED. THE WARHOONS BEGAN TO RAID M'RKASSA AND SLOWLY GUTTED THE CITY. WE SUFFERED FOR MANY YEARS... AND LOST EVERYTHING.

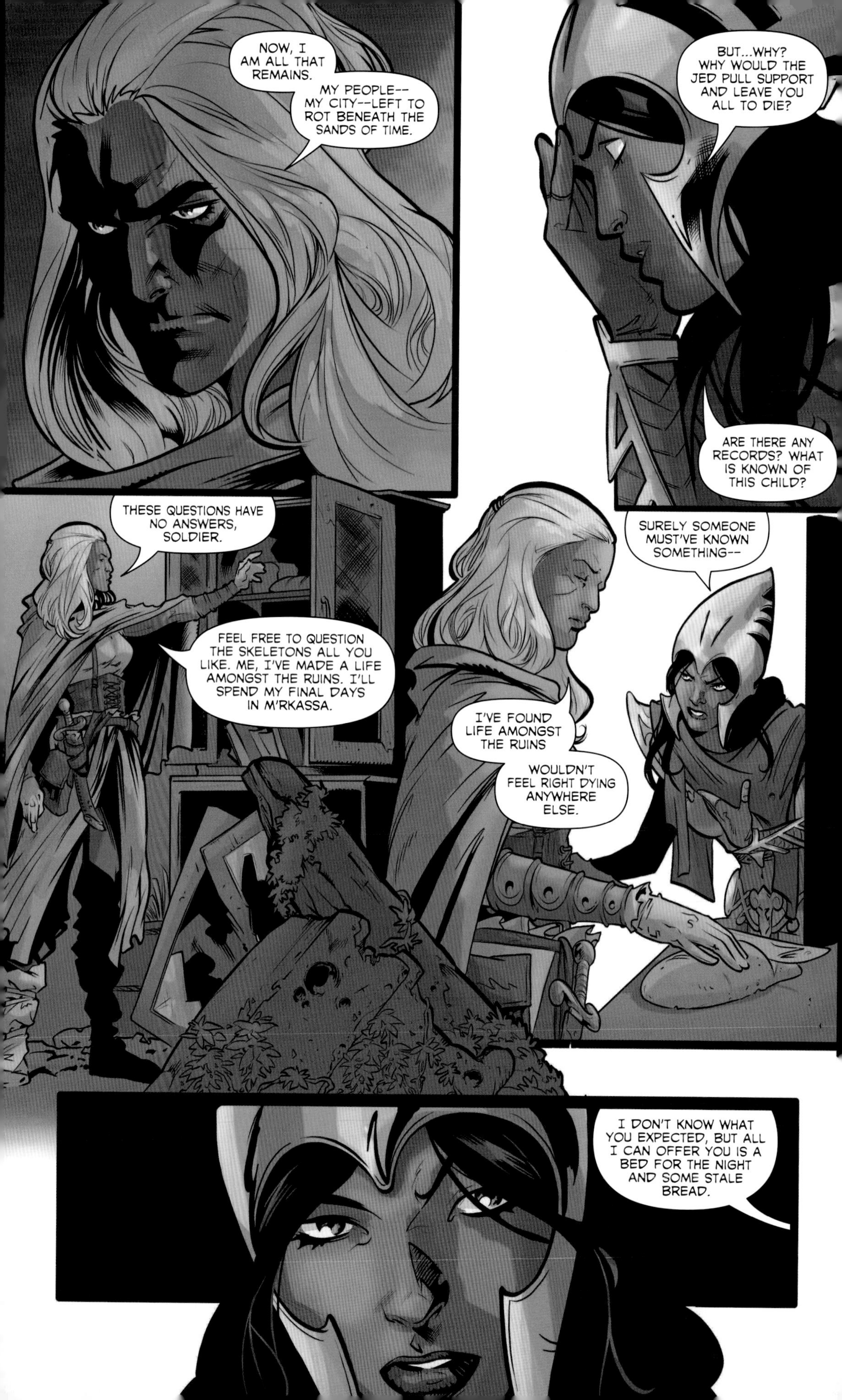
NOW, I AM ALL THAT REMAINS.
MY PEOPLE-- MY CITY--LEFT TO ROT BENEATH THE SANDS OF TIME.
BUT...WHY? WHY WOULD THE JED PULL SUPPORT AND LEAVE YOU ALL TO DIE?
ARE THERE ANY RECORDS? WHAT IS KNOWN OF THIS CHILD?
THESE QUESTIONS HAVE NO ANSWERS, SOLDIER.
FEEL FREE TO QUESTION THE SKELETONS ALL YOU LIKE. ME, I'VE MADE A LIFE AMONGST THE RUINS. I'LL SPEND MY FINAL DAYS IN M'RKASSA.
SURELY SOMEONE MUST'VE KNOWN SOMETHING--
I'VE FOUND LIFE AMONGST THE RUINS
WOULDN'T FEEL RIGHT DYING ANYWHERE ELSE.
I DON'T KNOW WHAT YOU EXPECTED, BUT ALL I CAN OFFER YOU IS A BED FOR THE NIGHT AND SOME STALE BREAD.

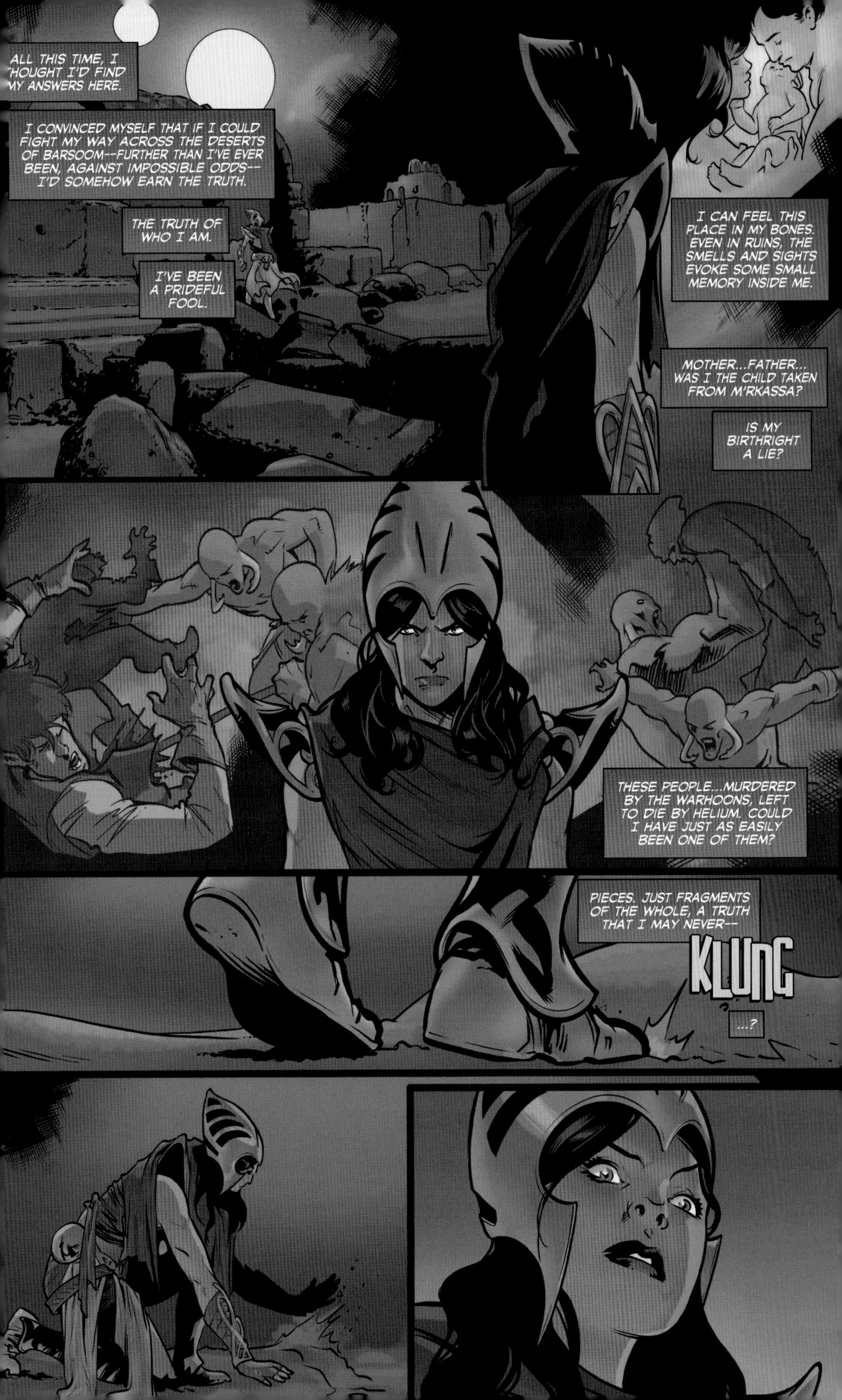
ALL THIS TIME, I THOUGHT I'D FIND MY ANSWERS HERE.
I CONVINCED MYSELF THAT IF I COULD FIGHT MY WAY ACROSS THE DESERTS OF BARSOOM--FURTHER THAN I'VE EVER BEEN, AGAINST IMPOSSIBLE ODDS--I'D SOMEHOW EARN THE TRUTH.
THE TRUTH OF WHO I AM.
I'VE BEEN A PRIDEFUL FOOL.
I CAN FEEL THIS PLACE IN MY BONES. EVEN IN RUINS, THE SMELLS AND SIGHTS EVOKE SOME SMALL MEMORY INSIDE ME.
MOTHER...FATHER... WAS I THE CHILD TAKEN FROM M'RKASSA?
IS MY BIRTHRIGHT A LIE?
THESE PEOPLE...MURDERED BY THE WARHOONS, LEFT TO DIE BY HELIUM. COULD I HAVE JUST AS EASILY BEEN ONE OF THEM?
PIECES. JUST FRAGMENTS OF THE WHOLE, A TRUTH THAT I MAY NEVER--
KLUNG
...?

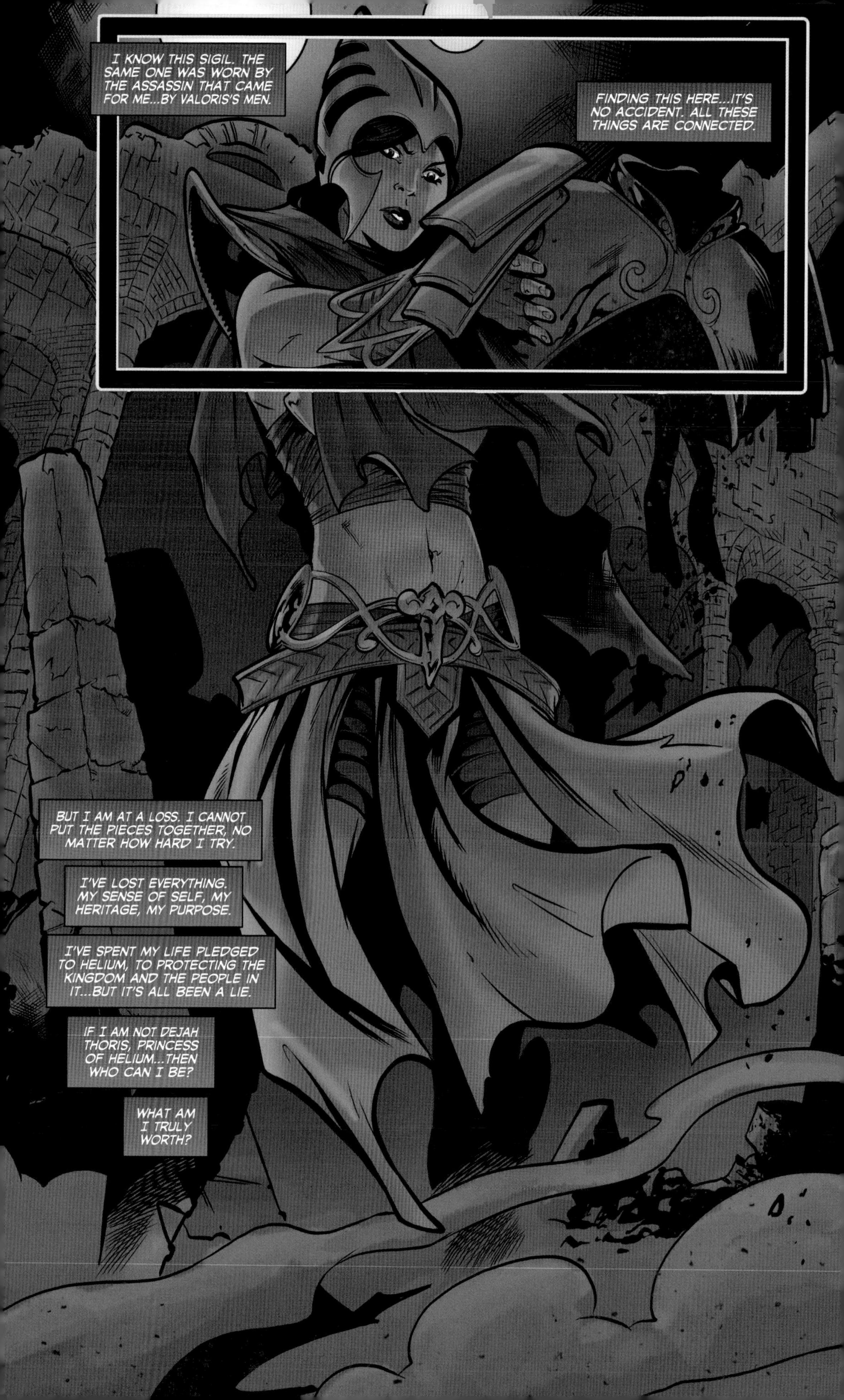
I KNOW THIS SIGIL. THE SAME ONE WAS WORN BY THE ASSASSIN THAT CAME FOR ME...BY VALORIS'S MEN.
FINDING THIS HERE...IT'S NO ACCIDENT. ALL THESE THINGS ARE CONNECTED.
BUT I AM AT A LOSS. I CANNOT PUT THE PIECES TOGETHER, NO MATTER HOW HARD I TRY.
I'VE LOST EVERYTHING. MY SENSE OF SELF, MY HERITAGE, MY PURPOSE.
I'VE SPENT MY LIFE PLEDGED TO HELIUM, TO PROTECTING THE KINGDOM AND THE PEOPLE IN IT...BUT IT'S ALL BEEN A LIE.
IF I AM NOT DEJAH THORIS, PRINCESS OF HELIUM...THEN WHO CAN I BE?
WHAT AM I TRULY WORTH?

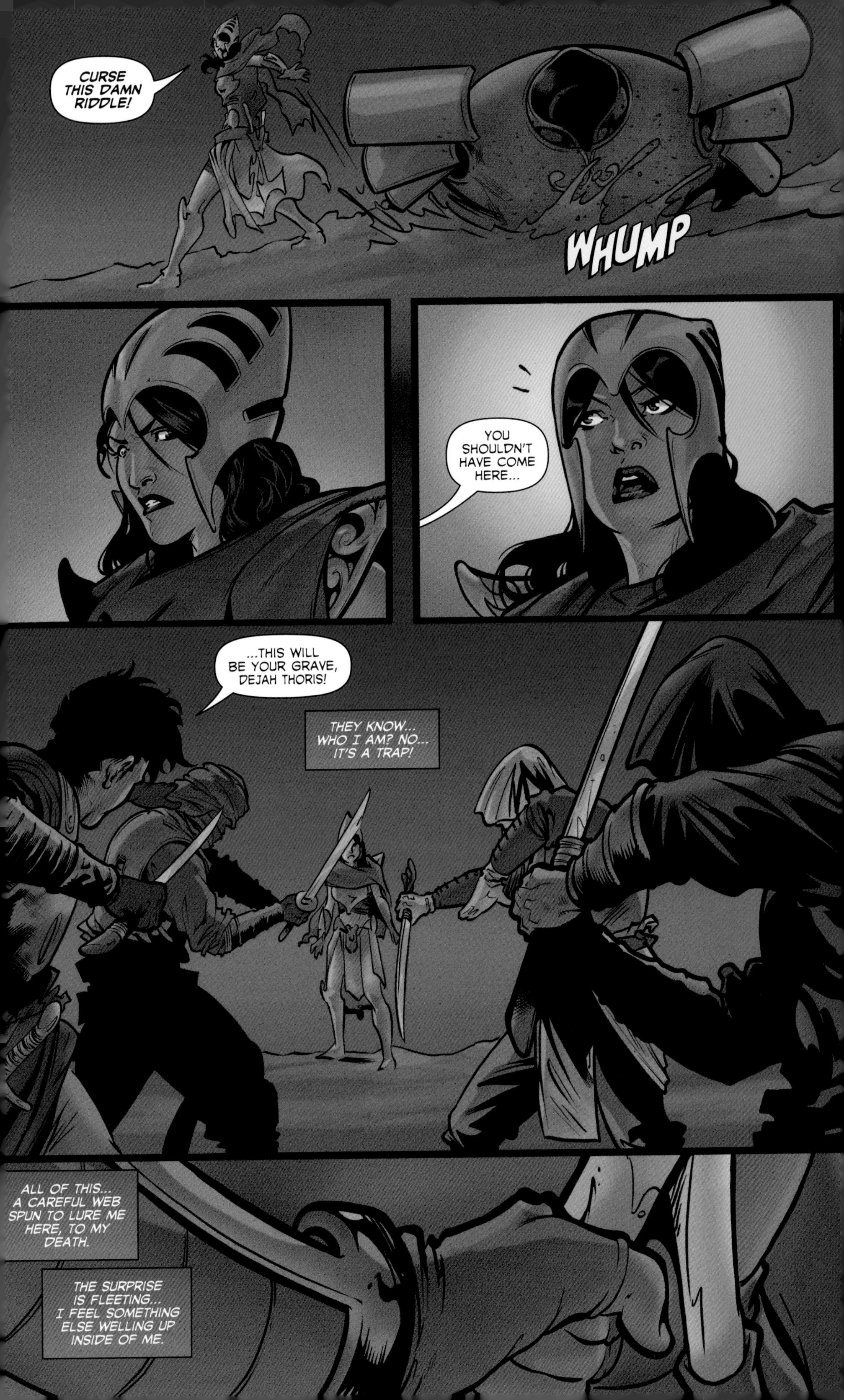
CURSE THIS DAMN RIDDLE!
WHUMP
YOU SHOULDN'T HAVE COME HERE...
...THIS WILL BE YOUR GRAVE, DEJAH THORIS!
THEY KNOW... WHO I AM? NO... IT'S A TRAP!
ALL OF THIS... A CAREFUL WEB SPUN TO LURE ME HERE, TO MY DEATH.
THE SURPRISE IS FLEETING... I FEEL SOMETHING ELSE WELLING UP INSIDE OF ME.

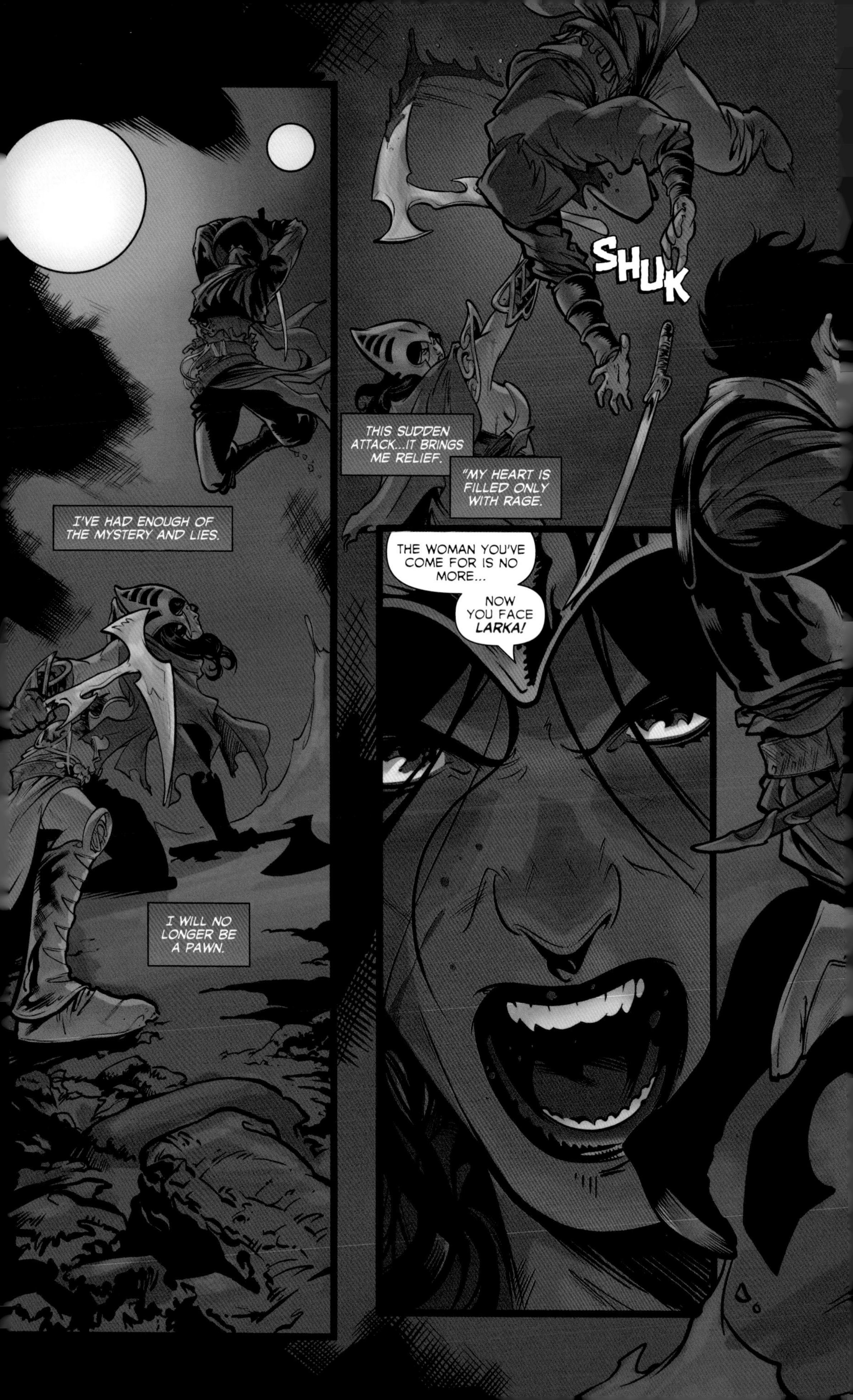
I'VE HAD ENOUGH OF THE MYSTERY AND LIES.
I WILL NO LONGER BE A PAWN.
SHUK
THIS SUDDEN ATTACK...IT BRINGS ME RELIEF.
"MY HEART IS FILLED ONLY WITH RAGE.
THE WOMAN YOU'VE COME FOR IS NO MORE...
NOW YOU FACE LARKA!

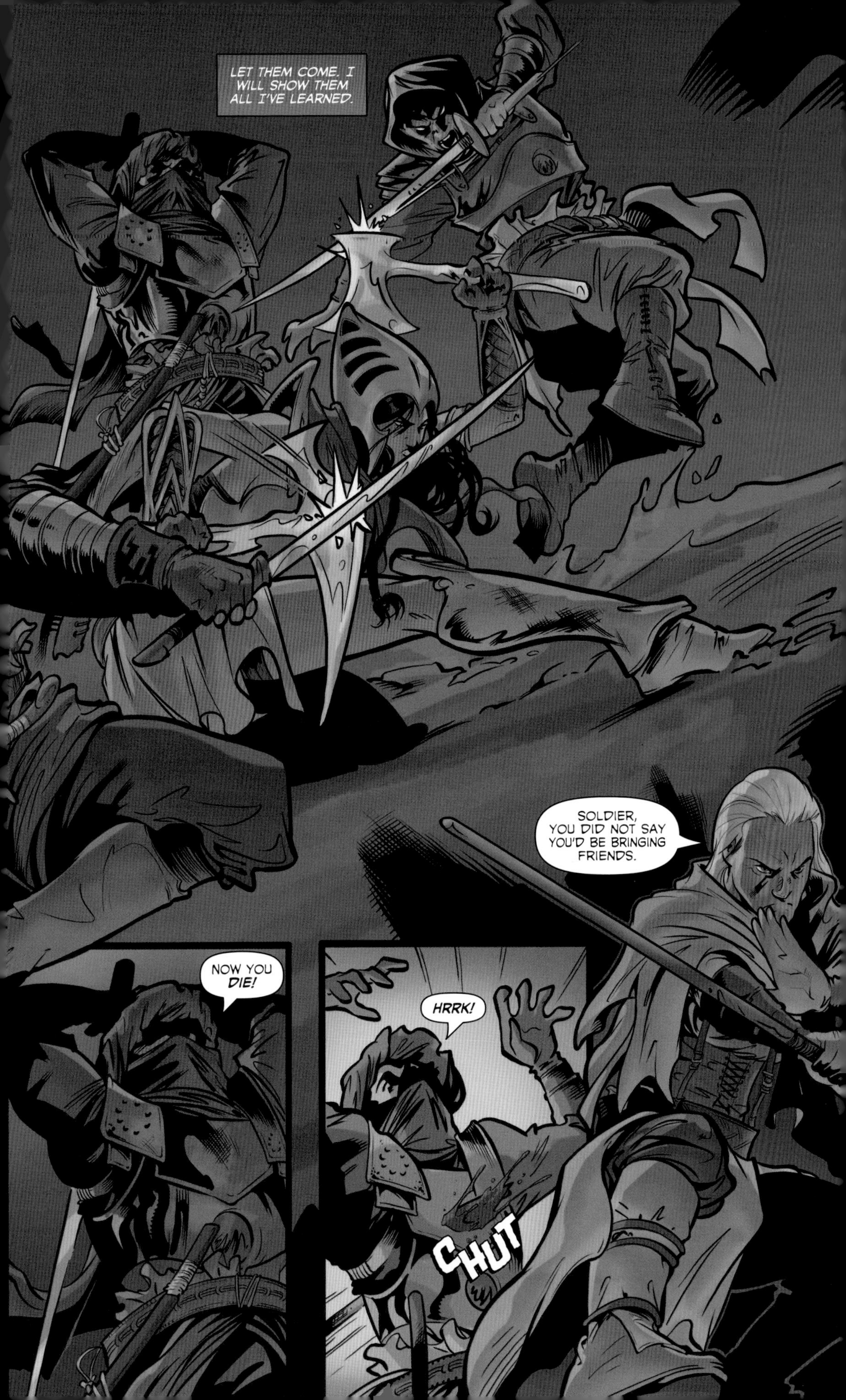
LET THEM COME. I WILL SHOW THEM ALL I'VE LEARNED.
SOLDIER, YOU DID NOT SAY YOU'D BE BRINGING FRIENDS.
NOW YOU DIE!
HRRK!
CHUT

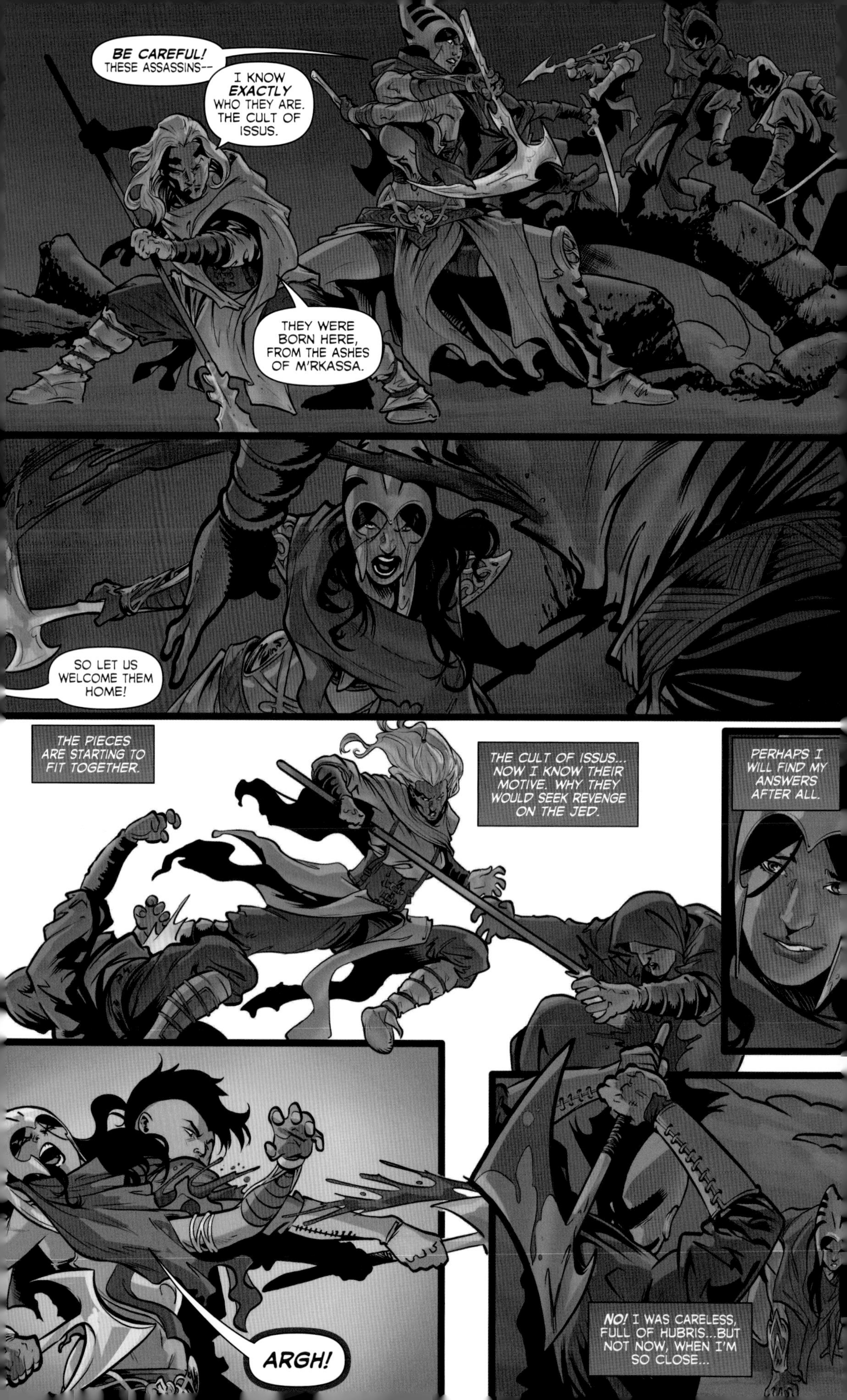
BE CAREFUL! THESE ASSASSINS--
I KNOW EXACTLY WHO THEY ARE. THE CULT OF ISSUS.
THEY WERE BORN HERE, FROM THE ASHES OF M'RKASSA.
SO LET US WELCOME THEM HOME!
THE PIECES ARE STARTING TO FIT TOGETHER.
THE CULT OF ISSUS... NOW I KNOW THEIR MOTIVE. WHY THEY WOULD SEEK REVENGE ON THE JED.
PERHAPS I WILL FIND MY ANSWERS AFTER ALL.
ARGH!
NO! I WAS CARELESS, FULL OF HUBRIS...BUT NOT NOW, WHEN I'M SO CLOSE...

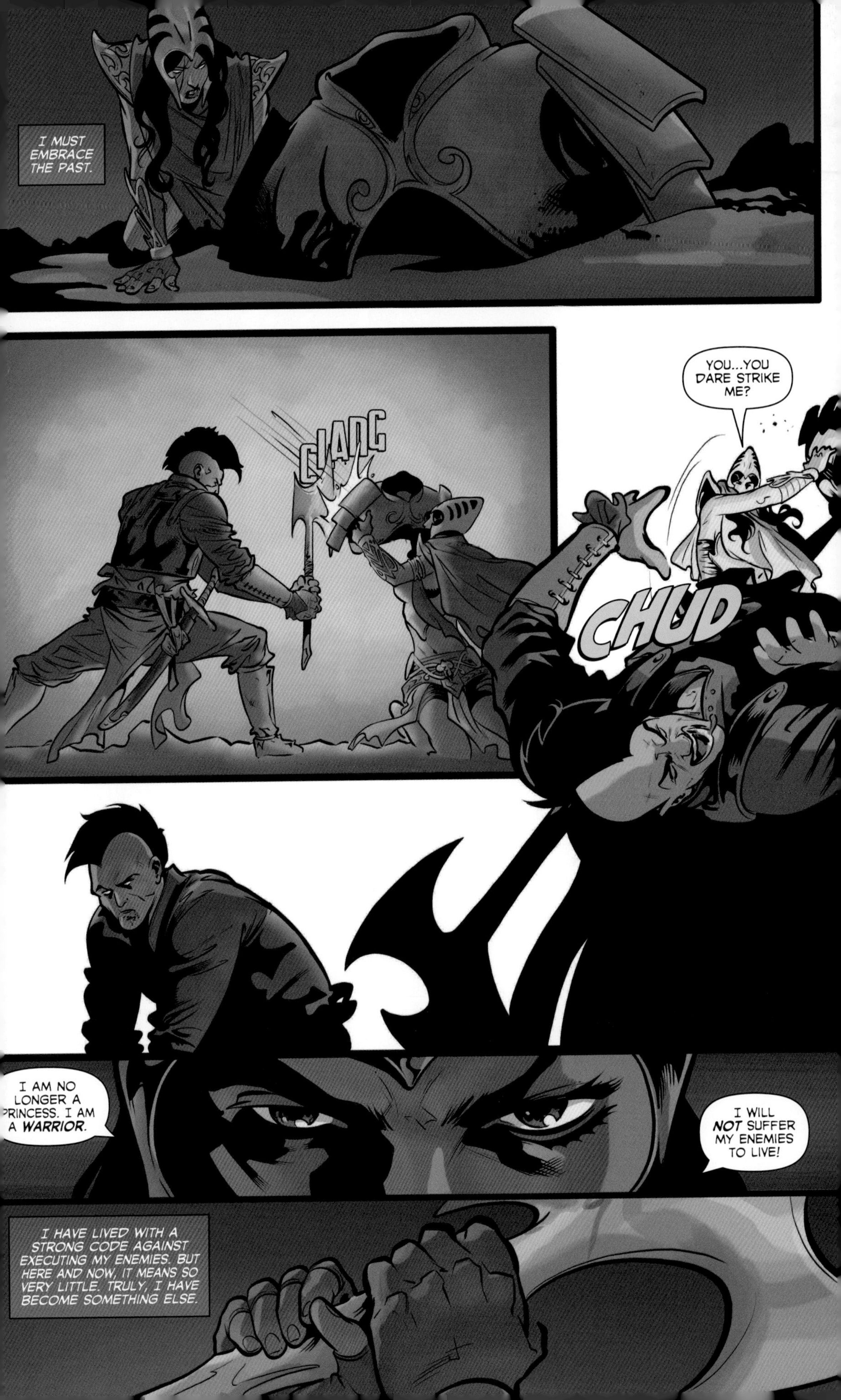
I MUST EMBRACE THE PAST.
CLANG
YOU...YOU DARE STRIKE ME?
CHUD
I AM NO LONGER A PRINCESS. I AM A **WARRIOR**.
I WILL **NOT** SUFFER MY ENEMIES TO LIVE!
I HAVE LIVED WITH A STRONG CODE AGAINST EXECUTING MY ENEMIES. BUT HERE AND NOW, IT MEANS SO VERY LITTLE. TRULY, I HAVE BECOME SOMETHING ELSE.

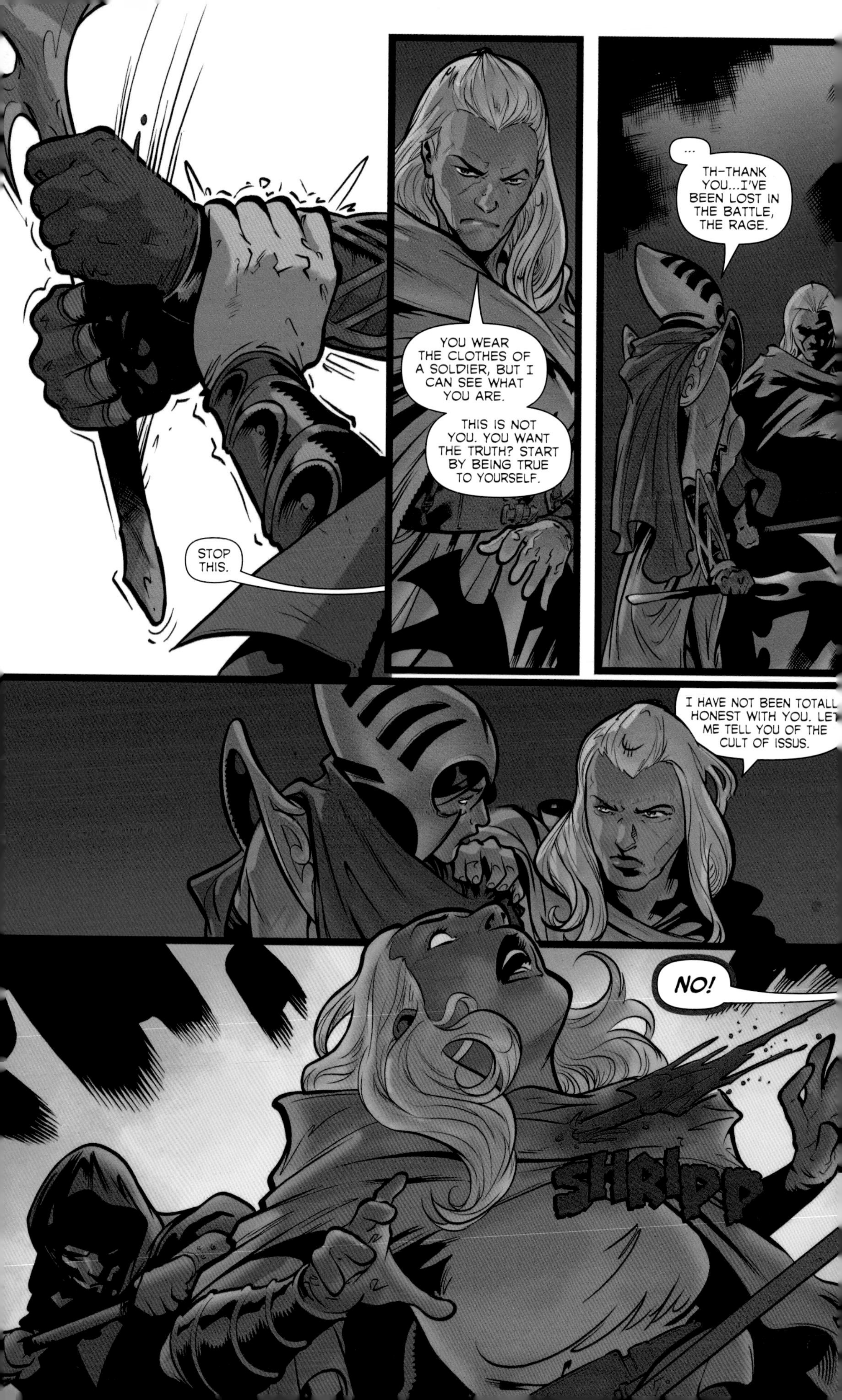

STOP THIS.
YOU WEAR THE CLOTHES OF A SOLDIER, BUT I CAN SEE WHAT YOU ARE.
THIS IS NOT YOU. YOU WANT THE TRUTH? START BY BEING TRUE TO YOURSELF.
...
TH-THANK YOU...I'VE BEEN LOST IN THE BATTLE, THE RAGE.
I HAVE NOT BEEN TOTALL HONEST WITH YOU. LET ME TELL YOU OF THE CULT OF ISSUS.
NO!
SHRIPP

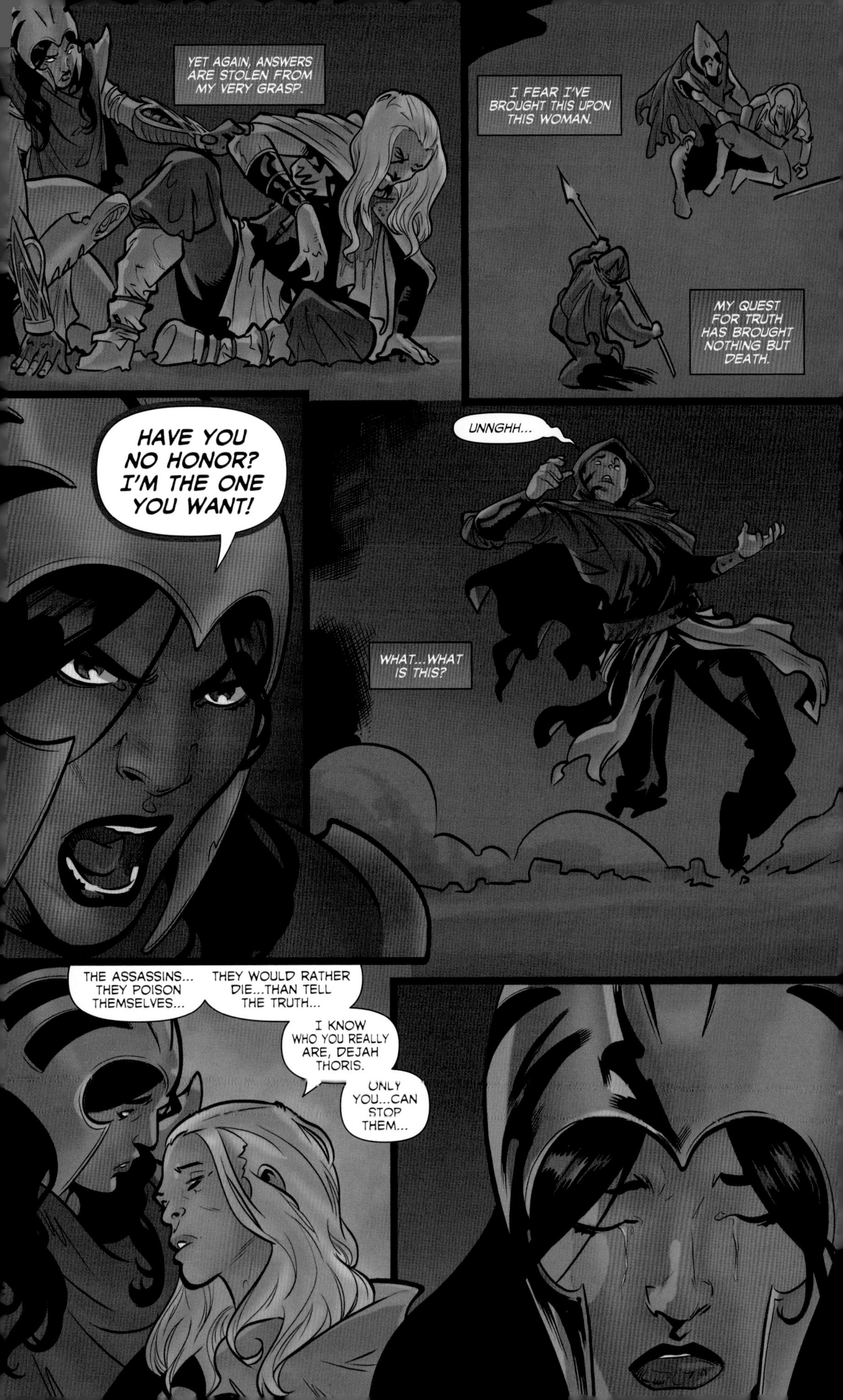
YET AGAIN, ANSWERS ARE STOLEN FROM MY VERY GRASP.
I FEAR I'VE BROUGHT THIS UPON THIS WOMAN.
MY QUEST FOR TRUTH HAS BROUGHT NOTHING BUT DEATH.
HAVE YOU NO HONOR? I'M THE ONE YOU WANT!
UNNGHH...
WHAT...WHAT IS THIS?
THE ASSASSINS... THEY POISON THEMSELVES...
THEY WOULD RATHER DIE...THAN TELL THE TRUTH...
I KNOW WHO YOU REALLY ARE, DEJAH THORIS.
ONLY YOU...CAN STOP THEM...

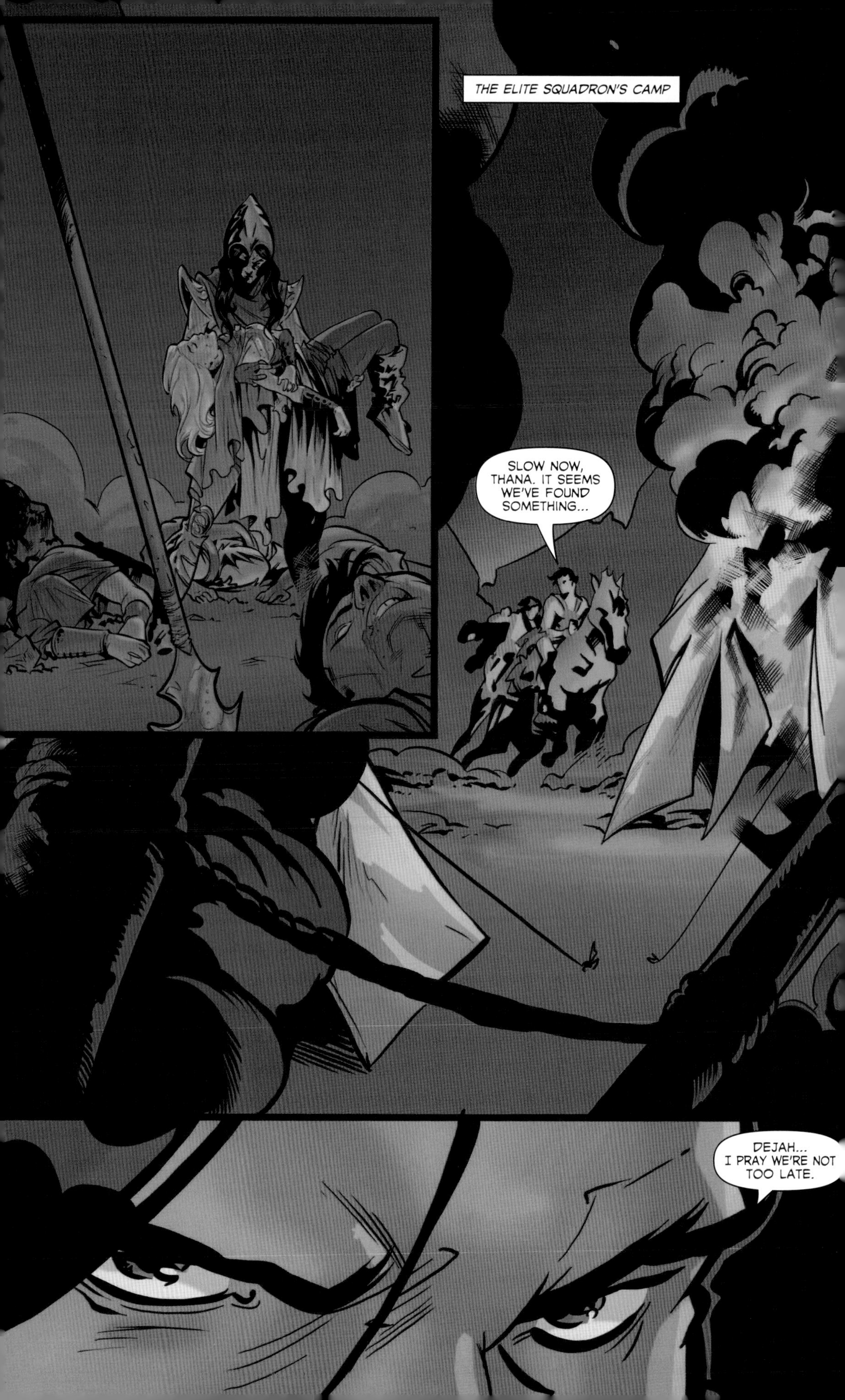
THE ELITE SQUADRON'S CAMP
SLOW NOW, THANA. IT SEEMS WE'VE FOUND SOMETHING...
DEJAH... I PRAY WE'RE NOT TOO LATE.

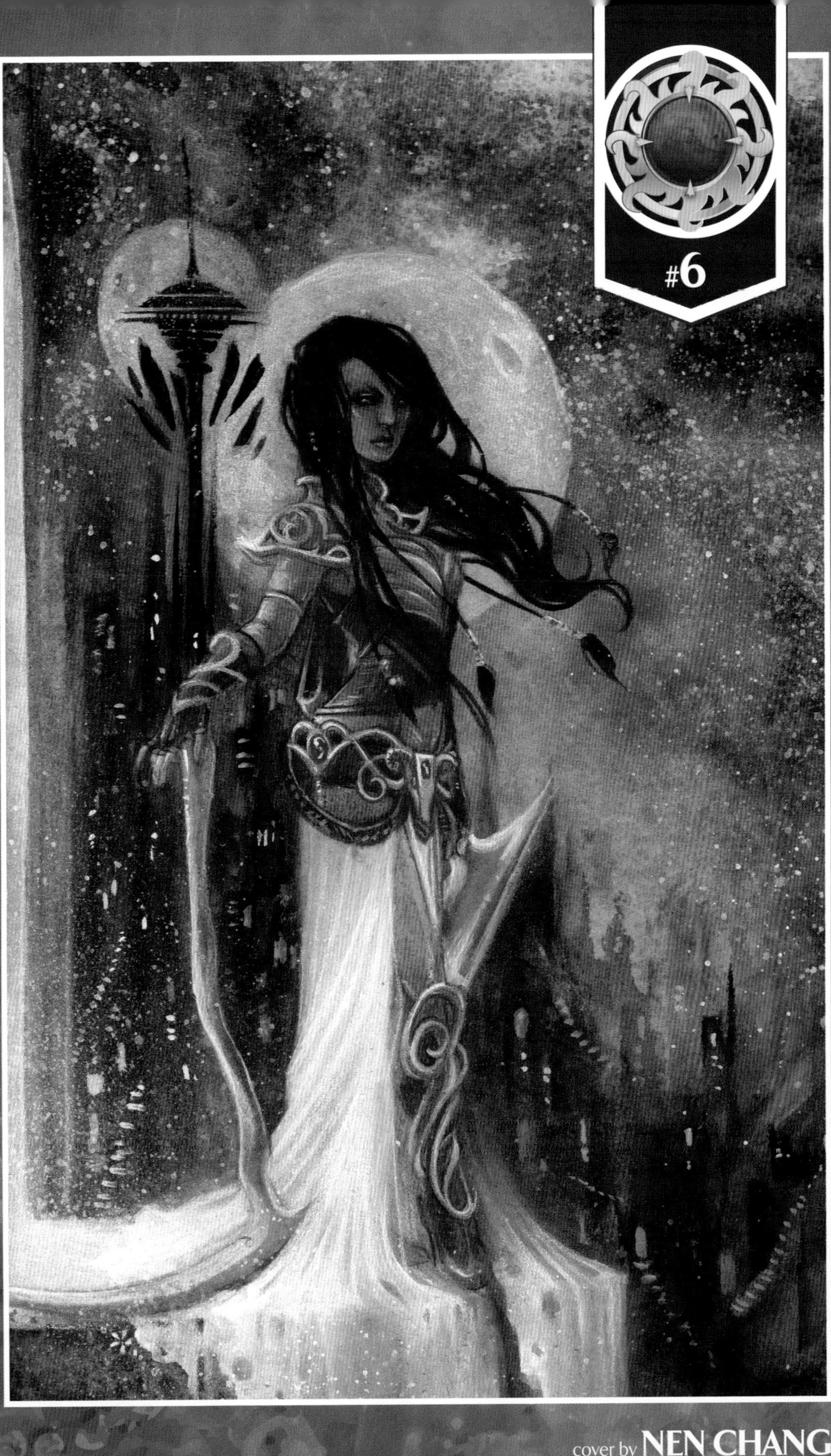
#6

cover by **NEN CHANG**

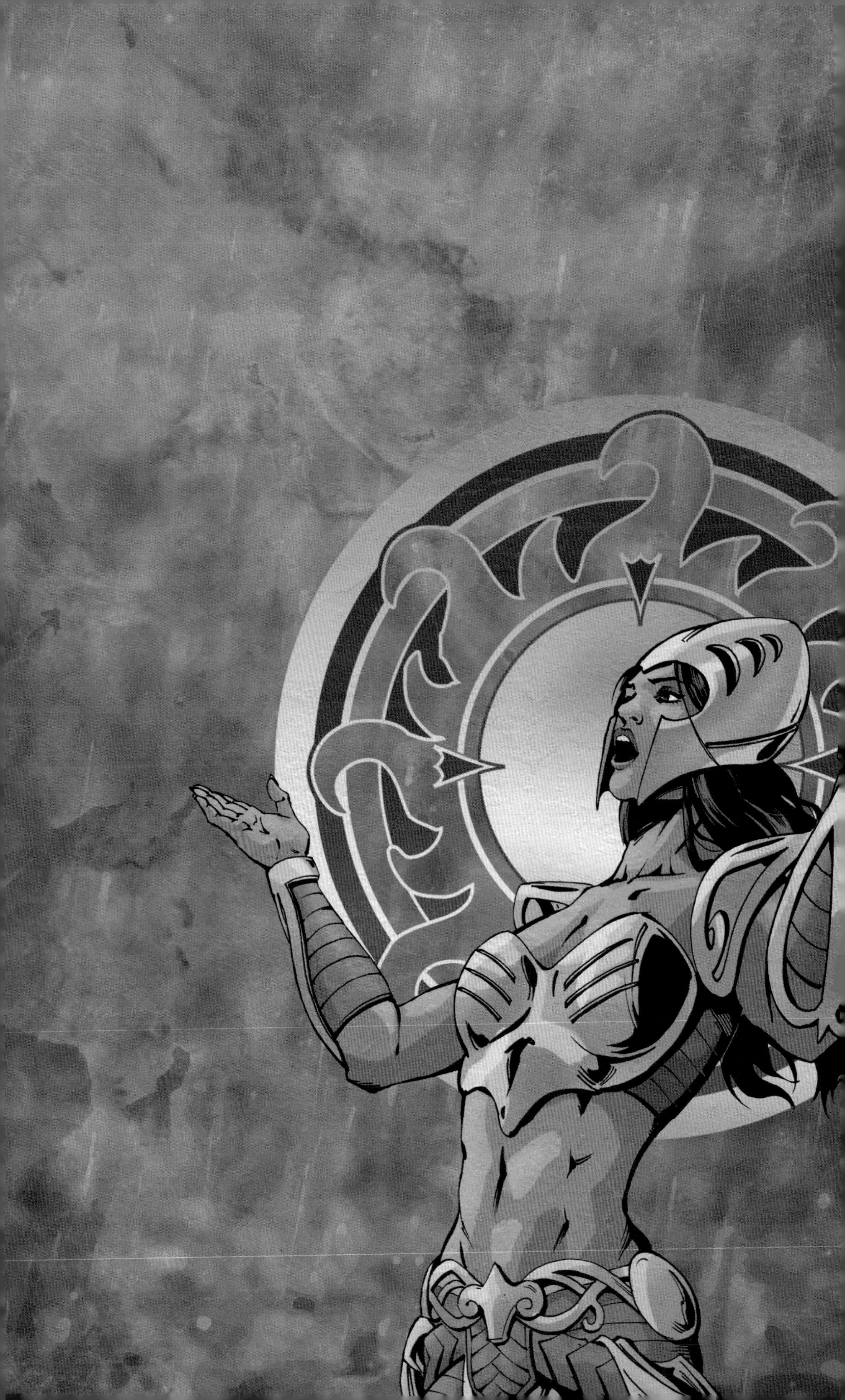

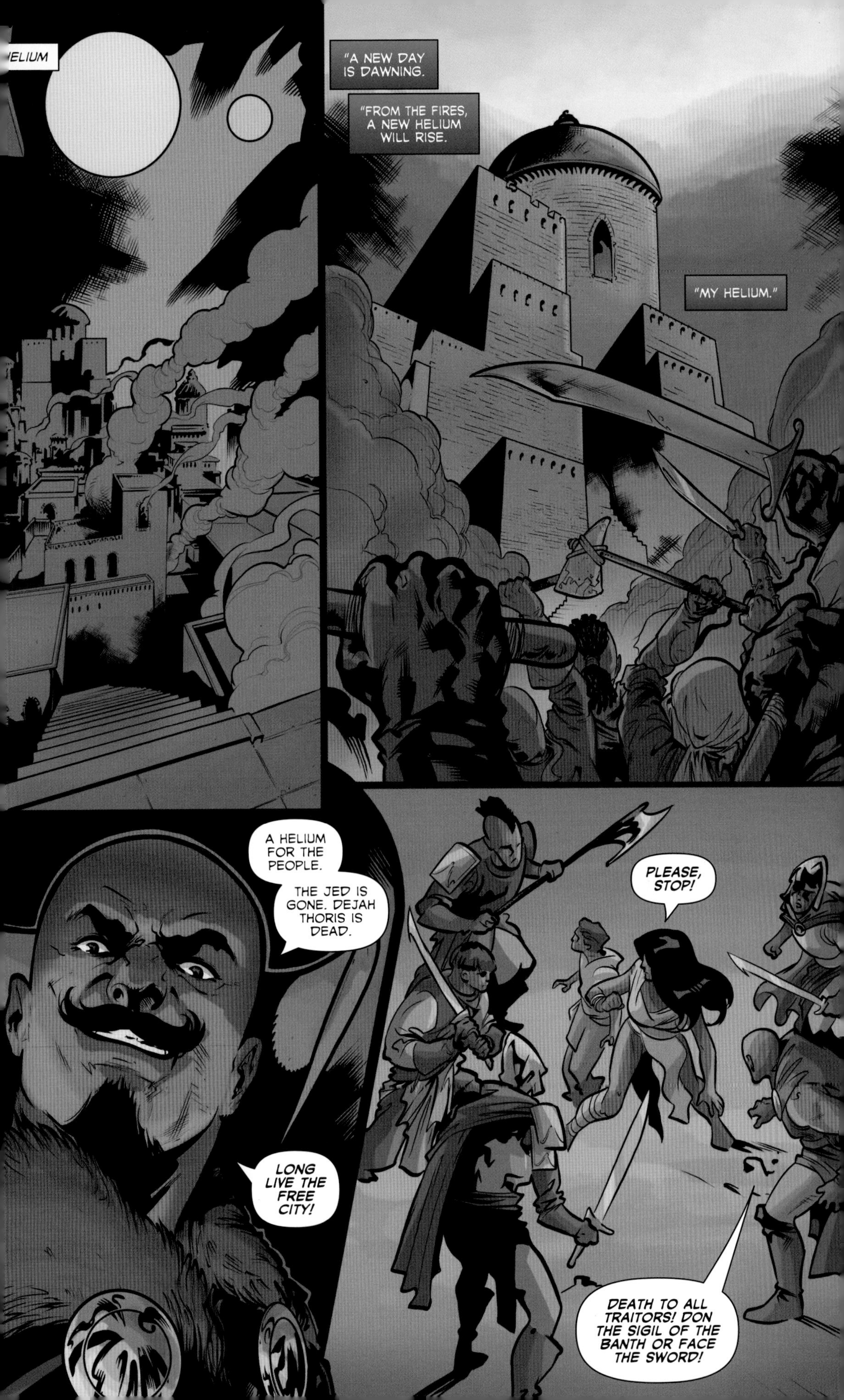
HELIUM
"A NEW DAY IS DAWNING.
"FROM THE FIRES, A NEW HELIUM WILL RISE.
"MY HELIUM."
A HELIUM FOR THE PEOPLE.
THE JED IS GONE. DEJAH THORIS IS DEAD.
LONG LIVE THE FREE CITY!
PLEASE, STOP!
DEATH TO ALL TRAITORS! DON THE SIGIL OF THE BANTH OR FACE THE SWORD!

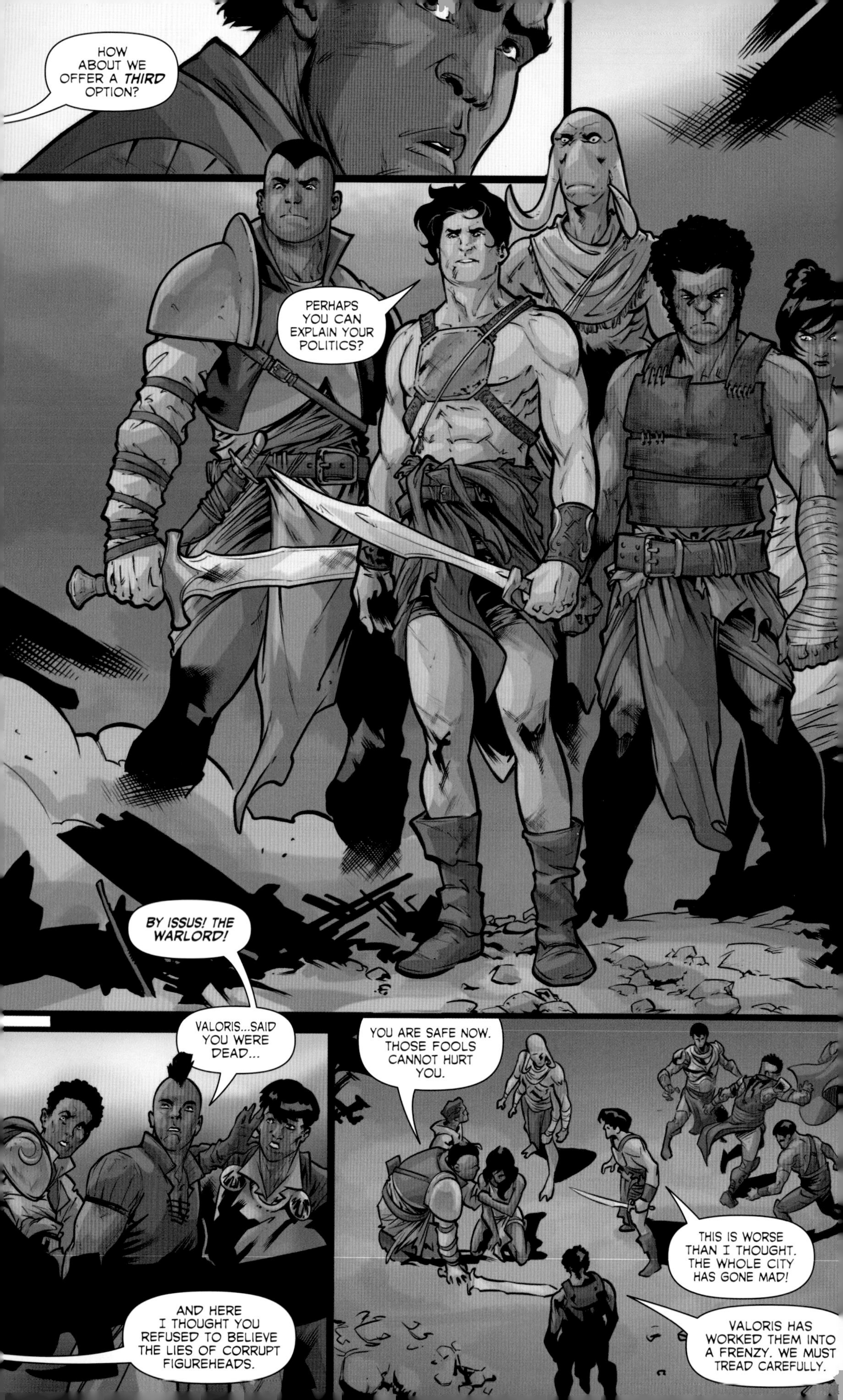
HOW ABOUT WE OFFER A *THIRD* OPTION?
PERHAPS YOU CAN EXPLAIN YOUR POLITICS?
BY ISSUS! THE WARLORD!
VALORIS...SAID YOU WERE DEAD...
AND HERE I THOUGHT YOU REFUSED TO BELIEVE THE LIES OF CORRUPT FIGUREHEADS.
YOU ARE SAFE NOW. THOSE FOOLS CANNOT HURT YOU.
THIS IS WORSE THAN I THOUGHT. THE WHOLE CITY HAS GONE MAD!
VALORIS HAS WORKED THEM INTO A FRENZY. WE MUST TREAD CAREFULLY.

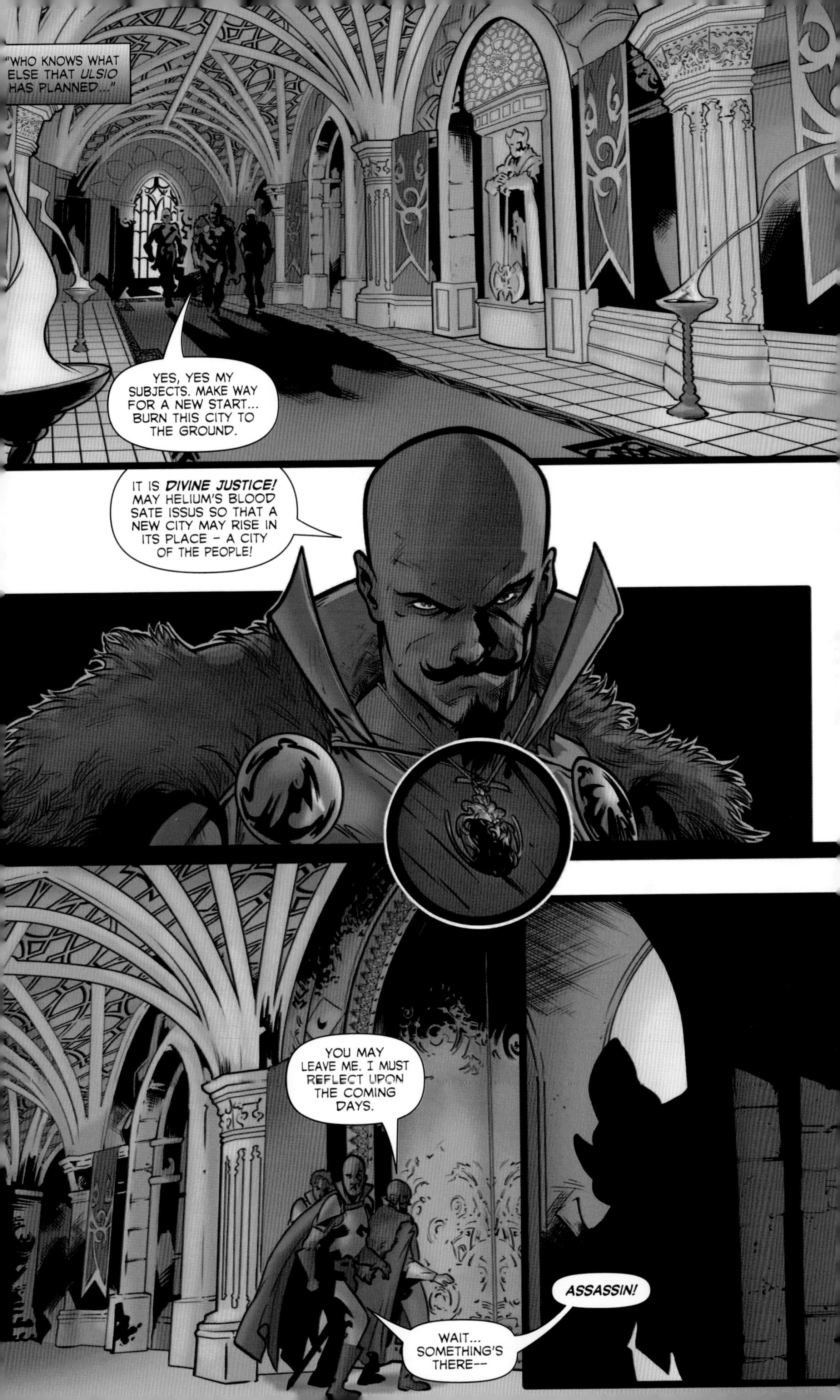
"WHO KNOWS WHAT ELSE THAT *ULSIO* HAS PLANNED..."
YES, YES MY SUBJECTS. MAKE WAY FOR A NEW START... BURN THIS CITY TO THE GROUND.
IT IS ***DIVINE JUSTICE!*** MAY HELIUM'S BLOOD SATE ISSUS SO THAT A NEW CITY MAY RISE IN ITS PLACE - A CITY OF THE PEOPLE!
YOU MAY LEAVE ME. I MUST REFLECT UPON THE COMING DAYS.
WAIT... SOMETHING'S THERE--
ASSASSIN!

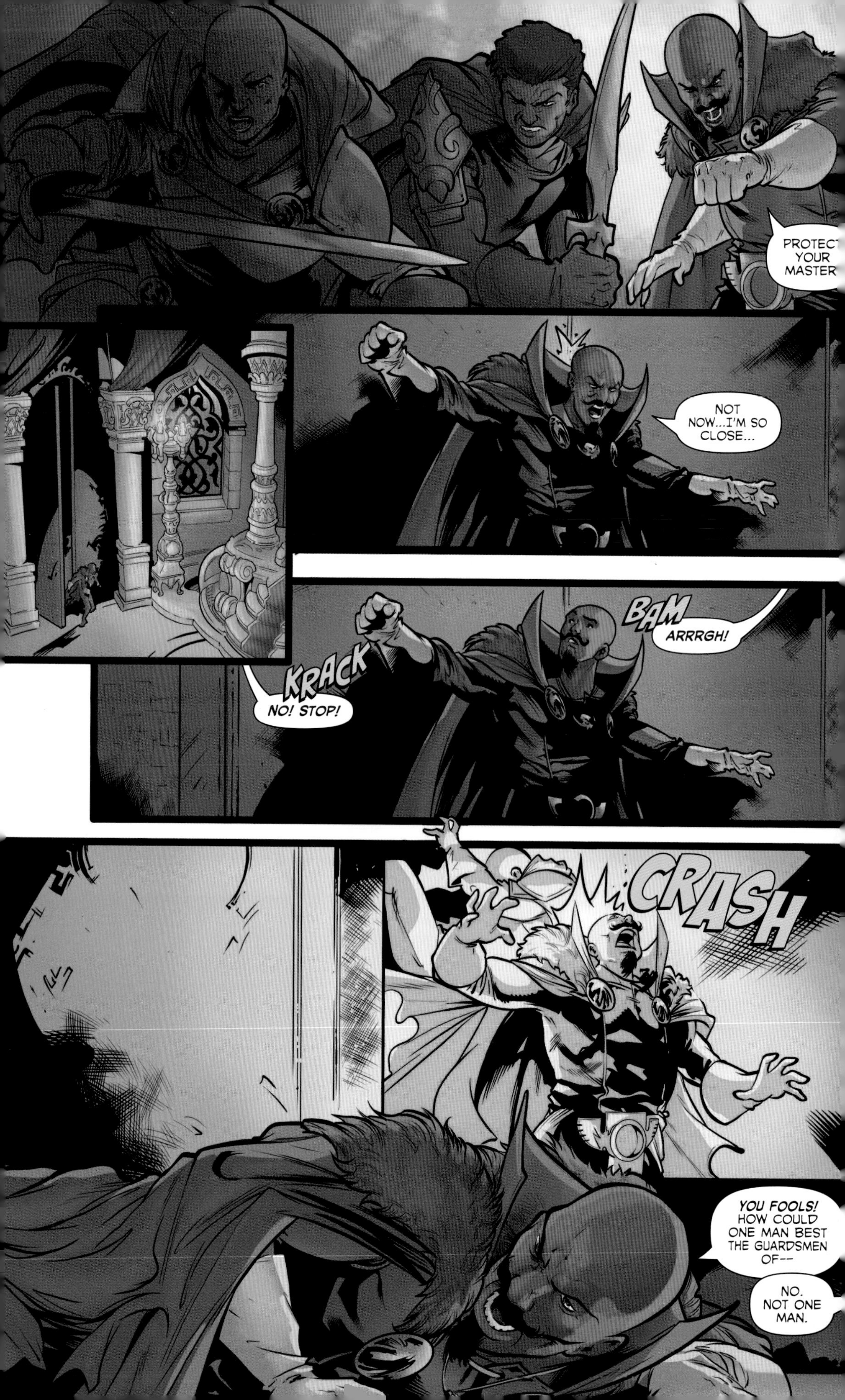
PROTECT YOUR MASTER
NOT NOW...I'M SO CLOSE...
BAM
ARRRGH!
KRACK
NO! STOP!
CRASH
YOU FOOLS! HOW COULD ONE MAN BEST THE GUARDSMEN OF--
NO. NOT ONE MAN.

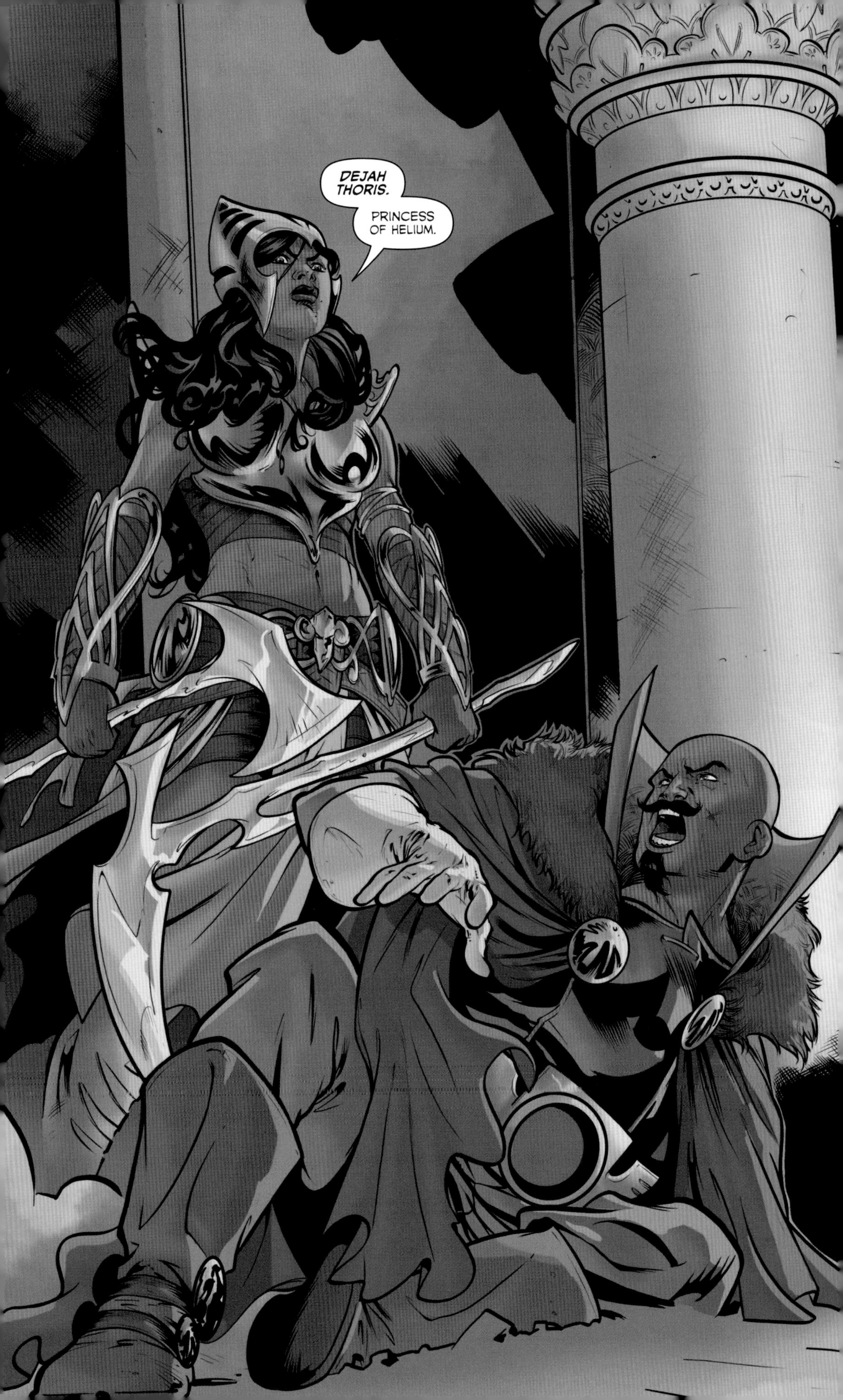
DEJAH THORIS.
PRINCESS OF HELIUM.

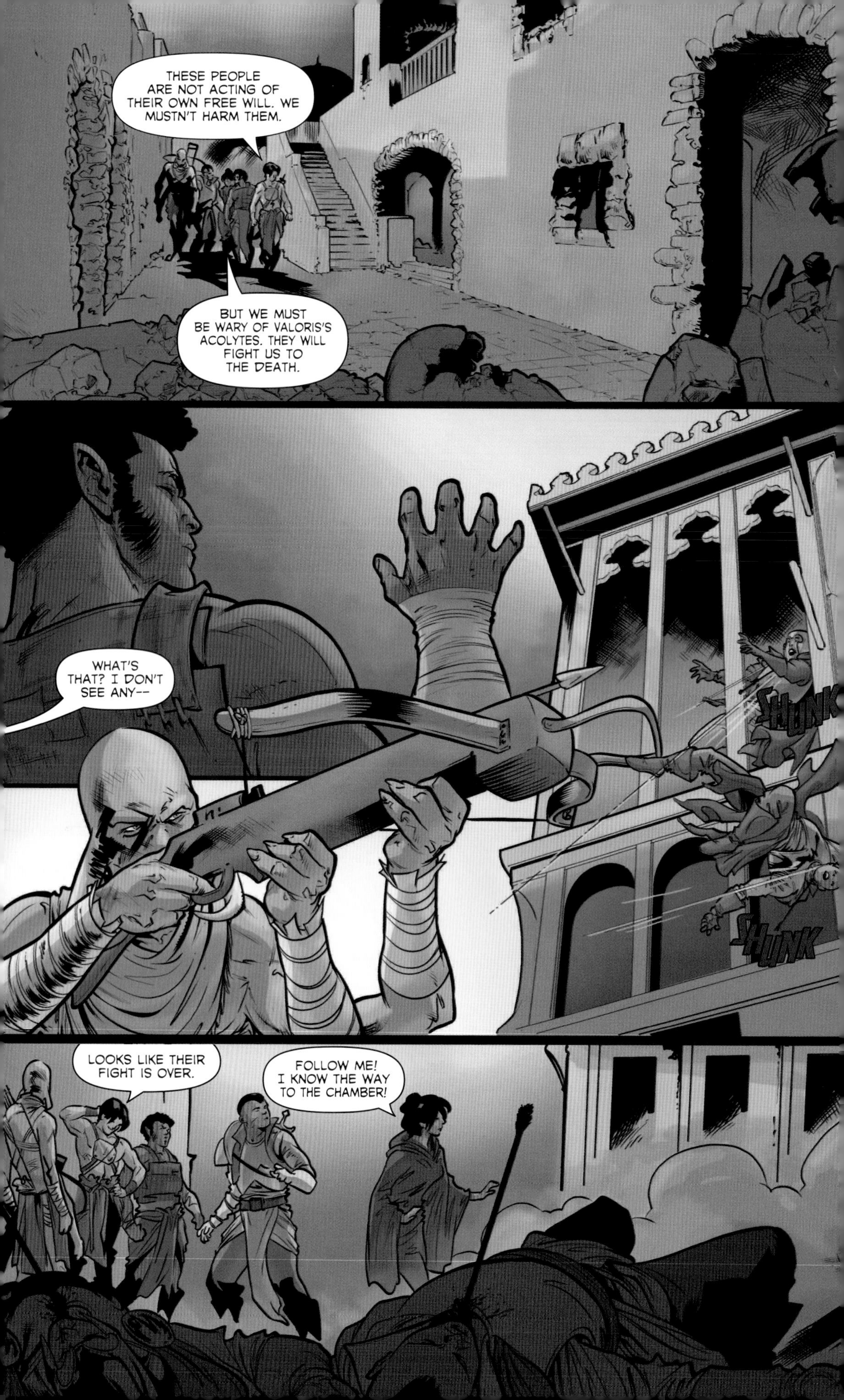
THESE PEOPLE ARE NOT ACTING OF THEIR OWN FREE WILL. WE MUSTN'T HARM THEM.
BUT WE MUST BE WARY OF VALORIS'S ACOLYTES. THEY WILL FIGHT US TO THE DEATH.
WHAT'S THAT? I DON'T SEE ANY--
SHUNK
SHUNK
LOOKS LIKE THEIR FIGHT IS OVER.
FOLLOW ME! I KNOW THE WAY TO THE CHAMBER!

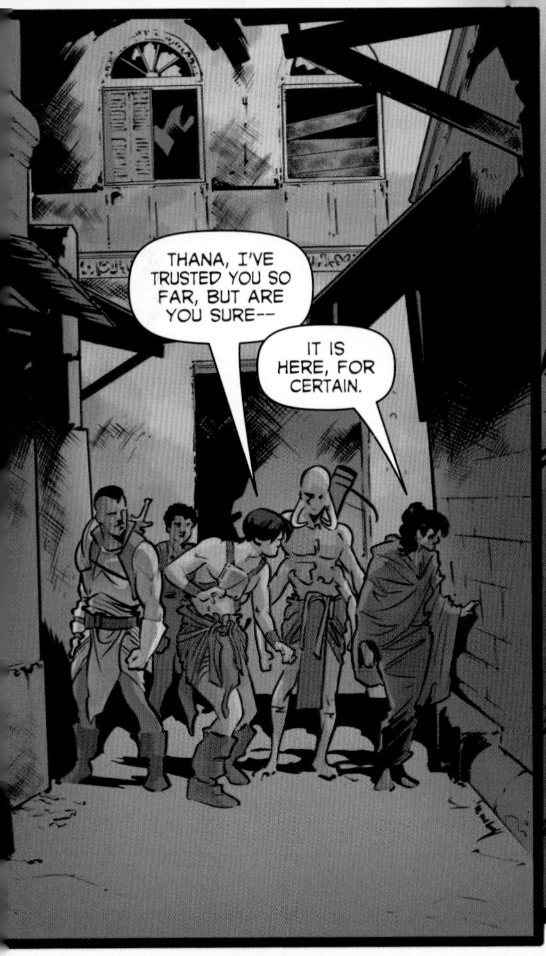
THANA, I'VE TRUSTED YOU SO FAR, BUT ARE YOU SURE--
IT IS HERE, FOR CERTAIN.

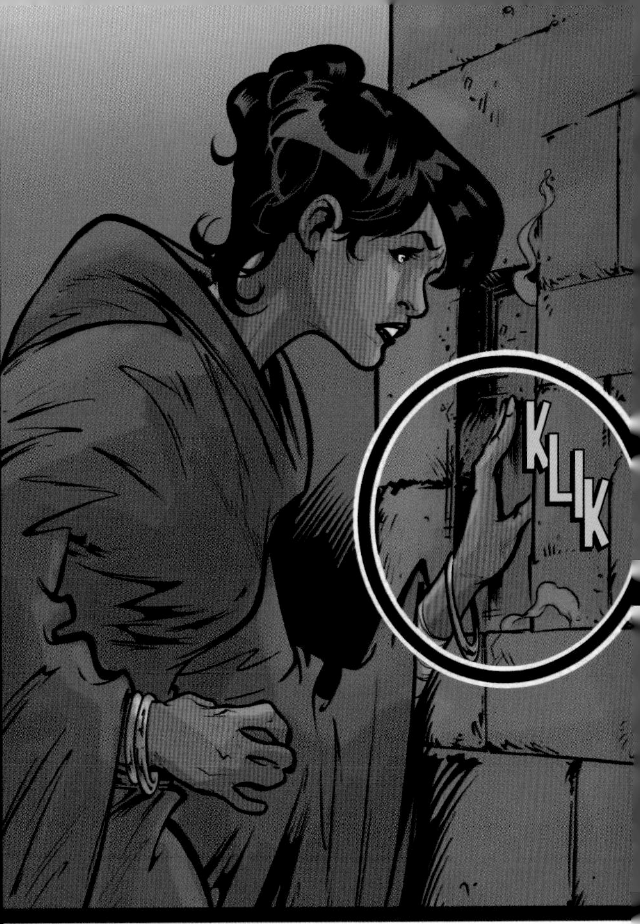
KLIK

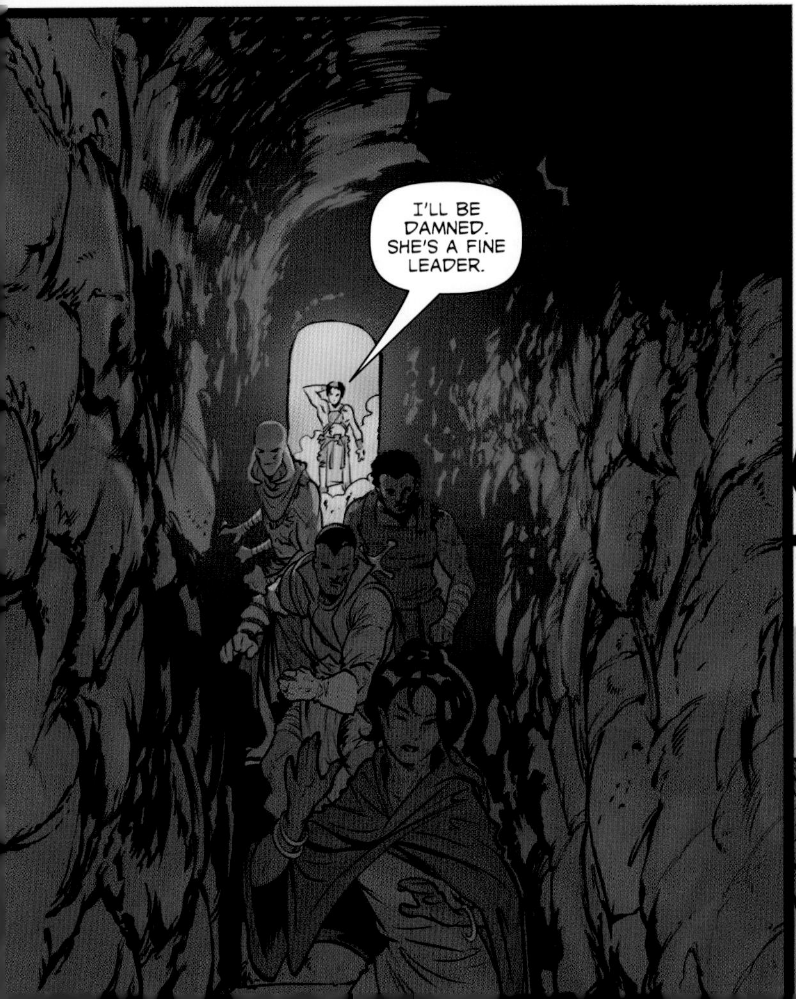
I'LL BE DAMNED. SHE'S A FINE LEADER.

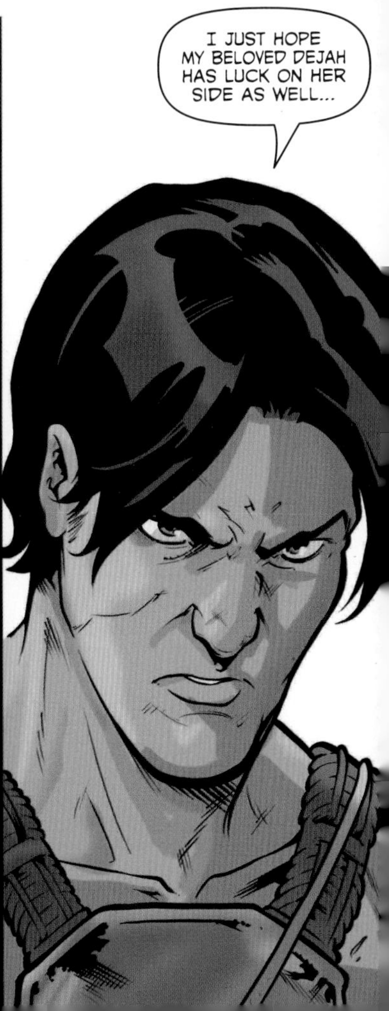
I JUST HOPE MY BELOVED DEJAH HAS LUCK ON HER SIDE AS WELL...

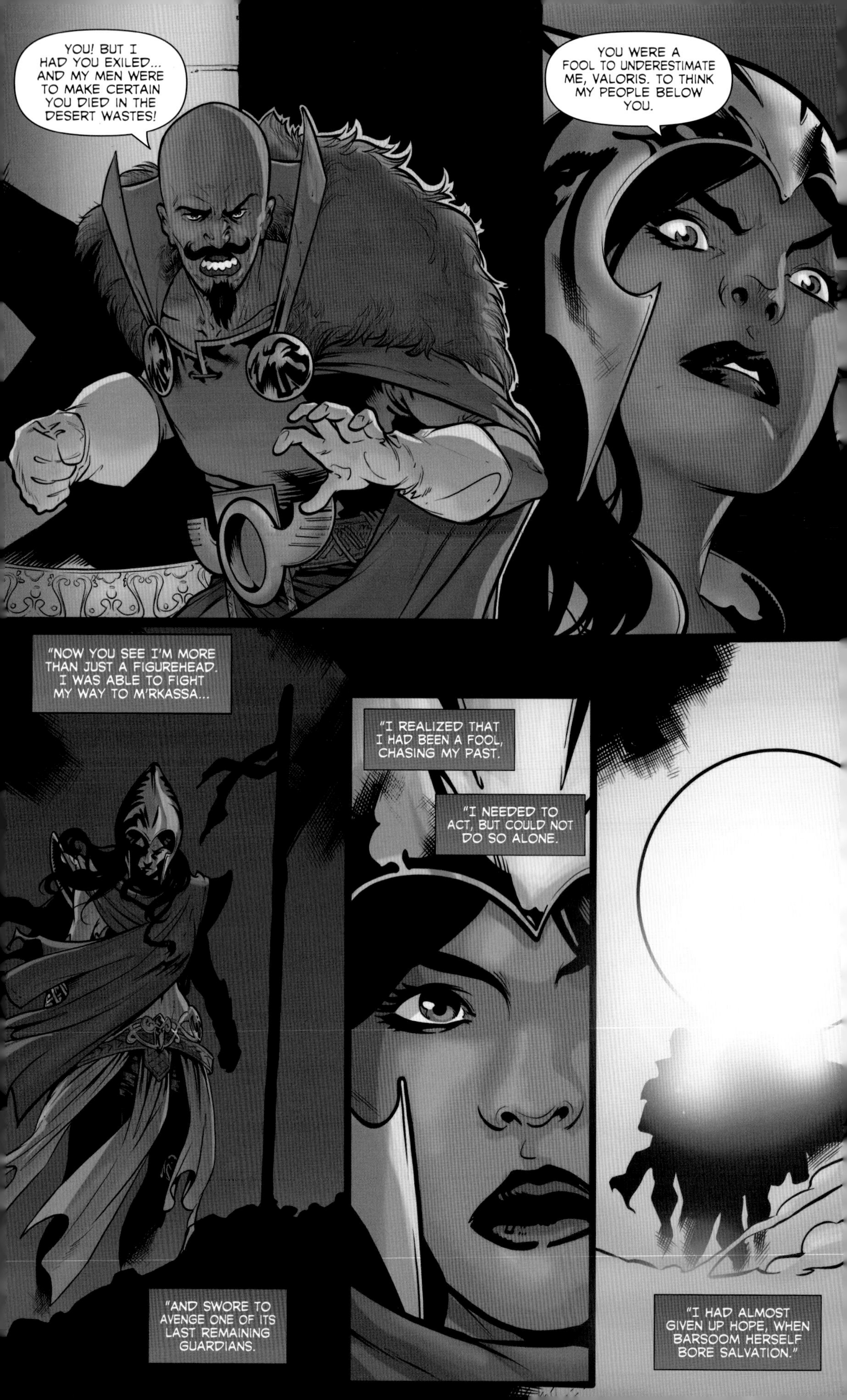
YOU! BUT I HAD YOU EXILED... AND MY MEN WERE TO MAKE CERTAIN YOU DIED IN THE DESERT WASTES!
YOU WERE A FOOL TO UNDERESTIMATE ME, VALORIS. TO THINK MY PEOPLE BELOW YOU.
"NOW YOU SEE I'M MORE THAN JUST A FIGUREHEAD. I WAS ABLE TO FIGHT MY WAY TO M'RKASSA...
"AND SWORE TO AVENGE ONE OF ITS LAST REMAINING GUARDIANS.
"I REALIZED THAT I HAD BEEN A FOOL, CHASING MY PAST.
"I NEEDED TO ACT, BUT COULD NOT DO SO ALONE.
"I HAD ALMOST GIVEN UP HOPE, WHEN BARSOOM HERSELF BORE SALVATION."

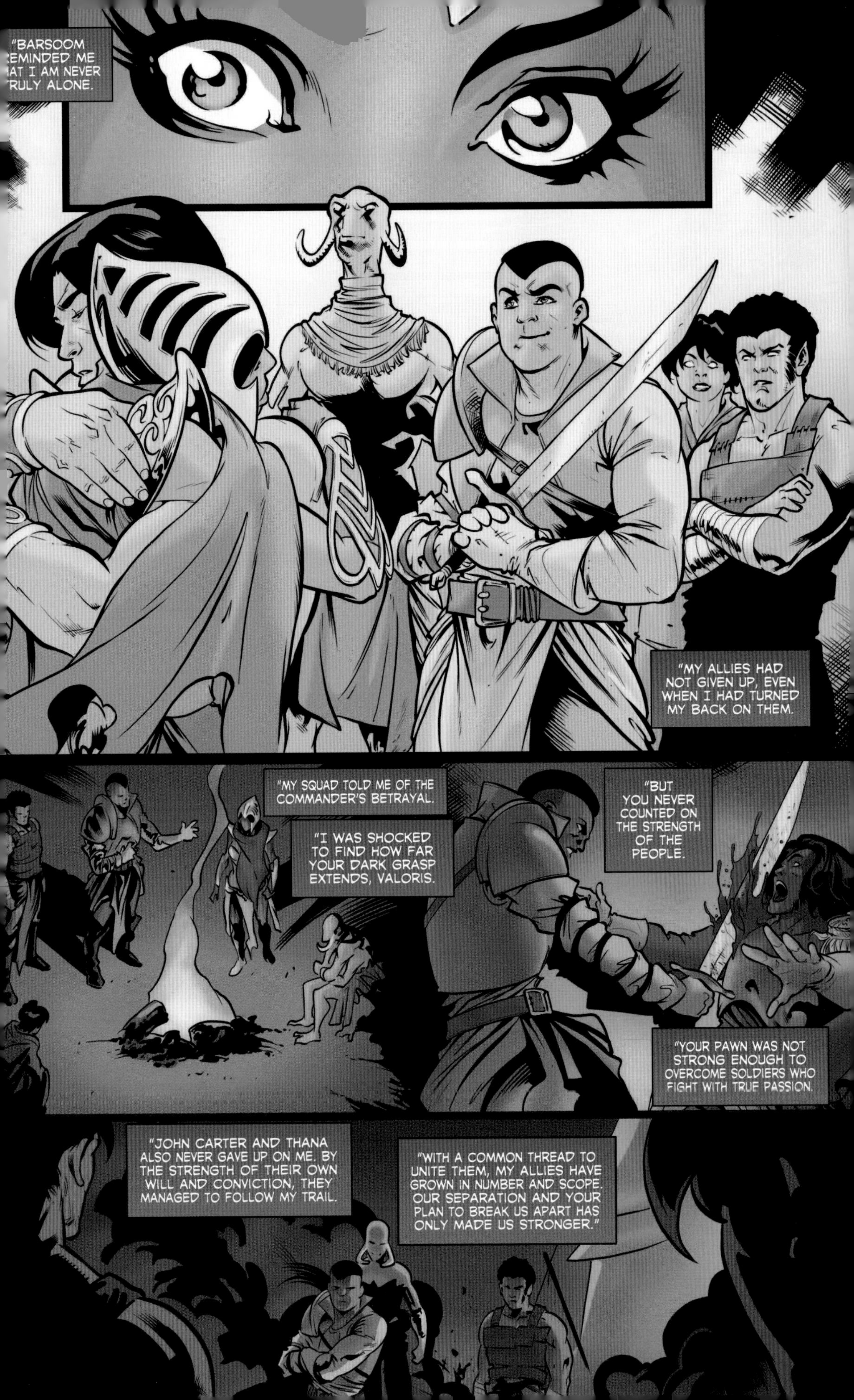
"BARSOOM REMINDED ME THAT I AM NEVER TRULY ALONE.
"MY ALLIES HAD NOT GIVEN UP, EVEN WHEN I HAD TURNED MY BACK ON THEM.
"MY SQUAD TOLD ME OF THE COMMANDER'S BETRAYAL.
"I WAS SHOCKED TO FIND HOW FAR YOUR DARK GRASP EXTENDS, VALORIS.
"BUT YOU NEVER COUNTED ON THE STRENGTH OF THE PEOPLE.
"YOUR PAWN WAS NOT STRONG ENOUGH TO OVERCOME SOLDIERS WHO FIGHT WITH TRUE PASSION.
"JOHN CARTER AND THANA ALSO NEVER GAVE UP ON ME. BY THE STRENGTH OF THEIR OWN WILL AND CONVICTION, THEY MANAGED TO FOLLOW MY TRAIL.
"WITH A COMMON THREAD TO UNITE THEM, MY ALLIES HAVE GROWN IN NUMBER AND SCOPE. OUR SEPARATION AND YOUR PLAN TO BREAK US APART HAS ONLY MADE US STRONGER."

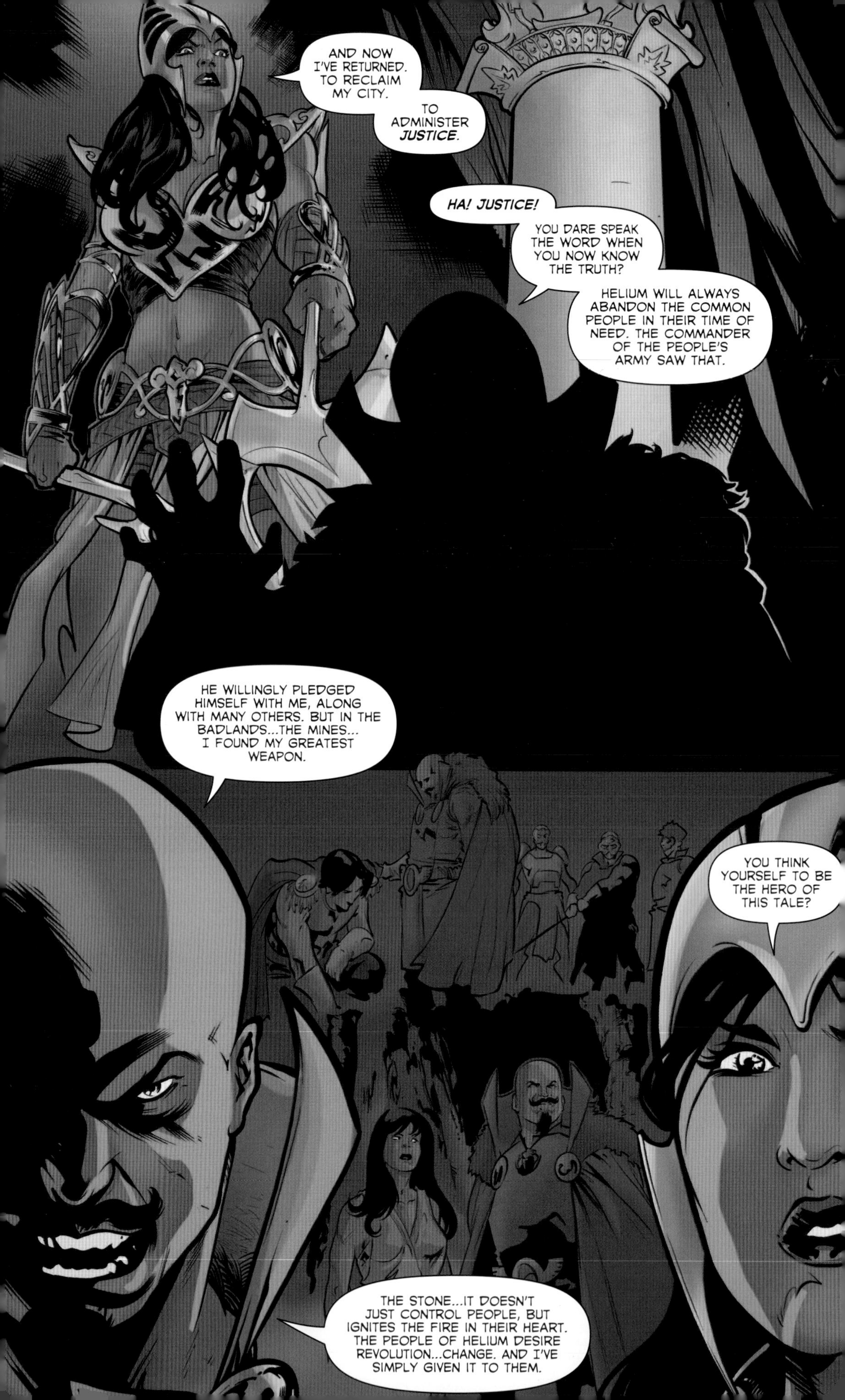
AND NOW I'VE RETURNED. TO RECLAIM MY CITY.
TO ADMINISTER *JUSTICE*.
HA! JUSTICE!
YOU DARE SPEAK THE WORD WHEN YOU NOW KNOW THE TRUTH?
HELIUM WILL ALWAYS ABANDON THE COMMON PEOPLE IN THEIR TIME OF NEED. THE COMMANDER OF THE PEOPLE'S ARMY SAW THAT.
HE WILLINGLY PLEDGED HIMSELF WITH ME, ALONG WITH MANY OTHERS. BUT IN THE BADLANDS...THE MINES... I FOUND MY GREATEST WEAPON.
YOU THINK YOURSELF TO BE THE HERO OF THIS TALE?
THE STONE...IT DOESN'T JUST CONTROL PEOPLE, BUT IGNITES THE FIRE IN THEIR HEART. THE PEOPLE OF HELIUM DESIRE REVOLUTION...CHANGE. AND I'VE SIMPLY GIVEN IT TO THEM.

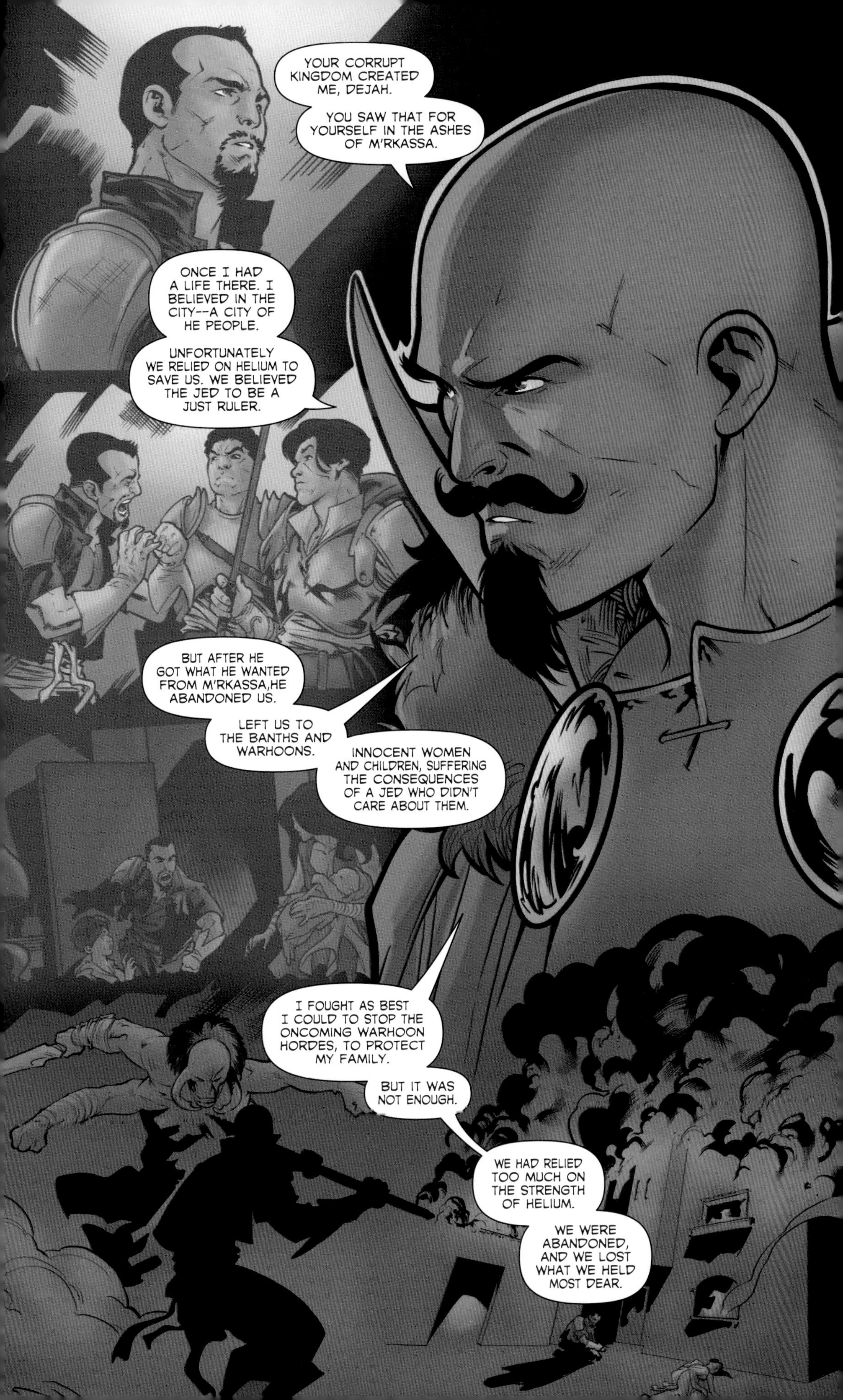
YOUR CORRUPT KINGDOM CREATED ME, DEJAH.
YOU SAW THAT FOR YOURSELF IN THE ASHES OF M'RKASSA.
ONCE I HAD A LIFE THERE. I BELIEVED IN THE CITY--A CITY OF HE PEOPLE.
UNFORTUNATELY WE RELIED ON HELIUM TO SAVE US. WE BELIEVED THE JED TO BE A JUST RULER.
BUT AFTER HE GOT WHAT HE WANTED FROM M'RKASSA,HE ABANDONED US.
LEFT US TO THE BANTHS AND WARHOONS.
INNOCENT WOMEN AND CHILDREN, SUFFERING THE CONSEQUENCES OF A JED WHO DIDN'T CARE ABOUT THEM.
I FOUGHT AS BEST I COULD TO STOP THE ONCOMING WARHOON HORDES, TO PROTECT MY FAMILY.
BUT IT WAS NOT ENOUGH.
WE HAD RELIED TOO MUCH ON THE STRENGTH OF HELIUM.
WE WERE ABANDONED, AND WE LOST WHAT WE HELD MOST DEAR.

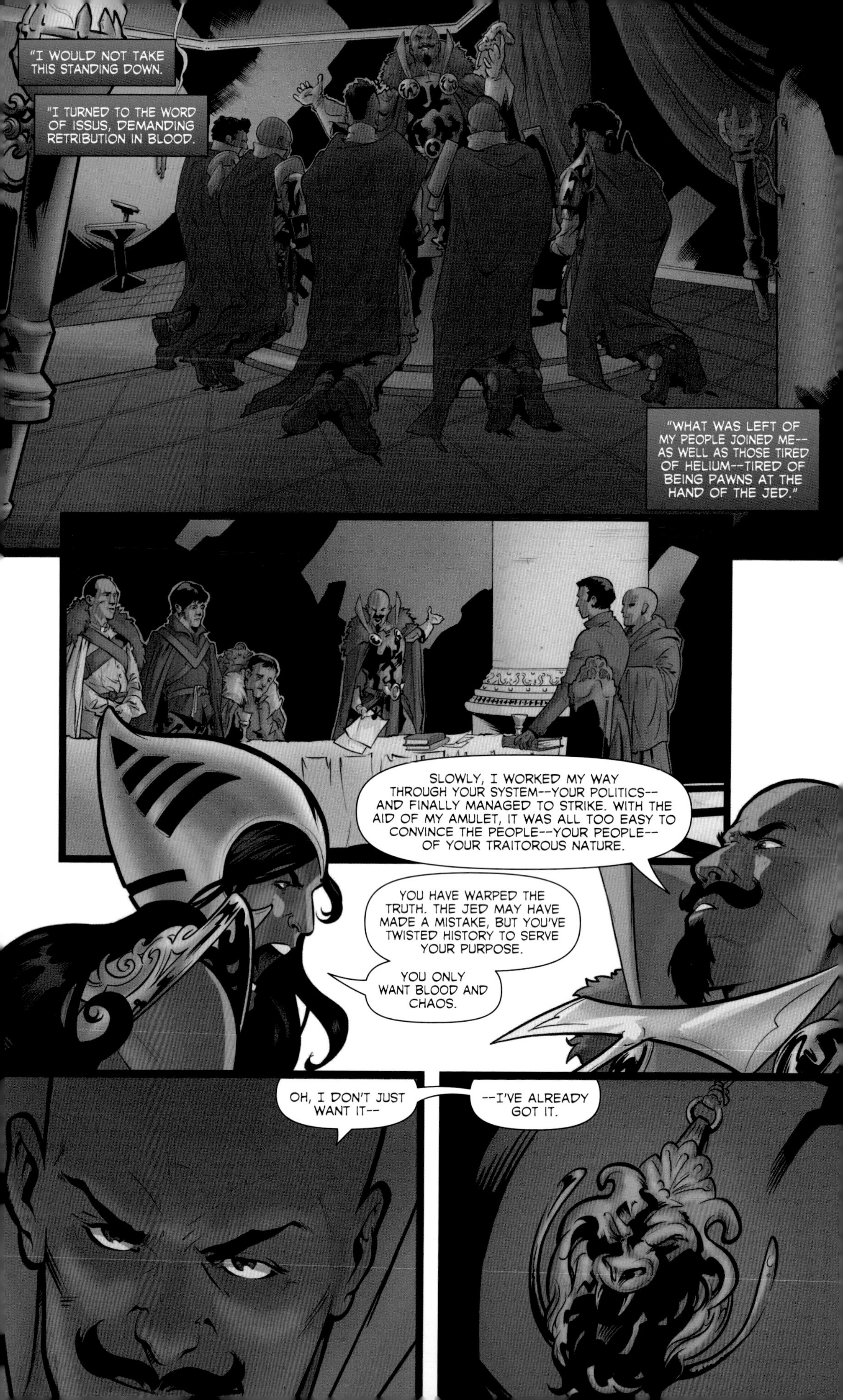
"I WOULD NOT TAKE THIS STANDING DOWN.
"I TURNED TO THE WORD OF ISSUS, DEMANDING RETRIBUTION IN BLOOD.
"WHAT WAS LEFT OF MY PEOPLE JOINED ME--AS WELL AS THOSE TIRED OF HELIUM--TIRED OF BEING PAWNS AT THE HAND OF THE JED."
SLOWLY, I WORKED MY WAY THROUGH YOUR SYSTEM--YOUR POLITICS--AND FINALLY MANAGED TO STRIKE. WITH THE AID OF MY AMULET, IT WAS ALL TOO EASY TO CONVINCE THE PEOPLE--YOUR PEOPLE--OF YOUR TRAITOROUS NATURE.
YOU HAVE WARPED THE TRUTH. THE JED MAY HAVE MADE A MISTAKE, BUT YOU'VE TWISTED HISTORY TO SERVE YOUR PURPOSE.
YOU ONLY WANT BLOOD AND CHAOS.
OH, I DON'T JUST WANT IT--
--I'VE ALREADY GOT IT.

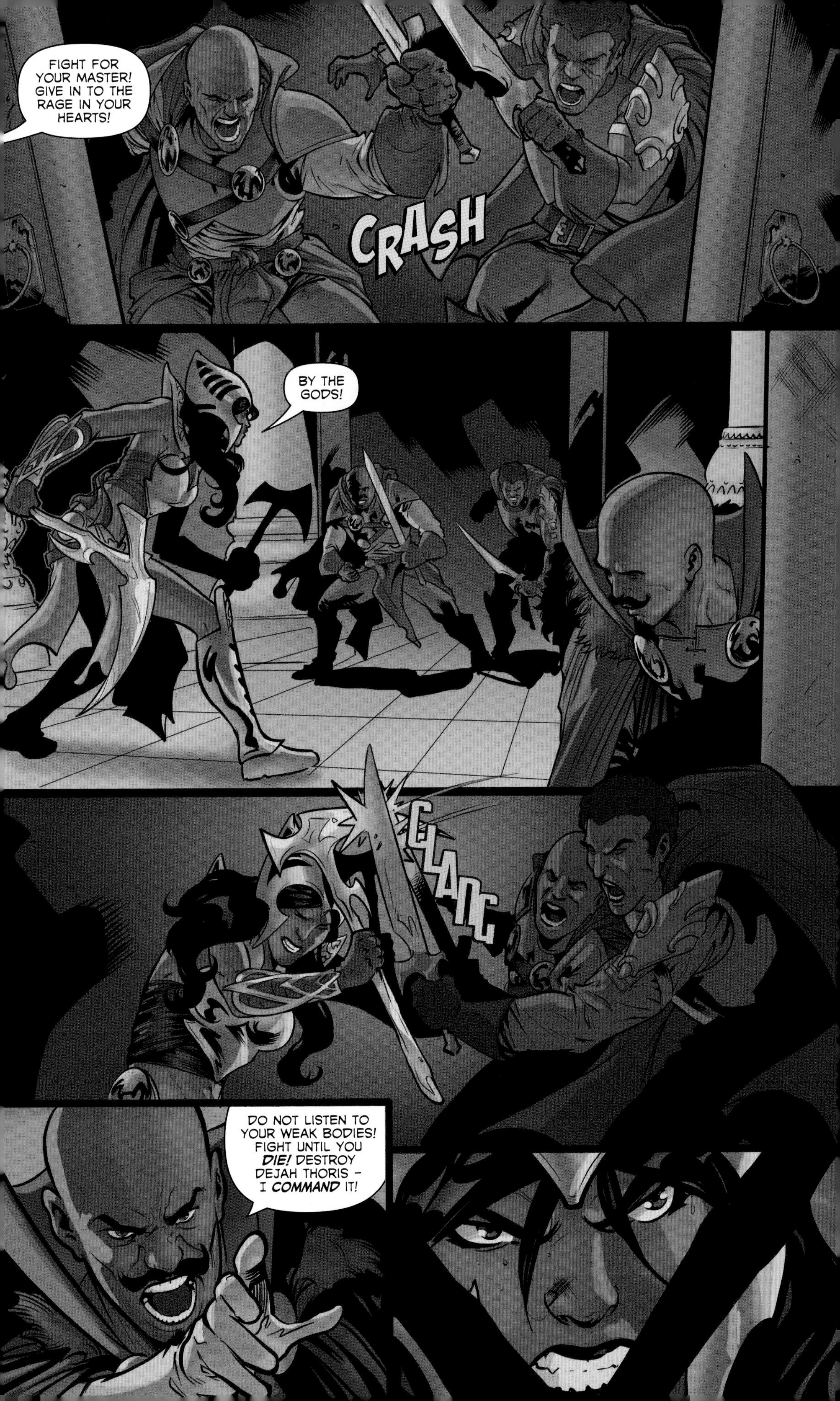

FIGHT FOR YOUR MASTER! GIVE IN TO THE RAGE IN YOUR HEARTS!
CRASH
BY THE GODS!
CLANG
DO NOT LISTEN TO YOUR WEAK BODIES! FIGHT UNTIL YOU *DIE!* DESTROY DEJAH THORIS – I *COMMAND* IT!

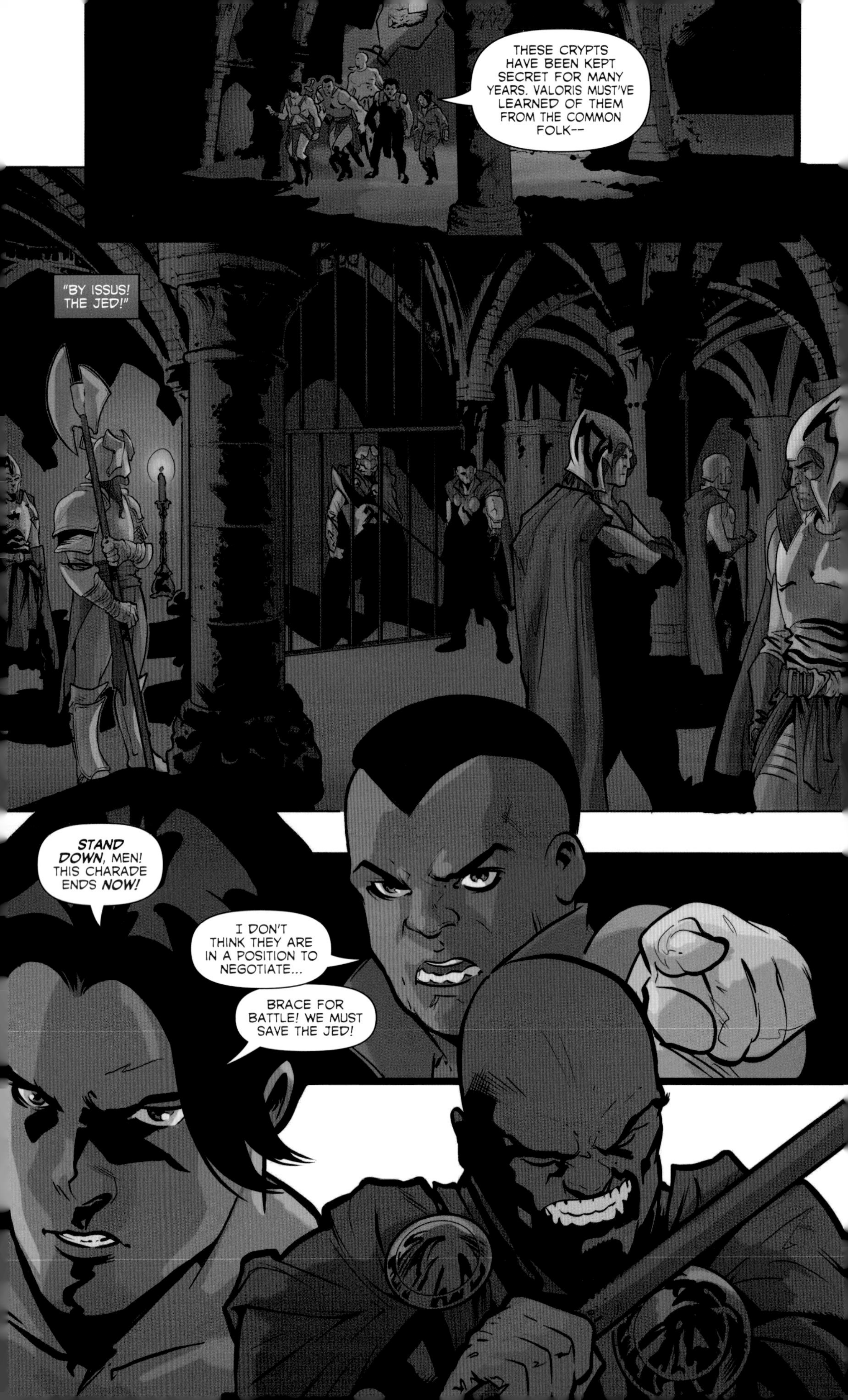
THESE CRYPTS HAVE BEEN KEPT SECRET FOR MANY YEARS. VALORIS MUST'VE LEARNED OF THEM FROM THE COMMON FOLK--
"BY ISSUS! THE JED!"
STAND DOWN, MEN! THIS CHARADE ENDS NOW!
I DON'T THINK THEY ARE IN A POSITION TO NEGOTIATE...
BRACE FOR BATTLE! WE MUST SAVE THE JED!

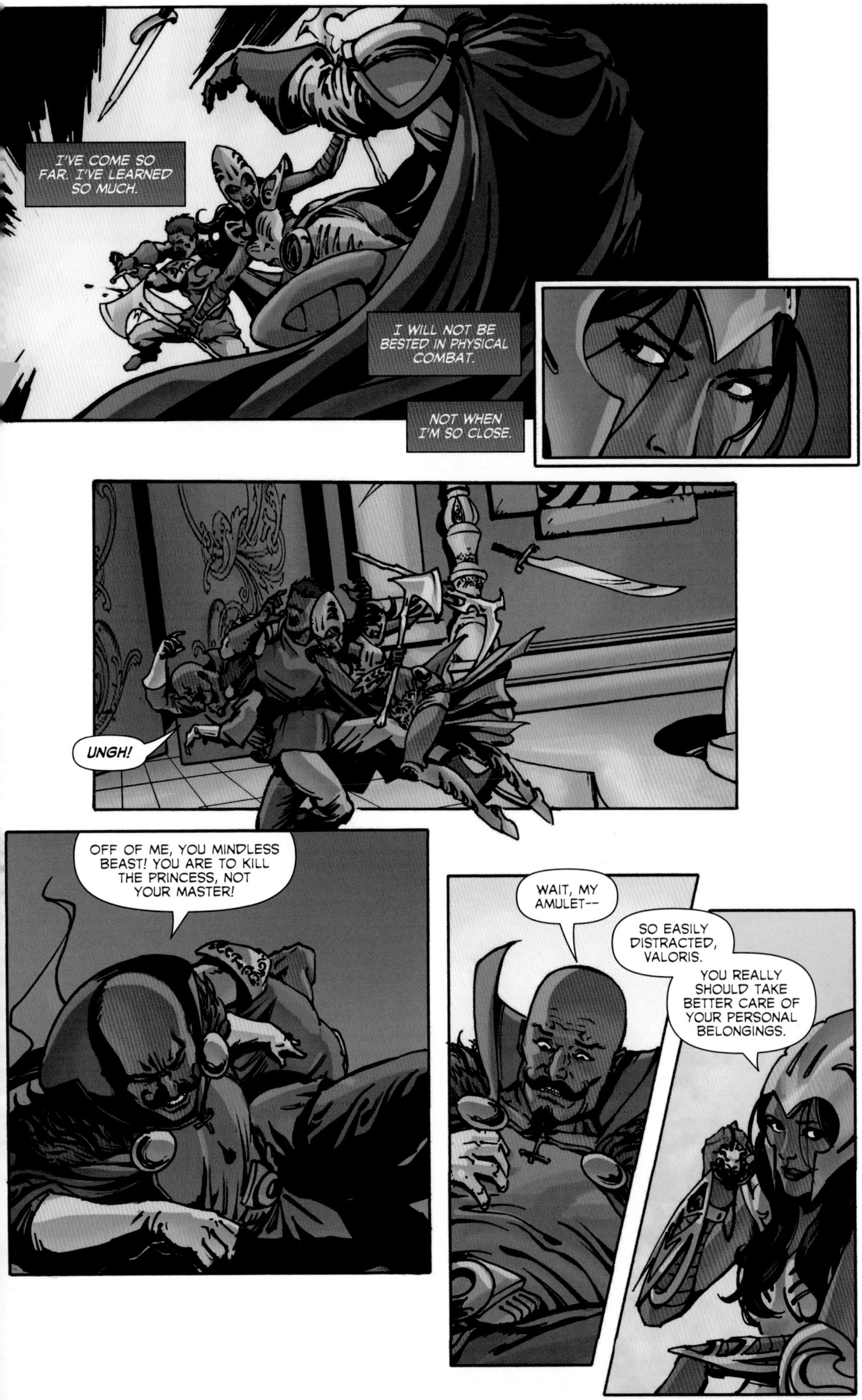
I'VE COME SO FAR. I'VE LEARNED SO MUCH.
I WILL NOT BE BESTED IN PHYSICAL COMBAT.
NOT WHEN I'M SO CLOSE.
UNGH!
OFF OF ME, YOU MINDLESS BEAST! YOU ARE TO KILL THE PRINCESS, NOT YOUR MASTER!
WAIT, MY AMULET--
SO EASILY DISTRACTED, VALORIS.
YOU REALLY SHOULD TAKE BETTER CARE OF YOUR PERSONAL BELONGINGS.

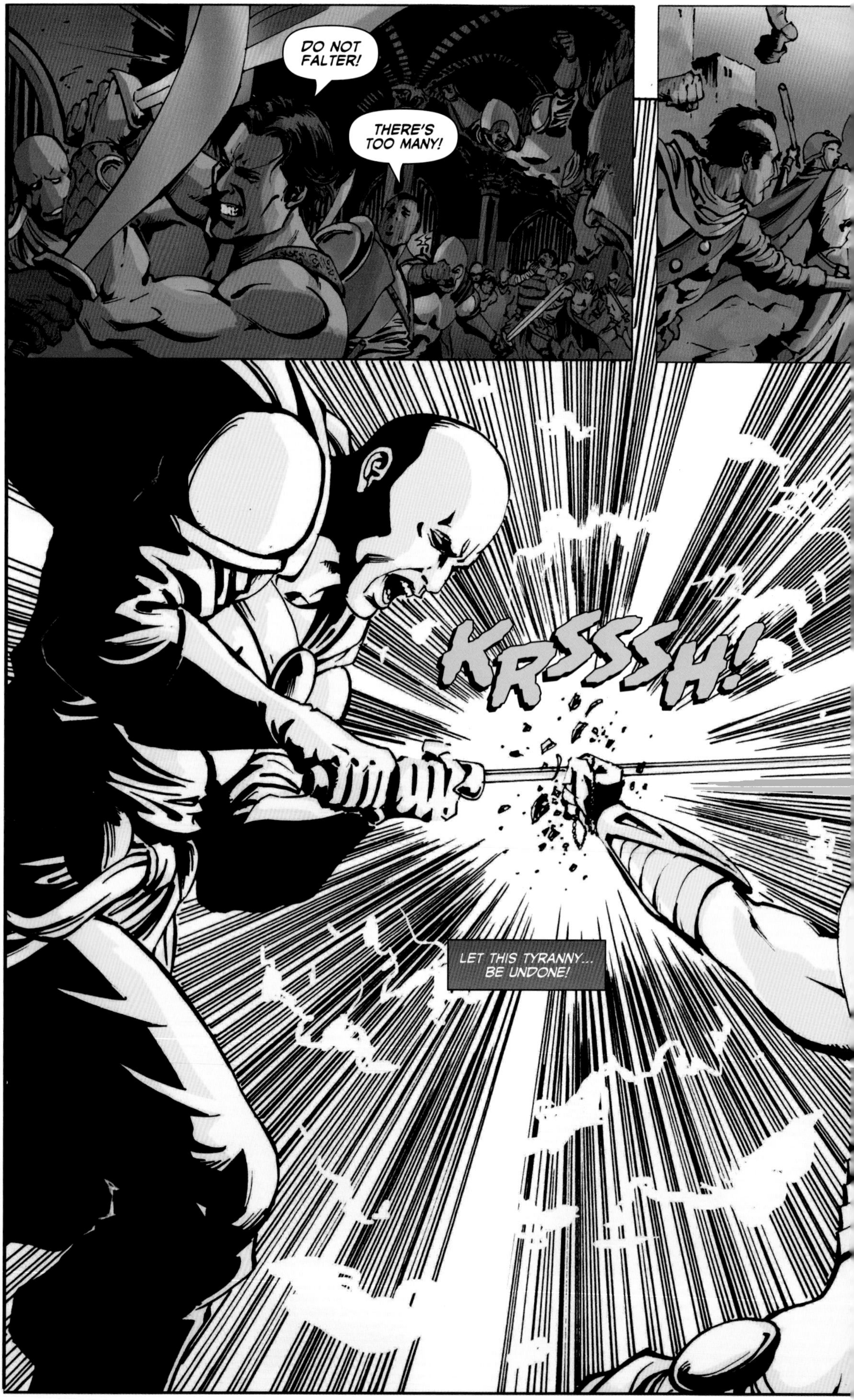
DO NOT FALTER!
THERE'S TOO MANY!
KRSSSH!
LET THIS TYRANNY... BE UNDONE!

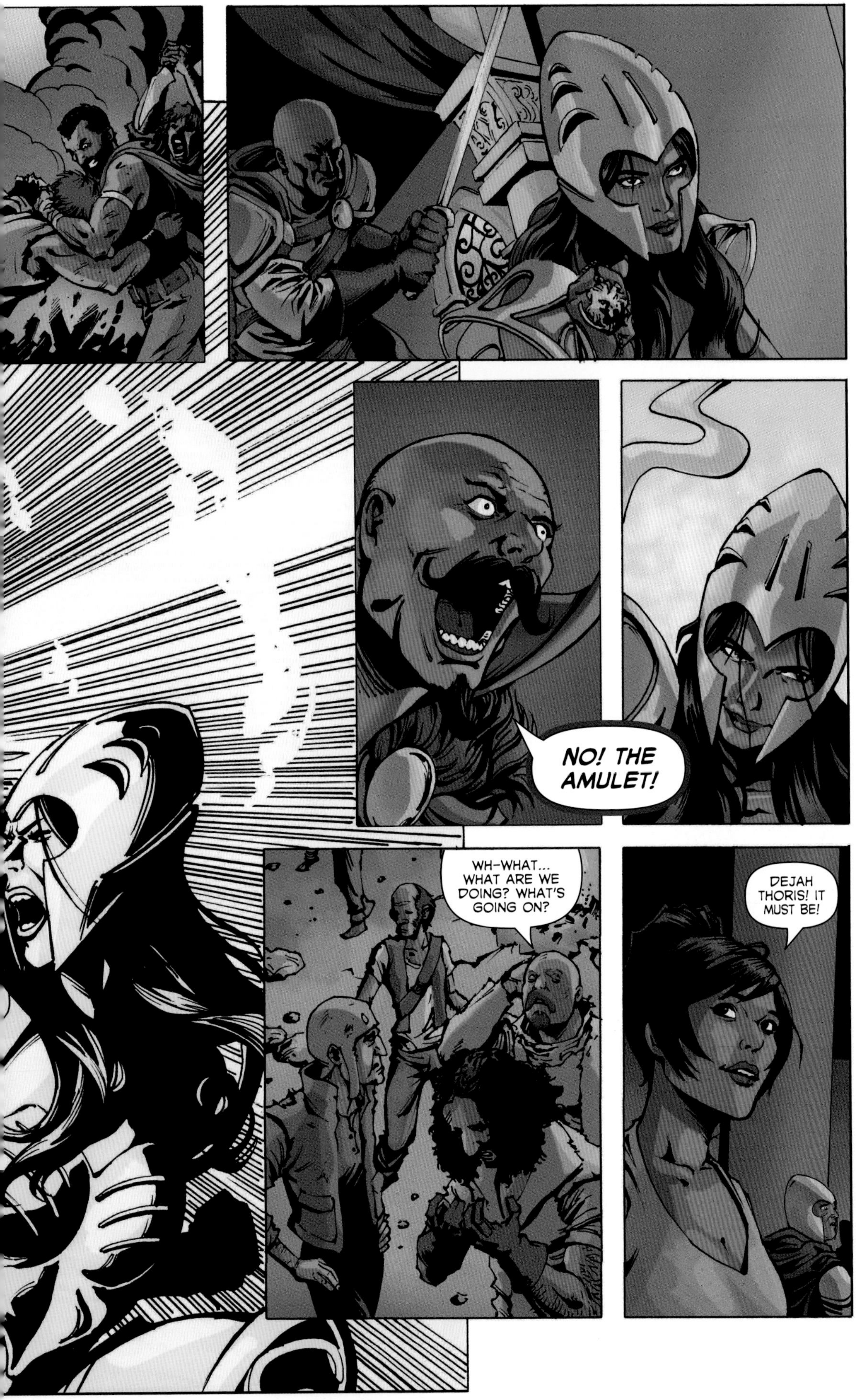
NO! THE AMULET!
WH-WHAT... WHAT ARE WE DOING? WHAT'S GOING ON?
DEJAH THORIS! IT MUST BE!

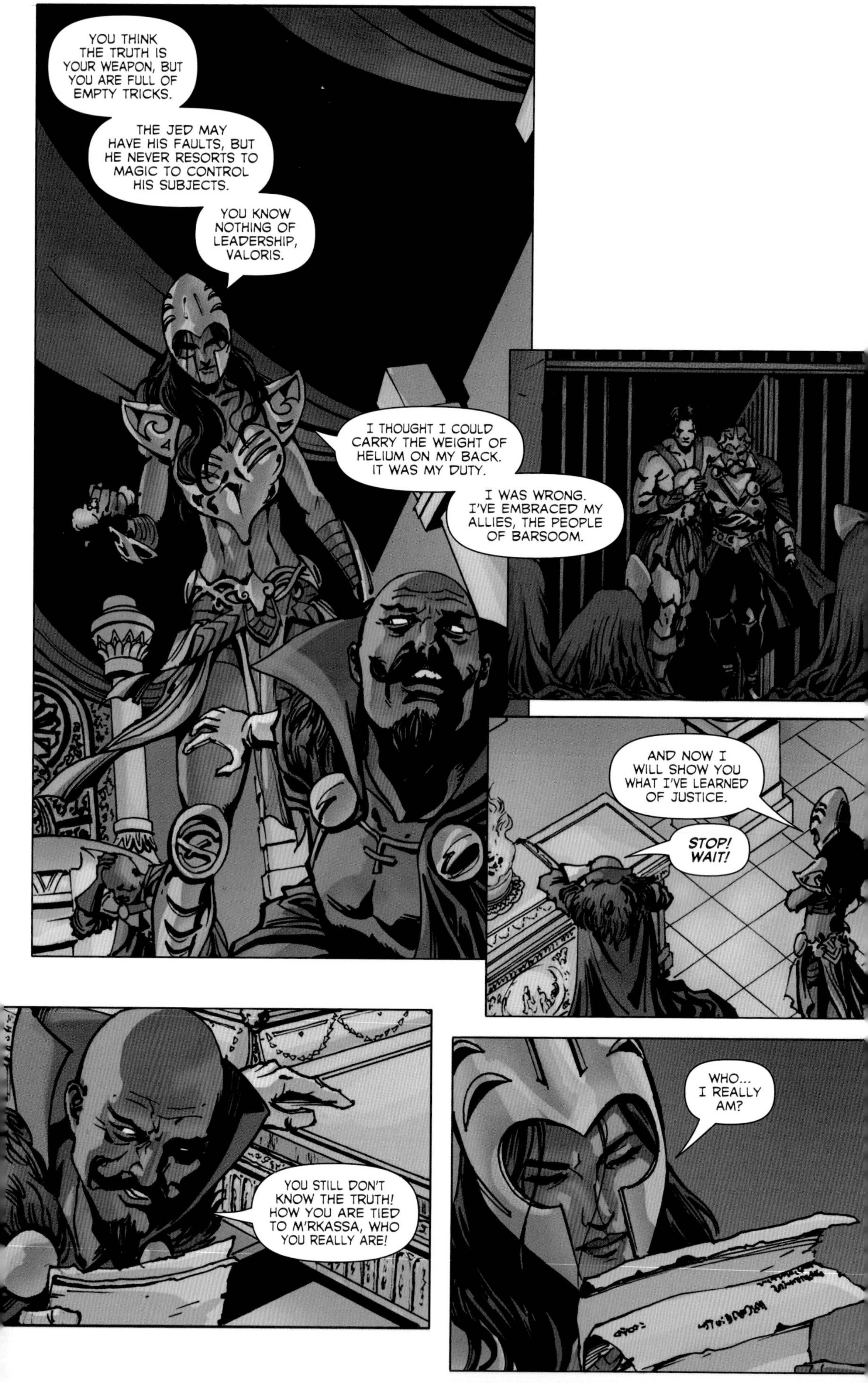
YOU THINK THE TRUTH IS YOUR WEAPON, BUT YOU ARE FULL OF EMPTY TRICKS.
THE JED MAY HAVE HIS FAULTS, BUT HE NEVER RESORTS TO MAGIC TO CONTROL HIS SUBJECTS.
YOU KNOW NOTHING OF LEADERSHIP, VALORIS.
I THOUGHT I COULD CARRY THE WEIGHT OF HELIUM ON MY BACK. IT WAS MY DUTY.
I WAS WRONG. I'VE EMBRACED MY ALLIES, THE PEOPLE OF BARSOOM.
AND NOW I WILL SHOW YOU WHAT I'VE LEARNED OF JUSTICE.
STOP! WAIT!
YOU STILL DON'T KNOW THE TRUTH! HOW YOU ARE TIED TO M'RKASSA, WHO YOU REALLY ARE!
WHO... I REALLY AM?

I KNOW *EXACTLY* WHO I AM, VALORIS.

IT'S TIME TO ADDRESS YOUR SUBJECTS. I THINK THEY'LL BE INTERESTED TO HEAR WHAT YOU'VE DONE.

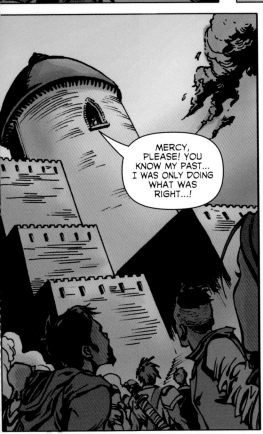

MERCY, PLEASE! YOU KNOW MY PAST... I WAS ONLY DOING WHAT WAS RIGHT...!

PEOPLE OF HELIUM. IT IS I, DEJAH THORIS, YOUR PRINCESS.

THIS MAN HAS BETRAYED THE KINGDOM.

HE FRAMED ME FOR MURDER, KIDNAPPED YOUR JED.

HE CONTROLLED YOU WITH STRANGE MAGICS AND TRIED TO TEAR THIS CITY APART.

I'VE TRAVELED FAR AND WIDE, AND SEARCHED DEEP WITHIN MYSELF.

AS YOUR PRINCESS, I DEMAND JUSTICE FOR WHAT THIS MAN HAS DONE.

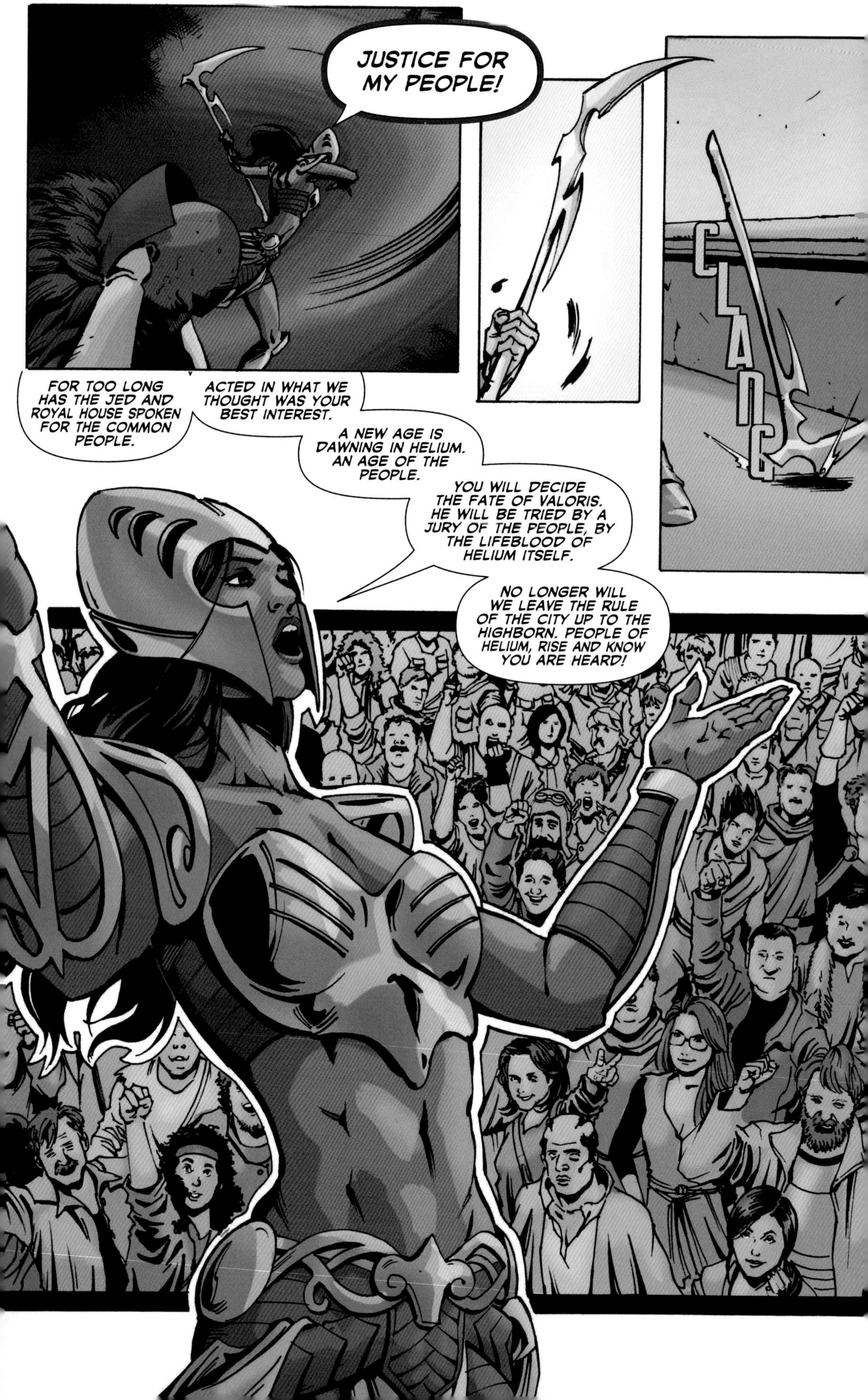
JUSTICE FOR MY PEOPLE!
CLANG
FOR TOO LONG HAS THE JED AND ROYAL HOUSE SPOKEN FOR THE COMMON PEOPLE.
ACTED IN WHAT WE THOUGHT WAS YOUR BEST INTEREST.
A NEW AGE IS DAWNING IN HELIUM. AN AGE OF THE PEOPLE.
YOU WILL DECIDE THE FATE OF VALORIS. HE WILL BE TRIED BY A JURY OF THE PEOPLE, BY THE LIFEBLOOD OF HELIUM ITSELF.
NO LONGER WILL WE LEAVE THE RULE OF THE CITY UP TO THE HIGHBORN. PEOPLE OF HELIUM, RISE AND KNOW YOU ARE HEARD!

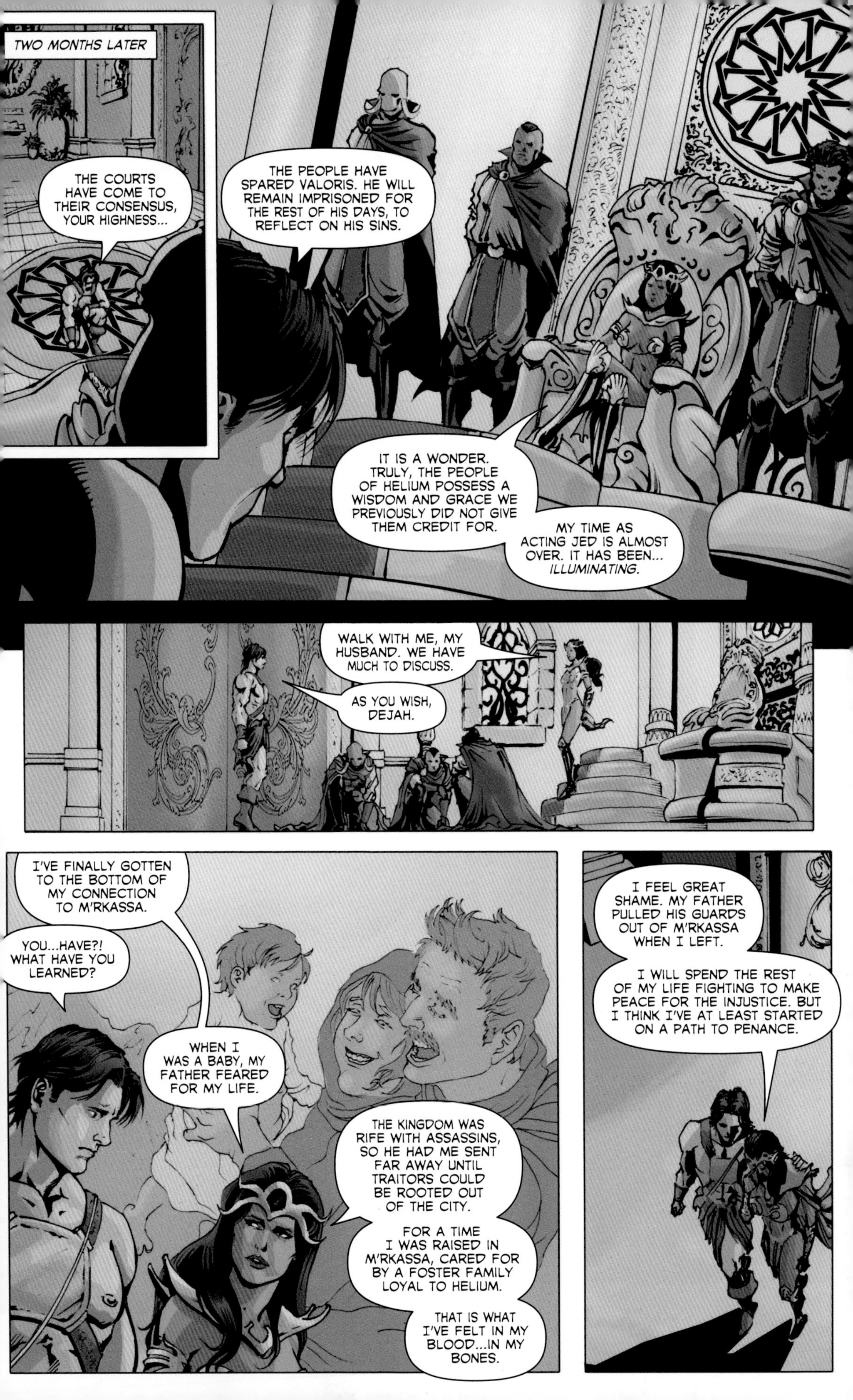
TWO MONTHS LATER
THE COURTS HAVE COME TO THEIR CONSENSUS, YOUR HIGHNESS...
THE PEOPLE HAVE SPARED VALORIS. HE WILL REMAIN IMPRISONED FOR THE REST OF HIS DAYS, TO REFLECT ON HIS SINS.
IT IS A WONDER. TRULY, THE PEOPLE OF HELIUM POSSESS A WISDOM AND GRACE WE PREVIOUSLY DID NOT GIVE THEM CREDIT FOR.
MY TIME AS ACTING JED IS ALMOST OVER. IT HAS BEEN... *ILLUMINATING.*
WALK WITH ME, MY HUSBAND. WE HAVE MUCH TO DISCUSS.
AS YOU WISH, DEJAH.
I'VE FINALLY GOTTEN TO THE BOTTOM OF MY CONNECTION TO M'RKASSA.
YOU...HAVE?! WHAT HAVE YOU LEARNED?
WHEN I WAS A BABY, MY FATHER FEARED FOR MY LIFE.
THE KINGDOM WAS RIFE WITH ASSASSINS, SO HE HAD ME SENT FAR AWAY UNTIL TRAITORS COULD BE ROOTED OUT OF THE CITY.
FOR A TIME I WAS RAISED IN M'RKASSA, CARED FOR BY A FOSTER FAMILY LOYAL TO HELIUM.
THAT IS WHAT I'VE FELT IN MY BLOOD...IN MY BONES.
I FEEL GREAT SHAME. MY FATHER PULLED HIS GUARDS OUT OF M'RKASSA WHEN I LEFT.
I WILL SPEND THE REST OF MY LIFE FIGHTING TO MAKE PEACE FOR THE INJUSTICE. BUT I THINK I'VE AT LEAST STARTED ON A PATH TO PENANCE.

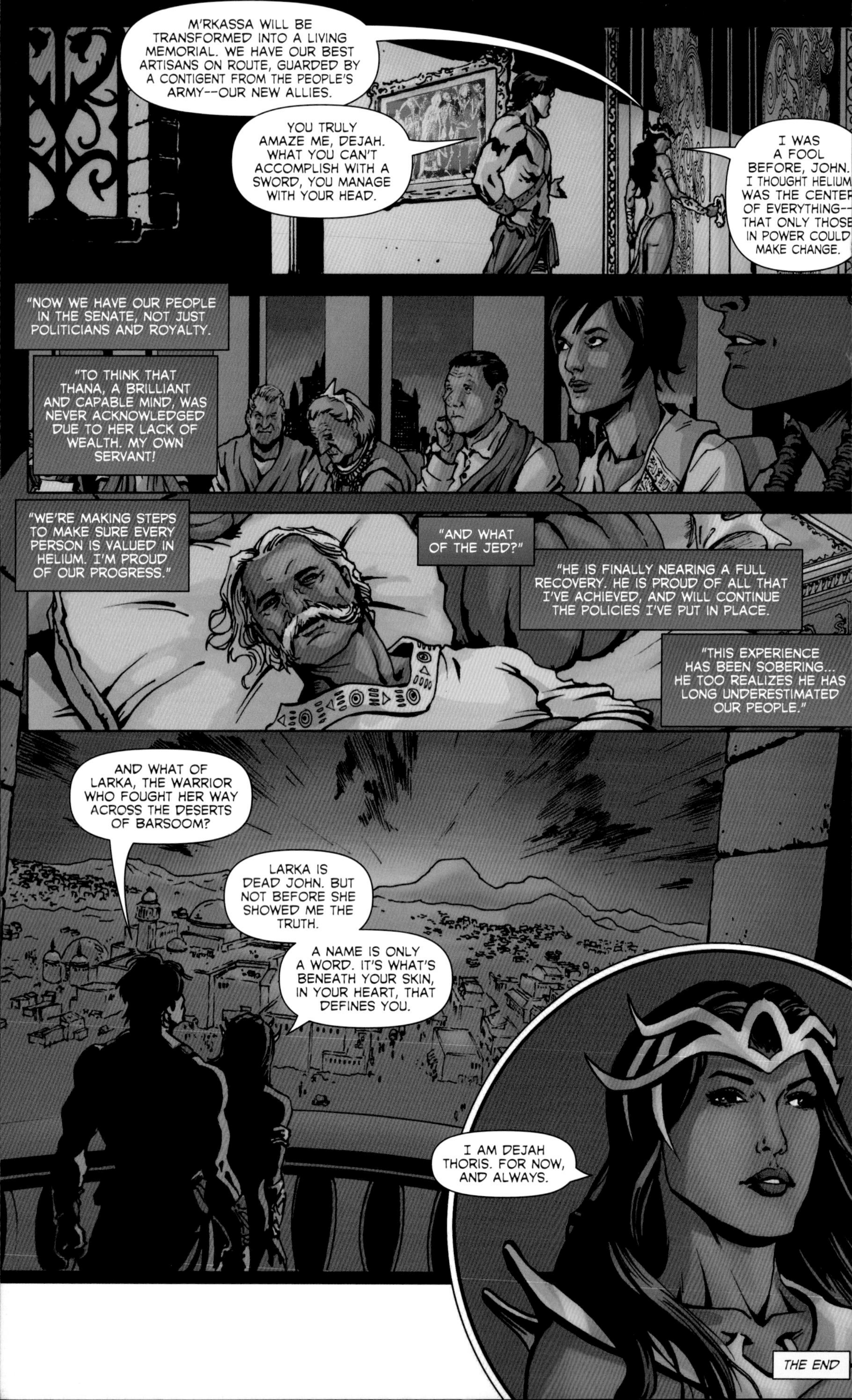
M'RKASSA WILL BE TRANSFORMED INTO A LIVING MEMORIAL. WE HAVE OUR BEST ARTISANS ON ROUTE, GUARDED BY A CONTIGENT FROM THE PEOPLE'S ARMY--OUR NEW ALLIES.
YOU TRULY AMAZE ME, DEJAH. WHAT YOU CAN'T ACCOMPLISH WITH A SWORD, YOU MANAGE WITH YOUR HEAD.
I WAS A FOOL BEFORE, JOHN. I THOUGHT HELIUM WAS THE CENTER OF EVERYTHING-- THAT ONLY THOSE IN POWER COULD MAKE CHANGE.
"NOW WE HAVE OUR PEOPLE IN THE SENATE, NOT JUST POLITICIANS AND ROYALTY.
"TO THINK THAT THANA, A BRILLIANT AND CAPABLE MIND, WAS NEVER ACKNOWLEDGED DUE TO HER LACK OF WEALTH. MY OWN SERVANT!
"WE'RE MAKING STEPS TO MAKE SURE EVERY PERSON IS VALUED IN HELIUM. I'M PROUD OF OUR PROGRESS."
"AND WHAT OF THE JED?"
"HE IS FINALLY NEARING A FULL RECOVERY. HE IS PROUD OF ALL THAT I'VE ACHIEVED, AND WILL CONTINUE THE POLICIES I'VE PUT IN PLACE.
"THIS EXPERIENCE HAS BEEN SOBERING... HE TOO REALIZES HE HAS LONG UNDERESTIMATED OUR PEOPLE."
AND WHAT OF LARKA, THE WARRIOR WHO FOUGHT HER WAY ACROSS THE DESERTS OF BARSOOM?
LARKA IS DEAD JOHN. BUT NOT BEFORE SHE SHOWED ME THE TRUTH.
A NAME IS ONLY A WORD. IT'S WHAT'S BENEATH YOUR SKIN, IN YOUR HEART, THAT DEFINES YOU.
I AM DEJAH THORIS. FOR NOW, AND ALWAYS.
THE END

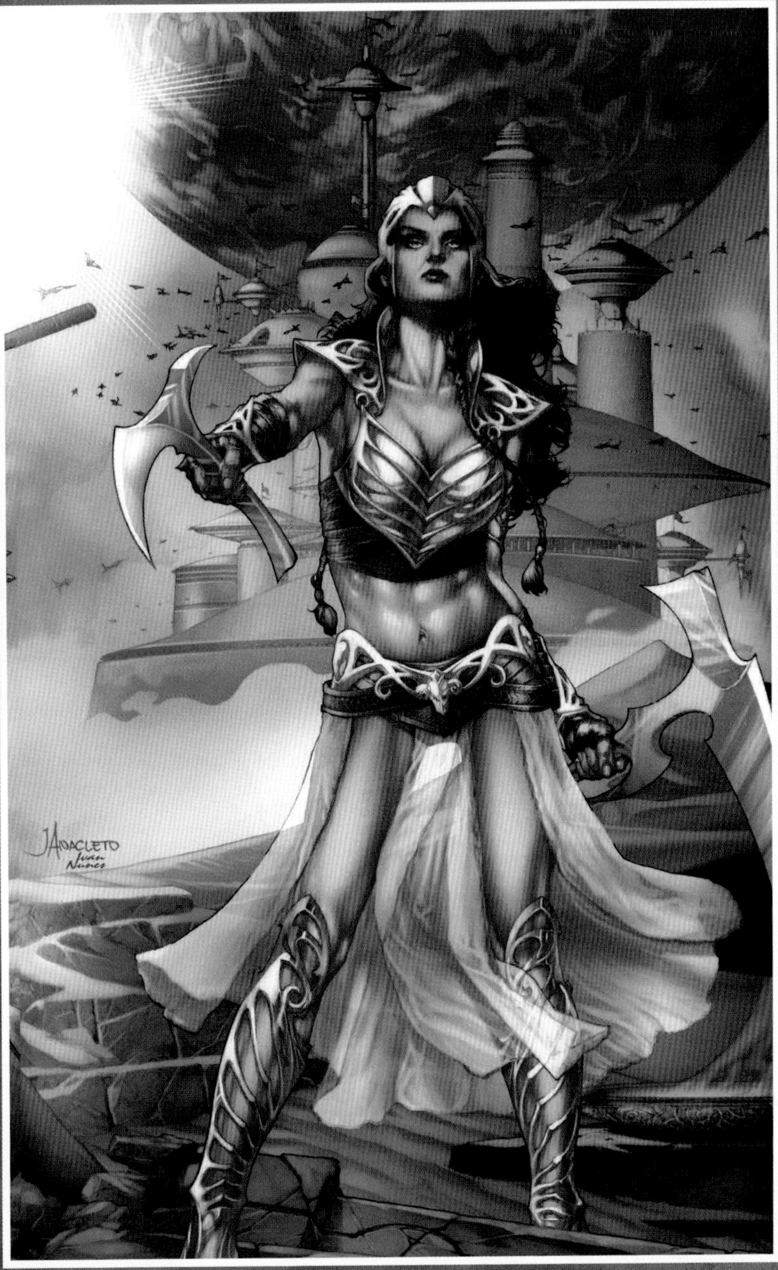
JAnacleto
Ivan Nunes

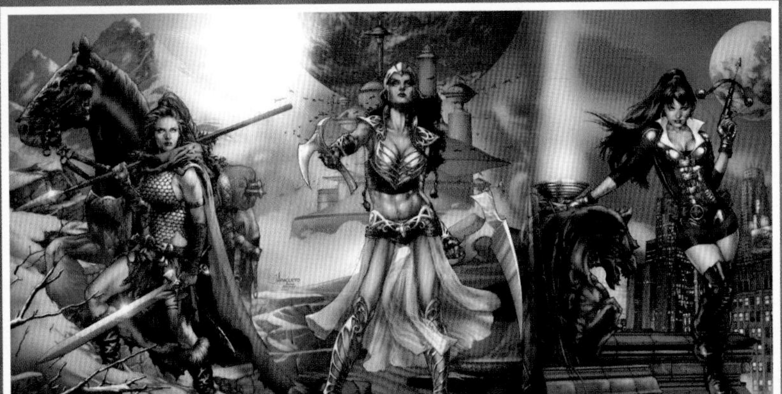

#1 variant cover by **JAY ANACLETO** and **IVAN NUNES**
connecting cover with Red Sonja #1 and Vampirella #1

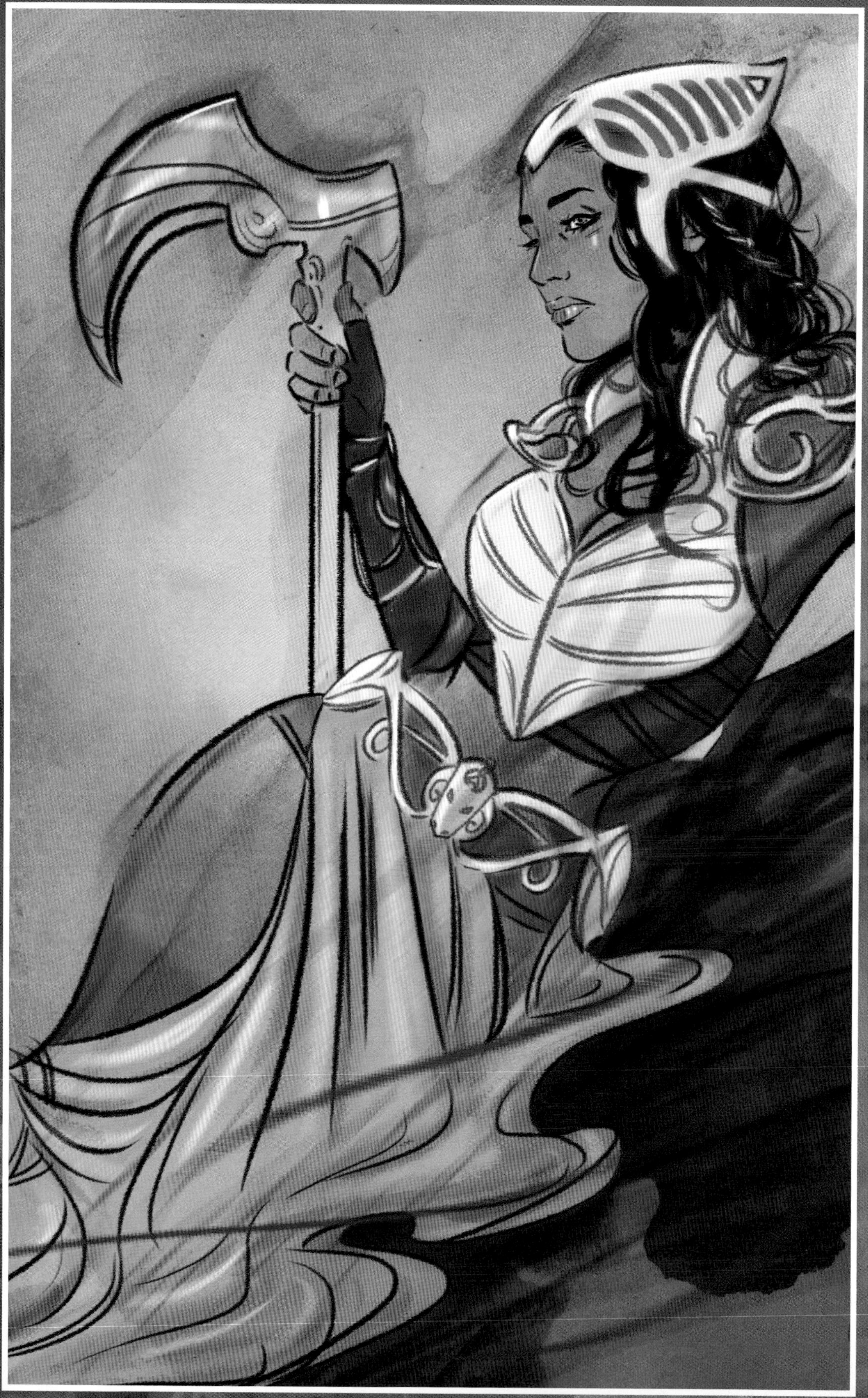

#1 variant cover by TULA LOTAY

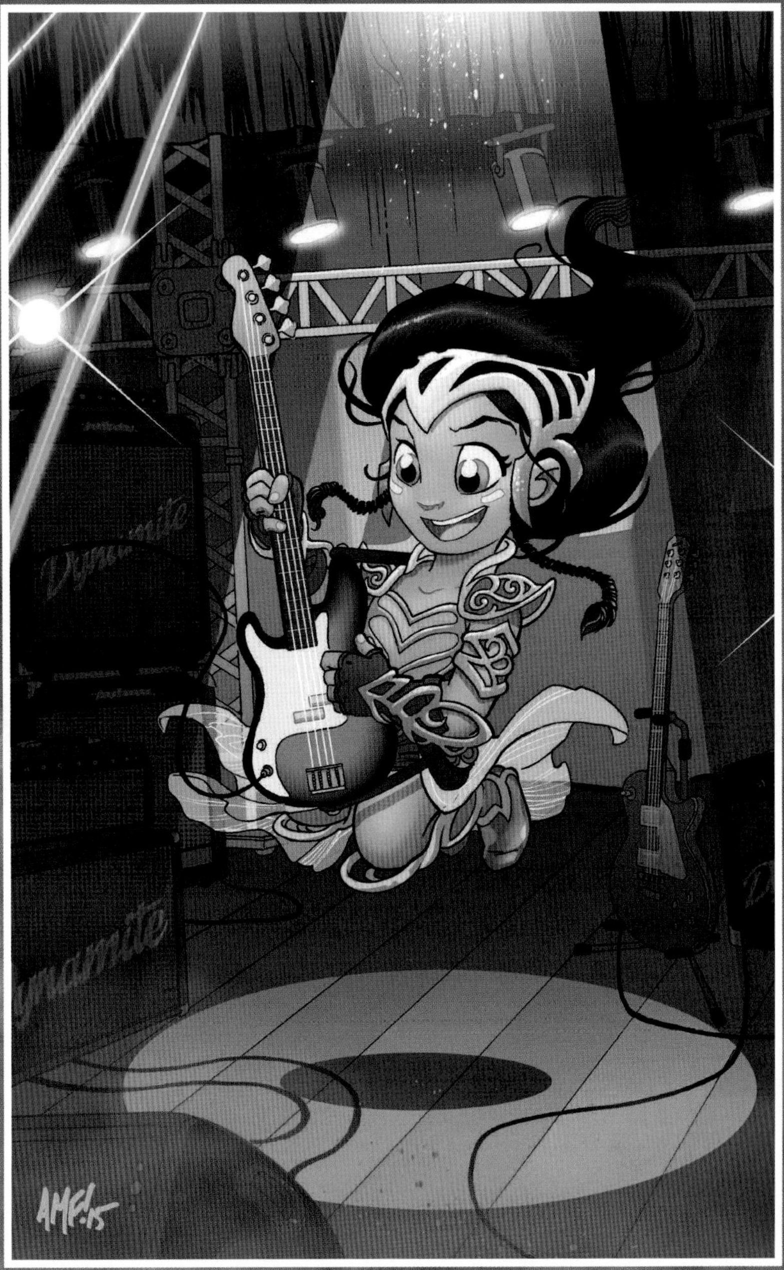
Dynamite
Dynamite
AMF! 15

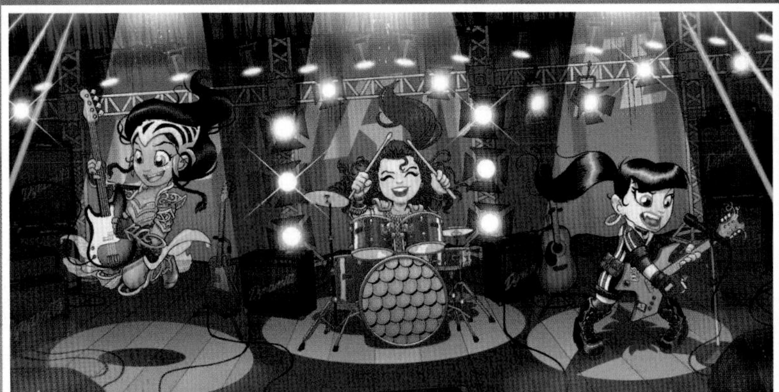

#1 subscription cover by **TONY FLEECS**
connecting cover with Red Sonja #1 and Vampirella #1

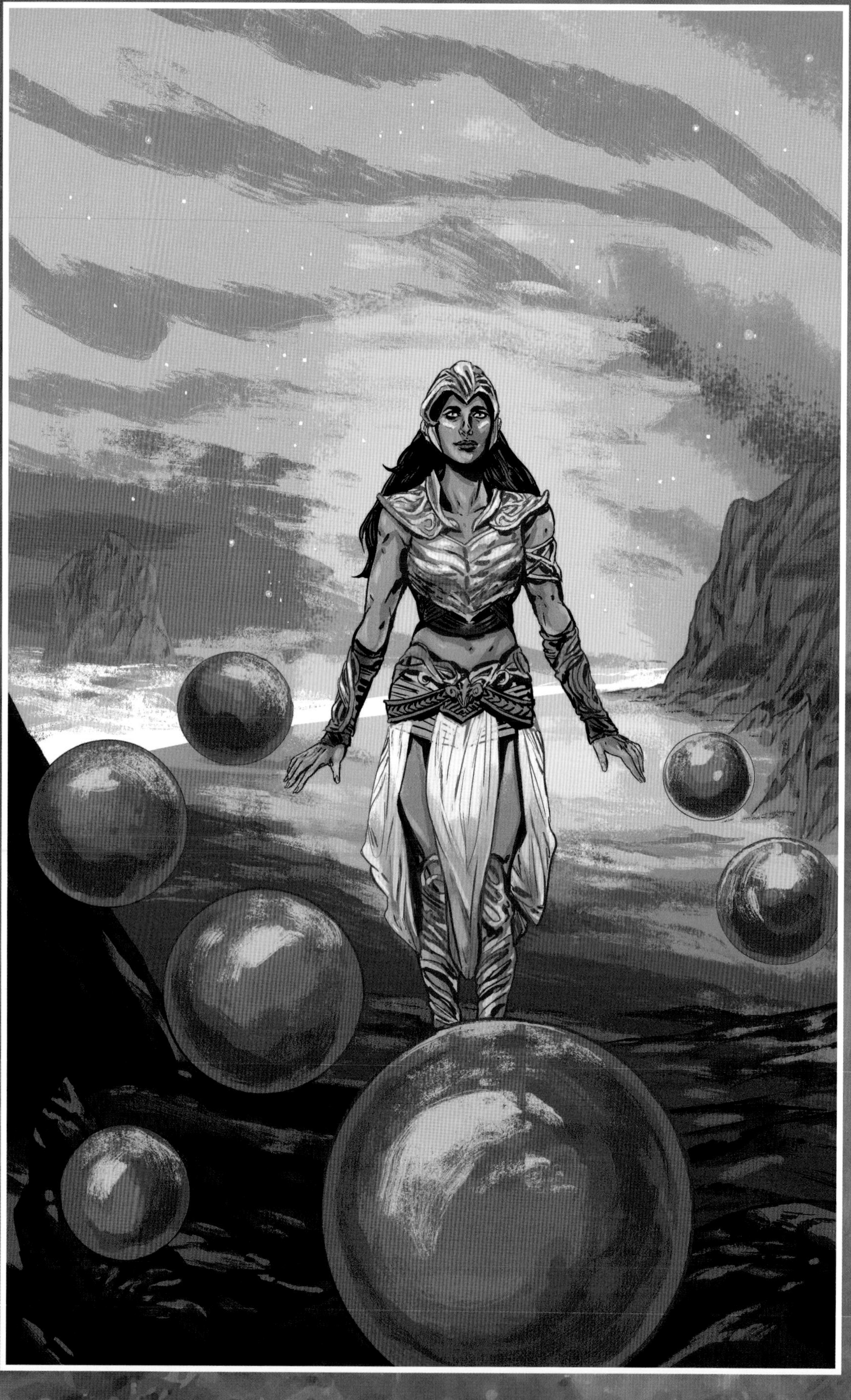

#1 variant cover by **MING DOYLE**

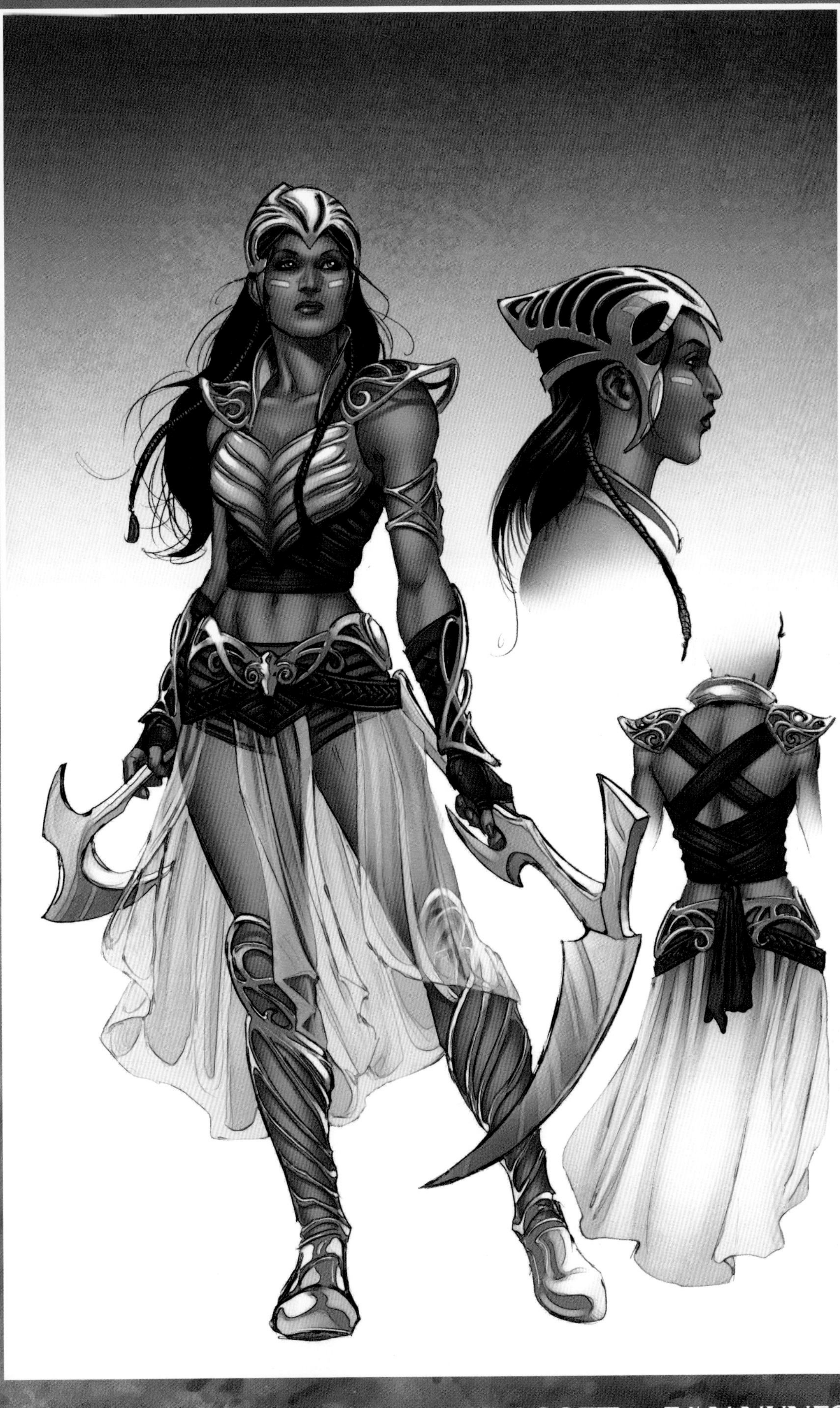

#1 variant cover by NICOLA SCOTT and IVAN NUNES

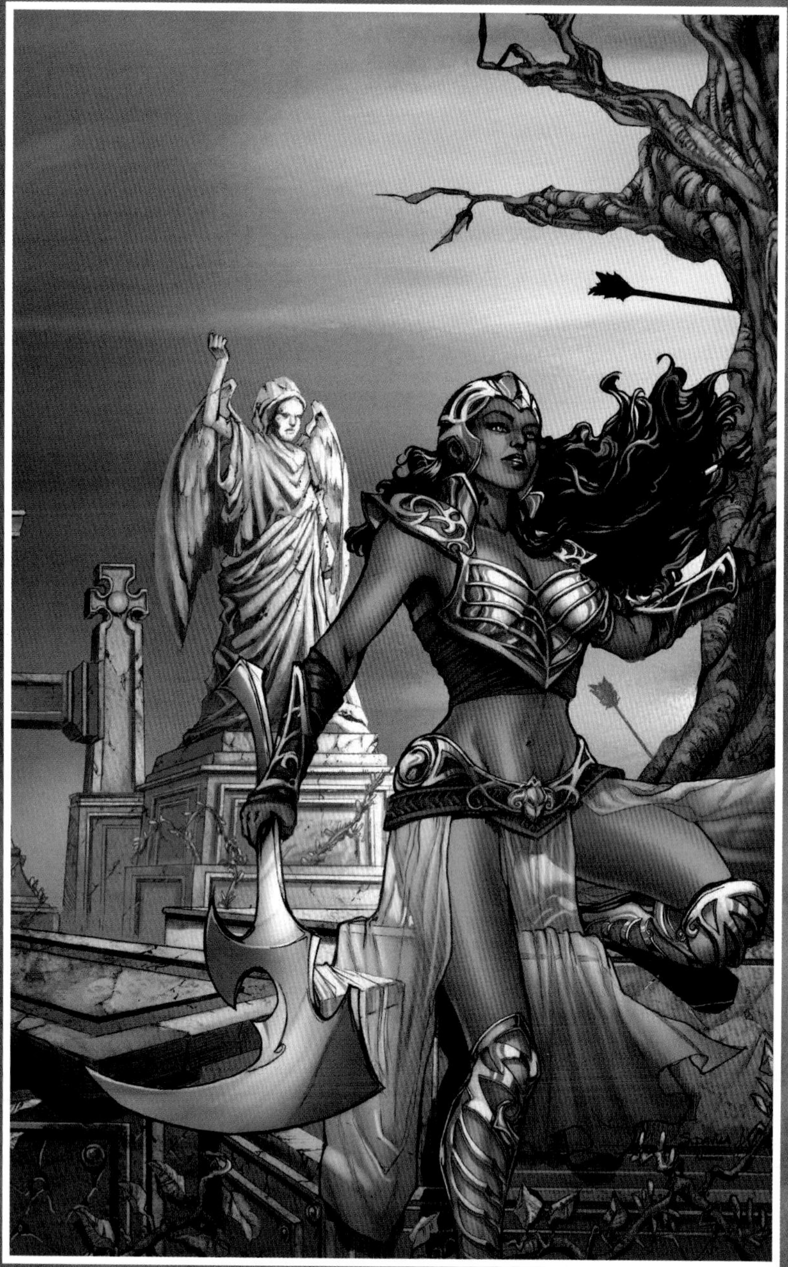

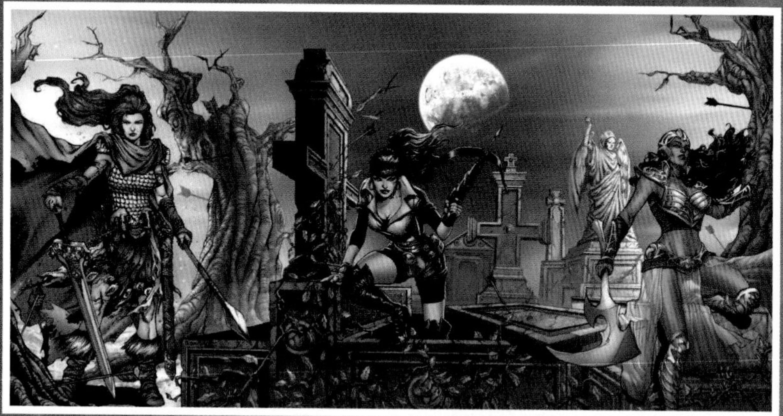

#1 In Your Dreams Collectibles cover by **SERGIO DAVÍLA** and **IVAN NUNES**
connecting cover with Red Sonja #1 and Vampirella #1

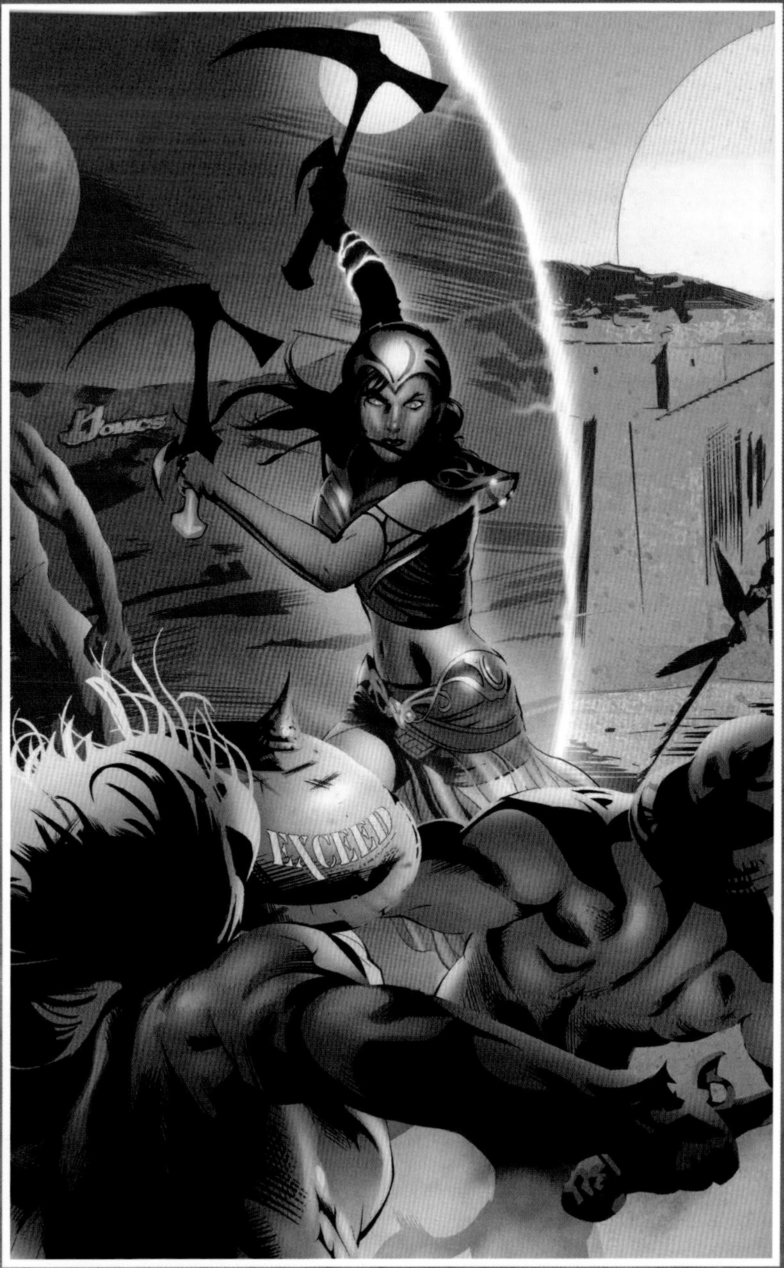
EXCEED

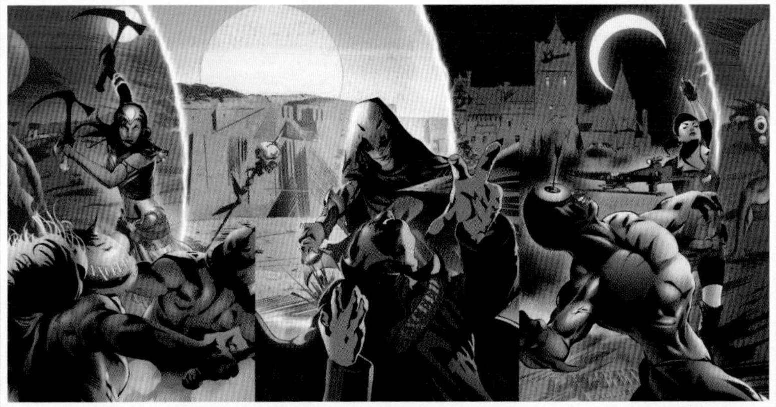

#1 Jesse James Comics exclusive cover by **DENNIS CALERO**
connecting cover with Red Sonja #1 and Vampirella #1

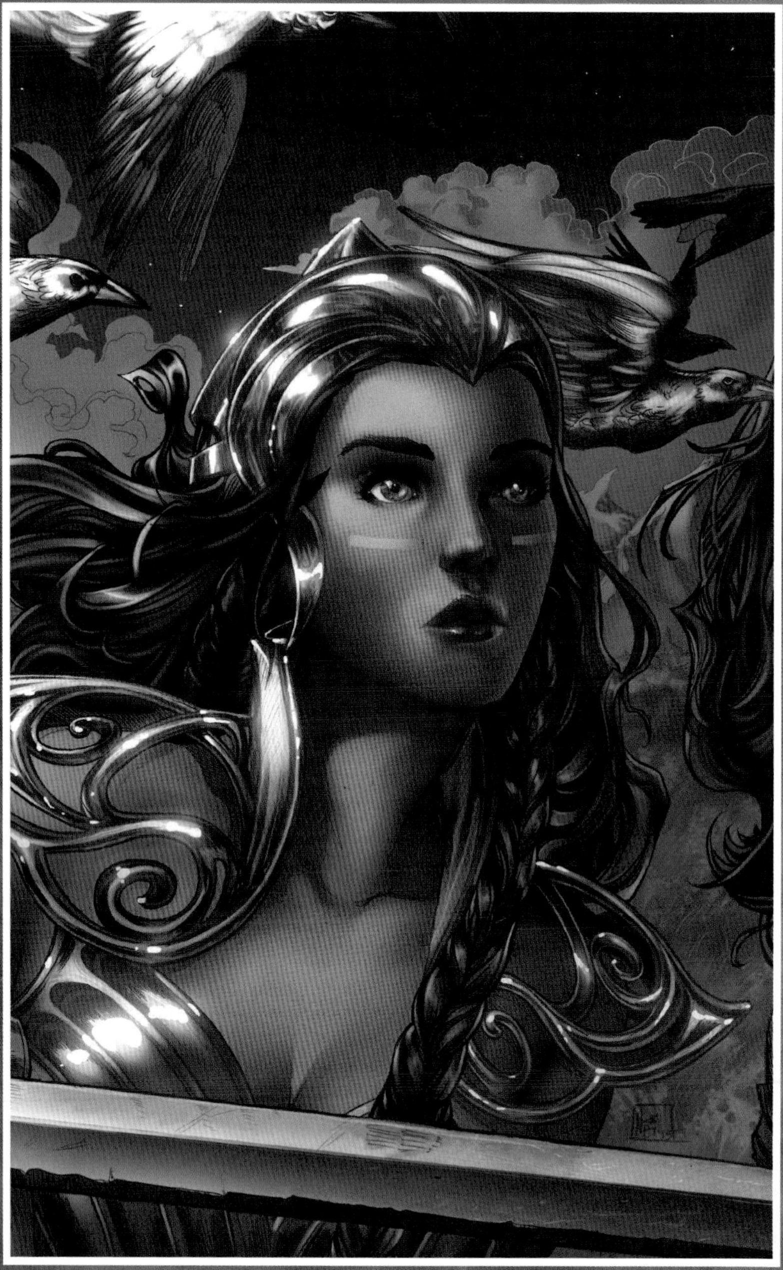

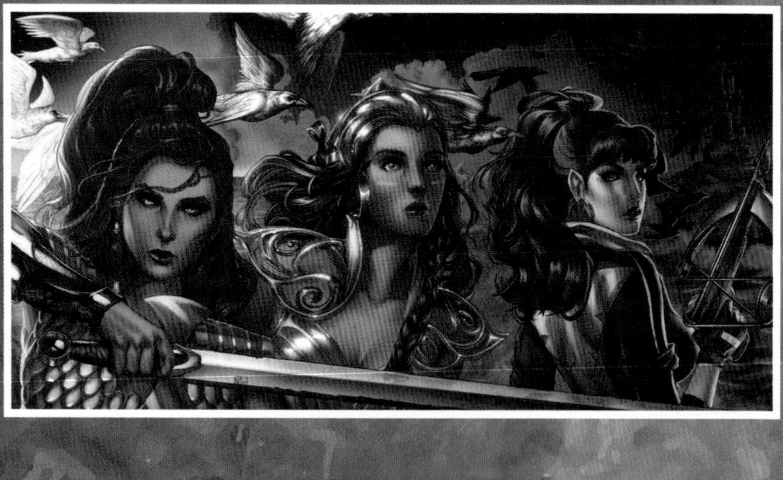

#1 Midtown Comics exclusive cover by **NEI RUFFINO**
connecting cover with Red Sonja #1 and Vampirella #1

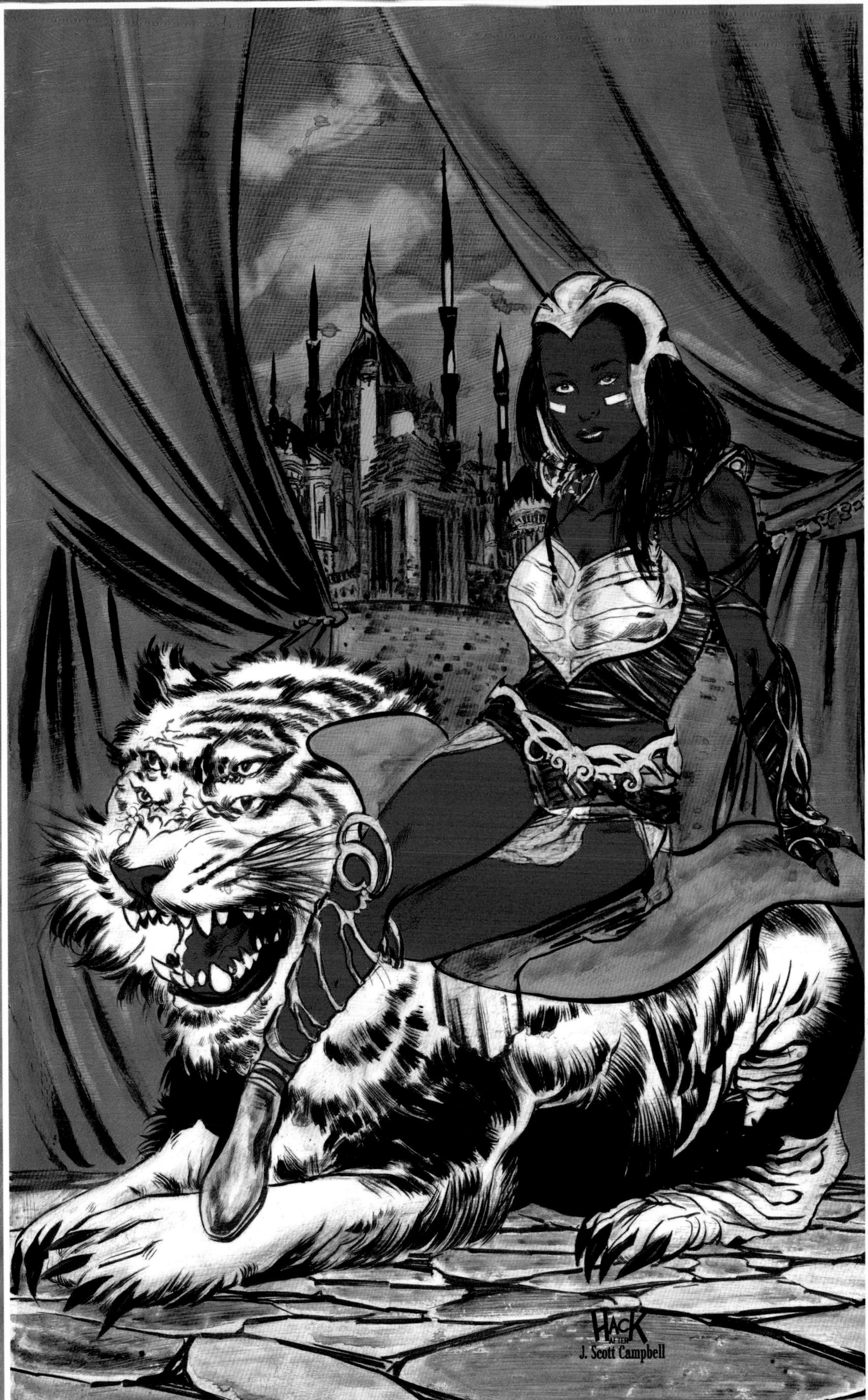
HACK
AFTER
J. Scott Campbell

#1 variant cover (second print) by **ROBERT HACK**

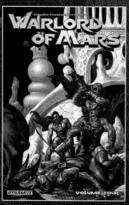

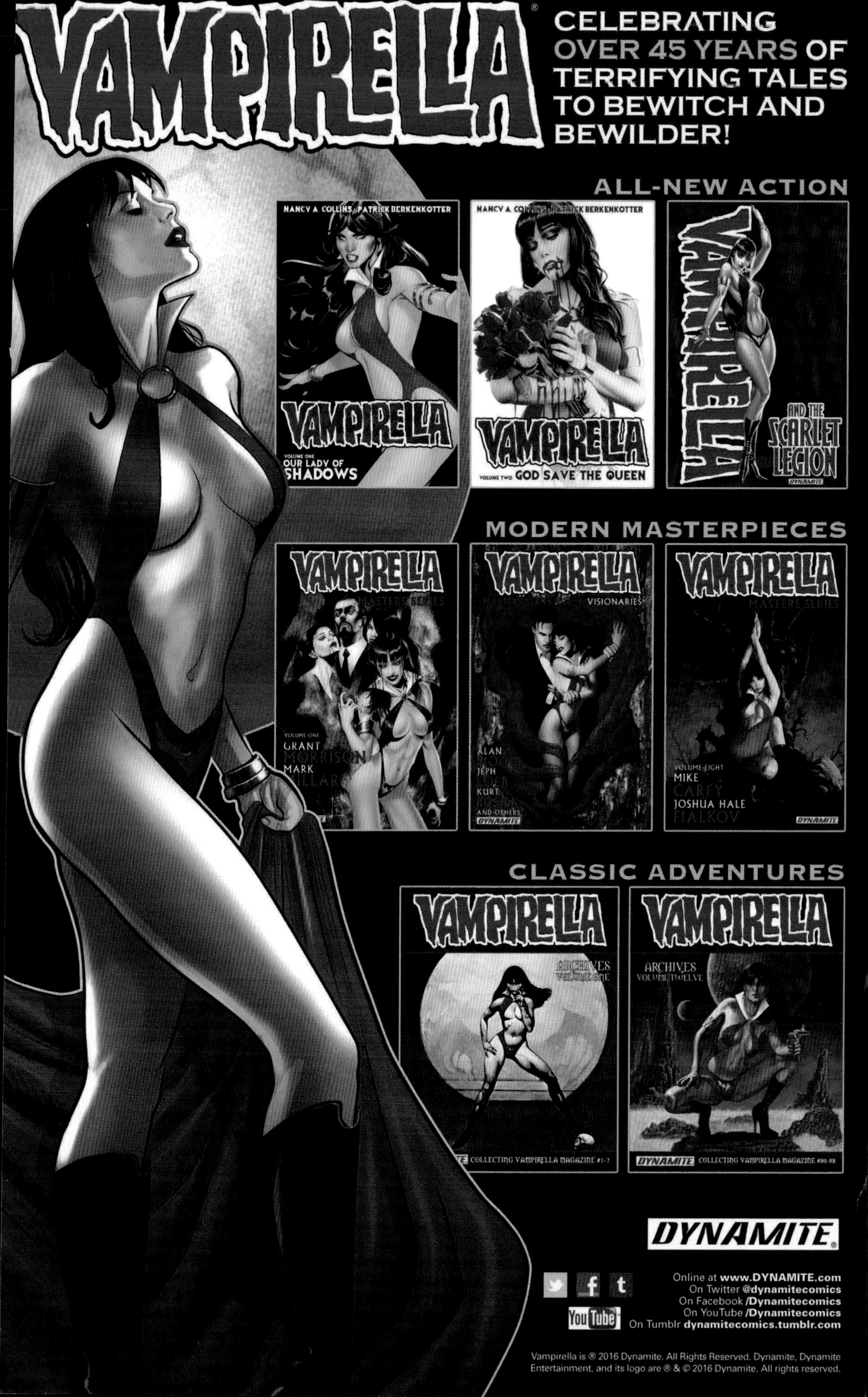

VAMPIRELLA®
CELEBRATING OVER 45 YEARS OF TERRIFYING TALES TO BEWITCH AND BEWILDER!
ALL-NEW ACTION
NANCY A. COLLINS · PATRICK BERKENKOTTER
VAMPIRELLA
VOLUME ONE OUR LADY OF SHADOWS
NANCY A. COLLINS · PATRICK BERKENKOTTER
VAMPIRELLA
VOLUME TWO GOD SAVE THE QUEEN
VAMPIRELLA
AND THE SCARLET LEGION
DYNAMITE
MODERN MASTERPIECES
VAMPIRELLA
MASTERS SERIES
VOLUME ONE
GRANT MORRISON
MARK MILLAR
VAMPIRELLA
VISIONARIES
ALAN MOORE
JEPH LOEB
KURT BUSIEK
AND OTHERS
DYNAMITE
VAMPIRELLA
MASTERS SERIES
VOLUME EIGHT
MIKE CAREY
JOSHUA HALE FIALKOV
DYNAMITE
CLASSIC ADVENTURES
VAMPIRELLA
ARCHIVES VOLUME ONE
COLLECTING VAMPIRELLA MAGAZINE #1-7
VAMPIRELLA
ARCHIVES VOLUME TWELVE
DYNAMITE COLLECTING VAMPIRELLA MAGAZINE #80-88
DYNAMITE®
Online at www.DYNAMITE.com
On Twitter @dynamitecomics
On Facebook /Dynamitecomics
On YouTube /Dynamitecomics
On Tumblr dynamitecomics.tumblr.com
Vampirella is ® 2016 Dynamite. All Rights Reserved. Dynamite, Dynamite Entertainment, and its logo are ® & © 2016 Dynamite. All rights reserved.

Dejah Thoris™

SOLDIER OF MEMORY